T0318333

New Venture Management

The third edition of this practical textbook provides an introduction to the world of new and emerging ventures and to the fundamentals of effective new venture management, including such diverse activities as planning, marketing, financing, and growth.

This textbook is divided into four distinct parts, guiding readers through the entire new venture management process and focusing in turn on ideas and opportunities, planning, finance, and management challenges. All chapters of this revised edition feature international cases, and the complete business plan has been replaced with a contemporary version. Other new elements to the third edition include:

- Expanded coverage of the Lean Startup methodology
- Improved focus on the development and importance of teams
- A new section on the emergence of equity crowdfunding
- Further discussion of ethics and the dangers of dramatic scaling

Presented in an easy-to-understand style, this book will be a valuable resource for undergraduate and postgraduate students in entrepreneurship and new venture management classes as well as active new venture owners and managers.

Online resources include an instructor's manual, test bank, PowerPoint slides, and additional materials to aid instructors and students in applying their knowledge.

Donald F. Kuratko is the Jack M. Gill Distinguished Chair of Entrepreneurship, Professor of Entrepreneurship, and Executive and Academic Director of the Johnson Center for Entrepreneurship & Innovation at the Kelley School of Business at Indiana University. He has authored over 200 articles and 30 books, including one of the leading entrepreneurship books in the world.

Jeffrey S. Hornsby is Executive Director of the Regnier Institute for Entrepreneurship and Innovation and Chair of the Department of Global Entrepreneurship and Innovation at the Bloch School of Management at the University of Missouri in Kansas City. He has authored or coauthored over 140 articles and five books on entrepreneurship, innovation, and human resource management topics.

New Venture Management

The Entrepreneur's Roadmap for Development, Management, and Growth

Third Edition

Donald F. Kuratko and Jeffrey S. Hornsby

Routledge
Taylor & Francis Group

NEW YORK AND LONDON

Third edition published 2021
by Routledge
52 Vanderbilt Avenue, New York, NY 10017

and by Routledge
2 Park Square, Milton Park, Abingdon, Oxon, OX14 4RN

Routledge is an imprint of the Taylor & Francis Group, an informa business

First edition published by Pearson 2008

Second edition published by Routledge 2017

Library of Congress Cataloging-in-Publication Data
Names: Kuratko, Donald F., author. | Hornsby, Jeffrey S. (Jeffrey Scott),
1959- author.
Title: New venture management : the entrepreneur's roadmap for development, management, and growth/Donald F. Kuratko and Jeffrey S. Hornsby.
Description: Third edition. | New York : Routledge, 2021. | Includes bibliographical references and index.
Identifiers: LCCN 2020035696 (print) | LCCN 2020035697 (ebook)
Subjects: LCSH: New business enterprises. | Venture capital. | Entrepreneurship.
Classification: LCC HD62.5. K853 2021 (print) | LCC HD62.5 (ebook) | DDC 658—dc23
LC record available at https://lccn.loc.gov/2020035696
LC ebook record available at https://lccn.loc.gov/2020035697

ISBN: 978-0-367-47236-8 (hbk)
ISBN: 978-0-367-46672-5 (pbk)
ISBN: 978-1-003-03429-2 (ebk)

Typeset in Times New Roman
by Apex CoVantage LLC

Visit the eResources: www.routledge.com/9780367466725

Contents in Brief

PART IV
New Venture Growth   217

Figures

Tables

Preface

New Ventures in the 3rd Decade of the 21st Century

The global revolution in entrepreneurship has spawned huge interest in new ventures and entrepreneurial businesses. Today, the entire global economy is focused on entrepreneurship and the development of new ventures. Individuals and giant corporations alike rely on smaller ventures for goods and services. Small entrepreneurial ventures greatly outnumber large businesses, and thousands of new ventures are formed each day throughout the world. Interest in entrepreneurial ventures continues to grow. Governmental bodies, public and private educational institutions, and a variety of economic development groups have joined the business community in recognizing the importance of entrepreneurial ventures to the global economy. As the world progresses through the 3rd decade of the 21st century, effectively developed and managed entrepreneurial ventures are critical for tomorrow's economic success.

Objectives of the Book

New Venture Management: The Entrepreneur's Roadmap for Development, Management, and Growth, 3rd edition, provides an introduction to the world of new and emerging ventures and to the fundamentals of effective new venture management—the fundamentals of such diverse activities as planning, marketing, financing, and growth. The book is designed as a "hands-on" practical approach for the collegiate market. This text is designed for courses in new ventures that involve three distinct but related constituencies. First, the textbook is designed to be useful to professors who relate the latest research to each topic as they teach the course. Second, the textbook has been written for students to *read*. The subject matter is presented in an interesting and easy-to-understand style. Finally, the specific needs of active new venture owner-managers have been considered. The book's coverage of the key aspects of new venture management will help them improve their management effectiveness on the job.

Distinguishing Features

A number of distinguishing features make this book informative, up-to-date, and useful.

Comprehensive Organization

The book has four distinct parts. Each chapter has a unique subtitle to indicate to the practicing entrepreneur what is really involved in the chapter.

Part I provides an examination of the aggregate picture of new ventures in today's economy, providing an inside look at the world of new and growing ventures. The focus of this section is on ideas and opportunities. It also discusses the various ways individuals find venture opportunities—by buying an ongoing concern, by establishing a home-based business, or by purchasing a franchise. The book also introduces the concept of building strong business models and uses this as a guide for the remaining sections of the book. We have called these chapters *The Quiet Giant*, *The Concept*, and *The Pathways*, respectively.

Part II discusses important elements of the venture development process. We focus on the planning that new ventures must pursue, with specific attention given to effective business models, marketing, legal issues, structures, and operations. We have called these chapters *The Customer*, *The Parameters*, and *The Hook*, respectively.

Part III deals with the challenges of venture finance. It covers the critical sources of capital, financial statements, record-keeping, and financial analysis. We have called these chapters *The Injection*, *The Scorecard*, and *The Gauges*, respectively.

Part IV focuses on the challenges of managing growing ventures. Attention is directed to unique challenges confronting the growing venture, including the human resource management functions and the need for planning. We have called these chapters *The People*, *The Compass*, and *The Future*, respectively.

The subject matter of the book moves from consideration of new ventures in general to the very specific needs of individual owner-managers who are focused on sustaining or growing their venture. The underlying theme is *effectiveness*; that is, the book tells the new venture owner-manager what he or she needs to know to manage a successful venture in the 21st century.

New Elements to the 3rd Edition

1. Organization of the Book

The book in the 3rd edition is updated for a flow from ideas to growth and development of a new venture. The major parts remain *opportunities*, *development*, *finances*, and *growth*. Within each of these major sections we have included a flow of topics that coincides with the development of a strong business model for a new venture. However, in this new edition we accepted many reviewer comments and suggestions for incorporation in each section. We detail some of those changes next.

2. Legitimacy of Ventures and Expanded Lean Startup Coverage

In Chapter 2, the entire ideation process is developed in the 3rd edition so students could gain an understanding of opportunity recognition and idea development. While the Business Model Canvas is presented as a tool for developing the idea into a business concept, that will be expanded upon to demonstrate its importance. We then cover the Lean Startup methodology to provide a scientific approach to creating an early venture concept and delivering a desired product to customers' hands faster. However, in this new edition that topic will also be expanded upon due to its growing popularity. We are adding a section on the strategies for new ventures to gain legitimacy with different audiences. This new section will emphasize how the Business Model Canvas must consider the particular audience the new venture must appeal to at different points of development.

3. **Teams**

The current Chapter 10 covers "HR and the Development of Teams: *The People*" to discuss the operations of the proposed venture. However, in this new edition the development and importance of teams have been added, which is reflected in the new title.

4. **Equity Crowdfunding**

In Chapter 9, a section on crowdfunding was added to the last edition to discuss all of the potential ways an entrepreneur can harness startup capital through social media processes. However, the emergence of equity crowdfunding has expanded dramatically, and this new edition will add a complete section on that phenomenon.

5. **Dangers of Scaling**

In Chapter 12, the concept of scaling was introduced. The future of the venture was discussed with some growth challenges. However, in this new edition we have added a section on "blitzscaling" and the dangers of dramatic scaling beyond the ability of the entrepreneur or the actual revenues of the company. Examples of recent tragedies like Theranos and WeWork are highlighted. The new edition also expands the small section on ethics to fit the discussion of blitzscaling and the examples discussed.

6. **Updated References**

The latest research articles from the entrepreneurship literature are examined to provide the latest aspects of venture development. Each chapter includes a thorough set of endnotes for easy reference.

7. **Updated Interest-Based Features**

Global Perspective for New Ventures

To emphasize the importance of the global environment for each topic in that particular chapter, we now feature a short international item that is designed to identify key issues that affect the new venture owner-manager across the globe. These global issues are adapted from some of the latest publications and relate to the chapter in which they appear.

New Venture Issues

Every chapter features an updated informational item that is designed to identify key issues that affect the new venture owner-manager. These helpful hints
are adapted from some of the latest publications.

The Venture Consultant

At the end of each chapter in the last edition, we developed a brief but challenging study entitled "The Venture Consultant." The problems posed by these
cases are comprehensive, and they call for the application of all the material
in the chapter as well as the student's experience and prior education. In this
new edition the issues will reflect some of the latest challenges that ventures
confront. Each chapter will have something that allows a specific problem to
be posed for student consultation.

An Updated Complete Business Plan

A complete business plan from 2019 is provided as an appendix. This is provided as a guide for the entrepreneur searching for the exact look and style of
a successful plan.

Acknowledgments

There are a number of people who contributed significantly to the final development of this book, and they deserve recognition. First, our wives, Debbie Kuratko and Peg Hornsby, and our families, who continually support all of our publishing endeavors. Second, our respective centers, the Johnson Center for Entrepreneurship & Innovation at Indiana University's Kelley School of Business and the Regnier Institute for Entrepreneurship and Innovation at the UMKC Henry W. Bloch School of Management, for their continued support of our entrepreneurial endeavors. Third, specific individuals who provided invaluable contributions and deserve special recognition would include Sandy Martin, Emily Wetzel, Max DeMumbrum, and David Banjavic from the Johnson Center for Entrepreneurship & Innovation at Indiana University's Kelley School of Business and Laura Moore and the Entrepreneurship Student Ambassadors from the Regnier Institute for Entrepreneurship and Innovation at the UMKC Henry W. Bloch School of Management. Finally, the professional editing team at Routledge/Taylor & Francis Group, including Sophia Levine, Commissioning Editor; Emmie Shand, Editorial Assistant; and Katie Hemmings, Deputy Production Editorial Manager. Our deepest gratitude to all of these professionals who helped turn this book into a reality.

—Donald F. Kuratko
Indiana University

—Jeffrey S. Hornsby
University of Missouri–Kansas City

Author Profiles

Dr. Donald F. Kuratko (Dr. K) is The Jack M. Gill Distinguished Chair of Entrepreneurship, Professor of Entrepreneurship, Executive & Academic Director, Johnson Center for Entrepreneurship & Innovation and the Institute for Entrepreneurship & Competitive Enterprise, Kelley School of Business, Indiana University–Bloomington. Dr. Kuratko is considered a prominent scholar and national leader in the field of entrepreneurship. He has published over 200 articles on aspects of entrepreneurship, new venture development, and corporate entrepreneurship. His work has been published in journals such as *Strategic Management Journal, Academy of Management Executive, Journal of Business Venturing, Entrepreneurship Theory & Practice, Small Business Economics, Journal of Management Studies, Journal of Operations Management, Journal of Product Innovation Management, Journal of Small Business Management, Family Business Review*, and *Journal of Business Ethics*. Professor Kuratko has authored or coauthored 30 books, including one of the leading entrepreneurship books in universities today, *Entrepreneurship: Theory, Process, Practice*, 11th edition (Cengage Publishers, 2020), as well as *Corporate Innovation* (Routledge Publishers, 2019); *Corporate Entrepreneurship & Innovation*, 3rd edition (Cengage Publishers, 2011); and *What Do Entrepreneurs Create?* (Edward Elgar Publishers, 2020). In addition, Dr. Kuratko has been consultant on corporate innovation and entrepreneurial strategies to a number of Fortune 500 corporations. Dr. Kuratko was the cofounder and Executive Director of the Global Consortium of Entrepreneurship Centers (GCEC), an organization comprised of over 400 top university entrepreneurship centers throughout the world. Under Professor Kuratko's leadership and with one of the most prolific entrepreneurship faculties in the world, Indiana University has consistently been ranked the #1 university for entrepreneurship research by the Global Entrepreneurship Productivity Rankings and a 12-year longitudinal journal study, the #1 University Entrepreneurship Program in the United States (public universities) by *Fortune*, and the #1 Graduate Business School (Public Institutions) for Entrepreneurship and the #1 Undergraduate Business School for Entrepreneurship (Public Institutions) by *U.S. News & World Report*. In addition, Indiana University was awarded the National Model MBA Program in Entrepreneurship for the MBA Program in Entrepreneurship & Innovation he developed. Professor Kuratko's honors include the George Washington Medal of Honor, the Leavey Foundation

Award for Excellence in Private Enterprise, the NFIB Entrepreneurship Excellence Award, and the National Model Innovative Pedagogy Award for Entrepreneurship. In addition, he was named the National Outstanding Entrepreneurship Educator by the U.S. Association for Small Business and Entrepreneurship, and he was selected one of the Top Entrepreneurship Professors in the United States by *Fortune*. He has been named a 21st Century Entrepreneurship Research Fellow by the Global Consortium of Entrepreneurship Centers. Dr. Kuratko was honored by his peers in *Entrepreneur* magazine as one of the Top Entrepreneurship Program Directors in the nation for three consecutive years, including the #1 Entrepreneurship Program Director in the nation. The U.S. Association for Small Business & Entrepreneurship honored him with the John E. Hughes Entrepreneurial Advocacy Award for his career achievements in entrepreneurship, and the National Academy of Management honored Dr. Kuratko with the Entrepreneurship Advocate Award for his career contributions to the development and advancement of the discipline of entrepreneurship. Professor Kuratko has been named one of the Top 10 Entrepreneurship Scholars in the world and was the recipient of the Riata Distinguished Entrepreneurship Scholar Award. In 2011 he was the inaugural recipient of the Karl Vesper Entrepreneurship Pioneer Award for his career dedication to developing the field of entrepreneurship, and in 2014 he was honored by the National Academy of Management with the Entrepreneurship Mentor Award for his exemplary mentorship to the next generation of entrepreneurship.

Dr. Jeffrey S. Hornsby holds the Henry Bloch/Missouri Endowed Chair of Entrepreneurship and Innovation and recently was named a University of Missouri System Curator's Distinguished Professor. He is the Executive Director of the Regnier Institute for Entrepreneurship and Innovation and Chair of the Department of Global Entrepreneurship and Innovation. Dr. Hornsby has authored or coauthored 78 refereed journal articles and 88 proceedings articles appearing in the top journals in entrepreneurship and management, including *Strategic Management Journal, Journal of Applied Psychology, Journal of Business Venturing, Entrepreneurship Theory and Practice, Strategic Entrepreneurship Journal*, and *Journal of Operations Management*. His research has earned five conference "best paper awards" and has been cited over 10,000 times. Recently, Dr. Hornsby and his coauthors were recipients of the *Journal of Operations Management* Ambassador Award for the best cross-discipline article in the past five years, awarded at the 2016 Academy of Management Meeting. Dr. Hornsby has coauthored seven books entitled *Corporate Innovation: Disruptive Thinking in Organizations, New Venture Management, Innovation Acceleration: Transforming Organizational Thinking, New Venture Management: The Entrepreneur's Roadmap, The Human Resource Function in Emerging Enterprises, Frontline HR: A Handbook for the Emerging Manager*, and *Training Systems Management*. He is co-editor of the *Journal of Small Business Management*. Dr. Hornsby is currently on the board of the Global Consortium of Entrepreneurship Centers and the Collegiate Entrepreneurs Organization. He recently served as 2016 Conference Chair, Senior Vice President of Programming (Anaheim and San Diego USASBE Conferences), Co-Program Chair, and a member of the Executive Board of the United States Association of Small Business and Entrepreneurship (USASBE). He has consulted with entrepreneurial startups to Fortune 500 companies in the areas of business planning, leadership, human resources, high performance work systems, corporate entrepreneurship, creativity and innovation.

Dr. Hornsby's awards and honors include the following: Named the Entrepreneurship Educator of the Year for the University of Missouri System; recipient of the 2016 John E. Hughes Award for Entrepreneurial Advocacy by the United States Association of Small Business and Entrepreneurship; named a United States Association of Small Business and Entrepreneurship Longenecker Fellow; named Henry W. Bloch/Missouri Endowed Chair in Entrepreneurship and Innovation at UMKC 2013; named Jack Vanier Chair of Innovation and Entrepreneurship, Kansas State University, 2008; founded the Center for the Advancement of Entrepreneurship at Kansas State University 2008; selected as the 2004 University Outstanding Faculty Member for Ball State University; Ball State University Graduation Commencement Speaker Summer 2005; named Ball Distinguished Professor of Management, Ball State University, 2004. Dr. Hornsby received his bachelor's degree from Miami University, M.S. from Western Kentucky University, and PhD from Auburn University.

Part I

New Venture Opportunities

1 New Ventures

The Quiet Giant

Introduction: The Entrepreneurial Imperative

Competitive enterprise is the economic basis for all entrepreneurial activity. It means that any individual is free to transform an idea into a business. The opportunities for potential entrepreneurs are unlimited across the world today. The constantly changing economic environment provides a continuous flow of potential opportunities *if* an individual can recognize a profitable idea amid the chaos and cynicism that also permeate such an environment. Thousands of alternatives exist since every individual creates and develops ideas with a unique frame of reference.

During the last two decades, new ventures have emerged at an exponential rate. Entrepreneurs have fueled innovation, and their new ventures have generated millions of jobs to offset the huge reductions by Fortune 500 firms. LinkedIn, Facebook, Twitter, Tesla, and YouTube illustrate the new generation of entrepreneurial ventures, as they captured the economic spotlight by demonstrating that new ideas from emerging ventures can create the giant institutions of tomorrow. Leading organizations like Apple, FedEx, Intel, Microsoft, Amazon, and Google were once entrepreneurial startups that changed the world forever. Thus, entrepreneurial ventures hold the greatest potential for continued innovation and economic prosperity across the globe. Harsh lessons have been learned over the years, and major corporations realized that the same entrepreneurial spirit in people who developed these new ventures may be present within the organizational boundaries. The entrepreneurial flame has caught on throughout the world, with former socialist economies searching for the competitive enterprise solution through entrepreneurial development. It is truly the entrepreneurial imperative of the 21st century.[1]

New Ventures: Energizing Global Economies

The past two decades have witnessed the most powerful emergence of entrepreneurial activity throughout the world. Many statistics illustrate this fact. For example, during the past ten years in the USA, new business incorporations averaged 400,000 *per year*. This trend clearly demonstrates the popularity of new venture activity, whether it is through startups, expansions, or development. More specifically, in the new millennium we have witnessed the number of smaller businesses in the USA soar to over 30 million, generating over 65 percent of net new jobs and employing over 57 million people.[2] Let's examine some of the historical numbers supporting this phenomenon.

Several methods are used to measure the impact of new ventures on the economy—for example, efforts to start a firm (which may not be successful), incorporation of a firm (which may never go into business), changes in net tax returns filed (reflecting new filings minus filings no longer received), and a substantial amount of full-time and part-time self-employment. Within the United States, the U.S. Small Business Administration reports that smaller firms reached a record total of 30.7 million in 2019. Of these, approximately six million were employing firms, and they accounted for 49.6 percent of U.S. private sector jobs. Small firms made up 99.7 percent of U.S. employing firms. Further, women- and minority-owned businesses increased. Minority-owned businesses numbered eight million, and women-owned businesses totaled 7.8 million, a 20.1 percent increase over the five-year span.[3]

According to the 2019 Global Entrepreneurship Monitor (GEM) United States Report, The highest rates of early-stage entrepreneurial activity in the developed world exist in the United States. Even with the low unemployment rate reported during 2018–2019, it is clear that American people have enough job options, but entrepreneurship represents a viable career path for many. In fact, 63 percent of Americans believe entrepreneurship is a good career choice. Entrepreneurial activity was found to be strong across the entire age spectrum of the 18–74 adult population. Furthermore, the year 2018 marked an all-time high for both men and women entrepreneurs, and the gender gap between men and women notably narrowed. Interestingly, the 35–44 age group, which is the most entrepreneurially active, is the same age group that in 2018 experienced one of the lowest discontinuance rates (4.3 percent). Among all entrepreneurs engaged in early-stage entrepreneurial activity, 87 percent expect to create jobs for others, driving overall economic growth.

While so much attention tends to be focused on technology or venture capital–backed businesses, it is important to understand that entrepreneurial behavior can benefit multiple contexts.[4] The GEM United States Report revealed that one-third of entrepreneurs started their business with family, 11 percent of the adult population is active in the gig/sharing economy, and eight percent of Americans are starting businesses for their employer. However, U.S. entrepreneurs continue to be among the world's leaders in new technology and innovation offerings, which means that early-stage startups are engaged in developing and delivering an innovative product or service as their base offering at a rate that is at least double that of established businesses.[5] According to the Kauffman Indicators of Entrepreneurship,[6] a leading indicator of new business creation in the United States, 0.32 percent of American adults created a business per month in 2019, or 565,000 new entrepreneurs emerged in the largest volume from ages 55–64, representing 26 percent of all new entrepreneurs.

From a worldwide perspective, the Global Entrepreneurship Monitor (GEM) studies over 50 economies and 100 countries, which account for over 75 percent of the world's population and 90 percent of the world's GDP. The belief and confidence in one's ability to succeed are indicators of one's readiness for entrepreneurship. In 36 of the 50 economies, more than half of the population consider that they have the skills, knowledge, and experience to start their own business, while in 42 of the 50 economies, less than half of those who see good opportunities would be deterred by fear of failure. In GEM's 2019–2020 report, it was found that multiple governments increasingly focused on putting into place policy frameworks and mechanisms to drive and promote entrepreneurship. Overall, GEM data suggest that entrepreneurship has been on the increase over the past two decades for most of the participating economies.

Thousands of new ventures have been founded, including many established by women, minorities, and immigrants. These new ventures have come from every sector of the economy and every part of the world. Together these new ventures make a formidable contribution to the world economy, as newer entrepreneurial ventures—some of which did not exist 15 years ago—have collectively created millions of new jobs during the past ten years. The world economy has achieved its highest economic performance during the last ten years by fostering and promoting entrepreneurial activity. All of these numbers illustrate how the entrepreneurial mindset has spread across the globe.[7]

In summary, new and emerging ventures make two indispensable contributions to the world economy. First, they are an integral part of the renewal process that pervades and defines market economies. New and emerging firms play a crucial role in the innovations that lead to technological change and productivity growth. In short, they are about change and competition because they change market structure. The world economy has become a dynamic organic entity always in the process of "becoming," rather than an established one that has already arrived. It is about prospects for the future, not about the inheritance of the past. Second, new and emerging ventures are the essential mechanism by which millions enter the economic and social mainstream of our global society. New ventures enable millions of people, including women, minorities, and immigrants, to access the "entrepreneurial dream." The greatest source of economic strength has always been the entrepreneurial dream of economic growth, equal opportunity, and upward mobility. In this evolutionary process, new ventures play the crucial and indispensable role of providing the "social glue" that binds together both high-tech and traditional business activities. New venture formations are the critical foundations for any net increase in global employment.

Overall, every study continues to demonstrate that entrepreneurs' ability to expand existing markets and create new markets makes entrepreneurship important for individuals, firms, and entire nations.

Entrepreneurs and New Ventures

Today, an entrepreneur is an innovator or developer who recognizes and seizes opportunities; converts those opportunities into workable/marketable ideas; adds value through time, effort, money, or skills; assumes the risks of the competitive marketplace to implement these ideas; and realizes the rewards from these efforts.

The entrepreneur is the aggressive catalyst for change in the world of business. He or she is an independent thinker who dares to be different in a background of common events. Many people now regard entrepreneurship as "pioneership" on the frontier of business.

In recognizing the importance of the evolution of entrepreneurship into the 21st century, researcher Donald F. Kuratko developed an integrated definition that acknowledges the critical factors needed for this phenomenon:

> Entrepreneurship is a dynamic process of vision, change, and creation. It requires an application of energy and passion toward the creation and implementation of new ideas and creative solutions. Essential ingredients include the willingness to take calculated risks—in terms of time, equity, or career; the ability to formulate an effective venture team; the creative skill to marshal the needed resources; the fundamental skill of building a solid business plan; and, finally, the vision to recognize opportunity where others see chaos, contradiction, and confusion.[8]

The current generation known as Generation Z (or Gen Z for short) is the demographic cohort succeeding millennials and preceding Generation Alpha. Studies of Generation Z reveal a strong entrepreneurial spirit. So what's empowering this group to adopt such an entrepreneurial mindset?

They are also considered "the internet generation" because this younger generation has used digital technology since a very young age, and they are comfortable with the internet and social media. Since social platforms have become ingrained in their lives, some platforms have provided a great way to share the excitement of the entrepreneurial spirit with this next generation. For example, the Entrepreneur Network began as a newsletter and has grown into a significant media brand with an audience encompassing more than 3 million print readers, 14 million unique visitors online, and 11 million followers from various social media platforms. Sharing entrepreneurial stories via blogs, videos, or social media has engaged this generation in the entrepreneurial sphere and teaches them how to get involved and start their own journey.[9] In addition, the exponential growth of university entrepreneurship programs has developed experiential aspects that allow these aspiring young entrepreneurs to test business ideas in an academic setting without the weighty fear of real-world failure. So, Generation Z is poised to become the most entrepreneurial generation we've ever seen—a new Generation Entrepreneur (Gen E).[10]

Every person has the potential and free choice to pursue a career as an entrepreneur. Exactly what motivates individuals to make a choice for entrepreneurship has not been identified, at least not as one single event, characteristic, or trait. A review of the literature related to entrepreneurial characteristics reveals the existence of a large number of factors that can be consolidated into a much smaller set of profile dimensions. For example, some of the most common characteristics can be identified:[11]

- Passion
- Vision
- Determination and perseverance
- Drive to achieve
- Opportunity orientation

- Initiative
- Tolerance for ambiguity
- Creativity and innovativeness
- Internal locus of control
- Calculated risk-taking
- High energy level
- Integrity

Entrepreneurship has also been characterized as the interaction of the following skills: Inner control, planning and goal setting, risk-taking, innovation, reality perception, use of feedback, decision-making, human relations, and independence. In addition, many people believe successful entrepreneurs are individuals who are not afraid to fail. New characteristics are continually being added to this ever-growing list.

Keep in mind that *entrepreneurship* is more than the mere creation of a business. Although that is certainly an important facet, it's not the complete picture. The characteristics of seeking opportunities, taking risks beyond security, and having the tenacity to push an idea through to reality combine into a special perspective that permeates entrepreneurs. An entrepreneurial perspective can be developed in individuals. This perspective can be exhibited inside or outside an organization, in profit or not-for-profit enterprises, and in business or non-business activities for the purpose of bringing forth creative ideas. Thus, the entrepreneurial process is an integrated concept that has revolutionized the way business is conducted at every level and in every country.

New Venture Issues

"The Rise of Exponential Organizations"

No one has quite captured the sheer magnitude of change, the reasons and how this change is impacting every industry quite as effectively as Salim Ismail of Singularity University and his team at Exponential Organizations. Today being "agile" is fast becoming the key factor of market competitiveness, with "lean" being the underlying dimension. Consider that since 2010 the cost of 3D printing has dropped by a factor of 400, industrial robots cost 1/23 of what they did then, drones are 143 times cheaper than they were then, and sequencing the human genome is 10,000 times less expensive.

The term "exponential organization" was first introduced in 2014 by Salim Ismail, Michael S. Malone, and Yuri van Geest in their book *Exponential Organizations: Why New Organizations Are Ten Times Better, Faster, Cheaper Than Yours (and What to Do About It)*. Whereas linear organizations are necessarily constrained by limited resources, exponential organizations are governed by an assumption of abundance. As an example, Airbnb, the popular short-term real estate rental market, is designed for rapid growth. Its low organizational demands are inversely proportional to its huge business potential. Airbnb doesn't own any property, but it has already accumulated over seven million listings in more than 100,000 cities and has been valued at $31 billion. Airbnb leverages abundance—in this case, an abundance of real estate. That orientation toward plenty, as opposed to dearth, multiplies everything else about the company's underlying value proposition. Another example is Uber, which leverages the abundance of available drivers and the power of algorithmic pricing software for a low-cost limousine service that is replacing traditional taxi service. One might think of scalability as the same concept, but exponential is more of a mindset or choice that firms will make, with scalability being one of its natural outcomes. Organizing around scalability begins with defining a massive transformative purpose or an aspirational goal for how the business will achieve radical transformation.

But exponential companies aren't simply more competitive. Given the continued penetration of mobile devices and mobile application software and the advent of the Internet of Things, these might be the only organizations set up for long-term survival.

Source: Salim Ismail, Michael S. Malone and Yuri van Geest, *Exponential Organizations: Why New Organizations Are Ten Times Better, Faster, Cheaper Than Yours (and What to Do About It)*, Diversion Books, 2014; also see Nabyl Charania, "Exponential Organizations Are the Future of Global Business and Innovation," TechCrunch, July 5, 2015, https://techcrunch.com/2015/07/05/exponential-organizations-are-the-future-of-global-business-and-innovation/ (accessed July 8, 2016); Biz Carson, "Old Unicorn, New Tricks: Airbnb Has a Sky-High Valuation. Here's Its Audacious Plan to Earn It," *Forbes*, October 3, 2018; and Jonathan Jeffery, "What Is An Exponential Organization?" *Entrepreneur*, October 29, 2019.

Entrepreneurial Motivation

Examining why people start new ventures and how they differ from those who do not may help explain how the motivation entrepreneurs exhibit during startup is linked to the sustaining behavior exhibited later. Lanny Herron and Harry J. Sapienza have stated, "Because motivation plays an important part in the creation of new organizations, theories of organization creation that fail to address this notion are incomplete."[12]

Thus, although research on the psychological characteristics of entrepreneurs has not provided an agreed-on "profile" of an entrepreneur, it is still important to recognize the contribution of psychological factors to the entrepreneurial process.[13] In fact, the quest for new venture creation as well as the willingness to *sustain* that venture is directly related to an ***entrepreneur's motivation***. One research study examined the importance of satisfaction to an entrepreneur's willingness to remain with the venture. Particular goals, attitudes, and backgrounds were all important determinants of an entrepreneur's eventual satisfaction.[14] In that context, Figure 1.1 illustrates the key elements of an approach or model that examines the motivational process an entrepreneur experiences.[15]

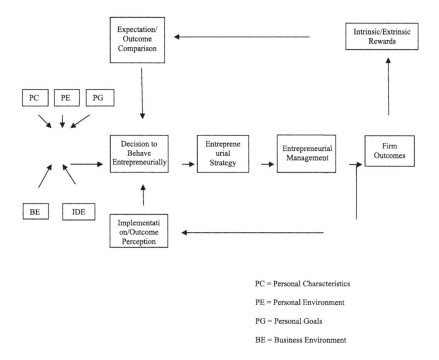

Figure 1.1 A Model of Entrepreneurial Motivation

Source: Naffziger, Douglas W., Jeffrey S. Hornsby, and Donald F. Kuratko, "A Proposed Research Model of Entrepreneurial Motivation," *Entrepreneurship Theory and Practice* (Spring 1994): 33.

The decision to behave entrepreneurially is the result of the interaction of several factors. One set of factors includes the individual's personal characteristics, the individual's personal environment, the relevant business environment, the individual's personal goal set, and the existence of a viable business idea.[16] In addition, the individual compares his or her perception of the probable outcomes with the personal expectations he or she has in mind. Next, an individual looks at the relationship between the entrepreneurial behavior he or she would implement and the expected outcomes.

According to the model, the entrepreneur's expectations are finally compared with the actual or perceived firm outcomes. Future entrepreneurial behavior is based on the results of all of these comparisons. When outcomes meet or exceed expectations, the entrepreneurial behavior is positively reinforced and the individual is motivated to continue to behave entrepreneurially, either within the current venture or possibly through the initiation of additional ventures, depending on the existing entrepreneurial goal. When outcomes fail to meet expectations, the entrepreneur's motivation will be lower and will have a corresponding impact on the decision to continue to act entrepreneurially. These perceptions also affect succeeding strategies, strategy implementation, and management of the firm.[17]

Another line of new research examined the specific motivations as to how and why entrepreneurs persist with a venture, defining *entrepreneurial persistence* as an entrepreneur's choice to continue with an entrepreneurial opportunity regardless of counterinfluences or other enticing alternatives. Researchers Daniel V. Holland and Dean A. Shepherd found that the decision to persist was influenced by personal characteristics as well as by feedback from the environment relative to certain thresholds of adversity. Their findings demonstrate that the decision policies of entrepreneurs regarding persistence differ based on their level of experience with adversity and individual values held.[18]

Thus, we are experiencing a phenomenon of new venture creation throughout the world today. It energizes economies around the globe and has become the most important business concept of the 21st century. Let's examine the advantages and disadvantages associated with starting these new and growing ventures.

Advantages to Starting a New Venture

Despite the failure record of businesses, the desire for individuals to own and operate their own new venture is still growing. As stated earlier, this continual creation of new businesses is at the heart of a free enterprise system. For individuals pursuing a career in business ownership, numerous benefits can be attained personally as well as professionally. The next section examines the following more common advantages of owning a new venture:

- Independence
- Financial opportunities
- Community service
- Job security
- Family employment
- Challenge

Independence

Most new venture owners enjoy being their own boss; they like the freedom to do things their way. Although often a great deal of responsibility is associated with this independence, they are willing to assume it.

Financial Opportunities

Another major reason for going into business for oneself is financial opportunity. Many new venture owners make more money running their own company than they would working for someone else.

Community Service

Sometimes an individual will realize that a particular good or service is not available. If the person has reason to believe the public will pay for such an output, he or she will start a company to provide it.

Job Security

When one owns a business, job security is ensured. The individual can work as long as he or she wants; no mandatory retirement exists.

Family Employment

Another advantage is the opportunity to provide family members with a place of employment. This has several benefits. First, many owner-managers want to perpetuate their business, and how better to do so than to get children or relatives to take it over? Second, higher morale and trust usually occur more in family-run businesses than in others. Third, in times of severe economic downturn, new venture owners can provide employment for family members.

Challenge

Many new venture owners are lured by the challenge that accompanies going into business for oneself. Research reveals that most successful new venture owners like to feel they have a chance to succeed (they want to know success is possible) and a chance to fail (success is not a sure thing). But one thing is certain: *The final outcome depends heavily on them*. They want to win or lose on their own abilities. This challenge gives them psychological satisfaction.

Disadvantages of Starting a New Venture

It should be recognized that some drawbacks to owning a new venture exist. Without proper preparation an individual may find the career path of business ownership frustrating. The major disadvantages of going into business include the following:

- Sales fluctuations
- Competition
- Increased responsibilities
- Financial losses
- Employee relations
- Laws and regulations
- Risk of failure

Sales Fluctuations

Working for a large firm that pays regularly allows the employee to budget food expenditures, plan vacations, and buy clothing. The venture owner/entrepreneur, however, often faces sales fluctuations. In some months sales are very high, while in others they drop off dramatically. The individual must balance cash inflows with cash outflows so that enough money to meet expenses always exists. Sometimes this will require the owner to take a short-term loan (30–90 days) to help the business get through a slack period. And virtually every new venture has sales fluctuations. For example, auto dealers have their best sales in months when the new models come out (November and December) and in the summer (June and July), when people again start thinking about buying a new car. Retail stores find that their greatest sales volume occurs during the end-of-year holiday season. Manufacturers of swimwear obtain their largest sales prior to summer, when they sell their merchandise to wholesalers and retailers. Construction firms have their best months during the summer, when the weather is good.

Competition

A second disadvantage of owning a business is the risk of competition. In particular, an individual may start a business and prosper for three or four years before meeting insurmountable competition. Or changes in market demand may occur, and the owner will find that this new demand is being satisfied by large competitors. For example, small restaurants and diners may find they have lost customers to fast-food chains.

Increased Responsibilities

New ventures face many responsibilities, especially as their operations get larger. For example, owners not only have to make more decisions on major matters but also have to become knowledgeable in many different areas. A successful owner is often a bookkeeper, accountant, salesperson, personnel manager, and janitor all rolled into one. The individual works long hours and, in many cases, six or seven days per week. This is in direct contrast to workers who hold full-time, nine-to-five jobs where salary is guaranteed and raises and promotions can be counted on.

Financial Losses

When the owner makes all major decisions, some of them will inevitably be wrong. On occasion, inventory will be too high (or low); a product line developed at great expense will not sell; a price reduction will not increase product demand, with a resulting decline in total revenue; an advertising campaign will not pay for itself; or an increase in the sales force will prove to be a mistake, and excess personnel will have to be laid off.

In all of these cases the owner will face a financial loss, and if enough of them occur, bankruptcy may result. However, this is not what usually happens. Rather, the owner simply ends up making less money, resulting in a small return on investment for a great deal of effort, work, and risk. Additionally, it is important to note that unless the business is incorporated, the owner is *personally* responsible for all losses. This means the individual could lose everything he or she owns, although in some states the person's home is protected from creditors until the individual chooses to sell it.

Employee Relations

The new venture owner also needs to be concerned with employee relations. If the workers are not content, sales will suffer. For example, in many retail stores employees are not allowed to talk or socialize on the job. Workers are expected to remain at their sales counters and stay alert for customers who need assistance. Management believes that if the employees begin talking to one another, they will lose potential sales. By contrast, research reveals that if employees feel isolated or alone, their attitudes toward the job will decline. This, in turn, will affect their sales ability. They will be rude or curt to the customer, who will then refuse to buy. Thus, a balance must be struck regarding how much socialization can be allowed. Solving this problem requires human relations skills.

Many other employee relations or human resource management issues are also faced by the entrepreneur. For example, friction among workers who do not like each other requires the owner to resolve the conflicts by either getting the employees to put aside their personal differences or by firing one or more of them. Another common problem is job assignment. Who will do what? The owner must be careful not to overload one person with work while another does virtually nothing. Financial compensation is also an issue. How much should each person be paid? When should raises be given? How large should each raise be? Finally, should salaries be secret, or should the owner let everyone know how much each person is being paid?

Questions such as these exemplify the employee relations problems the owner must resolve. As the enterprise grows and more people are hired, more issues arise. Some of the most common relate to medical insurance, retirement programs, other fringe benefits, and unionization. In short, company growth requires addressing more employee relations issues.

Laws and Regulations

New ventures are subject to a multitude of laws and regulations. For example, federal law requires the owner to pay Social Security taxes for all employees as well as to withhold federal taxes from each person's pay and remit these funds to the government. At the state level, in addition to employee taxes, often a state sales tax has to be collected and sent to the proper state agency. Also, for some fields the state requires that a license be secured before a business operates; typical examples include restaurants, barbershops, beauty salons, and liquor stores. At the local level, laws often regulate the days of the week and hours of the day during which business can be conducted. In addition, safety and health requirements cover fire prevention and the avoidance of job hazards. Finally, building and zoning regulations limit the type of structures that can be built and where they can be located. For example, in most cities, office and business buildings are not allowed in the same locale as residential homes.

Risk of Failure

The ultimate risk the new venture owner-manager faces is failure, usually with a loss of most, if not all, of the money invested in the enterprise. All entrepreneurs face this risk, and despite experience and business knowledge, many fail because of factors beyond their control. For example, a major recession hits most new ventures very hard. Moreover, despite precautions, every year some companies are forced into bankruptcy because their funds are embezzled by insiders who systematically drain their financial resources. In addition, disasters can strike, such as the terrible hurricanes that have ravaged so many cities, totally demolishing many businesses. In each of these cases, the company may be forced to close its doors. In most instances, however, failure is caused by poor management.

A Global Perspective

"Entrepreneurship as a Global Activity"

It is common to focus on entrepreneurial activity in the United States, with the reputation of geographic areas like Silicon Valley for fostering and growing entrepreneurial ventures into leading companies across a wide range of industries. However, it is important to recognize that entrepreneurial ambition spans beyond individual borders or cultures.

In June 2019, the U.S. Department of State's Global Innovation through Science and Technology (GIST) collaborated with the government of the Netherlands and corporate partners to host the second Global Entrepreneurship Summit in The Hague, Netherlands. Entrepreneurs from around the world gathered to offer solutions to the world's most pressing challenges with regard to food, connectivity, energy, health, and water under the conference's theme of "The Future *Now*." As part of the conference, over 4,000 entrepreneurs applied to take part in the GIST Catalyst Competition, with a final 30 chosen through expert review and a global public vote to compete at the conference for $650,000 in resources provided by corporate partners. The winners of the GIST Catalyst Competition came from around the world. One winner, Christina York, is CEO of SpellBound, a U.S.-based venture that created an augmented reality platform engineered for health care. It creates immersive visual experiences to increase pediatric patient cooperation with doctors and to facilitate patient education through procedure simulation (https://spellboundar. com). Sol Cabrera, a founder of Stent Intelligent Technology (STENTiT), was another winner. STENTiT is a Netherlands-based venture founded by Sol Cabrera and Bart Sanders that is focused on developing biodegradable stents that promote vascular tissue regeneration. The regenerative stents will be made out of a biodegradable structure that eventually degrades, leaving only repaired vascular tissue (www.stentit.com). The third winner was Syed Abrar, a founder of AzaadHealth. AzaadHealth is a Pakistani data platform that allows health care providers and patients to share and analyze health information (www. azaadhealth.com).

Meeting the world's challenges will require cross-cultural collaboration and the development of diverse entrepreneurial talent from across the world. The increasing interconnectedness of modern society pushes entrepreneurs to think more broadly about how to scale their ideas beyond their national borders.

Source: Adapted from "GIST Catalyst Competition Winners Take Home Over $650,000 in Entrepreneurial Resources–United States Department of State," U.S. State Department, June 5, 2019, www.state.gov/gist-catalyst-competition-winners-take-home-over-650000-in-entrepreneurial-resources/; SpellBound, www.spellboundar.com/; STENTiT, www.stentit.com/; and AzaadHealth, www.azaadhealth.com/.

New Venture Failure

Every year many new venture firms cease operations. The most frequent cause is failure to pay debts, in which case it is common for the owners to declare bankruptcy and to seek to accommodate the creditors, such as paying them 25¢ on the dollar. In other instances, businesses go out of existence because the owners realize that, although they are currently solvent, if they continue operations they will incur debts they cannot meet. In these instances, *business failure* can be defined as a *halt of operations*.

Specific Causes of Failure

Year after year, the major reason businesses fail is *incompetence*. The owners simply do not know how to run the enterprise. They make major mistakes that an experienced, well-trained entrepreneur would see quickly and easily sidestep.[19]

The second most common reason businesses fail is unbalanced experience. This means owners do not have well-rounded experience in the major activities of the business, such as finance, purchasing, selling, and production. Because the owner lacks experience in one or more of these critical areas, the enterprise gradually fails.

A third common cause of business failure is *lack of managerial experience*. The owners simply do not know how to manage people. A fourth common reason is *lack of experience in the line*; that is, the owner has entered a business field in which he or she has very little knowledge.

Other common causes of business failure include neglect, fraud, and disaster. *Neglect* occurs whenever an owner does not pay sufficient attention to the enterprise. The owner who has someone else manage the business while he or she goes fishing often finds the business failing because of neglect. *Fraud* involves intentional misrepresentation or deception. If one of the people responsible for keeping the business's books begins purchasing materials or goods for himself or herself with the company's money, the business might find itself bankrupt before too long. Of course, the owner can sue the individual for recovery of the merchandise and have him or her sent to jail, but that may all happen after the firm's creditors have demanded payment for their merchandise and the owner has had to close the business. *Disaster* refers to some unforeseen happening or "act of God." If a hurricane hits the area and destroys materials sitting in the company's yard, the loss may require the firm to declare bankruptcy. The same is true for fires, burglaries, or extended strikes.[20]

Failure Versus Survival: The Two Fates of Ventures

How great has business failure versus survival been in the recent past? To answer this question, we must first identify the two types of business failure: firm terminations and business bankruptcies. Firm termination means that an entity no longer exists. This can be for any reason, such as the owner grew tired of the business and simply decided to close the doors. However, business bankruptcy is quite different from firm termination. Business bankruptcies result from assets being liquidated and debts owed to creditors—the owner had no option but to quit the business. While firm terminations in the United States are hard to calculate, business bankruptcy rates are calculated on a yearly basis. Bankruptcies in the United States were 23,157 companies in 2017 but dropped to 22,232 in 2018 and 22,780 in 2019.[21]

As far as the failure versus survival question, the "births" and "deaths" of firms tend to be tracked over time—that is, the rate of new business establishments entering and old establishments exiting the economy. After the most recent recession in 2008, establishment births experienced the steepest decline in the history of the series. The downward trend reversed in early 2010, and establishment births have since returned to pre-recession levels.

Examining births and deaths more closely reveals two conclusions. First, termination and survival (birth and death) rates vary by region of the country and by industry. For example, the health care and social assistance industry consistently ranks among the industries with the highest survival rates over time, while construction ranks among the lowest.

As a final note in this section, we must acknowledge the surprising rate of survival by smaller ventures. Debunking many myths about the failure rates of smaller ventures, recent studies are demonstrating a much higher level of survival for these enterprises than ever envisioned. This is not to say that ventures are avoiding failure and experiencing only survival and success. Starting a new venture always has been and always will be a risk, and the two fates of failure and survival will always be a challenge for entrepreneurs. But remember that although 20 percent of new businesses fail in their first year and usually only 50 percent survive through five years, there are still close to 400 million entrepreneurs worldwide, which means the number of startups is always increasing by the year.[22] In addition, knowing the possible "failure traps" may be an effective way for entrepreneurs to prepare better for the survival of their firms.

Avoiding New Venture Management Traps

Over the years numerous studies of new venture failure have revealed a number of avoidable management traps. The following list provides ten of the more specific managerial causes of new venture failure based on a study of businesses that failed.

1. *Inadequate records:* Many bankrupt firms simply have inadequate records.
2. *Expansion beyond resources:* Some firms grow rapidly, and their bookkeeping systems were not designed to handle dramatic growth. In numerous cases, venture owners simply tried to save money on their bookkeeping system by taking shortcuts—with disastrous effects.
3. *Lack of information about customers:* Generally unsuccessful firms lack information about their customers. For example, one company had been shipping goods to customers without making credit investigations. In many cases, accounts were 90–120 days delinquent in their payments.
4. *Failure to diversify market:* A loss of any one customer could have a tremendous effect on overall revenue. Some firms have contracted *all* of their output to one buyer. When that buyer cancels the contract, the company could go bankrupt.
5. *Lack of marketing research:* There are major ventures started without conducting any market research. Changes in market conditions can leave a firm in a very poor position. Lack of market research can be a recipe for disaster.
6. *Legal problems:* Saving money on legal fees could be extremely shortsighted. When long, drawn-out patent infringement proceedings become necessary, firms are ill prepared to deal with them. Having the foresight to obtain competent legal advice from the beginning can prevent many problems.
7. *Nepotism:* Favoritism toward family members could actually cause the enterprise's failure. One of the most typical examples is the practice of carrying on the payroll family members who receive high salaries but contribute little to the overall running of the business.
8. *One-person management:* One-person management has led to company failure. One person's technical genius being the reason for the company's success is fine, but without that person will the business fail?
9. *Lack of technical competence:* Companies suffer from a lack of technical competence when the owners do not understand the basic technology or, worse, retain no one on their management team who does.
10. *Absentee management:* When the owner stays away for long periods, the operation gradually deteriorates. Financial records can be neglected, taxes fall behind, customers are ignored, etc. Given such developments, a company will fail.

Summary

Competitive enterprise is the economic basis for all entrepreneurial activity. It means that any individual is free to transform an idea into a business. The opportunities for potential entrepreneurs are unlimited. The constantly changing economic environment provides a continuous flow of potential opportunities *if* an individual can recognize a profitable idea amid the chaos and cynicism that also permeate such an environment.

The past two decades have witnessed the powerful emergence of entrepreneurial activity in the world. Many statistics illustrate this fact. For example, during the past ten years in the United States, new business startups averaged 400,000 *per year*. The entrepreneurial flame has caught on throughout the world, with almost every country searching for the entrepreneurial mindset solution for economic development.

New and emerging ventures make two indispensable contributions to the world economy. First, they are an integral part of the renewal process that pervades and defines market economies. New and emerging firms play a crucial role in the innovations that lead to technological change and productivity growth. Second, new and emerging ventures are the essential mechanism by which millions enter the economic and social mainstream of our global society.

The entrepreneur is the aggressive catalyst for change in the world of business. He or she is an independent thinker who dares to be different in a background of common events. Many people now regard entrepreneurship as "pioneership" on the frontier of business. Keep in mind that *entrepreneurship* is more than the mere creation of a business. Although that is certainly an important facet, it's not the complete picture. The entrepreneurial process is an integrated concept that has revolutionized the way business is conducted at every level and in every country.

The quest for new venture creation as well as the willingness to *sustain* that venture is directly related to an *entrepreneur's motivation*. The decision to behave entrepreneurially is the result of the interaction of several factors, which include the individual's personal characteristics, the individual's personal environment, the relevant business environment, the individual's personal goal set, and the existence of a viable business idea.

Individuals going into new ventures have a number of advantages. These include independence, financial opportunities, community service, job security, family employment, and challenge. However, disadvantages also exist. These include sales fluctuations, competition, increased responsibilities, financial losses, employee relations, laws and regulations, and the risk of failure.

In terms of management traps, ten management-related causes account for most new venture failures. Some of the specific traps are inadequate records, lack of marketing research, legal problems, and lack of information about customers.

When determining whether new venture ownership should be a career goal, a person should carefully weigh the expected growth in the particular industry and then analyze why some firms succeed and others fail.

Review and Discussion Questions

1. What is your personal definition of a new venture? What criteria did you use to formulate your definition?
2. Briefly describe what is meant by the term *entrepreneurship*.
3. Describe how new ventures are energizing the global economy.
4. New and emerging ventures make two indispensable contributions to the world economy. Identify each clearly.
5. How would you define an entrepreneur? Use specific characteristics from the chapter.
6. The decision to behave entrepreneurially is the result of the interaction of several factors. Describe these in relation to Figure 1.1.

7. What are the advantages of going into a new venture for oneself? List and explain at least four.
8. What are some of the disadvantages of going into a new venture for oneself? List and explain at least four.
9. Describe the two fates of new ventures—failure and success—in the United States. What do we know about the actual rates?
10. What are some other major reasons why new ventures fail? Explain them.

The Venture Consultant

Jumping Into Ownership?

Grant Hartzell is actively searching to buy a cloud storage firm. Grant has recently traveled across the country surveying cloud storage companies and believes he has found the winner in Cloud Enterprises. Cloud Enterprises has been solely owned by Adrian Snyder for five years. However, Adrian is now 73 years old and feels it's time to sell his business.

Grant ultimately found Cloud Enterprises to be his best option because of how personable Adrian was when he visited. Liking the open communication, Grant asked Adrian if he had considered selling his business. Luckily for Grant, he caught Adrian at the right time, as he had reached out to other potential buyers just a week earlier, leaving Grant ample time to place a bid. Grant was excited by Adrian's willingness to sell and the potential opportunity to own the business. To learn more about the business, Grant requested to hold separate one-on-one meetings with Adrian to discuss the financials and operations of the business. Adrian happily agreed.

Their first meeting was about Cloud Enterprises' financials. From their conversation, Grant learned that Adrian had 15 different customers. Adrian's largest customer, Vulanich Shrubbery, contributed over 50 percent of total revenue, as Adrian had been long-time college friends with the owner. Outside of these revenue specifics, Grant found Adrian's financial statements to lack key information, such as earnings before interest and taxes (which is necessary in company valuation). Additionally, Adrian's balance sheet was two full quarters behind the current date. When prompted about these potential issues, Adrian mentioned he had taken some accounting classes at a local university and prepared his own financial statements as sole owner.

Grant's second meeting started much better. Being a lifetime fisherman, Grant wanted to assume a role where no technical analysis was needed. Adrian assured him that his best employees were technology geniuses and could manage the technical aspect of the business. However, he did mention that the lead cloud advisor needed 12 weeks of vacation every year to stay with the business. Adrian also mentioned that he had been advertising through his local paper and felt the advertising was really working. Biweekly back page posts had been a staple of the business for years and really cut down the marketing expense. Adrian did not seem open to discussing the demographics of his customers but hinted his family and friends regularly referred their friends to the business.

After synthesizing the information, Grant is not sure if Cloud Enterprises has real potential. He lacks key information about the business, making his decision more difficult. Grant has notified Adrian that he will have made up his mind in seven days about whether he will place a bid to buy the company.

Your Consultation

What management traps has Adrian presented to Grant that have been discussed in the chapter? Explain. Also, what guidance would you give Grant on his decision to buy Cloud Enterprises? Why?

Notes

1 Donald F. Kuratko, "The Entrepreneurial Imperative of the 21st Century," *Business Horizons*, 2009, 52 (5): 421–428.

2 Alex Merkovich, "30 Insightful Small Businesses Statistics," *Fit Small Business*, March 18, 2019.

3 *Small Business Advocacy*. Washington, DC: U.S. Small Business Administration, Office of Advocacy, 2020.

4. Morris, M.H., Neumeyer, X., & Kuratko, D.F. 2015. "A Portfolio Perspective on Entrepreneurship and Economic Development," *Small Business Economics*, 45 (4), 713–728.

5 Niels Bosma, Stephen Hill, Aileen Ionescu-Somers, Donna Kelley, Jonathan Levie, and Anna Tarnawa, *Global Entrepreneurship Monitor: Global Report*. London: Global Entrepreneurship Research Association (GERA), 2019–2020.

6 Robert Fairlie, Sameeksha Desai, and A. J. Herrmann, *National Report on Early-Stage Entrepreneurship*. Kansas City, MO: Kauffman Indicators of Entrepreneurship, Ewing Marion Kauffman Foundation, 2019.

7 Julian E. Lange, Candida G. Brush, Andrew C. Corbett, Donna J. Kelley, Phillip H. Kim, Mahdi Majbouri, and Siddharth Vedula, *2018/2019 United States Report, Global Entrepreneurship Monitor: National Entrepreneurial Assessment for the United States of America*. Babson Park, MA: Babson College.

8 Donald F. Kuratko, *Entrepreneurship: Theory, Process, & Practice*, 11th ed. Boston, MA: Cengage Publishing, 2020, p. 5.

9 Serenity Gibbons, "Equipping Generation Z for an Entrepreneurial Future," *Forbes*, May 29, 2018; Aaron Paquette, "Gen Z Is Poised to Become the Most Entrepreneurial Generation Ever—Even More So Than Millennials," *Customer Insights*, April 27, 2019.

10 Donald F. Kuratko and Michael H. Morris, "Examining the Future Trajectory of Entrepreneurship," *Journal of Small Business Management*, 2018, 56 (1): 11–23; and Michael H. Morris, Donald F. Kuratko, and Jeffrey Cornwall, *Entrepreneurship Programs and the Modern University*. Cheltenham: Edward Elgar Publishing, 2013.

11 Kuratko, *Entrepreneurship*, pp. 33–36.

12 Lanny Herron and Harry J. Sapienza, "The Entrepreneur and the Initiation of New Venture Launch Activities," *Entrepreneurship Theory and Practice*, Fall 1992, 17 (1): 49–55.

13 Rik W. Hafer and Garett Jones, "Are Entrepreneurship and Cognitive Skills Related? Some International Evidence," *Small Business Economics*, 2015, 44 (2): 283–298; and J. Michael Haynie, Dean A. Shepherd, and Holger Patzelt, "Cognitive Adaptability and an Entrepreneurial Task: The Role of Metacognitive Ability and Feedback," *Entrepreneurship Theory and Practice*, 2012, 36 (2): 237–265.

14 Arnold C. Cooper and Kendall W. Artz, "Determinants of Satisfaction for Entrepreneurs," *Journal of Business Venturing*, November 1995, 10 (6): 439–458.

15 Douglas W. Naffziger, Jeffrey S. Hornsby, and Donald F. Kuratko, "A Proposed Research Model of Entrepreneurial Motivation," *Entrepreneurship Theory and Practice*, Spring 1994, 18 (3): 29–42.

16 A. Rebecca Rueber and Eileen Fischer, "Understand the Consequences of Founders' Experience," *Journal of Small Business Management*, February 1999, 30–45.

17 Donald F. Kuratko, Jeffrey S. Hornsby, and Douglas W. Naffziger, "An Examination of Owner's Goals in Sustaining Entrepreneurship," *Journal of Small Business Management*, January 1997, 35 (1): 24–33.

18 Daniel V. Holland and Dean A. Shepherd, "Deciding to Persist: Adversity, Values, and Entrepreneurs' Decision Policies," *Entrepreneurship Theory and Practice*, 2013, 37 (2): 331–358.

19 William P. Sommers and Aydin Koc, "Why Most New Ventures Fail (and How Others Don't)," *Management Review*, September 1987: 35–39; and Deniz Ucbasaran, Dean A. Shepherd, Andy Lockett, and S. John Lyon, "Life after Business Failure: The Process and Consequences of Business Failure for Entrepreneurs," *Journal of Management*, 2013, 39 (1): 163–202.

20 See Harriet Buckman Stephenson, "The Most Critical Problem for the Fledgling Small Business: Getting Sales," *American Journal of Small Business*, Summer 1984, 9 (1): 26–32; Erkki K. Laitinen, "Prediction of Failure of a Newly Founded Firm," *Journal of Business Venturing*, 1992, 7: 323–340; and Daniel P. Forbes and David A. Kirsch, "The Study of Emerging Industries: Recognizing and Responding to Some Central Problems," *Journal of Business Venturing*, 2011, 26 (5): 589–602.

21 "Business Employment Dynamics, Entrepreneurship and the U.S. Economy," *Bureau of Labor Statistics*, April 2016; and Erin Duffin, "Number of Business Bankruptcy Filings Nationwide in the U.S., 2000–2019," *Statista*, January 29, 2020.

22 Amanda Bowman, "Essential Facts and Statistics Every Entrepreneur Must Know," *Crowdspring*, June 25, 2018.

2 Ideation
The Concept

Introduction: Opportunities As a Source of Ideation

Opportunities are critical to the domain of ideation. Entrepreneurs must be alert to opportunities in the external and internal environments around them. They must be able to recognize potential opportunities that others simply do not see.[1] There are key sources that become the foundations for ideation. For example, one researcher suggests examining trends that could signal paradigm shifts in society (demographics), technology (mobile), economy (dual wage earners), or government (terrorism).[2] These trends may show the gap between expectations and reality. So many entrepreneurs begin their ideation with the simple question of, why not?

The trends may also show shifts in the marketplace caused by changes in consumer attitudes or redefinition of markets or industries. Again, these are sources of emerging opportunities that ideation can focus on. The insights gained from watching trends could produce a valuable source of potential entrepreneurial ideas. Whatever the source, entrepreneurs must begin the ideation process with some specific tools that can assist them in conceptualizing the eventual solution to a problem.

From Idea to Concept

The ideation and new venture development process as well as the processes associated with the development of new products and services is characterized by complexity and high levels of uncertainty. A plethora of data and information that at times may seem to be paradoxically related is available for use, adding to the difficulty in progressing in the development in a straightforward, strategic way. Although one could approach problems within these processes with a strategy in mind, it is by no means straightforward. Non-linear relationships can change the trajectory of the process if the information and complexity contained within it are not addressed or subdued. In this environment, entrepreneurs need to be equipped with processes and tools that are suited for this increasingly complex landscape. In this sense, viewing ideation as a problem-solving process would be a very useful exercise. Any entrepreneurial activity (such as ideation) involves solving a customer problem through a combination of knowledge sets and resources. This view also enables us to leverage an expanding body of methodologies designed to reduce complexity in problem-solving situations.

To propose a systemic problem-solving process to battle the complexity of the ideation entrepreneurial activity, we focus on opportunities. Opportunities are the heart of any ideation activity. In fact, without opportunities there is no ideation. Opportunities are central to delineating the meaning of ideation. This critical role is justified when we look at one of the most widespread definitions of entrepreneurship: "[H]ow, by whom, and with what effects opportunities to create future goods and services are discovered, evaluated, and exploited."[3] Opportunities themselves are defined as "those situations in which new goods, services, raw materials, and organizing methods can be introduced and sold at a greater price than their cost of production."[4] However, there has been a long-standing debate on whether opportunities are created or discovered. In other words, do opportunities exist independent of the entrepreneur (and he or she "discovers" them) or are opportunities created by the intersection of the qualities of the entrepreneur and the environment (the idea and those who support it)?[5]

In an attempt to resolve the discovery/creation debate, Davidsson (2015) conducted a comprehensive critical review of the state of research on opportunities and suggests that opportunities may consist of three subconstructs: The external enabler, new venture idea, and opportunity confidence. As a remedy, to identify the major barriers that have hindered the understanding of entrepreneurial opportunities,[6] Davidsson *et al.* suggested three opportunity-related constructs. The first one is *external enabler*, which is defined as "a single, distinct, external circumstance, which has the potential of playing an essential role in eliciting and/or enabling a variety of entrepreneurial endeavors by several (potential) actors."[7] Examples of this include changes in technology, institutional environments, and macroeconomic conditions. The next construct is *new venture idea*, which is "an imaginary combination of product/service offerings, markets, and means of bringing the offerings into existence."[8] Finally, *opportunity confidence* is "the result of an actor's evaluation of a stimulus ([external enabler] or [new venture idea]) as a basis for the creation of new economic activity."[9]

Considering the critical role of opportunity discovery and its multifaceted nature, as described earlier, this chapter covers a stage-based problem-solving model focused on the life cycle of an opportunity, as the evolving entity in the process of creating new venture ideas. More specifically, a brief review of the major elements of creative problem-solving methodologies is presented, and then the chapter shifts to design thinking as a more recent and widespread problem-solving methodology. In addition, a review of the Lean Startup, which is an application of design thinking in the entrepreneurship context, is covered. Being cognizant of different tools available from design thinking and creative problem-solving processes allows entrepreneurs to address the complexity and uncertainty inherent in the ideation and conceptualization processes. By following key concepts within these methodologies, entrepreneurs are able to quickly and relative cost-effectively apply different tools to try different approaches to solving a problem, failing early and thereby converging on the most optimal route in the journey to developing quality products and services that feasibly fit with market needs.

Examining the Methodologies

Creative Problem-Solving Methodology

Historically, many believed that creativity was an innate skill that some people have and others do not. Recently, this line of thinking has changed to focus on the notion that creativity skills are domain-specific and can be learned. Mihaly Csikszentmihalyi (1996) defined creativity as "[g]enerating novel ideas that are accepted in a domain."[10] Howard Gardner has an even broader definition:

> A person isn't creative in general—you can't say a person is creative. You have to say a person is creative in X, whether it's writing, being a teacher, or running an organization. People are creative in something. . . . People who are creative are always thinking about domains in which they work. They're always tinkering. They're always saying, "What makes sense here, what doesn't make sense? And if it doesn't make sense, can I do something about it?"[11]

These refined definitions allow the expansion of the focus of creative problem-solving into the ideation process. In entrepreneurship, the novel idea is a value proposition or hypothesis that evidences opportunity in a market. The creative problem-solving process enables entrepreneurs to create new value by solving real problems. The remainder of this section will focus on providing an overview of the creative problem-solving process and then present a process that helps entrepreneurs utilize skills for developing their entrepreneurial idea and concept

The Four Stages of the Creative Process

The creative problem-solving process flows through four stages.[12] Stage 1 is the generation of new problems and opportunities. Stage 2 is the conceptualization of new, potentially useful ideas. Stage 3 focuses on the optimization of new solutions. Finally, the innovation process ends with Stage 4, the implementation of new solutions. Each stage requires different kinds of thinking and problem-solving skills. If an entrepreneur hopes to mainstream and launch a successful product or service idea, they must develop and blend a team that can exhibit problem-solving skills in all four stages.

> *Generation* involves getting the creative problem-solving process rolling. Generative thinking involves gathering information through direct experience, questioning, imagining possibilities, sensing new problems and opportunities, and viewing situations from different perspectives. People who are strong in generating skills prefer to come up with options, or diverge, rather than evaluate and select, or converge.
>
> *Conceptualization* keeps the creative problem-solving process going. Like generating, it involves divergence. But rather than gaining understanding by direct experience, it favors gaining understanding by abstract thinking. It results in putting new ideas together, discovering insights that help define problems, and creating theoretical models to explain things. People who are strong in conceptualizing skills enjoy taking information scattered all over the map from the generator phase and making sense of it.

Optimization favors gaining understanding by abstract thinking, but it involves convergence rather than divergence. This results in converting abstract ideas and alternatives into practical solutions and plans. Individuals rely on mentally testing ideas rather than on trying things out. People who favor the optimizing style prefer to create optimal solutions to a few well-defined problems or issues.

Implementation completes the creative problem-solving process. Like optimization, it favors converging. However, it favors learning by direct experience rather than by abstract thinking. This results in getting things done. Individuals rely on trying things out rather than mentally testing them. People and organizations strong in implementing prefer situations in which they must somehow make things work. They do not need complete understanding to proceed and adapt quickly to immediate changing circumstances.

To succeed in creative problem-solving, an entrepreneur needs to focus on all four stages. They must learn to use their differing preferences or styles in complementary ways. Since skills in all four stages are equally valuable, entrepreneurs must appreciate the importance of all four stages and find ways to address each stage.

As shown in the following, each of the four stages in the creative problem-solving process is characterized by two activities:

Stage	Activities
Generation	Problem finding and fact finding
Conceptualization	Problem definition and idea finding
Optimization	Idea evaluation and action planning
Implementation	Gaining acceptance and implementation

These eight activities make up the complete creative problem-solving process in the form of a creative problem-solving wheel (Figure 2.1).[13] The following is a description of each of the eight creative problem-solving activities and a discussion of the three basic skills necessary to apply them.

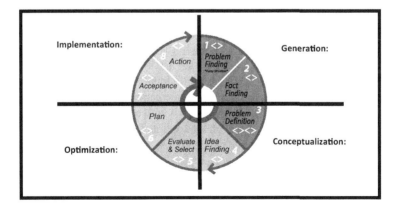

Figure 2.1 Creative Problem-Solving Process

Source: Adapted from Min Basadur and Michael Goldsby, *Disciplined Entrepreneurship*, New York, Routledge, 2016, p. 6. Reprinted with permission.

Generation

STEP 1: PROBLEM FINDING

Effective ideation begins with finding good problems in the organization or the market to solve. However, problem finding is different from problem-solving. Problem finding is the continuous activity of seeking out new opportunities or challenges to attack. This requires a real mindset change from one that says problems are to be avoided or ignored; rather, it requires a proactive approach, seeking problems out and preemptively resolving them. In this step it is critical to not assume anything. Keep an open mind. Call these problems or opportunities "fuzzy situations" to emphasize that you should not prematurely assume anything about them.

STEP 2: FACT FINDING

The bridge between finding a problem and clearly defining it is fact finding. Fact finding involves actively seeking and gathering information that is potentially related to a fuzzy situation and selecting the most intriguing revelations and insights. The following six fact finding strategies help to remove the "fuzziness" from a problem:

1.   Divergently seek possibly relevant facts using several viewpoints
2.   Be aware of conscious assumptions
3.   Avoid a negative attitude toward "problems"
4.   Share information, listen to others, and say what you think
5.   Look for the truth rather than ways to boost your ego
6.   Use a number of different questions to help uncover important facts

Conceptualization

STEP 3: PROBLEM DEFINITION

While an entrepreneur may recognize a problem or opportunity, it is important to find the point of maximum leverage within a given situation. Problem definition means composing clear, insightful challenges from a few key facts. These challenges reveal directions for solutions. An individual skilled in defining problems can create unusual ways to view them. He or she can broaden the problem's scope by asking why it needs to be solved and narrow its scope by asking what stands in the way of solving it. This individual creates optional ways of formulating a problem until a superior angle has been developed.

STEP 4: IDEA FINDING

Once a problem has been clearly defined, the entrepreneur is now ready to search for possible solutions. Idea finding means creating a variety of ways to solve a defined problem. A skilled idea finder is never content with a single good idea but continues to hunt for more. They are able to build on and complete fragments of other ideas. Seemingly radical, even "impossible," ideas can be turned into more unusual but workable solutions. A few of the more promising ideas are selected for evaluation and further development into possible solutions.

Optimization

STEP 5: EVALUATE AND SELECT

After selecting the ideas to move forward for further evaluation, the entrepreneur works to understand the strengths and weaknesses of the various ideas before formulating a solution. Evaluating and selecting involve converting selected ideas into practical solutions. An individual skilled in evaluation and selection considers plenty of criteria to take an unbiased look at the ideas. He or she avoids leaping to conclusions based on a single criterion or unrelated hidden motives. Interesting but flawed solutions are creatively improved, then reevaluated.

STEP 6: ACTION PLANNING

As all successful entrepreneurs realize, good ideas that stay on the shelf have little or no value. To create value, they have to be implemented. Action planning means creating specific action steps that will lead to successful implementation of a solution. An individual skilled in action planning can see the end result in a specific, concrete way that motivates people to act on the plan. For an entrepreneurial venture this could be a business plan (more specifics on this topic are found in Chapter 11).

Implementation

STEP 7: GAINING ACCEPTANCE

For the plan to work, the entrepreneur is going to need support from other stakeholders. Gaining acceptance means understanding that even the best ideas and plans can be scuttled by resistance to change. Someone skilled in gaining acceptance creates ways to show people how a particular solution benefits them and how possible problems with the solution can be minimized.

STEP 8: ACTION

Now it's time to get the job done. Taking action means "doing" the steps in the action plan and continually revising and adapting the plan as things change to ensure that the solution is successfully implemented. An individual skilled in taking action avoids getting mired in unimportant details and minor roadblocks on the way to implementing the solutions. He or she does not fear imperfect solutions, knowing that even perfect solutions can be revised and continuously improved. Each solution you implement automatically changes things. It results in a new array of problems, trends, and opportunities for improvement, then you revert back to step 1 of the process.

Skills for the Creative Problem-Solving Process

To make this creative problem-solving process work, entrepreneurs must learn and apply several specific process skills within each of the four stages and within each of the eight steps. There are three basic skills for making the creative problem-solving process successful: deferring judgment, divergence, and convergence.[14]

Deferring judgment requires the following:

*   an open-mindedness to new opportunities
*   deferral of action on a problem to seek out facts
*   willingness to look for alternative ways to define a problem
*   willingness to try unusual approaches to solve a problem
*   open-mindedness to new solutions

Divergence requires the following:

*   continually seeking new opportunities for change and improvement
*   viewing ambiguous situations as desirable
*   seeking potential relationships beyond the known facts
*   showing awareness of gaps in your own experience and tolerating situations in which things are less than clear-cut
*   realizing that the early stages of innovation require the patience to discover the right questions before seeking the right answers
*   extending yourself to seek out additional possible solutions to problems and additional factors for evaluating solutions beyond the obvious

Convergence requires the following:

*   taking reasonable risks to proceed on an option instead of waiting for the "perfect" answer
*   showing willingness to help your team reach consensus by viewing differences of opinion as helpful rather than as a hindrance
*   following through on implementation plans
*   doing whatever it takes to ensure successful installation

This creative problem-solving process can be a strong tool for the entrepreneur and his or her team. It involves taking the time to get to a strong value proposition through vetting ideas, testing hypotheses, and creating strong implementation plans. However, while the creative problem-solving process provides great insights to inform the ideation and conceptualization processes, with increasing power of consumers and the growing importance of social and environmental concerns, a new design-based problem-solving approach has attracted the attention of decision makers. This new approach is the so-called design thinking. This new approach will be described in more detail in the next section.

The Design Thinking Methodology

Design thinking is a user-centered design approach, popularized by U.S. design firm IDEO and the Stanford University Design School, which is guided by the emotional response of users to a product or service and its constituent features. The origins of the term *design thinking* can be found in the fields of architecture and design. The term was first proposed in a book written by a professor of architecture at Harvard's School of Design.[15] Although the term has been in use for the past three decades, the origins of the design thinking concept go back to the design science movement in the late 1960s and early 1970s. Herbert Simon's *The Sciences of the Artificial*[16] was a major influence on the use of design methodology in engineering, computer science, architecture, urban planning, and medicine. Table 2.1 reviews some of the definitions of design thinking.

Table 2.1 Definitions of Design Thinking

Year	Author(s)	Definition
1996	Liu & Group[17]	How designers see and how they consequently think.
2002	Stempfle & Badke-Schaub[18]	A cognitive operation involving generation, exploration, comparison, and selection to solve problems.
2008	Brown[19]	A discipline that uses the designer's sensibility and methods to match people's needs with what is technologically feasible and what a viable business strategy can convert into customer value and market opportunity.
2009	Martin[20]	The productive mix of analytical thinking and intuitive thinking.
2009	Lockwood[21]	A human-centered innovation process that emphasizes observation, collaboration, fast learning, visualization of ideas, rapid concept prototyping, and concurrent business analysis.
2012	Razzouk & Shute[22]	An analytic and creative process that engages a person in opportunities to experiment, create and prototype models, gather feedback, and redesign.
2013	Seidel & Fixson[23]	The application of design methods by multidisciplinary teams to a broad range of innovation challenges.

Design thinking is grounded within entrepreneurial teams' observations of users' latent needs and addresses the hindering effects of locked-in mentality or process unfamiliarity/usability issues in novel approaches to creating value through the use of a product or market offering. With the rapid changes in technology, users are unable to fully understand or envision solutions themselves due to certain cognitive or path-dependent limitations that are unique to themselves or their archetype/demographic. With careful observation and understanding of the market, user needs, technology, and perceived constraints, design thinking is able to incorporate real-life limitations, visualize new concepts or solutions and go on to evaluate and refine them further before implementing them fully. In other words, this process enables the discovery of a problem and finding the cause in a way that is not dependent on only the product itself. By focusing on the ambient conditions under which it operates or the user who interacts with it, you can learn the reason for that cause and efficiently explore possibilities to eliminate that problem. Observations are codified in capturing real data, which are incorporated into these problem-solving processes. Some general steps from IDEO[24] are:

1. *Empathy* is the focus of a human-centered design. Empathy is necessary to understand people in the context of a design problem. It is the effort to understand the way users behave and why, their emotional needs, how they think, and what makes sense to them.
2. *Define* to focus on clarity. The goal of the define step is to craft a clear and implementable problem statement. This should be a guiding point that focuses on insights and needs of a specific user or multiple users. These insights are the result of a process of combining knowledge to discover new patterns. To summarize, the define step is sense making.
3. *Ideate* is concentration on generating ideas. It demonstrates a process of diverging in terms of new concepts and outcomes. Ideation offers both the energy and the resources for building prototypes and delivering innovative solutions to end users.
4. *Prototype* is for generating artifacts that help an entrepreneur get closer to the solution of the problem at hand. Early in the design process, the questions are broad in nature. In these stages, it is important to create low-fidelity prototypes that are fast and cheap but can trigger useful feedback from users and stakeholders. In later stages, prototypes can be improved in terms of degree of complexity and realness.
5. *Test* involves asking for feedback from the potential customer regarding the protototypes an entrepreneur has created. Testing offers another opportunity for an entrepreneur to better understand the needs of his or her users. Ideally, testing should be carried out within the real context in which the user is embedded. This process can be facilitated by developing scenarios in accordance with previously discovered customer problems. Testing is the chance to refine solutions and make them better.

In their book on design thinking strategies,[25] authors Jeanne Liedtka, Andrew King, and Kevin Bennett suggest that the design thinking approach consists of four key questions to be answered in order:

1. *What is?* Involves framing the problem definition and understanding needs being fulfilled.
2. *What if?* Involves more creative idea generation and hypothesis testing.
3. *What wows?* Focuses on convergence to two or three possible solutions that appear feasible.
4. *What works?* Results include developing solution prototypes and testing/refining to get to what works well.

New Venture Issues

"Design Thinking at Airbnb"

Airbnb is an example of an entrepreneurial venture that relied on design thinking concepts to go from near bankruptcy in 2009 to a $2.6 billion company with over 2 million users per night. In 2009, cofounder Joe Gebbia realized that he had to change the company's approach and figure out what they were doing wrong if they wanted to increase their "flatlined" revenue of approximately $200 per week. Their whole focus early on was on quick scale. He realized that they needed to change focus and listen to customers more regarding their user experience. Growing the business, Gebbia realized, involved more than coding and websites. Initially, they focused on a hunch that the photographs of their listed rentals were not high-quality enough to entice renters. Instead of using cell phone pictures, they switched to more high-resolution photographs, and sales doubled in a week. This experience reinforced the need to focus more on the customer, or what he called "the patient," and that this focus should be the core value of the design team. Their focus on "being the patient" led to the implementation of successful design thinking processes.

- They send every new employee on a trip during their second or third week with Airbnb. After the trip they answer a set of questions to share with the company. Gebbia believes the fact that the company goes to such expense to get this information helps reinforce the patient experience focus.
- Instead of just reacting to date and metrics, Airbnb implemented a process, including starting with a creative hypothesis, then implementing the change, and finally reviewing how it worked.
- Airbnb worked to change the culture to allow for focusing on ideas even if they do not scale. They emphasize being a "pirate," where employees go out and test ideas and report what they found. The focus is making small "bets" or changes, and if they work they put more resources in that direction.
- New employees are empowered to work on improving and/or developing new features right from the start. The goal is to reinforce the culture that great ideas come from anywhere.

Source: Adapted from Ahmed Mahmoud, "The Impact of Airbnb on Hotel and Hospitality Industry," HN hosptitalitynet, 2016, www.hospitalitynet.org/columnist/148002093/ahmedmahmoud.html (accessed August 19, 2016); http://firstround.com/review/how-design-thinking-transformed-airbnb-from-failing-startup-to-billion-dollar-business (accessed August 19, 2016); and Fast Facts, Airbnb Newsroom, https://news.airbnb.com/fast-facts/ (accessed March 17, 2020).

The Lean Startup Methodology

In recent years, a new design thinking–based movement has been conceptualized in the new venture creation context in response to traditional business planning methods, which have been discussed under the umbrella term *Lean Startup*.[26] Lean Startup provides a systematic approach for venture startup and management. The goal of this method is to expedite delivery of the product or service to customers and directly meet customer needs. The Lean Startup method provides a path for venture development and implementation.[27]

Too many venture startups begin with a predetermined idea that they think people want. Entrepreneurs may spend a long time and a lot of money developing a product or service without getting feedback that could help them better serve the customer. The lean startup process requires you to build a rough product and get feedback from customers. Based on the feedback, the entrepreneur can revise or pivot their idea and then test it again with customers. Without this iterative feedback form potential customers, the product or service idea has a higher probability of failure due to not meeting customers' needs.

A useful tool within Lean Startup is Business Model Canvas, developed by Alexander Osterwalder[28]. Using a design template, the Business Model Canvas describes a venture's infrastructure (activities, resources, partnerships), offerings (the value proposition of the products or service), customers (customer segments, channels, customer relationships), and finances (revenue, costs, and resources). See Table 2.2 for additional information on each element of the Business Model Canvas. The canvas was created as a tool that fosters understanding, discussion, creativity, and analysis for all team members, who are able to write down ideas in different sections of the canvas over time. Additionally, it allows the venture to align its activities by illustrating potential trade-offs of different decisions during the various stages of development. There are many resources online that provide video and written descriptions and examples.[29]

Table 2.2 Elements of the Business Model Canvas

Element	Description
Customer Segments	Consists of your most important users and customers. Focus is on your stakeholders, with focus on who is underserved or has the most to gain.
Value Proposition	How does your product or service idea add value to your stakeholders that does not already exist? Can your value proposition motivate a customer to buy?
Distribution Channels	How do you deliver this value to your customers and stakeholders?
Customer Relationships	How do you attract and retain customers? What are your specific marketing plans for each customer group?
Key Resources	What infrastructure and other resources do you need to deliver the promised value to each customer segment?

Element	Description
Key Activities	What major activities and deliverables must happen to deliver to your customers?
Key Partners	Who do you have to engage with to deliver to your customers? This includes suppliers, distributors, investors, etc.
Cost Structure	What are the critical costs to set up and operate your venture to deliver to each customer segment? Costs include fixed and variable costs.
Revenue Streams	What are the projected revenue streams from each customer segment?

In addition to tools like Business Model Canvas, there are a vast array of tools and techniques with a design theme that facilitate the incorporation of design thinking in the entrepreneurial context. Table 2.3 includes a number of useful tools in this respect.

Table 2.3 Design Tools and Techniques to Aid the Idea Development Process

---

1) Persona Construction

To construct a persona for a typical customer, it is imperative to collect both quantitative and qualitative insights to create a comprehensive picture of your typical customer. A combination of methods can be used to facilitate this process, including online surveys, focus groups, in-depth interviews, social media, and emails. In the next stage, based on the results, describe each persona in detail with a lot of characteristics. Examples include name, job title, age, gender, and education. Even though these are surface-level attributes, they might help in constructing an accurate picture of your customers. Next, leverage the qualitative part of your data to answer questions about the information they are looking for, their biggest challenges, and their online surfing. Be focused and detailed to construct this properly. Finally, put yourself in your customer's shoes and think in terms of their feelings, emotions, and pains. Incorporate these elements into your profile to make it as close as possible to your ideal customer persona.

2) Customer Journey Map

A customer journey map is a graphical statement of the overall story from a customer's perspective with regard to their interaction with a company and its value proposition across time and space. The role of narratives is crucial to construct a fine-grained account of customer experience. The story should be told with the customer's voice. A number of elements should be present in any customer journey map:

- Personas: This includes the needs, wants, pains, gains, feelings, and goals of the user
- Timeline: This could be time periods (e.g., day, week, year) or phases (e.g., selection, purchase, after sale).
- Emotions: These include ups and downs representing frustrations and happiness.
- Touchpoints: This involves customer behavior and his or her relationship with the company.
- Channels: This is the place of interaction (e.g., website, application, store).

An Integrated Model of Idea Development

In light of the preceding discussion, we present a creative problem-solving model borrowing from recent advancements in the design thinking approaches for ideation and problem-solving. We begin with the building block of any entrepreneurial journey: an opportunity.

The process begins with an embryonic opportunity, which is an inkling of a potential opportunity to be exploited or leveraged by the entrepreneur(s). At this stage, subjective parameters are at play: Knowledge of a technology, a process, a pain point a customer is acting unevenly upon our understanding of, or the existence of the said opportunity or problem. Whether a problem in fact needs a solution or exists in the first place is important for us as the venture team or product development personnel. See Figure 2.2 for the model. The remainder of this section will provide descriptions of each step of the model.

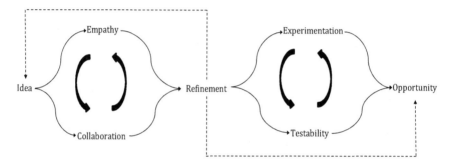

Figure 2.2 Integrated Model of Idea Development

Generation

The initial stages of idea generation are critical to the entire ideation and conceptualization process. Generative thinking involves gathering information through direct experience, questioning, imagining possibilities, sensing new problems and opportunities, and viewing situations from different perspectives. This is where ideas are born. Assumptions at this stage should not be made about an idea; rather, an idea that derives from such knowledge should be elaborated on through careful discourse and dialog with stakeholders both internal and external to the process. People and organizations strong in generating skills prefer to come up with options, or diverge, rather than converge (or to evaluate and select). They see relevance in almost everything and think of good and bad sides to almost any fact, idea, or issue. They dislike becoming too organized or delegating the complete problem but are willing to let others take care of the details. They enjoy ambiguity and are hard to pin down. They delight in juggling many new projects simultaneously. Every solution they explore suggests several new problems to be solved. Thinking in this stage includes problem finding and fact finding, generating solutions and ideas and then incorporating feedback loops to reevaluate the facts under different lenses, and, most importantly, being optimistic in face of challenging problems. This is a sizable portion of ideation, where brainstorming, entrepreneurial orientation, innovative mindset, and organization culture set the stage and attempt to be inclusive. The first part of the model thus shows an initial idea being refined through open communication and collaboration with internal and external stakeholders to vet its viability and to explore whether it is sound.

Conceptualization

After the generation of ideas in line with the problem at hand, the conceptualization stage keeps the innovation process going. Like generating, it involves divergence. But rather than gaining understanding by direct experience, it favors gaining understanding by abstract thinking. It results in putting new ideas together, discovering insights that help define problems, and creating theoretical models to explain things. People and organizations strong in conceptualizing skills enjoy taking information scattered all over the map from the generator phase and making sense of it. Conceptualizers need to "understand." To them, a theory must be logically sound and precise. They prefer to proceed only with a clear grasp of a situation and when the problem or main idea is well defined. They dislike having to prioritize, implement, or agonize over poorly understood alternatives. They like to play with ideas and are not overly concerned with moving to action. Thinking in this stage includes problem defining and idea finding. As the idea is better formulated, it helps to revisit the assumptions or parameters regarding said opportunity to evaluate if it still holds. If it does, the process proceeds to further stages after considerable iteration.

Evaluation

After multiple refinements, the idea is put to work. Like the stage of conceptualization, it favors gaining understanding by abstract thinking. But it now involves convergence rather than divergence, as was seen previously. This results in converting abstract ideas and alternatives into practical solutions and plans. Individuals rely on mentally testing ideas rather than on trying things out. People who favor the optimizing style prefer to create optimal solutions to a few well-defined problems or issues. They prefer to focus on specific problems and sort through large amounts of information to pinpoint "what's wrong" in a given situation.

They are usually confident in their ability to make a sound, logical evaluation and to select the best option or solution to a problem. They often lack patience with ambiguity and dislike "dreaming" about additional ideas, points of view, or relations among problems. They believe they "know" what the problem is. Thinking in this stage includes idea evaluation, development, selection, and action planning. More elaboration of the dynamics or usage of visuals or prototypes is therefore developed by the team. The developments are crucial in providing more context to the information and knowledge generated during the collaborative discussions and empathetic elaboration in consultation with potential stakeholders/users/payers. Affordable loss principles and customer interviews from lean methodologies are then used to maximize information while minimizing time, effort, and costs. This is crucial since a dominant design has yet to emerge, and significant resources should not be expended on trials or features that may not form key parts of the resulting concept. Experimenting with results garnered thus far in the process is of particular importance at this stage.

Iteration

As a concept that appropriately leverages a viable opportunity seems to emerge, a feedback system should once again reassess the parameters to see if it is still in line with the problem statement or the solution the idea proposed that resulted from the first few stages of development. These are iterative steps, and the team/unit/innovator loops through the process until an optimal design or concept arises. This implementation stage can be thought of as one that completes the innovation process. Like optimizing, it favors converging. However, it favors learning by direct experience rather than by abstract thinking. This results in getting things done. Individuals rely on trying things out rather than mentally testing them. People and organizations strong in implementing prefer situations in which they must somehow make things work. They do not need complete understanding to proceed and adapt quickly to immediate changing circumstances. When a theory does not appear to fit the facts, they will readily discard it. Others perceive them as enthusiastic about getting the job done but also as impatient or even pushy as they try to turn plans and ideas into action. They will try as many different approaches as necessary and follow up as needed to ensure that the new procedure will stick. Thinking in this stage includes gaining acceptance and implementation. Amid these stages lies the imperative for developing appropriate skills and for teams to develop capabilities that enhance the venture's ability to effectively incubate and develop ideas.

The creative problem-solving wheel presented in this chapter provides a tool for the entrepreneur to answer these questions in a systematic but iterative process. When the entrepreneur utilizes these concepts it can mean the difference between success and failure.

A Global Perspective

"Design Thinking For Global Strategy"

"Design Thinking is a human-centered approach to innovation that draws from the designers toolkit to integrate the needs of people, the possibilities of technology, and the requirements for business success"—Tim Brown, Executive Chair of IDEO.

Building a business across national and cultural boundaries is challenging, as local laws, values, and social norms often shift from region to region. A business model or way of doing business may be accepted and popular in one part of the world and be completely unacceptable in another. For example, differences in political structure, business culture, and local values have led to strict and uniform data privacy laws in the European Union, while laws in the United States offer users a patchwork of varying protections. In the European Union there is a prevailing belief that individuals have a "right to be forgotten" so that individuals are not connected to past mistakes in perpetuity. American values emphasize a belief in freedom of speech, which makes limiting information challenging.

For those entrepreneurs thinking of establishing a venture or expanding abroad, design thinking offers a planning framework that can help them identify potential problems in advance and create strategies to resolve them. Design thinking, as implemented by IDEO, involves six mindsets: Empathy, iteration, creative confidence, making, embracing ambiguity, and learning from failure. Design thinking emphasizes use of methods like interviewing, observation, and secondary research to gain insights from customers and clients, which can then be used to develop innovative solutions. This focus on gaining insight from customers through understanding the intricacies of their lives and decision-making helps to identify cultural and social norms that may be different than the entrepreneur's and accounted for when considering international expansion.

Developing business strategy using design thinking is a useful tool for organizations large and small, including PepsiCo. Former PepsiCo CEO Indra Nooyi credits design thinking with helping to focus product development at PepsiCo on customers' experience to ensure products are designed to delight customers and to ensure consumer preferences drive manufacturing decisions rather than manufacturing decisions driving product design.

Source: Adapted from Tony Wagner, "The Main Differences Between Internet Privacy in the US and the EU," Marketplace, April 24, 2017, www.marketplace.org/2017/04/24/blog-main-differences-between-internet-privacy-us-and-eu/; IDEO Design Thinking, www.designthinking.ideo.com/; and Adi Ignatius, "How Indra Nooyi Turned Design Thinking Into Strategy: An Interview With Pepsi-Co's CEO," Harvard Business Review, September 2015, www.hbr.org/2015/09/how-indra-nooyi-turned-design-thinking-into-strategy.

Summary

In this chapter, ideation and conceptualization, specifically using design thinking and creative problem-solving methodologies in the search for new venture ideas and opportunities, are examined. This chapter summarizes models used over the years for brainstorming and designing solutions for problems that organizations and businesses have leveraged over the last few decades. The chapter then presents a new model to assist in charting out the problem-solving process for a new venture, with attention to concepts in creative problem-solving and design thinking. The focus is on how an idea becomes a validated opportunity by going through various stages of design and development. Developing team and personal skills to impact these processes is also discussed within these concepts. The chapter concludes by suggesting some tools and techniques to aid the proposed model.

Review and Discussion Questions

1. What is an opportunity? Is it discovered or created?
2. What is design thinking? What are some of the popular approaches to design thinking?
3. Describe the model for design thinking suggested in this chapter.
4. List and describe the elements of design thinking.
5. How does the concept of creative problem-solving fit with design thinking?
6. What are the four stages of creative problem-solving? Briefly describe them.
7. What is a Business Model Canvas, and do you think it represents a good approach to design thinking?
8. Explain the specific elements of the Business Model Canvas (refer to Table 2.2).
9. How can the Lean Startup methodology assist in the design process?

The Venture Consultant

Choosing a Winner

Samuel is a serial entrepreneur. He has made a career of creating and launching several ventures from the ideation stage as the sole employee to the sale of the business. Samuel recently sold his last idea and finds himself in a familiar position—full of potential business ideas but uncertain which is the best choice. Samuel currently has two thoughts that he wants to home in on and gauge their feasibility.

Drone Data Collection: Samuel's family owned a small copper mine for three generations. Growing up, his job was to count the inventory of copper the mine produced. At the end of each month, Samuel would spend two full days estimating the level of copper. In prior generations, his family would not have made efforts to count the copper, but the government recently passed legislation requiring all copper mine owners to report inventory levels on a monthly basis. In the past, his family would simply extract the amount of copper from their mound when a customer was looking to make a purchase.

The strenuous and tedious process got Samuel thinking. He reasoned that there should be a faster way to make an estimate of a copper mound. Two days of painstaking labor and monotonous counting for one worker didn't seem right. How did larger companies do it? After a bit of research and networking phone calls, Samuel found drone technology may be able to better measure the inventory. After speaking with drone experts, they agreed. Samuel has since run beta tests for the idea, and the results have been extremely accurate, not to mention the two-day job now takes just 30 minutes. Samuel also likes the idea that drone technology is a relatively new industry and the potential he has to take advantage of early in the life cycle.

Discount Meal Service: Once a college student, Samuel understands the importance of having cheap meal options on college campuses. Restaurants are also aware of this and have recently had trouble marketing themselves to students to gain market share. Samuel's idea is to provide a mobile application that offers students extreme discounts for a limited period of time—say for two hours of the day. In return, the restaurant would demand that students either dine in or pick up their food. Incentivizing students with lower prices to dine in or pick up the meals themselves would save the restaurant delivery costs, which have eroded profits from student delivery service companies. Additionally, the steep discounts would work to attract a new customer base and potentially provide additional revenue during quieter parts of the day.

Your Consultation

How would you conduct feasibility research for Samuel's two ideas? What are the initial advantages and disadvantages of each idea posed? If you had to choose one idea to start with, which would it be? Explain your rationale.

Notes

1 Ivan P. Vaghely and Pierre-André Julien, "Are Opportunities Recognized or Constructed? An Information Perspective on Entrepreneurial Opportunity Identification," *Journal of Business Venturing*, 2010, 25 (1): 73–86.

2 Donald F. Kuratko, *Entrepreneurship: Theory, Process, & Practice*, 11th ed. Boston, MA: Cengage Publishing, 2020.

3 Scott Shane and S. Venkataraman, "The Promise of Entrepreneurship as a Field of Research," *Academy of Management Review*, 2000, 25 (1): 217–226, p. 220.

4 Ibid.

5 Sharon Alvarez and Jay B. Barney, "Entrepreneurship and Epistemology: The Philosophical Underpinnings of the Study of Entrepreneurial Opportunities," *The Academy of Management Annals*, 2010, 4 (1): 557–583; Saras D. Sarasvathy, Nicholas Dew, S. Ramakrishna Velamuri, and Sankaran Venkataraman, "Three Views of Entrepreneurial Opportunity," in Zoltan J. Acs and David B. Audretsch (Eds.), *Handbook of Entrepreneurship Research, International Handbook Series on Entrepreneurship*, vol. 5. New York: Springer, 2003.

6 Per Davidsson, "Entrepreneurial Opportunities and the Entrepreneurship Nexus: A Re-Conceptualization," *Journal of Business Venturing*, 2015, 30 (5): 674–695.

7 Ibid., p. 683.

8 Ibid.

9 Ibid.

10 Mihaly Csikszentmihalyi, *Creativity: The Psychology of Discovery and Invention*. New York: Harper Collins, 2009. Mihaly Csikszentmihalyi, "Society, Culture and Person: A Systems View of Creativity," in Robert J. Sternberg (Ed.), *The Nature of Creativity: Contemporary Psychological Perspectives*. New York: Cambridge University Press, 1988. Mihaly Csikszentmihalyi and J. W. Getzels, "Creativity and Problem Finding," in Frank H. Farley and Ronald W. Neperud (Eds.), *The Foundation of Aesthetics, Art, and Art Education*. New York: Praeger, 1988.

11 Daniel Goleman, Paul Kauffman, and Michael Ray, *The Creative Spirit*. New York: Penguin, 1993, p. 26.

12 Min Basadur, Garry Gelade, and Tim Basadur, "Creative Problem-Solving Process Styles, Cognitive Work Demands, and Organizational Adaptability," *The Journal of Applied Behavioral Science*, 2014, 50 (1): 80–115.
13 Min Basadur and Michael Goldsby, *Disciplined Entrepreneurship*. New York: Routledge, 2016, p. 6.
14 Ibid.
15 Peter G. Rowe, *Design Thinking*. Cambridge, MA: MIT Press, 1991.
16 Herbert A. Simon, *The Sciences of the Artificial*. Cambridge, MA: MIT Press, 1996.
17 Yu-Tung Liu and Architecture Group, "Is Designing One Search or Two? A Model of Design Thinking Involving Symbolism and Connectionism," *Design Studies*, 1996, 17 (4): 435–449.
18 Joachim Stempfle and Petra Badke-Schaub, "Thinking in Design Teams-an Analysis of Team Communication," *Design Studies*, 2002, 23 (5): 473–496.
19 Tim Brown, "Design Thinking," *Harvard Business Review*, 2008, 86 (6): 84–92.
20 Roger Martin, *The Design of Business: Why Design Thinking Is the Next Competitive Advantage*. Boston, MA: Harvard Business Press, 2009.
21 Thomas Lockwood, *Design Thinking: Integrating Innovation, Customer Experience and Brand Value*. New York: Allworth Press, 2010.
22 Rim Razzouk and Valerie Shute, "What Is Design Thinking and Why Is It Important?," *Review of Educational Research*, 2012, 82 (3): 330–348.
23 Victor P. Seidel and Sebastian K. Fixson, "Adopting Design Thinking in Novice Multidisciplinary Teams: The Application and Limits of Design Methods and Reflexive Practices," *Journal of Product Innovation Management*, 2013, 30 (1): 19–33.
24 dschool.stanford.edu
25 Jeanne Liedtka, Andrew King, and Kevin Bennett, *Solving Problems with Design Thinking: 10 Stories of What Works*. New York: Columbia Business School Publishing, 2015.
26 Eric Ries, *The Lean Startup: How Today's Entrepreneurs Use Continuous Innovation to Create Radically Successful Businesses*. New York: Crown Books, 2011.
27 Ibid.
28 Alexander Osterwalder and Yves Pigneur, *Business Model Generation: A Handbook for Visionaries, Game Changers, and Challengers*. Hoboken, NJ: John Wiley & Sons, 2010.
29 Go to www.youtube.com/watch?v=QoAOzMTLP5s for a very good presentation of the canvas with an example.

3 Venture Choices

The Pathways

Introduction: Starting a New Venture

In Chapter 2, we covered the entire process of idea generation and the selection of potential venture concepts. In looking at the most effective way to approach a new business venture, an individual should create a unique product or service—one that is not being offered today but, if it were, would be in great demand.[1] However, the next best way may be to adapt something that is currently on the market or extend the offering into an area where it is not presently available. The first approach is often referred to as *new-new*, the second as *new-old*. Remember, each approach can lead to entrepreneurial success

New-New Approach

We are always hearing about new products or services entering the market. Typical examples include smartphones, iPads, tablet computers, social media sites (Facebook, Twitter, Instagram, etc.), and the global positioning system (GPS). All of these products, and more, have been introduced as a result of research and development (R&D) efforts by major corporations or the new innovative developments of upstart ventures (such as Facebook, Waze, Twitter, or Instagram). See Table 3.1 for a list of emerging trends that will open up new ideas for businesses. In this new world of constant innovation, it is clear that unique ideas are not produced only by large companies. Moreover, the rate at which new products enter the market has caused the public to expect many of their household goods to be innovated and improved continuously. Figure 3.1 presents the life cycle stages of some common products. Note that some are beginning to be accepted, some are in the maturity stage, and others are no longer in demand.

How does one discover or invent new products? One of the easiest ways is to make a list of annoying experiences or hazards encountered during a given period of time with various products or services. Common examples include objects that fall out of one's hand, household chores that are difficult to do, and items that are hard to store. Can some innovations alleviate these problems? This is how some people get ideas for new products. As an historical example, James Ritty once observed the mechanism for recording the revolutions of a ship's propeller. As he watched the device tally the propeller's revolutions, he realized that the idea could be adapted to the recording of sales transactions, a problem he had been trying to solve for some time. The result led eventually to development of the modern cash register.

Most business ideas tend to come from people's experiences. Figure 3.2 illustrates the sources of new business ideas from a study conducted by the National Federation of Independent Business a number of years ago.

Table 3.1 Trends Creating Business Opportunities

Emerging Opportunities	*Emerging Internet Opportunities*
Green Products	**Mobile Advertising**
Organic foods	iPhones
Organic fibers/textiles	PDAs
Alternative Energy	**Concierge Services**
Solar	**Niche Social Networks**
Biofuel	Seniors
Fuel cells	Music fans
Energy conservation	Groups of local users
	Pet owners
Health Care	Dating groups
Healthy food	
School and government-sponsored programs	**Virtual Economies**
Exercise	Online auctions
Yoga	**Educational Tutoring**
Niche gyms	
Children	**Human Resources Services**
Non-medical	Matchmaking
Pre-assisted living	Virtual HR
Assisted living transition services	Online staffing
Niche Consumables	**Emerging Technology Opportunities**
Wine	*Nanotechnology*
Chocolate	*Mobile technology*
Burgers	*Health care technologies*
Coffee products	
Exotic salads	
Home Automation and Media Storage	
Lighting control	

Emerging Opportunities	*Emerging Internet Opportunities*
Security systems	
Energy management	
Comfort management	
Entertainment systems	
Networked kitchen appliances	

One hot area on the internet is social media sites such as Facebook and LinkedIn. Facebook was founded by Mark Zuckerberg, a Harvard University student who was frustrated by the lack of networking facilities on campus. The company was founded in February 2004 and is now the largest source of photos and one of the most trafficked sites on the internet. Users can create a user profile, add other users as "friends," exchange messages, post status updates and photos, share videos, use various apps, and receive notifications when others update their profiles. Facebook, Inc., held its initial public offering in February 2012 and began selling stock to the public three months later, reaching an original peak market capitalization of $104 billion. On July 13, 2015, it became the fastest company in the Standard & Poor's 500 Index to reach a market cap of $250 billion. Facebook had grown to more than two and a half billion monthly active users by 2020, with a market cap of $485 billion. This demonstrates the innovative power of new ideas in today's world.

In general, the main sources of ideas to create something new for both men and women are prior jobs, hobbies or interests, and personally identified problems. This indicates the importance of people's awareness of their daily lives (work and free time) for developing new business ideas.

New-Old Approach

Most small ventures do not start with a totally unique idea. Instead, an individual "piggybacks" on someone else's idea by either improving a product or offering a service in an area where it is not currently available. Some of the most common examples are setting up restaurants, clothing stores, or similar outlets in sprawling suburban areas that do not have an abundance of these stores. Of course, these kinds of operations can be risky because competitors can move in easily. Potential entrepreneurs considering this kind of enterprise should try to offer a product or service that is difficult to copy. For example, software as a service handling billing and reimbursements for medical doctors can be successful if the business has a sufficient number of doctors in a practice to justify the initial expense and monthly service fee while making an adequate profit. Or perhaps another type of enterprise is likely to be overlooked by other would-be entrepreneurs.

Regardless of whether the business is based on a new-new or new-old idea, the prospective entrepreneur cannot rely exclusively on gut feeling or intuition to get started. Market analysis is the key to a successful venture.

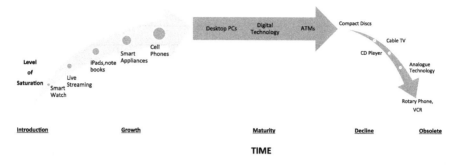

Figure 3.1 Life Cycle Stages of Various Products

Market Analysis

Market analysis can help a prospective business entrepreneur determine whether a demand for a particular good or service exists and whether this demand is sufficient to justify starting a business operation. Large firms do a great deal of market analysis, but such efforts are not restricted to them. New smaller ventures can, and must, conduct market research to assess the best product or service offerings and acceptable pricing structure. It need not cost much money, for the prospective entrepreneur-manager can perform most of the data gathering and analysis.[2] All the person needs to do is accurately formulate the questions that need to be answered and then objectively analyze the data received in response to these questions. In essence, *market analysis* is the application of the scientific method to business problems. The following steps comprise the scientific method that can be used to evaluate a good or a service:

1. State the problem or question in as clear a manner as possible.
2. Gather all the necessary facts about the problem or question.
3. Organize and analyze the facts.
4. Develop one or more courses of action, keeping in mind the pros and cons of each.
5. Select the best alternative and implement it.
6. Observe the progress of this alternative and adjust it as required.

This method can be used not only by people entering a new venture for the first time but also by business people who are already conducting operations and looking at the possibility of expanding their business into new lines or products. However, our attention here is confined to new ventures. The prospective entrepreneur can analyze a business opportunity by breaking the scientific method into four basic steps:

1. Fact gathering
2. Organization of the facts
3. Analysis of the facts
4. Implementation of an action plan

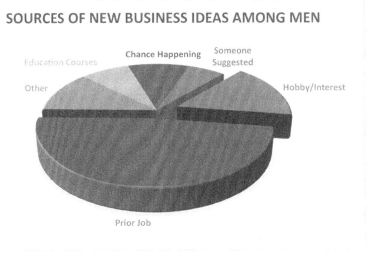

SOURCES OF NEW BUSINESS IDEAS AMONG MEN

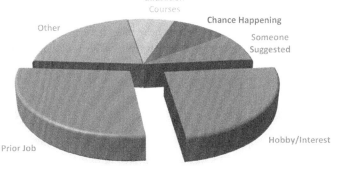

SOURCES OF NEW BUSINESS IDEAS AMONG WOMEN

Figure 3.2 Sources of New Business Ideas Among Men and Women

Fact Gathering

The first step in analyzing a business opportunity is to gather information about the proposed venture. Who would be attracted to this product or service? How many people in the area would buy it? What market trends may affect the product or service? (See "Megatrends That Will Revolutionize Industries" in the New Venture Issues box.) What sales volume would be needed to break even? Do any competitors exist in the area? How well established are they? What does the future of the business look like? Answers to these types of questions can be obtained by reading industry journals, getting data from the Small Business Association, and talking to a local banker who is knowledgeable about the area.

Organization of the Facts

After all the facts have been gathered, they must be organized in a logical fashion. Facts related to costs and revenues should be put together because this information will help the individual compute the break-even point for operations. Competition and projected sales in the local area go together because this information can be used to project an estimate of market share. Facts related to industry growth can be used to make projections regarding future sales and profit potential.

New Venture Issues

"Megatrends That Will Revolutionize Industries"

At the turn of the decade, technological advancements have never been more pronounced. These advancements dovetail into "megatrends"—movements that are expected to revolutionize industries and the way that stakeholders in those industries conduct business. These megatrends will serve as the bedrock for solving complex challenges, transforming day-to-day operations and altering the trajectory of our domestic economy. Following are 12 of the biggest megatrends that will influence our society's future.

Global Abundance

Will increase as the number of individuals in extreme poverty continues to decline. Imminent rise of middle-income demographics comes as access to digitized goods and services becomes easier and cheaper.

Human Life Span

Is expected to increase by roughly 10 years, due mostly to revolutionary enhancements in the biotechnology and pharmaceutical fields. Stem cell advancements, new vaccines, and expedited clinical trials are all contributing factors.

Access to Capital

Will increase for entrepreneurs. Democratizing funding through new platforms like crowdfunding and spotlighting current funding issues (like lack of access to capital for minorities) will continue to improve access options for all entrepreneurs.

AI Outlook

Will improve and should reach human-level intelligence by 2030, according to technology futurist Ray Kurzweil. Algorithms and machine learning will continue to be made open source, and AI partnership will become more normalized and, in some industries, even a requirement.

Renewable Energy

Will continue to advance in prominence and productivity. Solar, wind, geothermal, hydroelectric, nuclear, and localized grids will continue to steer civilizations toward cheaper and more renewable energy strategies.

Instant Economy

Will continue to become an expectation, especially for those living in urban environments. Use of drones, same-day delivery, and deployment of robots will become more normalized and necessary as punctual consumerism reaches new heights.

Advertising Disruption

Will continue, as programmatic advertising and custom AI will continue to map spending patterns. Machines will better help companies understand consumers' needs, and targeted advertising will continue to become more prominent. This trend is driven by the convergence of machine learning, sensors, augmented reality, and new 5G networks.

Cellular Agriculture

Will be an innovation in the coming decade, as protein production will become more ethical, nutritious, and environmentally friendly than it has ever been before. Biotechnology and materials science will increase nutritional content and access across the globe.

Focus on Environmental Sustainability

Will drive companies to reduce waste and pollution. Innovations in materials science will make reduction in environmental contamination a realizable goal.

Gene Therapies

Will minimize the disease burden on the world's population. Gene-editing technologies will continue to increase ease of use and allow families and individuals to cure hereditary disorders.

Cocooning

Finding ways to protect oneself from the harsh, unpredictable realities of the outside world, such as the COVID-19 pandemic.

"EVE"olution

The way women think and behave is impacting business, causing a marketing shift away from a hierarchical model toward a relational one.

Source: Adapted from Tech Blogs, www.diamandis.com/blog/20-metatrends-2020s (accessed March 18, 2020), and Faith Popcorn's official website, www.faithpopcorn.com/ (accessed March 16, 2020).

Organizing the facts in this fashion allows for a more thorough analysis of the information at hand.

Analysis of the Facts

In the analysis stage, the prospective entrepreneur answers the question, what does it all mean? In some cases, answering this question is not difficult because the information speaks for itself. For example, is the return on investment in this business high enough to justify the risk? Does the operation's future look promising? Answers to such questions provide the individual with insights about the potential of certain businesses.

Analysis of sales and cost data will provide the would-be entrepreneur with an idea of the profit margin. This can be compared with data on typical profit margins in the industry, which can be obtained from resources found in any business college library or from the Small Business Administration.

Another common analysis involves determining the number of competing firms in the area and the number of total customers. Is the population large enough to support another business? This approach can be used to estimate the potential sales volume of a proposed store.

Still another way to analyze data is to use an index of sales potential, such as an index of consumer purchasing power. For example, the Buying Power Index is available each year on the internet and provides an index of percentage of total retail sales occurring in a given geographical area. This index is used to predict demand for new stores and evaluate the performance of existing retail businesses. In addition, *Sales and Marketing Magazine* is available online and contains information useful for setting sales quotas, planning distribution, and studying sales potential. Information on population and income is provided for every state by county and city. This type of information can help the prospective entrepreneur-manager predict sales in the area and determine whether the business would be an acceptable risk.

Still another type of analysis involves consumer surveys. These surveys attempt to learn what customers want. They do not have to be conducted by the prospective entrepreneur; consumer surveys are often conducted by colleges and universities or Chambers of Commerce and generally are available for the asking. These surveys provide important information about local consumer demand, often revealing data that contradict national norms. For instance, although an area may have twice as many outlets as the national average, local consumer demand might be such that room still exists for another outlet.

Implementation of an Action Plan

If the analysis reveals that the business venture is a wise one, the entrepreneur can go ahead and begin operations. The specific procedures to follow during this action phase will be discussed in the next section. For the moment, however, it is imperative to remember that the plan may not work perfectly. Some modification may be necessary. Thus, the entrepreneur has to be flexible in planning. If something does not work out, a contingency or backup plan should be available. The worst thing the entrepreneur can do is adopt an "all or nothing" perspective. After the analysis is complete and the entrepreneur is ready to proceed, an action plan is needed. What will be done, and how will it be done? This plan should cover three areas:

1. The entrepreneur as a person
2. The financial picture
3. Other key factors (marketing, insurance, building, etc.)

The Entrepreneur as a Person

Before making the final decision about going into business, the entrepreneur needs to ask a number of personal questions. Ten of the most important ones are listed here. As you read, mark the response that best describes you.

1. Are you a self-starter?

   - I can get going without help from others.
   - Once someone gets me going, I am just fine.
   - I take things easy and do not move until I have to.

2. How do you feel about others?

   - I can get along with just about anyone.
   - I do not need anyone else.
   - People irritate me.

3. Can you lead people?

   - I can get most people to go along with me once I start something.
   - I can give the orders if someone tells me what should be done.
   - I let someone else get things done and go along if I like it.

4. Can you take responsibility?

   - I take charge and see things through.
   - I'll take over if necessary but would rather let someone else be responsible.
   - If someone is around who wants to do it, I let him or her.

5. Are you an organizer?

   - I like to have a plan before I begin.
   - I do all right unless things get too confusing, in which case I quit.
   - Whenever I have things all set up, something always comes along to disrupt the plan, so I take things as they come.

6. Are you a hard worker?

   - I can keep going as long as necessary.
   - I work hard for a while, but then that's it.
   - I cannot see that hard work gets you anywhere.

7. Can you make decisions?

   - I can make decisions, and they usually turn out pretty well.
   - I can make decisions if I have plenty of time, but fast decision-making upsets me.
   - I do not like to be the one who has to decide things.

8. Can people rely on your word?

   - Yes, I do not say things I do not mean.
   - I try to level with people, but sometimes I say what is easiest.
   - Why bother? The other person does not know the difference.

9. Can you stick with it?

   - When I make up my mind to do something, nothing stops me.
   - I usually finish what I start.
   - If things start to go awry, I usually quit.

10. How good is your health?

    - Excellent.
    - Pretty good.
    - Okay, but it has been better.

Now count the number of checks you have made next to the first responses and multiply this number by 3. Count the checks next to the second responses and multiply by 2. Count the number of times you checked the third answer. Total these three numbers. Out of a total possible 30 points, a successful entrepreneur will have at least 25 points. If not, the prospective entrepreneur-manager should consider bringing in a partner or abandoning the idea of going into business alone. The potential entrepreneur should keep in mind these personal factors while formulating the action plan.

The Financial Picture

The next plan area the prospective entrepreneur-manager must cover is an evaluation of the enterprise's financial picture. How much will it cost to stay in business for the first year? How much revenue will the firm generate during this time period? If the outflow of cash is greater than the inflow, how long will it take before the entrepreneurial venture turns the corner?

Answering these questions requires consideration of two kinds of expenses: Startup and monthly. Table 3.2 illustrates a typical worksheet for making the necessary calculations of startup expenses. Notice that this worksheet is based in the assumption that no money will flow in for about three months. Also, all startup costs are totally covered. If the firm is in the manufacturing business, however, it will be three to four months before any goods are produced and sold, so the factors in column 3 have to be doubled, and the amount of cash needed for startup will be greater. This may be the same situation in some service businesses as well.

Much of the information needed to fill in this worksheet already should have been gathered and at least partially analyzed. Now, however, it can be put into a format that allows the entrepreneur to look at the overall financial picture.

At this point the individual should be concerned with what is called *upside gain and downside loss*. This term refers to the profits the business can make and the losses it can suffer. How much money will the enterprise take in if everything goes well? How much will it gross if operations run as expected? How much will it lose if operations do not work out well? Answers to these questions provide a composite picture of the most optimistic, the most likely, and the most pessimistic results. The entrepreneur has to keep in mind that the upside may be minimal, while the downside loss may be great.

It is necessary to examine overall gains and losses. This kind of analysis is referred to as *risk versus reward* analysis and points out the importance of getting an adequate return on the amount of money risked.

Other Key Factors

The third planning area the prospective entrepreneur-manager must be concerned with consists of operational information, which will be examined throughout the remainder of this book. However, these factors warrant attention here because of their importance in startup activities. Some of the major considerations, put in the form of questions, include the following:

- The location/building
  - o   Is it currently adequate?
  - o   Can it be fixed up without spending too much money?
  - o   Does it have room for expansion?
  - o   Can people get to it easily from parking spaces, bus stops, or their homes?
  - o   Has a lawyer checked the lease agreement and zoning ordinances?
- Merchandise and equipment
  - o   Have suppliers who will sell at reasonable prices been located?
  - o   Have the prices and credit terms of suppliers been compared?
- o   Have all the equipment and suppliers needed for operation been purchased?

Table 3.2 Checklist for Estimating Startup Expenses

MONTHLY Item	EXPENSES Estimate based on sales of $___ per year	CASH NEEDED TO START THE BUSINESS (see column 3)	WHAT TO PUT IN COLUMN 2 (These figures are estimates. The entrepreneur-manager must decide how many months to allow depending on the type of business.)
Salary of entrepreneur-manager	Column 1 $	Column 2 $	Column 3 3 times column 1
Other salaries and wages			3 times column 1
Rent			3 times column 1
Advertising			3 times column 1
Delivery expense			3 times column 1
Supplies			3 times column 1
Telephone or iPhone			3 times column 1
Other utilities			3 times column 1
Insurance			6 times column 1
Taxes, Social Security			4 times column 1
Interest			3 times column 1
Maintenance			3 times column 1
Legal and other professional assistance			3 times column 1
Miscellaneous			3 times column 1

STARTUP COSTS		
Item	Estimate	TO ARRIVE AT ESTIMATE
Fixtures and equipment	$	Determine what is typical for this kind of business; talk to suppliers.
Decorating and remodeling		Talk to a contractor.
Installation of fixtures, equipment		Talk to suppliers.
Starting inventory		Talk to suppliers.
Deposits with public utilities		Talk to utility companies.
Legal and other professional fees		Talk to a lawyer, accountant, or other professional.
Licenses and permits		Contact appropriate city offices.
Advertising and promotion		Decide what will be used; talk to media.

MONTHLY Item	EXPENSES Estimate based on sales of $___ per year	CASH NEEDED TO START THE BUSINESS (see column 3)	WHAT TO PUT IN COLUMN 2 (These figures are estimates. The entrepreneur-manager must decide how many months to allow depending on the type of business.)
Accounts receivable			Estimate how much will be tied up in receivables by credit customers and for how long.
Cash			Allow for unexpected expenses and losses, special purchases, and other expenditures.
Other expenses			List and estimate costs.
TOTAL CASH NEEDED TO START	$_____		Add all estimated amounts.

Source: U.S. Small Business Administration, "Management Aids" MA. 2.025 (Washington, DC: U.S. Government Printing Office).

- Record-keeping
  - o Has a record-keeping system been planned for income and expenses, inventory, payroll, and taxes?
  - o Has an accountant been found to help with records and financial statements?
  - o Have all the financial statements needed for control purposes been identified? Does the entrepreneur-manager know how to use them?
- Insurance and legal concerns
  - o Have plans been made for protecting against insurable losses?
  - o Have all licenses and permits been obtained?
  - o Has a lawyer been hired to assist with the legal aspects of the operation?
- Marketing and personnel
  - o Have prices for all goods been determined?
  - o Has a buying plan been worked out?
  - o Is an advertising program or some form of promotion ready to go?
  - o Will credit be given to customers? On what basis?
  - o Will salespeople be used? If so, how will they be recruited? Is a training program planned for them? How much will they be paid?

If questions like these can be answered, the entrepreneur-manager is in a good position to begin. However, in most cases it is necessary for the individual to look more closely into one or more of these operational areas; perhaps the individual does not fully understand some aspects of the operation.

Buying An Ongoing Venture

One of the most frequent opportunities individuals confront is the purchase of an ongoing business. This may be one of the easiest ways for an entrepreneur to get started. A lot of headaches can be avoided with this approach. For example, startup problems will have been taken care of by previous entrepreneurs. Additionally, the business has a track record the buyer can examine to determine the types of products to sell, the prices to charge, etc. But buying an existing business also has potential pitfalls. Examples include buying a company whose success has been due to the personality and charisma of the entrepreneur-manager, buying a company when the market for its product has peaked, or simply paying more for a company than it is worth. In this section, we will examine the advantages of buying an ongoing business as well as the key valuation methods that help individuals determine a fair price to pay for someone else's business.

Advantages of Buying an Ongoing Venture

Of the numerous advantages to buying an ongoing business, three of the most important are as follows:

1. Since the enterprise is already in operation, its successful future operation is likely.
2. The time and effort associated with starting a new enterprise are eliminated.
3. It is sometimes possible to buy an ongoing business at a bargain price.

Each of these three advantages is discussed next.

Less Fear About Successful Future Operation

A new business faces two great dangers: The possibility it will not find a market for its goods or services and the chance it will not be able to control its costs. If either event occurs, the new business will go bankrupt.

Buying an existing concern, however, alleviates most of these fears. A successful business has already demonstrated the ability to attract customers, control costs, and make a profit. Additionally, many of the problems a newly formed firm faces are sidestepped. For example, Where should the company be located? How should it advertise? What type of plant or merchandise layout will be the most effective? What type of service does the potential customer base desire? How much should be reordered every three months? What types of customers will this business attract? What pricing strategy should the firm use? Questions such as these have already been asked and answered. Thus, when buying an ongoing operation, the new entrepreneur is often purchasing a *known quantity*. Of course, it is important to check whether hidden problems exist in the operation. Barring something of this nature, however, the purchase of an existing successful operating venture can be a wise investment.

Time and Effort Can Be Reduced

An ongoing enterprise has already assembled the inventory, equipment, personnel, and facilities necessary to run it. In many cases this has taken the entrepreneurs a long time to do. They have spent countless hours "working out the bugs" so that the business is as efficient as possible. Likewise, they probably have gone through a fair number of employees before getting the right type of personnel. Except for the top management in an operating venture, the personnel usually stay with the sale. Therefore, if the new owners treat the workers fairly, they should not have to worry about hiring, placing, and training personnel.

In addition, the previous owners undoubtedly have established relations with suppliers, bankers, and other businesspeople. These individuals can often be relied on to provide assistance to the new owners. The suppliers know the type of merchandise the business orders and how often it needs to be replenished. They can be a source of advice about managing the operation, as can the bankers with whom the enterprise has been doing business. These individuals know the enterprise's capital needs and often provide new owners with the same credit line and assistance they gave the previous owners. The same holds true for the accountant, the lawyer, and any other professionals who served the business in an advisory capacity. Naturally, the new owners may have their own bankers, accountant, or lawyer, but these old relationships are there if the new owners need them.

Buy at a Good Price

Sometimes it is possible to buy an ongoing operating venture at a very good price. The entrepreneur may want to sell quickly because of a retirement decision or illness. Or the entrepreneur may be forced to sell the business to raise money for some emergency that has occurred. Or the entrepreneur may seek a greater opportunity in another type of business and therefore be willing to sell at a low price to take advantage of the new opportunity. Ideally, when one is looking to buy an ongoing, successful operating venture, one of these three advantages (especially the last one) is present. However, seldom does someone in business sell a successful firm at an extraordinarily low price. The entrepreneur of a successful small venture built the enterprise through skillful business practices, knows how to deal with people, and has a good idea of the operation's fair market value. The person will rarely sell for much below the fair market value. Therefore, the prospective entrepreneur must avoid bidding high on a poor investment or walking away from a good bargain because it seems too good to be true. The way to prevent making the wrong decision is to evaluate the existing operation in a logical manner.

Key Questions to Ask

When deciding whether to buy, the astute prospective entrepreneur needs to ask and answer a series of "right questions."[3] The following section discusses questions and provides insights into the types of actions to take for each response. While some of these questions may be more pertinent to manufacturing ventures, keep in mind that service and internet operations may still benefit from some of these questions.

Why Is the Business Being Sold?

One of the first questions that should be asked is *why* the owner is selling the business.[4] Quite often a difference exists between the reason given to prospective buyers and the real reason. Typical responses include "I'm thinking about retiring"; "I've proven to myself that I can be successful in this line of business, so now I'm moving to another operation that will provide me with new challenges"; and "I want to move to California and go into business with my brother-in-law there."

Any of these statements may be accurate, and if they can be substantiated, the buyer may find that the business is indeed worth purchasing. However, because it is difficult to substantiate this sort of personal information, the next big thing to do is to check around and gather business-related information. Is the owner in trouble with the suppliers? Is the lease on the building due for renewal and the landlord planning to triple the rent? Worse yet, is the building about to be torn down? Other site-location problems may relate to competition in the nearby area or zoning changes. Is a new shopping mall about to be built nearby that will take much of the business away from this location? Has the city council passed a new ordinance that calls for the closing of business on Sunday, the day of the week when this store does 25 percent of its business?

Financially, what is the owner going to do after selling the business? Is the seller planning to stay in town? What employment opportunities does he or she have? The reason for asking these questions is that the new owner's worst nightmare is finding out that the previous owner has set up a similar business a block away and is drawing back all of the customers. One way to prevent this from happening is to have an attorney write into the contract a covenant not to compete clause that lasts for a period of at least five years. This is known as a legal restraint of trade—an "agreement not to compete" or "non-compete clause." Doing this helps the new owner retain the customers.

What is the Current Physical Condition of the Business?

Even if the asking price for the operation appears to be fair, it is necessary to examine the *physical condition of the assets*. Does the company own the building? If it does, how much repair work needs to be done? If the building is leased, does the lease provide for the kinds of repairs that will enhance the successful operation of the business? For example, if a flower shop has a somewhat large refrigerator for keeping flowers cool, who has to pay to expand the size of the refrigerator? If the landlord agrees to do so and to recover the investment through an increase in the lease price, the total cost of the additional refrigerated space must be compared to the expected increase in business. By contrast, if the landlord does not want to make this type of investment, the new owners must realize that any permanent additions to the property remain with the property. This means that if something simply cannot be carried out of the building, it stays. Pictures on the walls, chairs, and desks the previous business owner purchased can be removed. However, new bookshelves nailed to the wall, carpeting attached to the floor, a new acoustic ceiling installed to cut down on noise in the shop, and the new refrigerated area all become the permanent property of the building owner. Therefore, the overriding question while examining the physical facilities is, how much will it cost to get things in order?

What Is the Condition of the Inventory?

How much inventory does the current owner show on the books? Does a physical check show that inventory actually exists? Additionally, is inventory *salable* or is it out of date or badly deteriorated?

What Is the State of the Company's Other Assets?

Most operating ventures have assets in addition to the physical facilities and inventory. A machine shop, for example, may have various types of presses and other machinery. An office may have computers, copiers, and other technology belonging to the business. The question to ask about all of this equipment is, is it still useful or has it been replaced by more modern technology? In short, are these assets obsolete?

Another often overlooked asset is the firm's records. If the business has kept careful records, it may be possible to determine who is a good credit risk and who is not. Additionally, these records make it easy for a new owner to decide how much credit to extend to the prior customers. Likewise, sales records can be very important because they show seasonal demands and peak periods. This can provide the new owner with information for inventory control purposes and can greatly reduce the risks of over- or understocking.

Still another commonly overlooked asset is past contracts. What type of lease does the current owner have on the building? If the lease was signed three years ago and is a seven-year lease with a fixed rent, it may have been somewhat high when it came into effect but may be somewhat on the low side for comparable facilities today. Furthermore, over the next four years the rent should prove to be quite low considering what competitors will be paying. Of course, if the lease is about to expire, this is a different story. Then the prospective owner has to talk to the landlord to find out what the terms of the lease will be. Additionally, a prospective entrepreneur's lawyer should look at the old lease to determine if it can be passed on to a new owner and, regardless of the rent, how difficult it is to break the lease if the business should start to fail.

Finally, the prospective buyer must look at intangible assets such as *goodwill, patents, franchise rights,* and *non-compete agreements.* Goodwill is often defined as the value of the company beyond what is shown on the books. For example, if a software company has a reputation for quick and accurate service, the company has built up goodwill among its customers. If the owners were to sell the business, the buyer would have to pay not only for the physical assets in the software company (office furniture, computers, etc.) but also for the goodwill the firm has accumulated over the years. Patents, franchise rights, and non-compete agreements are also important in valuing a business, but it is very difficult to assess the future value of these assets. The key issue is that these intangible assets could be a major part of the value of any business and should not be overlooked.[5] The reputation of the business has a value.[6]

How Many of the Employees Will Remain?

It is often difficult to give customers the good service they have come to expect if seasoned employees decide they do not want to remain with the new owner. The owner is certainly an important asset of the firm but so are the employees; they play a role in making the business a success. Therefore, one question the prospective buyer must ask is, If some people will be leaving, will enough be left to maintain the type of service the customer is used to getting? In particular, the new owner must be concerned about key people who are not staying. Key employees are part of the value of the business. If it is evident these people will not be staying, the prospective buyer must subtract something from the purchase price by making some allowance for the decline in sales and the accompanying expense associated with replacing *key personnel.*

Also, when purchasing an existing business, you should conduct an assessment of the current group of employees. Review existing performance evaluations and talk with current owners about the quality of each employee and their value to the business. It may be easier to retain valuable employees by seeking them out before the purchase to ensure they feel secure. As the incoming new owner, interview all the current employees and make decisions on who to keep and who to let go before you actually take over the enterprise.

What Type of Competition Does the Business Face?

No matter what goods or services the business provides, the number of people who will want it and the total amount of money they will spend for it is limited. Thus, the greater the competition, the less the business's chance of earning large profits. As the number of competitors increases, the cost of fighting them usually goes up. More money must be spent on advertising. Price competition must be met with accompanying reductions in overall revenue. Simply too many companies are pursuing the same market.

Additionally, the *quality of competition* must be considered. If nine competitors exist, you could estimate a market share of ten percent. However, some of these competitors undoubtedly will be more effective than others. One or two may have very good advertising and know how to use it to capture 25 percent of the market. A few others may offer outstanding service and use this advantage to capture 20 percent of the market. Meanwhile, the remaining six fight for what is left. Then the location of the competition must be considered. In many instances, a new venture does not offer anything unique, so people buy on the basis of convenience. A service located on the corner may get most of the business of local residents. One located across town will get virtually none. Since the product is the same at each location, no one is going to drive across town. This analogy holds true for groceries, notions, drugs, and hardware. If competitors are located near each other, each will take some of the business the others could have expected, but none is going to maximize its income. But if the merchandise is items such as furniture, people will shop very carefully, so a competitor in the immediate area can be a distinct advantage. For example, two furniture stores located near each other tend to draw a total number of customers greater than they would if located ten blocks apart. When people shop for furniture, they go where a large selection is available. With adjacent stores, customers will reason that if the furniture they are looking for is not in one, it might be in the other. Additionally, since they can step from one store to the next, they can easily compare prices and sale terms. Finally, the emergence of the internet has introduced another competitive threat that must be considered. How effective are internet sales in this particular industry? Are customers likely to "shop at home" using the internet as their source?

Finally, any analysis of competition should look for *unscrupulous practices*. How cutthroat are the competitors? If they are very cutthroat, the prospective buyer will have to be continually alert to practices such as price fixing and kickbacks to suppliers for special services. Usually, if the company has been around for a couple of years, it has been successful dealing with these types of practices. However, if some competitors are getting bad reputations, the new owner will want to know this. After all, over time customers are likely to form a stereotyped impression of enterprises in a given geographic area and will simply refuse to do business with any of them: "It's no use looking for clothing in the Eighth Street area." In this case the customers are retaliating against unethical business practices by boycotting the entire area where these firms are located. In short, an unethical business competitor can drag down other firms as well.

What is the Status of the Firm's Financial Picture?

It may be necessary for a prospective buyer to hire an accountant to look over the company's books. It is important to get an idea of how well the firm is doing financially. One of the primary areas of interest should be the *company's profitability*.[7] Is the business doing anything wrong that can be spotted from the statements? If so, can the prospective buyer eliminate these problems?

Individuals who are skilled in buying companies that are in trouble, straightening them out, and reselling them at a profit know what to look for when examining the books. So do good accountants. Both also know that the seller's books alone should not be taken as proof of sales or profits. One should insist on seeing records of bank deposits for the past two to three years. If the current owner has held the firm for only a short time, the records of the previous owner should also be examined. In fact, it is not out of line to ask for the owner's income tax return. The astute buyer knows that the firm's records reflect its condition.

Another area of interest is the firm's *profit trend*. Is it making more money year after year? More importantly, are profits going up as fast as sales or is more and more revenue necessary to attain the same profit? If the latter is true, this means the business may have to increase sales five to ten percent annually to net as much as it did the previous year. This spells trouble and is often a sign the owner is selling because "there are easier ways to make a living."

Finally, even if the company is making money, the prospective buyer should compare the firm's performance to that of similar companies. For example, if a small retail shop is making a 22 percent return in investment this year in contrast to 16 percent two years ago, is this good or bad? It certainly appears to be good, but what if competing stores are making a 32 percent return on investment? Given this information, the firm is not doing as well.

One way to compare a company to the competition is to obtain comparative information put out by firms such as Dun & Bradstreet that gather data on retail and wholesale firms in various fields and provide businesspeople with an overall view of many key financial ratios. For example, one of the most important ratios is the comparison of current assets (cash or items that can be turned into cash in the short run) to current liabilities (debts that will come due in the short run). This key ratio reflects a business's ability to meet its current obligations. A second key ratio is the comparison of net profits to net sales (net profit margin). How much profit is the owner making for every dollar in sales? A third key ratio is net profit to net worth (return on net worth). How much profit is the individual making for every dollar invested in the firm? Table 3.3 shows the key ratios and other data for numerous types of business.

By comparing the accounting information obtained from a business's books to financial data such as those illustrated in Table 3.3, it is possible to determine how well the business is doing. If the facts look good, then the prospective buyer can turn to the question of how much to offer the seller. In Chapter 9, we will cover all the needed aspects of financial ratios.

Determining the Price

After the previously mentioned questions and issues have been resolved, the prospective entrepreneur must answer one final question: "How much are you willing to pay for the business?" This is not an easy question to answer. However, because the enterprise is small, fewer factors need to be considered than if a large corporation were being purchased. Additionally, some commonly accepted indicators can be used to establish an enterprise's value.

Table 3.3 Key Data by Business

Line of Business	Quick Ratio (times)	Current Ratio (times)	Collection Period (days)	Accounts Payable to Net Sales (%)	Overall Gross Profit (%)	Net Profit Margin (%)	Asset Turnover (times)	Return on Net Worth (%)
Automotive dealers	0.6	1.8	16.4	4.5	22.5	2.8	5.5	14.6
Book stores	0.5	2.4	6.9	8.7	36.9	2.9	4.3	12.5
Children's clothing stores	0.6	3.6	6.9	3.8	36.0	4.6	4.2	12.8
Department stores	1.0	3.4	11.7	5.5	32.7	1.7	4.4	6.0
Eating places	0.6	1.0	4.0	3.2	52.6	3.8	74.5	18.5
Employment agencies	2.1	2.4	44.9	1.6	29.6	5.2	109.7	35.4
Fitness facilities	0.7	1.0	24.1	3.3	74.4	5.6	83.1	16.0
Florists	1.1	2.1	18.5	4.0	48.9	4.0	15.3	12.2
Furniture stores	0.9	2.7	25.2	5.0	37.4	3.9	4.8	9.2
Gift & novelty shops	0.7	3.2	6.2	4.4	42.2	5.2	4.7	17.0

Line of Business	Quick Ratio (times)	Current Ratio (times)	Collection Period (days)	Accounts Payable to Net Sales (%)	Overall Gross Profit (%)	Net Profit Margin (%)	Asset Turnover (times)	Return on Net Worth (%)
Grocery stores	0.5	1.6	2.9	3.2	21.6	1.7	19.2	12.6
Hardware stores	0.7	3.0	18.3	5.2	33.8	3.0	4.5	8.9
Hobby, toy & game shops	0.6	3.1	3.1	4.7	39.9	4.1	4.6	13.2
Hotels & motels	0.8	1.2	9.5	3.1	66.0	8.1	92.2	14.7
Mail-order houses	0.8	2.1	14.1	6.2	38.5	3.3	7.9	17.5
Medical equipment rental facilities	1.5	2.3	63.0	5.0	63.7	6.8	19.1	18.0
Men's & boys' clothing stores	0.9	2.0	32.5	5.7	24.6	3.7	8.1	18.2
Public golf courses	0.8	1.5	6.8	2.8	71.7	3.2	31.3	8.4
Radio, TV & electronics stores	0.7	2.0	13.5	5.3	35.5	3.8	7.1	17.1
Shoe stores	0.5	3.7	6.2	5.9	37.2	5.0	3.7	14.1
Sporting goods stores	0.8	1.9	35.4	6.8	26.7	2.7	5.8	3.7
Tobacco stores	0.4	2.3	6.6	3.6	31.4	6.6	9.3	44.8
Variety stores	p.8	3.8	4.8	4.4	35.2	4.2	4.7	11.3
Women's clothing stores	0.9	3.7	11.7	4.2	37.4	5.1	5.2	12.3

For a more thorough and updated analysis see Steven M. Bragg, Business Ratios and Formulas: A Comprehensive Guide, 3rd edition (Wiley Publishers, 2012).

Assessing the Price

A number of indexes reflect an operating venture's value. Five of the most important are as follows:

1. Book value
2. Replacement value
3. Liquidation value
4. Past earnings
5. Cash flow

Book Value

Book value refers to the value of the company's assets from an accounting standpoint. For example, if the firm bought a new machine for $25,000 last year and it has been in operation for one year, its book value would be $20,000, assuming five-year, straight-line depreciation. Likewise, if the business has bought 1,000 shirts for $7 each, they would be carried in the books for $7,000. However, if something has lost value, its book value should be written down; assets should be carried at *cost* or *present value*, whichever is *lower*. For example, if the enterprise has just learned that 1,000 shirts it bought are now out of style, it may be lucky to get $4 each for them, and the shirts should be written down from $7,000 to $4,000.

Replacement Value

Replacement value refers to how much it would cost to buy the same machinery, materials, or merchandise on the market today. In many cases, the use of replacement value increases the asking price for a business. For example, land is seldom in the books at replacement value. If the land was bought ten years ago for $150,000, it may be worth double that today.

Liquidation Value

Liquidation value reflects the worth of the business's assets if they were thrown on the market today and purchased by knowledgeable buyers. This value is usually the lowest of those discussed here because most assets sell for far less than their original purchase price. Consider, for example, that most people expect to buy things at an auction more cheaply than anywhere else. *Auction value* is another term for the liquidation value. It is what the owner can get for the assets in a competitive bidding situation.

Past Earnings

Past earnings are important because the bottom-line reason for buying someone's business is to make money. Therefore, the prospective entrepreneur would be wise to choose a business that has been profitable. Of course, to obtain these earnings, the *physical assets* (building, machinery, material, inventory) are also needed, but in the final analysis the prospective entrepreneur must be concerned with what he or she can earn with these assets.

Cash Flow

Cash flow is still another measure of value. In most service and internet businesses, this measure is the most widely used. It is equal to net profit after taxes plus any "noncash" expenses, such as depreciation, depletion, or amortization. *Noncash expenses* are items that can be written off on the company's income tax, thus saving it money while not requiring a layout of cash. We will discuss these later, but, for the moment, keep in mind that these expenses help free up cash for the firm. The reason many people use cash flow as an index of value is that high cash flows are instrumental in reducing debt and helping the firm expand. A company with a high cash flow, therefore, is preferable to one whose cash flow is moderate or low.

None of these five indexes of value is likely to be used exclusively for determining a fair price for an operating venture. However, liquidation value tends to be favored over book value or replacement value if the firm is going out of business. Likewise, in any computation of purchase price, past earnings will play a major role. Before looking at a formula for determining a fair purchase price, however, we must consider asset pricing.

Asset Pricing

A prospective buyer first needs to approach the purchase of a business from a rational standpoint. Some common assets and the ways to evaluate them are discussed here.

- *Building:* If the company owns the building, what value does it have on the company books? Deduct the cost of any repairs or alterations that are needed to keep the facility in working shape.
- *Inventory:* Adjust the purchase price to account for slow-moving or obsolete items.
- *Equipment:* Deduct depreciation of equipment from the purchase price. If some of the equipment is not usable because of age or obsolescence, pay no more than liquidation value for it.
- *Prepaid expenses:* Buy prepaid expenses at face value. These include fire and theft insurance premiums the owner pays annually that have coverage remaining.
- *Supplies:* If supplies are usable, buy them at the price the owner paid, unless the price has changed. In that case, adjust upward or downward to reflect the change.
- *Accounts receivable:* Purchase customer obligations after first deducting those so old they are deemed uncollectible. Also, if it appears it will take 60 days, on average, to collect the rest, deduct two to three percent from the total as an expense for the investment in these receivables, unless a monthly charge is added to outstanding accounts. Remember, time is money, and unless the business charges the customer monthly interest, the new owner is buying accounts receivable that will not be turned into cash for 60 days. Since most retail credit cards charge one to two percent per month, the buyer should make a similar charge to the seller.
- *Goodwill:* This is the excess of the selling price over the value of the physical assets. Goodwill depends on factors such as (1) how long it would take to set up a similar business and the expense and risk associated with such a venture, (2) the amount of income to be made by purchasing an ongoing concern rather than starting a new one, (3) the price the owner of this business is asking for goodwill compared to what owners of similar businesses ask, and (4) the value associated with the seller's agreement to remain out of the same business within the competitive area.

Of these assets, goodwill is the only *intangible* one. The buyer cannot *see* goodwill; the individual can only try to assess its presence and assign a value to it. Before illustrating how this can be done, one final point merits discussion: The buyer should not pay more for goodwill than can be recovered from profits within a reasonable period. Usually this period is three to five years, although if one were purchasing a major corporation such as Microsoft, the goodwill price might take 10 years to recover because the product is continuously innovating and may be valuable for a longer period.

One Acceptable Formula?

No one has a surefire way to attach a price to the value of an ongoing operating venture. However, one formula is straightforward and may prove the most understandable for a prospective entrepreneur. The seven steps of the formula are described here and illustrated with a real-life situation. Refer to Table 3.4 as you read the steps.

Table 3.4 Determining a Purchase Price

	Step	Amount
1.	Liquidation or market value of all assets minus liabilities	$100,000
2.	Earning power of ten percent	$10,000
3.	Salary for the entrepreneur-manager	$30,000
4.	Average annual earnings before subtracting	
	Entrepreneur-manager's salary and earning power	$30,000
5.	Extra earning power of the business (step 4 minus step 3)	$5,000
6.	Value of intangibles using a five-year profit figure (five times step 5)	$25,000
7.	Final price (step 1 plus step 6)	$125,000

Step 1 Determine the value of the business by identifying the liquidation or market value of all the assets and then subtracting the debts or liabilities of the business. This has been determined to be $100,000 for this example.

Step 2 Determine how much the buyer could earn with this money if it were invested somewhere else. If the risk in the current business is very high, this percentage should be set at ten percent or $10,000.

Step 3 To the figure must be added a salary for the entrepreneur-manager. This figure has been set at $30,000. The sum of steps 2 and 3 represents the total the prospective buyer could expect to earn if the investment were placed elsewhere and if the efforts involved in working in the business are taken into account. This total amount would be 40,000.

Step 4 Determine the average net profit before taxes and the average salary the entrepreneur-manager can obtain from this business over the next few years. This is a key calculation because it forces the buyer to answer the question, how long will it take to recoup the investment? This figure has been determined to be $30,000.

Step 5   Subtract the earning power and the salary (steps 2 and 3) from the average net earnings in step 4. This represents the "extra earning power" the buyer will obtain by owning the business.

Step 6   Take this extra earning power and estimate the number of years it will exist. This, in effect, represents what the buyer is willing to pay for the firm's goodwill. In our example, a five-year profit figure has been used. This means the buyer is willing to pay $25,000 for the firm's intangible assets. If the firm is well established, five is a reasonable multiplier. If it is a new company, it is common to find the multiplier varying between one and three. Obviously, the more established the business, the more the buyer should be willing to pay for goodwill.

Step 7   This is the final price. It is equal to the net market value of the assets plus the value of the intangibles. In this case, the buyer has set a purchase price of $125,000 as fair and reasonable.

An advantage of this formula is that it helps the buyer arrive at a fair price for intangible assets, specifically goodwill. In our example (Table 3.4), the total of the earning power and the entrepreneur-manager's salary was less than the average annual new earnings. This can be easily verified by comparing the total of steps 2 and 3 with that in step 4: The latter is larger. However, if the latter is not larger, the seller should not assign any value to goodwill because the earning power of the investment and the amount the buyer can earn from personal effort are greater than can be obtained from running the business. How, then, does the buyer decide on a final selling price?

In this case, the buyer needs to recalculate the price by determining the average annual profit and capitalizing it by the desired rate of return. For example, assume the initial data in Table 3.4 are the same except that the average annual net earnings before subtracting the earning power and entrepreneur-manager's salary are only $20,000. In this case the business has no extra earning power (step 5), so the value of the intangibles (step 6) will be zero. Additionally, since the buyer wants to obtain an earning power of ten percent (step 2), it is necessary to take the average annual net earnings and subtract the entrepreneur-manager's salary:

$$\$20,000 - \$15,000 = \$5,000 \text{ proft}$$

After the new entrepreneur takes a salary of $15,000, only $5,000 will be left as a return on the original investment. Since the individual wants to secure a ten percent return on the original investment, the purchase price must be ten times the profit:

$$\$5,000 / 0.10 = \$50,000 \text{ purchase price.}$$

Since this may be difficult to grasp without practice, another example is in order. This time, still using the data in Table 3.4, assume the average net earnings before the entrepreneur-manager's salary and earning power are subtracted are $23,000. In this case, then, the buyer's profit after salary is deducted will be $8,000:

$23,000 - $15,000 = $8,000$ profit

Since the individual wishes to make a ten percent profit on the investment, the purchase price is equal to ten times the profit:

$8,000 / 0.10 = $80,000$ purchase price

Finally, consider an example for which the basic data in Table 3.4 still apply, but the average annual net earnings before the entrepreneur-manager's salary and earning power are $25,000. How much should the individual now pay for the business? The answer is $100,000 because the firm will have no extra earning power. The person will just clear the desired ten percent on investment, or $10,000, after the $15,000 salary is deducted from the $25,000 profit before taxes.

Before we close this discussion about buying an ongoing concern, a final point is in order. The formula presented here provides a reasonable estimate of what to pay for a business. However, this price must be tempered by how badly a seller wants to get rid of the business and how much the buyer wants to acquire it. Quite often the desire of either or both parties dictates the final selling price, and a mathematical formula is just the beginning, Thus, in the first example, where a final selling price of $125,000 was reached, the buyer would have to compare this price with the asking price. If the seller wants $130,000, the buyer might offer $120,000 and then negotiate up to $125,000. This does not mean, however, that the final price will always be the midpoint between the original asking price and the original bid. If the seller refuses to accept less than $130,000, the buyer should either walk away from the deal or agree to pay a premium for the business. In this case, the individual's return on investment will be reduced slightly because of paying more for the business. Would such a purchase be wise? This question can be answered only by the prospective entrepreneur, for in the final analysis "fair price" is whatever the buyer is willing to pay.[8] However, buyers must educate themselves to identify the "fair" price. One suggestion is for buyers to follow a six-step process when determining the value of a business.[9] These steps are:

1. Prepare the financial statements and determine the SDE.

Gather the financial records for the past three years, including an income statement, a cash flow statement, and a balance sheet. Next, work with an accountant to transform the income statement into a seller's discretionary earnings (SDE) statement, which takes into account non-recurring purchases and discretionary expenses to more accurately reflect the value of your business.

2. Establish the asset value of the business.

First, estimate the value of the company's tangible assets by taking inventory of all the physical aspects of the business, such as fixtures, equipment, and inventory.

Then estimate the value of the company's intangible assets, including intellectual property, contracts, partnerships, and brand recognition.

3. Use price multiples to estimate the value of the business.

This bases the value of the business on a multiple of its potential earnings. Price multiples provide buyers with a tool to estimate their return on investment. Once you've established the asset valuation of the business, the next step is to determine the multiple that applies to the geographical region and type of industry. These numbers combine to form an equation that results in a fair estimate of the business's sale price. For example, nationally, the average business sells for around 0.6 times its annual revenue.

4. Use comparables of sold businesses.

By identifying examples of similar businesses that have sold in the same area, you can get a better sense of a realistic selling price. These data can be accessed through several online sources as well as through business brokers, who can help provide you with the right multiplier for your market.

5. Consult with a professional appraiser and get a formal valuation.

Many brokers are experienced at conducting a formal valuation or have connections with qualified professionals. Valuing a business correctly is essential in a competitive market, and enlisting the help of a third-party professional will not only eliminate seller sentiment from the sales process but will also shorten the sales process by aligning the business value with up-to-date market conditions.

6. Use the final business valuation formula.

Use the following formula to come to an estimated business value:

$$\textit{Business' Estimated Value} = (SDC) \times (\textit{Industry Multiple}) + (\textit{Real Estate})$$
$$+ (\textit{Accounts Receivable}) + (\textit{Cash on Hand}) + (\textit{Other Assets Not in SDE}$$
$$\textit{or Multiplier}) - (\textit{Business Liabilities})$$

Negotiating the Deal

After a proper valuation of the business is completed, the potential buyer must negotiate the final deal.[10] This negotiation process, however, involves a number of factors. Four critical elements should be recognized: Information, time, pressure, and alternatives.

Information may be the most critical element during negotiations. The performance of the company, the nature of its competition, the condition of the market, and clear answers to all the key questions presented earlier are all vital components in the determination of the business's real potential. Without reliable information, the buyer is at a costly disadvantage. The seller should never be relied on as the sole information source. Although the seller may not falsify any information, he or she is likely to make available only the information that presents the business in the most favorable light. Therefore, the buyer should develop as many sources as possible. The rule should be to investigate every possible source.

Time is also a critical element. If the seller has already purchased another business and you are the only prospect to buy the existing firm, then you have the power to win some important concessions from the seller. If, however, the owner has no such deadline but is simply headed to retirement, or if your financial sources wish to invest in the project quickly, then you are at a serious disadvantage. In short, having more time than the other party can be very beneficial.

Pressure from others will also affect the negotiation process. If the company is owned by several partners, then the individual who is selling the company may not have complete autonomy. If one of the owners is in favor of accepting an offer, the negotiator for the company must decide whether to accept the bid on behalf of all owners or attempt to hold out for more money. This causes a distraction during the negotiation process.

Finally, the alternatives available to each party become important factors. The party with no other alternatives has a great deal of interest in concluding negotiations quickly. Table 3.5 outlines some additional considerations a person should keep in mind when purchasing a business.

Table 3.5 The "Always" of Buying a Business

Buying an ongoing business provides many advantages for a prospective purchaser, such as a proven track record, established credit, ongoing operations, and a significantly lower chance of failure. However, without careful analysis, a person buying an ongoing business may suffer from hidden problems inherited with the business. The following "always" list provides some tips to consider before signing over the check.

1. *Always have a seller "earn out" some of the purchase.* If a seller receives 100 percent of the purchase money, it is highly unlikely he or she will give you any help running the business in the future. Another option would be to have the ultimate purchase price of the business dependent on the performance of the business over the next two- to three-year period ("earn out clause").
2. *Always have the seller sign a "covenant not to compete" or "non-compete agreement."* This prevents the seller from conducting the same business within a reasonable distance and time period.
3. *Always get everything in writing.* Oral promises have no legal substance after you have purchased the business.
4. *Always have an accountant examine the books.* An accountant must examine the seller's financial statements to determine actual revenues and cash flows.
5. *Always investigate everything.* Find out as much as you can about the business before you sign the contract. Check vendors, suppliers, customers, and even the competition to get all the facts. Also, investigate the entire industry, looking for possible major shifts that could affect future business. The better your research, the better your decision.
6. *Always interview the employees.* All employees have valuable information about the company. The seller should never be afraid to let buyers communicate with employees. Remember to conduct confidential interviews so the employees are honest.

For the seller, alternatives include finding another buyer in the near future or not selling at all. He or she may continue to run the business, hire a manager to do so, or sell off parts of the company. Likewise, the buyer may choose not to purchase this business or may have alternative investment opportunities available. In any event, the negotiating parties' alternatives should be recognized because they impact the ability to reach an agreement.

Once the negotiation process is complete and the price is agreed on, the new owner ought to have an action plan already outlined. This plan should have two parts. First, financing of the business should be arranged. How is the money to be raised? If some of the funds are to be borrowed, the individual should have already discussed the matter with a banker and should know how much money the bank is willing to lend. Otherwise, personal capital should be investigated.

Second, will business continue as before or must some specific changes be made in the operation? If the new owner has decided to change some things, the plan for implementing these changes should be operational so that it can be put into effect immediately. These key action steps prepare a buyer to assume control of his or her new business.

A Global Perspective

"Problem-Solving with Entrepreneurship"

Opportunities for new ventures come from a wide variety of places, but the best ideas often come from entrepreneurs seeking solutions to problems they have experienced.

The loss of a family pineapple farm in the Philippines pushed the founder of Cropital, Rachel de Villa, to seek solutions to help stop financially stressed farmers from losing their livelihood.

Farmers in developing nations often have limited access to financial markets and are vulnerable to exploitation by predatory lending practices. In addition, farmers in developing nations often have limited access to markets for their agricultural products, depending on traders and middlemen, who may not offer fair value to sell their goods. Beyond societal risks, farmers in developing nations are also exposed to risk related to extreme weather, with limited insurance options if they lose a crop to flood—which in turn leads to more debt. Cropital facilitates loans as low as about U.S. $100 to farmers from investors around the world. Cropital does not guarantee returns, but it has seen a very high rate of loan repayment overall. Cropital offers a source of needed funding for farmers in developing countries while offering investors an alternative opportunity to obtain a return.

Mexican chemical engineer Javier Larragoiti was inspired to pursue avenues to develop a sugar substitute after his father was diagnosed with diabetes. Obesity is a leading cause of death in Mexico, and high-calorie, sugary snacks and drinks are ubiquitous in the country. Sugar substitutes have the opportunity to help address this issue. Javier's solution also has the added value of reducing greenhouse gas emissions. The sugar substitute, xilinat, is derived from corn alcohol. In Mexico, corn waste from agricultural production is often burned, releasing greenhouse gases. Redirecting this corn waste to develop xilinat helps turn what was previously an agricultural waste product into a beneficial product.

What's a problem in your life in need of a better solution? There may be a business idea for solving it.

Source: Adapted from Casey Hynes, "For Poor Filipino Farmers Reliant on Predatory Lending, This Startup Offers an Alternative," *Forbes*, June 19, 2017, www.forbes.com/sites/chynes/2017/06/19/this-filipino-startup-banks-on-alternative-investing-to-spark-an-agricultural-renaissance/#5220f2256d80; and Senay Boztas, "A Sweet Tale: The Son Who Reinvented Sugar to Help Diabetic Dad," The Guardian, May 28, 2019, www.theguardian.com/world/2019/may/28/a-sweet-tale-the-son-who-reinvented-sugar-to-help-diabetic-dad.

Summary

The easiest and best way to approach a new business venture is to design a unique product or service. Sometimes this involves what is called a new-new approach—that is, the development of an entirely new idea for a product or service, as was the case with the first Polaroid camera. In most instances, however, the prospective entrepreneur-manager must be content to use a new-old approach by "piggybacking" on someone else's ideas. This involves either expanding on what the competition is doing or offering a product or service in an area where it is not presently available.

In either event, market analysis can help a prospective entrepreneur-manager determine whether a demand for a particular good or service exists and, if so, whether this demand is sufficient to justify starting operations. Market analysis is carried out through the scientific method. The steps in this method are to state the problem or question in a clear manner, to gather all necessary facts about the problem or question, to organize and analyze these facts, to develop one or more courses of action, to select the best alternative and implement it, and then to observe the progress of this alternative and adjust it as required. These steps can be classified into four basic groups: Fact gathering, organization of the facts, analysis of the facts, and implementation of an action plan.

In particular, the action plan should cover three primary areas: The entrepreneur's personality, the financial picture, and other major factors vital to the action plan. To deal with the first of these, the entrepreneur needs to assess his or her strengths and work habits. On the financial side, the prospective entrepreneur-manager needs to examine the enterprise's financial picture and determine the costs of setting up the operation and the amount of revenue that will be generated during the initial period. Finally, the prospective entrepreneur-manager must review a series of other operational considerations, ranging from the building, merchandise, and equipment needed for operations to record-keeping, insurance, legal, marketing, and personal matters.

Another opportunity is the purchase of an existing successful firm, which has a number of advantages. Three of the most important are that successful future operation is likely, the time and effort associated with starting a new enterprise are eliminated, and a bargain price may be possible.

Before deciding whether to buy, however, the prospective entrepreneur needs to ask and answer a series of "right questions," some of which are as follows: Why is the business being sold? What is the physical condition of the business? What is the condition of the inventory? What is the state of the company's other assets? How many of the employees will remain? What competition does the business face? What is the firm's financial picture?

After all questions have been answered satisfactorily, the prospective buyer must determine how much he or she is willing to pay for the business. Some of the indexes of an operating venture's value are book value, replacement value, liquidation value, past earnings, and cash flow. In the final analysis, however, the prospective entrepreneur should be concerned with buying the company's assets at *market value* and then paying something for *goodwill* if it is deemed an asset.

Review and Discussion Questions

1. What is the new-new approach to starting a new venture? How does this approach differ from a new-old approach?
2. What are the six steps in the scientific method?
3. Of the six steps in the scientific method, which is the most important for the prospective new venture entrepreneur-manager? Support your answer.
4. Market analysis can help a prospective new venture entrepreneur-manager determine whether a demand for a particular good or service exists. What does this statement mean?
5. What kinds of questions should the new venture entrepreneur be able to answer when developing an action plan? List as least five.
6. How can an individual who is thinking of going into business evaluate the financial picture of the enterprise? Use the methodology of Table 3.2 to prepare your answer.
7. In addition to personal and financial issues, what other factors should the prospective entrepreneur be concerned with? Describe at least four.
8. What are the advantages of buying an ongoing business? Explain them.
9. What "right questions" need to be answered when deciding whether to buy a business?
10. What is book value? Replacement value? Liquidation value? Past earnings? Cash flow?
11. How should a prospective buyer price the assets of a company? Explain.
12. What are the seven steps involved in pricing an operating venture?
13. A prospective buyer is thinking about purchasing a business. The following facts have been gathered: The liquidation value of all assets minus liabilities

is $500,000; the earning power desired is 20 percent; the prospective buyer needs a yearly salary of $40,000; the average annual earnings before subtracting the entrepreneur-manager's salary and earning power are $100,000; and any extra earning power is estimated to be of value for five years. How much should the buyer be willing to pay for the business?

14.   What is a "covenant not to compete"?

The Venture Consultant

Give the Customer What They Want

Lilah's goal since graduating from college has been to start her own ridesharing service. Her interest stems from a summer internship at a ridesharing company called PickMeUp during her freshman, sophomore, junior, and senior summers. Her dedication to the company earned her direct access to the CEO for her junior and senior summers. Perhaps naively, Lilah believes that she has ample knowledge to be the CEO of her own ridesharing company.

During her internship, Lilah learned a lot. She knew the industry was competitive and took a defined, niche service to attract customers. She experienced this first hand with PickMeUp. While PickMeUp's mobile application could compete with the competitors in the market, it hadn't aggressively marketed itself as a low-cost service in major cities. Learning from PickMeUp's downfall, Lilah knew she couldn't compete with larger players in the industry that already benefitted from economies of scale. The major players were able to cut costs below her potential threshold. Still dedicated to starting her own business, Lilah's service needed to be unique and different.

Lilah believed the way to stand out was to provide *exactly* what the customer wanted. During her time at PickMeUp, she worked directly with the CEO on gathering consumer research. The statistic she found most interesting was how customers wanted PickMeUp to improve their service. Specifically, the three areas where customers thought PickMeUp could improve and differentiate were (1) offering food and drinks, (2) offering free mobile charging devices, and (3) providing television access to deliver news. The results were telling, and Lilah believed consumers would respond to a slightly higher price point if she showed she was listening.

Expanding on this idea, Lilah also strived to offer a specified ridesharing service that was based on real-time consumer feedback. So, in addition to offering services like food, water, charging stations, and in-car entertainment, Lilah would poll customers through survey and conversation to see what they desired, her idea being that each month, based on consumer demands and survey results, she would create a new type of service her ridesharing business can offer. For example, if there was a large percentage of customers who showed interest in riding in Jeeps in the summer, she would lease Jeeps to the fleet of vehicles for that month. Lilah thinks this unique value proposition could demand a higher ridesharing premium that customers would pay for. Data at PickMeUp backed up the assertion that 90 percent of rideshare users would be willing to pay more for an increase in services.

Your Consultation

What type of business model is Lilah attempting to institute? How does revenue function within this model? What are the benefits and risks associated with adopting a model that depends heavily on customer feedback? Do you believe this business model is fit for such a competitive industry? Explain your rationale.

Notes

1 See "World Changing Ideas," *Fast Company*, 2020. www.fastcompany.com/section/world-changing-ideas

2 ESOMAR, Peter Mouncey, and Frank Wimmer, *Market Research Best Practice: 30 Visions for the Future*. Hoboken, NJ: John Wiley & Sons, 2007; see also Jonas Dahlqvist and Johan Wiklund, "Measuring the Market Newness of New Ventures," *Journal of Business Venturing*, 2012, 27 (2): 185–196.

3 See Donald F. Kuratko, *Entrepreneurship: Theory, Process, & Practice*, 11th ed. Boston, MA: Cengage Publishing, 2020, pp. 163–166.

4 Fred Steingold and Emily Dostow, *The Complete Guide to Buying a Business*. Berkeley, CA: Nolo Press, 2005.

5 "Intangible Assets List: Top 6 Most Common Intangible Assets," *Wall Street Mojo*, accessed on March 16, 2020 at www.wallstreetmojo.com/intangible-assets-list/; Chris B. Murphy, "How Do Tangible and Intangible Assets Differ?," *Investopedia*, March 7, 2020.

6 Jay B. Abrams, *How to Value Your Business and Increase Its Potential*. New York: McGraw-Hill Publishing, 2005; see also Ted Koller, Marc Goedhart, and David Wessels, *Valuation: Measuring and Managing the Value of Companies*. New York: McKinsey & Company, 2015.

7 For a good discussion of buying or selling a small business, see Rene V. Richards, *How to Buy and/or Sell a Small Business for Maximum Profit*. Ocala, FL: Atlantic Publishing Group, 2013.

8 For a thorough analysis on valuation of a business, see James R. Hitchner, *Financial Valuation: Applications and Models*, 3rd ed. Hoboken, NJ: John Wiley & Sons, 2011; Shannon P. Pratt, *Business Valuation: Body of Knowledge*. Hoboken, NJ: John Wiley & Sons, 2003; see also Jean Murray, "Here Are the Steps to Buy a Business," *Small Business*, January 2, 2019, accessed March 16, 2020, at www.thebalancesmb.com/want-to-buy-a-business-here-are-the-steps-398893; and J. Gerard Legagneur, "Steps to Buying a Business," *Nolo*, accessed on March 16, 2020, at www.nolo.com/legal-encyclopedia/steps-to-buying-a-business.html.

9 Luba Kagan, "Six Rules of Thumb for Business Valuation," *BizBuySell*, accessed March 16, 2020, at www.bizbuysell.com/learning-center/article/6-rules-of-thumb-for-business-valuation.

10 See Roy J. Lewicki, David M. Saunders, and John W. Minton, *Negotiation*, 3rd ed. New York: McGraw Hill/Irwin Publishers, 2002. This paperback gives practical examples and advice about negotiating. Also see Michael Wheeler, *The Art of Negotiation*. Boston, MA: Harvard Business School Press, 2013; and Michael Sommerville, "Here Are 14 Negotiating Tips You Need to Know When Buying a Business," *Small Business.co.uk*, accessed on March 16, 2020 at https://smallbusiness.co.uk/tips-on-negotiating-when-buying-a-business-20695/.

Part II

New Venture Development

4   Marketing

The Customer

Introduction: Foundations of Marketing

Marketing is a key component that must be understood for any entrepreneur to succeed.[1] So, what is a market? A *market* is a group of consumers who behave in a similar way. For example, after Christmas, many stores have sales to clear out merchandise left over from the holiday shopping season. In particular, they offer holiday cards and wrapping paper at large discounts. Some people start shopping for the next year's holidays on December 26. Those people constitute a market. Other market examples include those who buy suits that cost between $300 and $400, those who purchase only Nissans, and those who camp out in front of electronics stores to get the latest video game system. In each instance, a classification or market niche exists where these people can be categorized.[2]

Determining Market Niches

People buy all sorts of products and services. Thus, they fall into *many* market niches. For example, using price as the determinant of demand, consider the following individuals and the price ranges within which they buy goods:

	Mr. A	*Ms. B*	*Mr. C*
Suits	$300–$400	$175–$275	$70–$150
Books	$5–$50	$3–$20	$3–$10
Automobiles	$26,000–$52,000	$18,000–$34,000	$11,000–$17,000
Homes	$325,000–$595,000	$180,000–$220,000	$85,000–$95,000
Restaurant meals	$40–$75	$25–$35	$15–$22
Watches	$124–$3000	$50–$150	$30–$60

Mr. A appears to be the most affluent. Certainly, he is willing to spend more money for the goods and services he buys. Mr. C appears to be the least affluent. He buys much less expensive products than Mr. A and is more likely than Mr.

A to be a bargain shopper. Ms. B falls somewhere between. In all, three different market niches for goods are described in this example: High price, medium price, and low price.[3]

Relevant Price Range

When analyzing market niches, the entrepreneur launching a new venture needs to be concerned with both relevant price range and competition. This price range is important because current customers will not buy *above* certain levels, nor will they buy *below* certain levels. Additionally, the entrepreneur cannot sell at a profit below a specific level. These three factors help determine the *relevant price range*.[4] If the current price is above the minimum level for customer acceptance and owner's profit and below the level judged as "too high," the price is within the relevant range. How high or low can the owner set a price? It depends on the customers in the market niche. For example, using the graph in Figure 4.1 as an illustration, any price higher than A is too high; current customers will not buy the suits for that much money. Meanwhile, any price below point B is too low; customers will consider the suits to be of inferior quality. Note in the graph that point B is above the acceptable profit level. In this example, customers are willing to pay high prices, and unless the owner wants to lose this market niche, price should remain within the relevant range. Other stores can cater to those who want to pay more and less than this range.

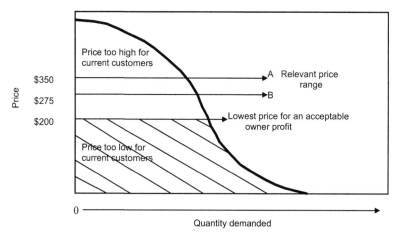

Figure 4.1 Suit Purchases

Note in the graph that the relevant price range is $275–$350. Although this price is relatively high, a strong demand exists for suits in this range; that is, the high price does not scare away customers. The reason is undoubtedly the high quality of the suits. They are regarded by these buyers as *specialty* items; the customers seek them out and pay whatever (within the range of relevance) the seller asks.

However, not all products fit into this category. In many cases, customers will substitute one good for another. For example, if the price of leather belts triples, suspenders might come back in style; if hardcover books cost too much, readers will wait for paperback editions. Food is another example. Hamburger, for instance, will be substituted for steaks if the cost of steaks rises too much. Likewise, if the price of hamburger rises, people will stop buying it and will substitute with something else, such as chicken. Then, if the price of hamburger drops while the price of other meats remains the same, people are likely to increase their purchase of hamburger. This demand curve is illustrated in Figure 4.2

The relevant price range is much broader for hamburger than for specialty items. People will pay more for a pound of hamburger than they are paying currently, and if the price declines, they will buy *more*. Nonetheless, even here a price can be too high or so low the store owner cannot afford to stock the product and earn a profit. Additionally, keep in mind that as the price of hamburger drops, it is likely that the price of other meats will also drop. As the price of hamburger approaches the bottom of the relevant price range (Figure 4.2), some customers will buy less hamburger and purchase more steaks. They will trade off the lower-priced meats for more expensive ones because if they can afford all of these products, they will prefer T-bone and filet mignon at least as often as hamburger. In short, some people will not buy below a certain price, preferring to substitute.

The term *price elasticity* is something to be considered here. Researchers Kotler and Armstrong[5] describe price elasticity as how responsive demand will be in response to a change in the price.

$$\text{Price elasticity of demand} = \frac{\% \text{ change in quantity demanded}}{\% \text{ change in price}}$$

If the price is elastic, a firm may consider lowering its price to increase revenues by selling more goods or services.

Competition

In a market evaluation, it is important to examine not only the relevant price ranges but also the presence of competition.[6] People usually base their buying decisions on need, prices competing firms charge, and availability of substitute products. Also, knowing and understanding your competition directly impact the "profit impact" of your competition strategy. The entrepreneur must decide between a strategy of cost leadership and differentiation of some sort based on the type and amount of competition for the product or service being delivered. Generally, new ventures should try to avoid cost leadership since they are not large enough to take advantage of economies of scale and focus more on promotional differentiation, where they show how they satisfy a need better than the competition.[7]

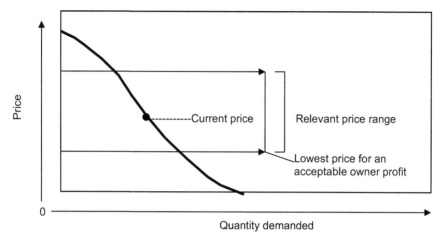

Figure 4.2 Hamburger Demand

The more competition a particular product has, the more likely it is that a range of prices exist and numerous similar goods can be substituted for it. Putting this into perspective, it is useful to look at the four possible economic conditions affecting new ventures. Most businesses operate in a competitive environment. However, the *degree of competition* tells the story. The local natural gas utility has no competition, whereas the local furniture store is in a highly competitive market, and the chance of long-term survival might be at risk. The different types of market situations are as follows:

1. Monopoly
2. Oligopoly
3. Monopolistic competition
4. Pure competition

Monopoly

A monopoly has only one seller or producer, and no substitutes for the desired good or service exist. One must either do business with this firm or forego the good or service. Various ways of developing a monopoly range from having it given to the business through legislation, such as a public utility that has the exclusive right to sell electricity in an area, to obtaining it through a patent right, such as Intel, which dominated the computer chip market for years. A new venture seldom has a monopoly, although if a restaurant has such a loyal following it always has a waiting line, it has a monopoly for all practical purposes: Customers are unwilling to accept another restaurant as a substitute.

Oligopoly

An oligopoly is a market with a few dominant firms. Often, these companies account for a large percentage of industry sales. Obviously, no new ventures are oligopolies, at least not at the national level. However, if a few dominate a local market, they can be considered an oligopoly, in that they follow the same basic strategies as their giant counterparts. For example, although the businesses in an oligopoly do not have a unique good or service for sale, they know that the strategies of each will affect the others. As a result, they tend to have a philosophy of "live and let live." They often do not compete on the basis of price but use advertising and personal selling to draw customers into their establishments.

Monopolistic Competition

Monopolistic competition exists when an industry has many firms, each producing only a small share of the output demand. To capture as large a share of this market as possible, each firm attempts to distinguish its goods and services from those of the competition. Advertising, credit, personal selling, and reputation are all used to draw people away from other products and businesses. Competition is vigorous. Common illustrations of monopolistic competition include restaurants, cleaning establishments, service stations, shoe stores, and grocery stores. Most new ventures fall into this category.

Pure Competition

Pure competition exists when many independent sellers offer products in the same basic way. The products are standardized—they are almost identical—and buyers are indifferent to which one they purchase. In addition, no firm can exercise significant control over the product's price because none supplies more than a small fraction of the total output demand. The most common example of this is in agriculture. Farmers who sell corn, wheat, or barley find that sellers buy their produce on the basis of weight (bushels) because very little difference exists, if any, between corn grown in one field and corn grown in the next.

These market models are contrasted in Table 4.1. As noted earlier, the market model that most new ventures fall within is monopolistic competition. A business survives in this type of market by examining the current needs of the customers, determining which goods and services appeal to them, and then giving them what they want. This is done by examining the firm's market niche and continually conducting marketing research.

Table 4.1 Comparison of the Market Models

	Monopoly	*Oligopoly*	*Monopolistic Competition*	*Pure Competition*
Number of Firms	One	A few	Many	Very many
Control Over Price	Much	Depends on what the others do	Some	None
Type of Product	Unique	Unique or standardized	Unique or standardized	Standardized
Access to the Industry	Impossible	Difficult	Fairly easy	Very easy

(Continued)

	Monopoly	Oligopoly	Monopolistic Competition	Pure Competition
Use of Non-Price Competition	Public relations advertising	Much	Much	None

Examining the Current Market Niche

Once the new venture owner-manager understands a market and the ways in which it is affected by both price and competition, he or she is in a position to examine the venture's current *market niche*.[8] Who are the customers? Do they pay for their purchases with cash or credit? Who are the bargain shoppers? What do they buy? How often do they buy? Answers to questions such as these provide a customer profile. Based on the results, the owner-manager can determine what to stock, how to price, where to advertise, and what service to provide.[9]

Market Niche Analysis: An Example

One of the first ways to examine a business's market niche is to break down the types of customers and their shopping habits. For example, consider the case of a pharmacy store owner who gathered age data on customers who frequented the store during a recent two-week period. A breakdown of customers' ages revealed the following information:

Adolescents and children	960
Males aged 20–40	1,140
Males aged 41–60	940
Males aged 60+	830
Females aged 20–40	1,250
Females aged 41–60	1,440
Females aged 60+	1,600

In addition, a breakdown of their buying habits, based on information gathered by store employees and the owner, reveals the profile shown in Table 4.2.

From this information, the owner knows that many of the customers like to charge purchases and that traffic is much heavier on weekends than during the week. Additionally, whereas everyone buys some product lines (staples and cosmetics), less than one-third of the customers purchase fad items.

Data like these are useful for examining customer purchasing habits. By collecting more such data at a later time, the owner can find relevant consumer information, in particular *changes* in customer buying habits that indicate *trends*.

Table 4.2 Breakdown of Pharmacy Customers' Buying Habits

Type of Customer	Cash Purchases	Charge Purchases	Bargain Shoppers	Daytime Shoppers	Evening Shoppers	Weekend Shoppers	Online Shoppers	Buy Staples (Candy, Laundry Detergent, etc.)	Buy Health and Cosmetic Products
Adolescents and Children	X			X		X	X	X	X
Males, 20–40		X			X	X		X	X
Males, 60+		X			X	X		X	X
Males, 41–60	X			X		X		X	X
Females, 20–40			X	X	X	X	X	X	X
Females, 41–60	X		X		X	X		X	X
Females 60+	X		X	X			X	X	X

Based on the data, the store owner can assess which types of inventory provide the best *return on investment (ROI)*. Since store space is limited, the store owner should stock those items desired by the customer that yield the highest profit margin. This is referred to as *ROI control*, and it is one of the most effective control procedures. In essence, it tells the owner-manager to keep only product lines that provide at least a minimum return on investment. The owner must establish what this minimum is, but let us assume the drugstore offers ten major product lines and wants a return of at least 12 percent from each. At the end of the year, the accountant closes the books and then makes the calculations, which reveal the following:

Major Line	Return on Investment (%)
1	17
2	13
3	21
4	29
5	11
6	14
7	28
8	6

Major Line	Return on Investment (%)
9	12
10	2

From the data, it is obvious items 5, 8, and 10 are not producing a desirable return. From this information, the owner must decide whether to drop them. If the lines are not new and do not hold some promise for the future, they should be dropped. The only exception to this is if they are *complementary products* bought by people who come into the store to buy something else. If that is the case, it may be wise for the store to carry both lines since customers may go elsewhere if they cannot obtain both kinds of products at this location.

Market Niche Danger Signals

In addition to the marketing analysis, the owner should use some qualitative criteria to judge whether the store is meeting the needs of its customers. This often can be determined by observing the behavior of customers and employees. Following are some danger signals:

1. Many customers leave the store without buying anything.
2. Many former customers no longer shop here.
3. Customers do not buy additional items or trade up to more expensive items.
4. Traffic (pedestrian and vehicular) in front of the store has fallen off.
5. Customers are returning more merchandise than they used to.
6. This month's sales are down from last year, and sales for the year to date are down from last year.
7. Employees are slow in greeting customers.
8. Employees appear indifferent and make customers wait unnecessarily.
9. Employees' personal appearance is not neat.
10. Salespeople lack knowledge of the store's merchandise.
11. The number of employee errors is increasing.
12. Because of high prices, the store has a reputation for greediness.
13. The better qualified employees are leaving for jobs with competitors.

Although knowledge of the current market niche and customer buying habits is very important, a more vital consideration is the changes that will occur in the next three to five years. How will the market change? Remember, today's successful products eventually will become marginal winners and then losers. Based on product availability and market trends, the owner should be willing to change the goods and services mix to continue to attract customers into the store. The appropriate product mix can be identified and cultivated through marketing research. The Global Issues for New Ventures box provides an interesting look at how smaller ventures compete with the big-box stores today.

Global Issues for New Ventures

"Competing with Giants"

How can a small retailer compete against the power, size, prices, and selection offered by giant mass merchandisers? Walmart, for example, generated more than $478.6 billion in global revenue for 2016, employed over 2.2 million people, and managed 11,534 stores in 28 countries, serving millions of customers each week.

To survive such competition and remain distinctive in the eyes of customers, new ventures need to apply the following strategies:

1. *Research:* Do your research on the big-box stores in your area to find out what they offer, then dare to be different in the following ways.
2. *High end:* Target higher end customers by offering higher quality items.
3. *Connect online:* Create an online presence by developing customer email lists, writing blogs, and getting involved in social networking.
4. *Specialize:* Offer specialty items and extra services that big-box retailers do not.
5. *Involvement:* Make connections in the community and get involved.
6. *Provide meaning:* Carry merchandise that is meaningful to customers looking for a special gift.
7. *Establish convenience:* Provide shoppers a smaller atmosphere for shopping quickly and easily.
8. *Personal attention:* Treat each customer as your best customer and truly care about their needs.
9. *Family:* Constantly stress the "family" part of the family business by using expressions, such as "locally owned," when promoting or advertising.

These tips for competing with big-box stores can help level the playing field. However, even with exceptional customer service and unique products, many customers will still pursue low prices at the big-box stores.

Source: Adapted from Peter Gasca, "5 Ways Small Retailers Can Compete (& Win)," Inc. Online, www.inc.com/peter-gasca/5-ways-small-retailers-can-compete-win.html; Shari Waters, "Competing With Big Box Stores," Business News Daily, May 29, 2016, http://retail.about.com/od/competition/a/big_box_stores.htm (accessed July 6, 2016); and Tim Parker, "How Small Business Can Compete With Big Box Stores," Business Know How, www.businessknowhow.com/marketing/bigbox.htm (accessed March 16, 2020).

Marketing Research

Marketing research is the systematic study of the factors that affect a venture's sales in its particular market niche. If the entrepreneur operating the new venture is astute, he or she has been conducting some kind of marketing research from the first day the business opened, if not earlier during the business planning process.[10] Location, customer needs, competition, and product lines have long been recognized as areas of concern. The problem with most businesses, however, is that conditions change over time, and owners may not be aware of them. In general, marketing research can confirm hunches, reveal additional information, identify opportunities, and clarify advertising targets and the types of media necessary to reach them.

In particular, *marketing habits* change. For example, in metropolitan areas, many people used to take public transportation to shop downtown. However, massive movement of people to the suburbs and increasing automobile ownership have led to the emergence of the suburban shopping center as the dominant retail outlet in most parts of the country. This same mobility, in conjunction with the advent of larger and better refrigerators and freezers, has changed the food-buying habits of many people. Instead of making a few purchases at the neighborhood grocery each day, most people now do large-scale food shopping at a supermarket, at lower prices, once or twice a week.

Likewise, trends toward shorter working hours, online shopping, and greater interest in convenience products, do-it-yourself foods, and sports equipment have been noted. The rising purchasing power in the world's developed countries has increased the demand for luxury products and services. All of these changes have a tremendous effect on buying habits and add up to the need for a business to remain flexible. This is where marketing research enters the picture.[11]

How to Conduct Marketing Research

The data collected through market research efforts should be decision-oriented rather than background-oriented. Specifically, the data gathered are used to solve specific problems or make a particular decision.[12] How can the new venture owner obtain the necessary marketing research? Three broad sources should be considered. First, trade associations, regular business advisors, business agencies, and, to a limited extent, suppliers can offer factual information. Second, the entrepreneur can acquire the services of an independent marketing research service. Third, the entrepreneur can organize a marketing research effort within the firm itself. The best method for a particular business depends on its resources, the availability of needed information, the complexity and size of the problem, and, most important of all, the cost involved.[13]

Secondary Sources

Regardless of who conducts the research, a good place to begin is with data from currently available secondary sources. These documents present statistics compiled about the industry, the competition, and the local area as well as information gleaned from business publications. Secondary sources are fundamental for marketing research and often yield great value for the investment. However, they should *never* be the *only* sources tapped because they seldom provide all the information the owner-manager needs. Two of the most important secondary sources are local statistics and sales analysis.

Local Statistics

One way to begin a marketing research effort is to get statistics on the local community. These can often be obtained from the Chamber of Commerce (local and state), the city government, and census data (www.census.gov). Analyzing these data can help the owner compile a profile of the local population by age distribution, average income, family size, automobile ownership, home ownership, and number of school-age children.

Another important area of consideration is the changing population. Currently, more than half the population of the United States is younger than 45 years of age. These people have different buying habits than older people. The geographic breakdown of this population can tell the new venture owner-manager where people are moving to and from. For example, in recent years, Arizona, Florida, California, and Colorado have been increasing in population. States that have either been losing population or are growing very slowly are North Dakota, South Dakota, Virginia, and Wyoming. By studying population changes, the business owner can determine whether the firm is located in a growing area or one that is likely to become economically stagnant in the next five to ten years.

Another way to get local statistics without expending a lot of time and effort is by reading the local newspaper and subscribing to trade journals and business publications. The local newspaper often carries reports of income levels for the community and the region, and its financial section is another ready source of important statistical information. Additionally, publications such as *Business Week*, *The Wall Street Journal*, and *Fortune* offer a wealth of information that can prove useful for making marketing decisions. The astute business owner-manager will cut out and file statistics that directly affect his or her business. In this way, the individual can compile a *market fact file* for marketing research.

Sales Analysis

A type of marketing research that can be conducted within the place of business is sales analysis. By analyzing sales data, the owner-manager can answer many questions, such as the following: How many dishwashers did we sell last year? How many freezers did we sell? What is our most profitable product line? What is our biggest seller? Did most people pay cash or charge it? Do most of our customers live close by or more than ten miles away? These questions are answered easily by examining sales slips with customer's names and addresses, date, item sold, and amount paid for the item recorded.

Primary Sources

Statistics and sales analysis can provide important information, but the data are limited, in that they are historical. No "new" facts are considered; just old information is studied. Also, data are not specific to the target market in which you plan to do business. Collecting current data requires some form of survey research. This can be done by the new venture itself, or an outside survey research firm can be hired. In either case, the steps in the research are the same.

Survey Research

Conducting marketing survey research involves six steps:

1. *Analyze the situation.* What are the conditions in the industry and in the local area? For example, assume the new venture owner provides rug cleaning services. The first task of the owner-manager or the marketing survey organization is to get background information. This can be done by asking the trade association or national industry group to which the business owners belong if any national or area surveys have been conducted. Then the Chamber of Commerce and other local sources of data can be consulted. During this background research, investigators should get information that will help with the second step.

2. *Formulate a statement of the problem or goal.* Obviously, the entrepreneur is having the research conducted with a purpose in mind. Sometimes this is nothing more than a desire to know whether to expand services by moving into another geographic area.

3. *Design the research.* How will further information be collected so that the situation can be analyzed in sufficient depth?

4. *Carry out the survey.* Numerous methods can be used. Among the most common are interviews and questionnaires. Regardless of who carries them out, however, the issue of bias must be addressed. Sometimes the way a person asks a question generates a particular response. The same is true for the way a question is written in a questionnaire. For example, if the owner of the rug cleaning firm decides to interview 100 people in the local area to ask them questions about rug cleaning, the owner will get different answers depending on how the questions are phrased. If the owner asks, "Would you consider using my firm to clean your rugs?" the respondent will probably say yes. However, the person is not saying that he or she *will* do so, merely that he or she will *consider* it. A better way to gather marketing research data is to ask open-ended questions, such as "How do you clean your rugs?" The answer will tell the owner how many people hire professionals or do it themselves. This answer will indicate something about how area homeowners value their time and who can afford such services. These data, in turn, will provide some bases for distinguishing potential customers from people who will do it themselves.

5. *Tabulate, analyze, and report the information.* At this stage, the information is put into some meaningful form. Once the information is recorded, it should be analyzed to determine the overall critical responses form the participants.

6. *Apply the data to the purpose.* What percentage of interviewees said that they hire professionals for rug cleaning services? How many potential homes will use this service every year? How many competing firms offer rug cleaning? What percentage of this market can the firm capture? By answering these

questions, for example, the new venture owner is in a position to determine whether it is a good idea to expand the business into another geographic area.

Focus Groups

Focus groups are small groups of usually seven to ten participants selected from a broader population and "interviewed" through facilitator-led discussions for opinions and attitudes about a particular issue. Focus groups are a common market research tool that yield qualitative data in a condensed amount of time. Conducting effective focus groups requires attention to five steps:

Step 1. Prepare for the Session

1. Identify the major objective(s) of the meeting.
2. Develop four to six questions.
3. Invite potential participants to the meeting.
4. About three days before the session, call each participant who initially said they would participate to remind them to attend.

Step 2. Develop Questions

1. Develop four to six questions. The session can last up to two and a half hours, and during this time one can ask at most six questions.
2. Allow time for follow-up and probing of answers to the four to six questions.
3. Ask yourself what problem or need will be addressed by the information gathered during the session.

Step 3. Plan the Session

1. Scheduling: Plan meetings to be one to two and a half hours long. Avoid lunch meetings, where participants could be distracted. If you provide food, serve it before, during a break, or after the meeting.
2. Setting and refreshments: Hold sessions in a conference room or other setting with adequate lighting, comfortable chairs, and space for a facilitator to work the crowd. Configure chairs so that all participants face each other and provide name tags or name cards.
3. Set the ground rules: It is important that all participants participate as much as possible, but you need to keep the meeting moving to cover all the questions. A few rules should include (1) staying focused, (2) maintaining a timeline, and (3) getting closure and summarizing each of the questions.
4. Agenda: Use an agenda that includes a welcome, review of the agenda, review of the purpose of the meeting, review of focus group rules of engagement, introductions, questions, and wrap-up.
5. Number of participants: Focus groups are usually conducted with seven to ten participants who have similar characteristics (e.g., similar age group, status, income, target market).

6. Record the session with either a note taker or some sort of audio or audio-video recorder. Also, use flip charts, postcards, story boards, or other tools that provide a record of what was said.

Step 4. Facilitate and Manage the Session

1. Stick to the agenda/goals of the meeting.
2. Introduce yourself and others who are helping you.
3. Explain how you will record the information and protect confidentiality where necessary.
4. When you are finished with each focus group question, summarize your findings for the group.
5. Ensure participation. If one or two people are dominating the meeting, then call on others. Consider using a round-table approach, including going in one direction around the table, giving each person a minute to answer the question.
6. Close the session. Tell participants that they will receive a copy of the report generated from their answers (if necessary), thank them for coming, and adjourn the meeting.

Step 5. Follow Up Immediately After the Session

1. Transcribe all responses into a report. Do not delay because some of the nuances of the meeting may be forgotten.
2. Have a few selected participants review your report to check for accuracy.
3. Take action on suggestions if possible.

If conducted properly, focus groups yield a great deal of information in a very short period of time. However, the data are qualitative in nature and cannot be statistically analyzed.

Other Data Collection Methods

Step 4 in the section on survey research used one of the most common methods of data collection: Home interviews. Another method of gathering data—probably the simplest method of all—is the *store interview* or questionnaire. Retail stores in particular can use this approach with very little trouble. A common technique is to have a personable, pleasant interviewer approach customers and ask them to answer a few simple questions. Usually, these questions are limited in number and take only a few moments to answer. The information is recorded on an easily marked interview sheet or tablet so that a permanent record of the comments exists. Typical questions include "How often do you visit this store?" "Where do you live?" "How many times a week do you shop?" "What kind of products do you come to this store to buy?" and "Why do you like shopping at this store?" If the owner experiences some resistance from interviewed shoppers, other methods can overcome it. For example, instead of asking shoppers a series of questions, the business can use point-of-sale survey cards that shoppers fill out and drop in a box. On the survey card is a place for the person's name and answers to a few questions. Then the owner can draw a predetermined number of responses from the box, with these respondents receiving a prize. In this case, the survey instrument is used both to gather information and as a contest entry.

Another method new ventures often use is the *mail survey*. This type of questionnaire is sent to the respondent with a request to fill it out and return it in a pre-stamped or postage-paid envelope. Such surveys are usually cheaper than personal interviews and easier to tabulate. Indeed, many people respond to mail questionnaires, depending on the purpose of the survey and the party that is inquiring. In fact, some companies have found them more reliable than interviews. For example, one large consumer goods firm discovered that the results obtained from interview surveys were different from those obtained from a mail survey. After it analyzed the eventual buying habits of the consumers, it found the mail survey more accurate.

A third common form of survey is the *telephone interview*. Using this method, the owner-manager should ensure that respondents know they are being asked to participate in a survey. Prepared questions are asked and the answers are recorded. The obvious advantages of telephone interviews are that a single interviewer can handle a large number of respondents, and the overall cost is relatively low. Of course, the person carrying out the interview must have a pleasant voice, and the questionnaire the person reads should be simple, direct, and brief. If the call takes too long, the respondent is likely to terminate it. Also, many states have implemented no-call legislation that may regulate if and how phone surveys can be conducted.

Finally, owners should not overlook *specialized surveys* for collecting consumer data, some of which lend themselves to *demonstration approaches*. New products or product prototypes are often researched this way. A place is created where consumers can examine the products and ask questions about them. Supermarkets often set up demonstration tables where new food items are cooked and shoppers are urged to sample products. Department stores also do this. A salesperson shows how a new product works and encourages the shopper to buy one before leaving the store.[14]

Using Research Data

Having collected the data, the business owner must decide how to use the information. Until now, all the owner has done is collect a mass of facts and figures.

First, the data must be tabulated and arranged in some useful form. For example, if a new venture owner believes most shoppers in his toy store are children or young parents, he might be interested in the number of people in this section of town who are aged 0–9 (children) and 20–39 (the most common ages of parents) and whether the numbers are increasing or decreasing. Assume the owner has collected census data for the metropolitan area for ten years ago and for today and finds the data presented in Table 4.3.

Table 4.3 Age Distribution in the Local Area

10 Years Ago			Today	
Age (Years)	Number	Percentage of Population	Number	Percentage of Population
0–9	88,617	26.4	125,768	25.8
10–19	76,212	22.6	112,386	23.0
20–29	51,007	15.2	82,087	16.8
30–39	42,839	12.7	55,320	11.5
40–49	36,793	11.0	42,107	8.6
50–59	25,107	7.5	40,567	8.2
60+	15,361	4.6	29,138	6.1
Total	335,936	100.00	487,373	100.00

Note that the percentage breakdowns are about the same today as they were ten years ago. Approximately 26 percent of the group is children below the age of 10, while almost 30 percent of the group is between the ages of 20 and 39. Thus, no significant population shifts have occurred. Additionally, to the owner's advantage, the number of people in the local area has increased by 45 percent.

The foregoing leads to the other important step in using research data: The owner must *interpret the statistics*. What do they tell the owner that can help in making decisions? This is often the most difficult part of the research. The owner must evaluate the data objectively, not twist or distort their meaning.

Social Media Marketing

The traditional marketing approaches that we have presented are still important foundations to understand marketing, but in the new terrain of social media, they have to be adapted to fit this generation. For example, there is a distinction between *control* and *contributions*. Traditional marketing methods seek to control the content seen by the audience and attempt to dominate the competitors' message, whereas social media marketing emphasizes audience contribution for large parts of the content.

Another distinction is in the area of *trust*. Since ventures do not control the content users will create, they must develop trust with the customer audience. Unlike some traditional marketing efforts where consumers have grown to expect some exaggeration, social media demands complete honesty because ventures will be held accountable to explain their claims.

Remember that traditional marketing is "one-way," from the venture to the customers, whereas social media involves "*two-way communication*" with an audience that is interested in responding. Thus, social media creates an ongoing conversation between the new venture and the customer.

In developing a social media marketing plan, the creation of solid marketing strategies is critical. Here are some key elements to keep in mind:

Identify the target market (*niche*) so marketing strategies can be organized to efficiently reach the most receptive customers and, eventually, advocates.

Categorize social media platforms by target market relevancy. In other words, a company should focus its efforts on the social media sites where its target audience resides in the greatest numbers, resulting in a higher return on investment (ROI).

Collaborate with platform members as a means of establishing a mutually beneficial relationship with the platform participants. Social media is a key way to build relationships. People who feel a personal connection with a company are apt to like and trust the associated brand or product.

Contribute content to build reputation and become a valued member, helping to improve the community. A brand or company can be positioned as a thought leader or expert in an industry by showcasing its unique knowledge.

Convert strategy execution into desired outcomes such as brand building, increasing customer satisfaction, driving word-of-mouth recommendations, producing new product ideas, generating leads, handling crisis reputation management, integrating social media marketing with advertising, and increasing search engine ranking and site traffic.[15]

These key steps for a social media marketing plan are only the beginning. The specifics will depend on information from observing and interacting with the target market.

Mobile Marketing

Mobile computing—the use of portable wireless devices to connect to the internet—is fast becoming the wave of the future. Experts estimate that in 2014 there were eight billion internet-connected devices and that by 2024 that number will jump to 50 billion! They further estimate that a decade after that the number of internet-connected devices will reach a trillion. Our world will be completely connected and mobile with smartphones, tablet PCs, notebooks, and wearable technologies such as wristbands and headbands.[16]

Today, mobile social media marketing is a fast-paced and high-impact marketing tool that many companies are now using as a standard communication strategy to connect with consumers. Through mobile social media, text messaging, mobile applications, and mobile advertising are all possible marketing opportunities. In addition, mobile social media can be a vehicle to gather data about consumers' geographical position in time or space. In other words, consumers can be differentiated based on location sensitivity (does the message take into account the specific location of the user?) and time sensitivity (is the message received and processed by the user instantaneously or with a time delay?). The most sophisticated forms of mobile social media applications are those that account for both time and location simultaneously.[17]

While a comprehensive mobile social media marketing strategy can be complicated, one researcher recommends the "4 I's" to help build the approach. These are *integration* into the daily life of the user by offering incentives, prizes, or discounts to the user of the application; *individualization* of company-to-consumer communication by directing customized messages to different users based on location, taste preferences, and shopping habits; *involvement* of the user interactively with a type of story or game, often involving prizes for the winners (but even without prizes, users are still motivated to win one of these interactive games because their social media network "friends" will see if they have won); and *initiation* of a meaningful dialogue between different consumers as they communicate online with the creation of user-generated content.[18]

Simply stated, the future of mobile social media marketing is immense, and ventures must capitalize on this type of marketing as soon as possible. The future will bring continued technology enhancements, and the integration of virtual life and real life is inevitable. Mobile marketing using social media will be revolutionary and potentially more important than almost any other type of marketing.[19]

A Global Perspective

"The Alternative Meat Wars"

Recent scientific advances, concerns about the negative impact of animal livestock on the climate and environment, and societal interest in new sources of dietary protein not derived from animals have led to the development of plant-based meat alternatives.

U.S. companies such as Beyond Meat and Impossible Foods have developed products derived from plant proteins that mimic the taste and texture of animal-based products, such as beef and pork. Both companies have focused their initial product development on developing an offering that approximates a favorite American dish: The beef burger. Beyond Meat's and Impossible Foods' plant-based burgers have found their way into grocery stores and onto restaurant menus across the country.

The initial success to upend the animal protein market of pioneers Beyond Meat and Impossible Foods has not gone unnoticed. These startups, both interested in disrupting the disrupters and the legacy food companies, have been quick to pursue opportunities to develop their own meat alternative products. Tyson Foods, a major U.S. producer of beef, pork, and poultry, after having initially invested in Beyond Meat, has launched its own line of meat alternative products under the brand Raised & Rooted.

As these U.S.-based companies seek to spread to large international markets, such as China, they will need to adapt to market dynamics different than the United States, where market competition and consumer tastes are significantly different. Chinese consumers are major consumers of pork, and the spread of disease in Chinese hog stock has led to rising pork prices. This has spurred interest in development of meat alternatives. However, where U.S. companies have focused on initially developing products that meet Americans' tastes, such as the burger, Chinese competitors have focused on developing similar plant-based meat alternatives targeted toward the tastes of Chinese consumers. This includes products such as dumplings and sausage.

Beyond modifying the product to meet the expectations of consumers, U.S. companies will have to contend with the different structure of the Chinese market. In China, state-backed companies can receive preferential treatment, and consumers may feel a preference to "buy local."

Understanding local market dynamics and adapting to local consumers' expectations are key to successfully competing in international markets.

Source: Adapted from Impossible Foods, www.impossiblefoods.com/; Products, Beyond Meat, www.beyondmeat.com/products/; Raised & Rooted Plant-Based Protein, Raised & Rooted, www.raisedandrooted.com/; "Beyond Meat vs Zhenmeat: The Battle for China's Meatless Market," CNBC, November 18, 2019, www.cnbc.com/2019/11/19/beyond-meat-vs-zhenmeat-the-battle-for-chinas-meatless-market.html; and Jacob Bunge, "Beyond Meat Books First Profit as Competition Mounts," *The Wall Street Journal*, October 28, 2019, www.wsj.com/articles/beyond-meat-books-first-profit-as-competition-mounts-11572292802.

Summary

A market is a group of consumers who behave in a similar way. However, since people buy all sorts of goods and services, many market niches exist. In analyzing market niches, the owner-manager needs to consider the relevant price range and competition. The relevant price range is the minimum to maximum price customers will pay. Competition represents the threat to this niche, and the degree of competitiveness tells the story. Thus, of four types of markets—monopoly, oligopoly, monopolistic competition, and pure competition—it is monopolistic competition and its high degree of competitiveness that most concerns the new venture owner-manager. In addition to understanding price and competition, the new venture owner needs to understand the firm's current market niche. The development of a customer profile is one of the best ways to do this.

Marketing research is the systematic study of factors that affect a business's sales. Analyzing these factors is important because customer buying habits are continually changing. Secondary sources such as local statistics and sales analyses are good places to begin marketing research. These can then be supplemented with primary sources, such as market survey research, with which previously unavailable data are gathered. After these new data are available, the owner-manager must know how to objectively arrange, analyze, and interpret them to draw valuable conclusions. The individual must not allow personal biases or opinions to alter an objective evaluation of the data. If the owner-manager can do this, maximum value can be derived from the survey. Today, mobile social media marketing is a fast-paced and high-impact marketing tool that many companies are now using as a standard communication strategy to connect with consumers. Through mobile social media, text messaging, mobile applications, and mobile advertising are all possible marketing opportunities.

Review and Discussion Questions

1. What are the meanings of the terms *markets* and *market niche*?
2. Explain what a new venture owner-manager needs to know about relevant price range.
3. How do monopoly, oligopoly, monopolistic competition, and pure competition differ from one another?
4. Explain how a customer profile can be useful to an owner-manager who is interested in examining a market niche.
5. What is meant by the term *marketing research*?
6. How is market survey research carried out? Explain the six steps.
7. What are the most common data collection methods new ventures use for their marketing research? Describe at least two.
8. Specifically, what should a new venture owner know about using research data? How can the information be useful? Explain.
9. Explain some of the key steps to remember with social media marketing.
10. Describe the rise in mobile social media. How should a new venture utilize this dimension for marketing purposes?

The Venture Consultant

Who's Buying My Fries?

"I will have the double bacon cheeseburger, cooked medium, and a side of your famous Mudd Fries, thank you." But before the waiter could turn away, the customer made a quick inquiry: "Your menu says you have been in business for five years, but this is the first time I have heard of your restaurant. I have been living in Chesterton for 25 years and am wondering if you changed locations?"

The waiter and sole owner, Jesse, responded, "Why, yes, we moved here two months ago because we felt the location was better for business."

Jesse had recently moved his burger joint from the outskirts of Chesterton to the center of town. He had an inclination that he was missing out on business because people were less willing to drive the 15 minutes from town to his restaurant. He also thought families that lived in town were more likely to stay closer to home when looking for a place to dine out. Jesse had always been an impulsive decision maker and owner, but that is what has kept his business alive for 25 years.

When Jesse returned with the customer's burger and fries, he was met with another question: "So, how much better has business been in the new location?" Jesse responded, "It has been much better. I have noticed more middle-aged couples dining at the restaurant. This uptick in customer traffic has also translated into more profits. Times are good, thanks for asking!"

The customer countered, "How do you know there have been more middle-aged couples? Also, what demographic do you see yourself growing in the future? I apologize for all the questions, but I am a marketing professor, and I have noticed a trend in successful businesses—they often lose sight of their customer of tomorrow!" Jesse nodded in agreement and pondered the customer's initial question. Thinking clearly and honestly, Jesse didn't know what customer base had been growing the fastest because he never tracked his customers' demographics.

Amid his pondering, the professor interrupted again and kindly offered to perform a marketing study on his restaurant—completely free of charge. "I have some students who are eager to earn real-world experience, and I think your restaurant would be an exciting case study. They are also intrigued at the idea of creating a marketing campaign for the restaurant if you are open to that?"

Jesse was taken aback by this customer's generosity and immediately accepted the offer. He had never conducted an analysis on his customers' spending habits, ages, location, or thoughts about his food other than through conversation. It was time that he had some hard data about his customers to make his burger joint more appealing.

Your Consultation

What is marketing research and how can it help Jesse improve his burger joint? What type of research do you think the professor and his students will conduct? Why? Finally, what types of marketing tactics would you recommend the professor and students consider in their recommendation to Jesse? How will this campaign attract more customers?

Notes

1 Jonas Dahlqvist and Johan Wiklund, "Measuring the Market Newness of New Ventures," *Journal of Business Venturing*, 2012, 27 (2): 185–196.
2 See Philip Kotler and Gary Armstrong, *Principles of Marketing*, 16th ed. Upper Saddle River, NJ: Pearson/Prentice Hall, 2016; and William M. Pride and O. C. Ferrell, *Marketing*, 18th ed. Mason, OH: Cengage/South-Western, 2016.
3 See Louis E. Boone and David L. Kurtz, *Contemporary Marketing*, 17th ed. Mason, OH: Thomson/South-Western, 2016.
4 Marco Bertini and John T. Gourville, "Pricing to Create Shared Value," *Harvard Business Review*, 2012, 90 (6): 96–104.
5 Philip Kotler and Gary Armstrong, *Principles of Marketing*, 16th ed. Upper Saddle River, NJ: Pearson/Prentice Hall, 2016.
6 See Stephanie Prause, "The True Value of Market Research," *NZ Business*, 2006, 20 (9): 21.
7 Shelby D. Hunt and Robert M. Morgan, "The Comparative Advantage Theory of Competition," *Journal of Marketing*, 1995, 59 (2): 1–15; see also Matthew Bumgardner, Urs Buehlmann, Albert Schuler, and Jeff Crissey, "Competitive Actions of Small Firms in a Declining Market," *Journal of Small Business Management*, 2011, 49 (4): 578–598.

8   William G. Zikmund and Barry J. Babin, *Exploring Marketing Research*, 11th ed. Mason, OH: Cengage/ South-Western, 2016; see also Boyd Cohen and Monika I. Winn, "Market Imperfections, Opportunity, and Sustainable Entrepreneurship," *Journal of Business Venturing*, January 2007, 22 (1): 29–49.

9   See Frans J. H. M. Verhees and Matthew T. G. Meulenberg, "Market Orientation, Innovativeness, Product Innovation, and Performance in Small Firms," *Journal of Small Business Management*, 2004, 42 (2): 134–154.

10   Zikmund and Babin, *Exploring Marketing Research*.

11   See Bret Golann, "Achieving Growth and Responsiveness: Process Management and Market Orientation in Small Firms," *Journal of Small Business Management*, July 2006, 44 (3): 369–385.

12   See Raguragavan Ganeshasundaram and Nadine Henley, "The Prevalence and Usefulness of Market Research: An Empirical Investigation into 'Background' versus 'Decision' Research," *International Journal of Market Research*, 2006, 48 (5): 525–550.

13   For a detailed discussion of marketing research, see Minet Schindehutte, Michael H. Morris, and Leyland F. Pitt, *Rethinking Marketing*. Upper Saddle River, NJ: Pearson/Prentice Hall, 2009.

14   For examples of various approaches, see Philip Kotler and Kevin Lane Keller, *Marketing Management*, 15th ed. Upper Saddle, NJ: Pearson/Prentice Hall, 2016; see also Andy Lockett, "Conducting Market Research Using the Internet: The Case of Xenon Laboratories," *Journal of Business & Industrial Marketing*, 2004, 19 (3): 178–187.

15   Melissa S. Barker, Donald I. Barker, Nicholas F. Borman, and Krista E. Neher, *Social Media Marketing: A Strategic Approach*, 2nd ed. Mason, OH: South-Western/Cengage, 2017; see also Maria Teresa Pinheiro Melo Borges Tiago and José Manuel Cristóvão Veríssimo, "Digital Marketing and Social Media: Why Bother?," *Business Horizons*, 2014, 57 (6): 703–708.

16   See Salim Ismail, *Exponential Organizations*. New York: Diversion Books, 2014.

17   Mary Lou Roberts and Debra Zahay, *Internet Marketing: Integrating Online and Offline Strategies*. Mason, OH: South-Western/Cengage, 2013.

18   Andreas Kaplan, "If You Love Something, Let It Go Mobile: Mobile Marketing and Mobile Social Media 4x4," *Business Horizons*, 2012, 55 (2): 129–139; see also Eileen Fischer and A. Rebecca Reuber, "Online Entrepreneurial Communication: Mitigating Uncertainty and Increasing Differentiation via Twitter," *Journal of Business Venturing*, 2014, 29 (4): 565–583.

19   Jordi Paniagua and Juan Sapena, "Business Performance and Social Media: Love or Hate?," *Business Horizons*, 2014, 57 (6): 719–728; and William C. Moncrief, Greg W. Marshall, and John M. Rudd, "Social Media and Related Technology: Drivers of Change in Managing the Contemporary Sales Force," *Business Horizons*, 2015, 58 (1): 45–55.

5   Legal Considerations

The Parameters

Introduction: Forms of Business

Entrepreneurs are often perplexed by the issues involved in selecting the correct form of business to operate, and the various tax implications add to their confusion. Owners of new ventures often select the sole proprietorship business form by default, but as the business grows, they begin to consider a change. Instead of selection by default, each form of business organization should be examined carefully, weighing the advantages and disadvantages of each against the owner's needs as well as the venture's needs. Whether an entrepreneur is starting a venture that is manufacturing-, service-, or internet-based, the legal aspects surrounding the forms of organization are the same. A change in the legal form of a business can be made at different points in the life of the business, if the original selection becomes inappropriate. However, careful consideration should be given to current and future needs as well as to the cost of formation.[1]

This chapter examines the advantages and disadvantages of the different forms of business organization:

1. Sole proprietorships
2. Partnerships
3. Corporations

Figure 5.1 shows the predominance of the three major types of business organizations in the United States today. When examining these legal forms of organizations, entrepreneurs need to consider a few important factors:

*   how easily the form of business organization can be implemented
*   the amount of capital required to implement the form of business organization
*   legal considerations that might limit the options available to the entrepreneur
*   the tax effects of the form of organization selected
*   the potential liability to the owner of the form of organization selected[2]

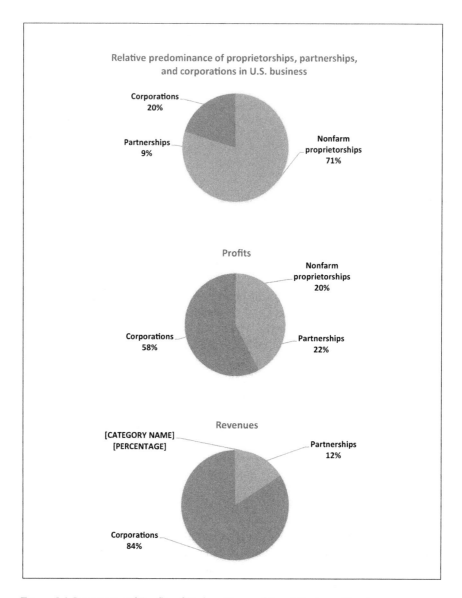

Figure 5.1 Revenues and Profits of Various Types of Legal Business Structure

Sole Proprietorship

A sole proprietorship or proprietorship is a business that is owned and controlled by only one person. This is the most common form of ownership in the United States by far, with over 23 million sole proprietorships, representing 73 percent of all U.S. businesses.[3] Why is this form of ownership so popular? The answer is found in the many advantages it offers.

Advantages of Proprietorships

Numerous advantages are associated with proprietorships, but *four* are particularly important:

1. Complete control and decision-making
2. Lack of restrictions
3. Minimum legal costs of formation
4. Personal satisfaction

Complete Control and Decision-Making

Perhaps the major advantage of a proprietorship is that the owner-manager owns the entire business and the profits belong to him or her. In this type of business, there are no specific business taxes paid by the company. The owner pays taxes on income from the business as part of his or her personal income tax payments. So if a sole proprietor coffee shop earns $150,000 in operational income in 2021, the sole proprietor simply pays the tax rate that he or she would pay if that $150,000 was coming from a salary.

Lack of Restrictions

Another advantage of proprietorships is the lack of restrictions. The individual has a great deal of freedom in deciding how the firm will be run. No partners or stockholders must be consulted. Additionally, because the operation is usually much smaller than that of other forms of business, a proprietorship is often much easier to manage. It has fewer people and fewer complicated business dealings. Finally, although in some cases a license must be obtained from the state (such as in the operation of a bar or barbershop), proprietorships have no serious restrictions on either starting or terminating operations. Thus, an individual can form a proprietorship and then close the business without having to get permission from a state or federal agency.

Minimum Legal Costs of Formation

While businesses need to comply with licensing requirements, local regulations, and zoning ordinances, sole proprietorships have far less legal paperwork than corporations. In addition, there is very little cost involved with choosing this form of organization. Thus, it is relatively easy to open a sole proprietorship and usually less costly from an administrative perspective.

Personal Satisfaction

Many proprietors report that the best aspect about owning their own business is the personal satisfaction they derive from it. The individual can work as many, or as few, hours a week as he or she wants. Additionally, the goals pursued are the proprietor's own. If the business is a success, the owner knows it is due to his or her own contributions.

Disadvantages of Proprietorships

Despite the advantages just described, some drawbacks are also associated with proprietorships. In determining whether this type of operation will be best for the business, the owner needs to consider factors such as these:

1. Unlimited liability
2. Limited size
3. Limited life

UNLIMITED LIABILITY

Perhaps the greatest drawback of the sole proprietorship is unlimited liability: The individual is responsible for all debts incurred. Creditors have a claim against these debts and can exercise it against both the business assets and personal assets of the proprietor. As a result, if the owner's operation is worth $80,000 and the individual has debts of $125,000, creditors can sue the proprietor and force him or her to liquidate personal assets to pay the financial obligations. This explains why a sole proprietor may have a higher credit rating than other business owners. For example, the president of a corporation may find that the bank will lend the corporation up to 75 percent of the firm's value. If the company suffers a financial setback, the only property the bank has a claim against is the assets of the corporation. But in the case of a sole proprietor, the bank can also claim the owner's personal assets. When a bank determines a fair line of credit for a sole proprietorship, it adds together the owner's business and personal assets.

LIMITED SIZE

Because a proprietorship has only one owner, the amount of capital that can be raised for operations is limited. For example, assume a bank has a policy of lending up to 50 percent of the value of a business and a sole proprietorship has personal and business assets worth $150,000. The bank will lend the company up to $75,000. However, this is as far as the bank is willing to go. If the owner needs an additional $25,000 to take advantage of a business opportunity, one of the few ways to get the money is to take in another partner who has personal assets of $50,000, with the bank lending 50 percent of that value. This may of course vary by industry type or by the degree of the entrepreneur's experience.

To a large degree, the growth of a proprietorship is dependent on reinvested profits. Financially speaking, the business's growth is limited. In particular, sole proprietorships are virtually excluded from entering areas where large capital expenditures are required, such as mass production operations and large manufacturing plants.

An additional problem arises from the business having only one owner. That individual is responsible for doing everything: Buying, selling, extending credit, advertising, hiring, firing, and handling all other business-related matters. This amount of work can be quite a burden, and as the business increases in size, the owner may find that he or she is weighed down. One way to deal with these duties is to delegate authority to subordinates, but the owner still must make the major decisions. When all of these tasks are considered, it is evident that the proprietorship is indeed limited in size. Any attempt to grow beyond this limit will result in uncontrollable operations.

LIMITED LIFE

The life of the proprietorship depends entirely on the proprietor. If the individual dies, is imprisoned, goes bankrupt, or simply chooses to cease operations, the business dies. This presents a risk to the people who work for the firm and to the creditors. To offset some of these risks, it is common for creditors to require the proprietor to carry life insurance sufficient to cover all financial obligations. Then, if the owner should die unexpectedly, the face value of the policy can be used to pay all of the firm's debts. If the policy size is sufficiently large, it may even be possible for someone else to continue operating the business, but this is unlikely. The major reason is that a proprietor usually leaves the estate to his or her spouse. In most cases the spouse does not know enough about the business to keep it going or does not care to.

The Partnership

A partnership, as defined by the Revised Uniform Partnership Act (RUPA), is "an association of two or more persons to carry on as co-owners of a business for profit."[4] In recent years, the partnership has declined in popularity. At present, only about ten percent of all business firms in the United States are partnerships. Nevertheless, millions of them currently exist, and they account for billions of dollars in sales.

In most cases, partnerships consist of two owners, although they can involve any number of partners. For example, advertising agencies, stock brokerages, and public accounting firms often have five or more partners. In addition, master limited partnerships have evolved, which blend the interests of several private partnerships into one larger "master" partnership.

A partnership can be formed by people simply getting together and agreeing to operate a business. However, such an informal arrangement is unlikely. If only to protect themselves in case one of the partners dies, most partners prefer to have a formal partnership contract drawn up. An example of a simple partnership contract is provided in Figure 5.2. More specific terms are usually spelled out after item 5. These typically cover areas such as these:

1. The division of profits and losses
2. The method to be followed if original partners withdraw from the firm or new ones enter the business

3. The division of assets in case the partnership is dissolved
4. The duties of the partners
5. The manner in which any controversies arising out of the contract will be set-tled (a typical approach is arbitration)

This agreement is executed on this _____ day of _____ 20____ between

_____ and _____, all of

_____.

  1. The name of the partnership will be

     _____.

  2. The principal place of business of the partnership will be at

     _____.

  3. The partnership will engage in the business of

     _____ and in such other related business as

     agreed upon by the partners.

  4. The partnership will begin operations _____, 20 __, and will continue until

     terminated as herein provided.

  5. The initial capital of the partnership shall be $_____. Each person agrees to

     contribute cash or property as agreed upon valuation as follows:

PARTNER	AMOUNT	PERCENT
_____	$_____	_____
_____	_____	_____
_____	_____	_____
_____	_____	_____

Figure 5.2 Example of Partnership Contract

At the bottom of the agreement, after all of the provisions are listed, the partners sign their names. The document is then a legally binding contract for all of the parties involved.

Types of Partnerships

A partnership can involve various types of partners. Members of the general public tend to think of all partners as equally responsible for the debts of the business and as equally entitled to the profits. However, this is a simplistic view. Actually, the rights, duties, and obligations of the partners are usually determined by factors such as how much money each has invested in the partnership, how much liability each is willing to assume, and whether each partner wants his or her membership known to the general public. In all, the three categories of partners are general partners, limited partners, and other types of partners.

GENERAL PARTNERS

General partners have unlimited liability and are usually very active in the operation of the business. Each partnership must have at least one general partner. In this way, someone assumes ultimate responsibility for all of the firm's obligations and is authorized to enter into contracts for the firm. If all of the partners fall into this category, the organization is commonly known as a *general partnership*.

LIMITED PARTNERS

Under the provisions of the Revised Uniform Limited Partnership Act (RULPA), which has been enacted by most states, individuals who want to invest in a partnership but do not want to risk all of their assets can do so as limited partners. Their liability is limited to the amount of money they have invested in the company. For example, if Bob puts $5,000 into his uncle's firm and is a limited partner, the most Bob can lose in case of bankruptcy is $5,000. However, his uncle, assuming he is the general partner, can lose all of his business and personal assets.

OTHER TYPES OF PARTNERS

Although the most common types of partners are general and limited, other categories include silent, secret, dormant, and nominal. A *silent partner* is one who is known as a partner by the general public but who does not play an active role in the operation of the business. A *secret partner* is just the opposite: He or she is not known as a partner by the general public but does play an active role in the operation of the business. A *dormant partner* is not known as a partner by the general public and does not play an active role in the operation of the business. A *nominal partner* is a partner in name only. This typically occurs when a well-known person allows his or her name to be used by a partnership. The individual invests no money in the firm and plays no role in its management.

Before we continue, it is important to know that some people may have limited liability according to the partnership contract but may end up with unlimited liability because of some action they take. For example, a limited partner is not empowered to act in the name of the firm; he or she plays no active role in the operation. However, if a limited partner enters into a contract for the partnership by passing himself or herself off as a general partner, the individual can become liable for any losses resulting from this action.

Likewise, a nominal partner can get into the same bind. For example, Anita Gomez, an investor, has been asked for a loan by the general partner, David Smith. Gomez would not ordinarily lend money to a partnership, but in this case she is willing to do so because she knows that Ben Arturo, a local millionaire, is a partner, and if the business gets into trouble, she believes Arturo will bail it out. Smith has told her that, although Arturo is a general partner, some of his funds are tied up in a big European deal, and thus he is unable to come up with the money right now. Unbeknownst to Gomez, she is being told a lie. Arturo is Smith's cousin, and in an effort to help him out in his business, he has allowed the Arturo name to be used. The business is called Arturo Hardware. However, Arturo does not have a financial interest in the store: He is a nominal partner. Given this information, can Arturo be held responsible if Gomez lends Smith the money and the store goes bankrupt? Without getting into the legal ramifications of the problem, let us introduce one final fact. Arturo knows Smith has passed him off as a general partner. Because of this, Arturo *can* be held liable for the firm's obligations. If a nominal partner knows he (or she) is being passed off as a general partner and does not step forward to reveal himself to be a nominal partner, he loses his liability protection.

In short, if a nominal or limited partner passes herself or himself off as a general partner, the courts will rule that the nominal or limited partner is now a general partner and can be held responsible for any debts that arise because of the misrepresentation.

The *limited liability partnership (LLP)* is a form of partnership that allows professionals to enjoy the tax benefits of a partnership while avoiding personal liability for the malpractice of other partners. If a professional group organizes as an LLP, innocent partners are not personally liable for the wrongdoing of the other partners. The LLP is similar to a limited liability company (LLC), discussed later in the chapter. The difference is that LLPs are designed more for professionals who normally do business as partners in a partnership. Like limited liability companies, LLPs must be formed and operated in compliance with state statutes. LLP statutes vary from state to state. Generally, a state statute limits in some way the normal individual collective liability of partners. One of the reasons LLPs are becoming so popular among professionals is that most statutes make it relatively easy to establish an LLP. This is particularly true for an existing partnership. Converting from a partnership to an LLP is easy because the firm's basic organizational structure remains the same. Additionally, all of the statutory and common law rules governing partnerships still apply (apart from those modified by the LLP statute). Normally, LLP statutes are simply amendments to a state's already existing partnership law.[5]

The *limited liability limited partnership (LLLP)* is a relatively new variant of the limited partnership. An LLLP has elected limited liability status for all of its partners, including general partners. Except for this liability status of general part-ners, limited partnerships and LLLPs are identical.

Advantages of Partnerships

Numerous advantages are associated with partnerships.[6] The most important ones are as follows:

1. Increased sources of capital and credit
2. Improved decision-making potential
3. Improved chances for expansion and growth
4. Definite legal status

INCREASED SOURCES OF CAPITAL AND CREDIT

The sole proprietor relies on his or her own personal funds to provide the capital the business needs. This capital also backs any credit others extend to the firm. How-ever, because only one person owns the proprietorship, the individual's capital and credit are limited. A partnership can overcome this problem, at least partially, by bringing in more people with capital to invest and personal assets that can be used as collateral for bank loans and credit. Banks and creditors often feel that less risk is involved in lending to a partnership than to a sole proprietorship because more people can pay the outstanding debts should the business suffer a financial setback.

Improved Decision-Making Potential

The saying "two heads are better than one" has particular application to partner-ships. Three or four partners have a greater chance of making better decisions col-lectively than the proprietor operating alone. This is particularly true if each partner is a specialist in some area. For example, if one is a salesperson, another is an accountant, and a third is the "idea" person, the partnership may be able to outper-form any competitive sole proprietorship.

IMPROVED CHANCES FOR EXPANSION AND GROWTH

Thanks to increased sources of capital and credit and improved decision-making potential, the partnership is usually in a much better position to expand and grow than is the sole proprietorship. In particular, the partnership has the money and managerial expertise to supervise more employees and manage larger facilities. Therefore, as the operations increase in size, the owners are able to maintain opera-tional control.

DEFINITE LEGAL STATUS

Because partnerships have been in existence for centuries, many court decisions have been rendered in regard to all sorts of legal problems. Thus, a good lawyer can answer virtually any question that might arise about partner ownership, liability, or continuity of operations.

Disadvantages of Partnerships

Although partnerships have many advantages, they also have some disadvantages. A few are very similar to the disadvantages of a sole proprietorship. Here are four in particular:

1. Unlimited liability
2. Problem of continuity
3. Managerial problems
4. Size limitations

UNLIMITED LIABILITY

As noted earlier, some partners are limited partners, and as long as they do nothing to jeopardize this status, they can lose only their investment should the business suffer a financial setback. The other partners are general partners, and they must assume unlimited liability for all obligations. However, it is important to remember that profits and losses are not always shared equally. It is common to share everything in relation to capital contribution. For example, the individual who puts up half the money gets half of the profits and, of course, must take responsibility for half of the losses. Yet this is not always the way profits and losses are divided because the general partners are considered *both individually and collectively liable* for the partnership debts. This means that if one of the general partners cannot contribute his or her share of the losses, the others must make it up. The latter, of course, can sue the delinquent partner, but, for the moment, it is they who must pay. Keeping this in mind, it should be obvious why wealthy persons do not like to be general partners in businesses where everyone else has only moderate wealth: They can end up carrying their poorer partners.

PROBLEM OF CONTINUITY

If one of the partners dies, goes to jail, is judged insane, or simply wants to withdraw from the business, the partnership is terminated. As the number of partners increases, the likelihood that one of these events will occur becomes increasingly greater. For example, consider the case of five partners when one of them dies. To reorganize the partnership, the remaining partners must buy out the deceased individual's share, the value of which may be difficult to determine. And if the partners do not have the necessary assets, such action is impossible. In this case, the only alternative may be to bring in a partner with the money to buy out the share of the deceased. Yet it is often difficult to find a person who is acceptable to all the partners—a requirement for any new partner. Such problems affect the continuity of partnerships.

MANAGERIAL PROBLEMS

Although all of the general partners have the right to contract in the name of the business, the firm may find that "too many cooks spoil the broth." One way to overcome this problem is to have each partner restrict his or her activities to one area of operations. For example, one works exclusively in purchasing, another handles the bookkeeping, and a third sells. Yet even when these agreements are spelled out in writing, it is common for problems to arise and for partners to interfere in each other's areas of responsibility.

SIZE LIMITATIONS

Although a partnership can usually raise more money than a sole proprietorship, the amount of capital and credit that bankers and suppliers will provide is limited. Sooner or later the firm reaches its limit. Thus, a partnership can grow larger than a sole proprietorship, but it cannot reach the size of large corporations because its financial assets will not permit it to do so.

The Corporation

Most large businesses in the United States today are corporations—for example, Google, Amazon, Netflix, Microsoft, and Starbucks. Although they constitute only about 20 percent of all businesses, corporations account for more than 90 percent of all business receipts and the largest percentage of wages paid.

What makes the corporation such a popular form of organization? One reason is that, legally, a corporation is an artificial being that has the right to conduct business affairs in its own name, to sue and be sued, and to exist indefinitely.

Organizing the Corporation

In contrast to sole proprietorships and partnerships, it is necessary to get permission from the state to create a corporation. The first step in this process is usually to file the necessary application form with the appropriate state official. Most states require at least three incorporators, each of whom must be an adult, and the payment of the necessary fees at filing time. Aside from this, little other paperwork usually has to be done.

Figure 5.3 shows the basic form of an application for incorporation. Usually the form is written so that the firm's activities and objectives are not very limited. Additionally, since the incorporators often want to minimize taxes, they will investigate the incorporation fees and taxes the various states levy. Because of their tax rates, Delaware, Maryland, and New Jersey are very popular states in which to incorporate, and the corporation does not have to operate in those states.

Once the filing is complete and the approval to incorporate has been given, the secretary of the state will issue the corporation a corporate charter. This charter relates facts such as the type of business the firm is in and the number of shares of stock it intends to issue. The business must operate within the confines of this

---

ARTICLES OF INCORPORATION OF

_____

We, the undersigned natural persons of the age of 21 years or more, acting as incorporators of a corporation under the _____ Business Corporation Act, adopt the following Articles of Incorporation for such corporation:

FIRST: The name of the corporation is

_____

SECOND: The period of its duration is

_____

THIRD: The purpose or purposes for which the corporation is organized are

_____

_____

___

FOURTH: The total number of shares that the corporation shall have authority to issue is

_____

FIFTH: The corporation will not commence business until at least one thousand dollars has been received by it as consideration for the issuance of the shares.

SIXTH: Provisions limiting or denying to shareholders the preemptive right to acquire additional or treasury shares of the corporation are

_____

SEVENTH: Provisions for the regulation of the internal affairs of the corporation are

_____

_____

___

EIGHTH: The address of the initial registered office of the corporation is

_____

_____ and the name of its initial registered agent at such address is

_____

_____

___

NINTH: The number of directors constituting the initial board of directors of the corporation is _____ and the names and addresses of the persons who are to serve as directors until the first annual meeting of shareholders or until their successors are elected and shall qualify are

Name   Address

_____   _____

_____   _____

_____   _____

_____   _____

_____   _____

TENTH: The name and address of each incorporator is

_____   _____

_____   _____

Date _____ , 20___   Incorporators

Figure 5.3 Application for Incorporation

charter, and any changes have to come from either the stockholders or new governmental regulations.

The Corporate Structure

The corporate charter provides the basis for the corporate structure. According to the charter, the stockholders own the firm and have the right to elect the board of directors. These individuals, in turn, choose the president, who appoints the top corporate officers. This process continues down the line, all the way to the workers' level.

The people who own the stock—the stockholders—are permitted to elect the members of the board of directors. For example, if Alice owns ten shares of stock in the Jones Corporation and a total of 10,000 shares are issued, she is the owner of 1/1,000 of the firm and can cast her ten votes for any director she wants. The same is true for those who hold the other 9,990 shares of stock. Under this procedure, the largest stockholders have the greatest amount to say about the management of the corporation.

The board of directors, meanwhile, is responsible for seeing that the business is managed properly. In this capacity, they are charged with formulating long-range direction, approving plans of top management, and seeing that overall policy is carried out. If some problem with the management occurs and the company is not doing well, the board of directors may decide to hire a new president. Thus, the board of directors, voted into office by the stockholders, is ultimately responsible for the overall management of the business.[7]

Advantages of Corporations

The corporate form of ownership offers five important advantages:

1. Limited liability
2. Indefinite life
3. Growth potential
4. Managerial efficiency
5. Transfer of ownership

LIMITED LIABILITY

Stockholders in a corporation are like limited partners, in that they can lose no more than they have invested in the business. For example, Andy and Sue buy 100 shares of stock for $1,000 in their cousin Bob's corporation. A year later, the business goes bankrupt. How much do Andy and Sue lose as a result? Only $1,000. Keep in mind, however, that *Bob* may lose a lot more because he *may* be personally responsible for the corporation's debts. Earlier we noted that some people in a partnership may be limited partners while others are general partners. Lenders are aware that the liability of the investors in a small corporation is limited. Therefore, to secure a large loan, banks or other lending institutions will require the owner to *sign* both personally and in the name of the business. This individual does *not* have limited liability. Yet this is only reasonable, for no bank would be foolish enough to lend a small corporation a great deal of money and then find in the case of financial failure that its ability to collect is restricted to the business's assets. Lenders want to ensure that the owner is as careful as possible with the money, and what better way to do this than to make the person personally liable for the obligation?

INDEFINITE LIFE

Unlike sole proprietorships or partnerships, corporations can exist indefinitely. If a major stockholder dies, the ownership is simply transferred to the heirs. If these people do not want the stock, they can sell it. In short, as long as a market for the stock exists—and it should if the corporation is doing well—the business ownership may change hands, but the corporation remains in existence. A look at some of the major corporations in the United States bears this out: Standard Oil of Indiana (1889), General Electric (1892), IBM (1911), General Motors (1916), and Ford Motor Company (1919).

GROWTH POTENTIAL

In contrast to sole proprietorships or partnerships, corporations generally have greater growth potential because they can raise more capital. By selling shares of stock, the company often can raise large amounts of money. Of course each stockholder may buy only ten or 20 shares, but if enough people are willing to invest, the corporation can raise enough capital to expand.

MANAGERIAL EFFICIENCY

As a business grows in size, it requires greater managerial expertise. The sole proprietorship is heavily dependent on the skills and abilities of the proprietor; the partnership relies greatly on the capabilities of the general partners. However, the corporation often separates ownership from management so that the people who own the company do not manage it. Even when they do, they still tend to bring in specialists, such as sales managers, accountants, and lawyers. In short, as the size of the firm increases, so, too, does the reliance on professional management.

TRANSFER OF OWNERSHIP

An individual who buys stock in a corporation is given a stock certificate. As long as a market for the stock exists, this certificate can be sold if the individual is not happy with the investment. Small corporations have limited markets, so it may be difficult for them to sell stock immediately. Large firms have ready markets for their stock and usually have no problem making immediate sales. The financial section of any newspaper gives the latest prices of many corporations' stock, from AT&T to General Motors to Home Depot. Regardless of the corporation's size, if the company is in good financial shape, the investor is generally able to sell the stock easily.

Disadvantages of Corporations

Some of the disadvantages associated with the corporate form of ownership are as follows:

1. Double taxation
2. High organizing expenses
3. Government restrictions
4. Lack of secrecy

DOUBLE TAXATION

Corporations are subject to heavier taxes on their earnings than either sole proprietorships or partnerships. In recent years, this rate has been as high as 39 percent, making it the highest corporate tax in the world today. Corporations are also subject to a state tax by the state where they are incorporated. Most significantly, there is a double taxation on dividends to stockholders. These individuals must pay a personal income tax on the dividend after the corporation pays the corporate income tax on the same money, thus subjecting corporate earnings to a *double taxation*.[8]

HIGH ORGANIZING EXPENSES

To incorporate, a business must pay certain fees. These include a charter fee to the state in which the business incorporates and corporate fees in all of the states where it operates. (These fees are sometimes in the form of a tax for the right to conduct business in the particular state.) Additionally, because of all the legal procedures and red tape, the company usually has to have an attorney. All of this can add up to a sizable incorporation bill.

GOVERNMENT RESTRICTIONS

Relative to proprietorships and partnerships, corporations face many more governmental restrictions. Their stock sales are regulated by federal and state governments, and the organization must maintain records and reports for examination by government agencies. Additionally, if it tries to merge or consolidate with another organization, the corporation is required to comply with certain laws.

LACK OF SECRECY

Since the corporation has to make various records available to the government, its operations are much less confidential than those of other organizational forms. Additionally, the corporation must provide an annual report to each stockholder so that, as the firm gets bigger, the degree of secrecy declines. Everyone, including the competition, can find out the firm's sales revenues, gross profit, total assets, net profit, and other financial data. Virtually nothing is secret.

New Venture Issues

"Critical Legal Mistakes"

New venture creation always involves many elements, such as searching for an idea, developing the concept, creating a prototype, establishing a market, generating sales, and hiring employees. One area that sometimes gets overlooked is the legal environment. Listed here are a few of the most common mistakes entrepreneurs encounter with new ventures.

1. **No Upfront Agreement With Cofounders**
   An early agreement with any cofounders should always be created. In this document certain key issues must be considered. For example, who gets what percentage of the company? What are the roles and responsibilities of the founders? What salaries (if any) are the founders entitled to? How can that be changed? How are key decisions and day-to-day decisions of the business to be made? How will a sale of the business be decided? What happens if one founder isn't living up to expectations under the founder agreement?

2. **Securities Regulations Issues With Angel Investors**
   Most securities laws require that the sale of any shares of the venture must comply with certain disclosure, filing, and form requirements unless such sales are exempt. Failure to comply with such requirements can result in significant financial penalties for the founders and the startup company, including requiring the startup company to repurchase all the shares at the original issuance price even if the company has lost most, if not all, of its money. Entrepreneurs must seek out knowledgeable lawyers who understand compliance with such laws.

3. **Ignoring Intellectual Property Protection**
   Entrepreneurs that develop a unique product, technology, or service, should consider the appropriate steps to protect the intellectual property and avoid infringing on the intellectual property rights of others. Patents, copyrights, and trademarks are all important legal issues that must be addressed if they apply to the particular venture.

4. **Problems With the Venture or Domain Name**
   When picking the venture's name, entrepreneurs must avoid trademark infringement or domain name problems, especially if the use of a name, domain name, or mark is likely to cause confusion among customers as to the source of the goods or services. To avoid such issues, consider doing a Google search on the name to see what other companies may be using the name. Also, do a search at the U.S. Patent and Trademark Office site for federal trademark registrations on your proposed name. Finally, do a search on GoDaddy.com or other name registrars to see if the desired domain name is available. If the ".com" domain name is taken, this is very problematic and a red flag.

5. **Failing to Outline Contingency Plans**

   What if a partnership experiences financial hardship that causes one partner to buy out the other at a discount? What if a corporation's working capital has deteriorated for years because the COO failed to exert adequate oversight? What if a sole proprietor is suddenly tasked with paying an extra 15 percent of rent expense? Challenges like these cause businesses to pivot every single day. Delegating responsibilities, chartering ownership documents early on, and developing operational hedging strategies are necessary for businesses to maintain their sustainability.

6. **Maintain a Healthy Balance to Confront Legal Issues**

   Many entrepreneurs rely on their business as their sole income stream. Oftentimes increased liability forces the entrepreneur to pour more time and resources into his or her venture. With the stakes raised, it can often be difficult for entrepreneurs to balance their ventures with their personal lives. This is why entrepreneurs are often more stressed, sleep less, and have higher divorce rates. By outlining expectations with personal stakeholders up front and practicing good mental health exercises, entrepreneurs can actively maintain better balance in their lives.

   All of these mistakes can be avoided if entrepreneurs keep the legal concerns in mind when they are initiating their new venture. The advice and counsel of experienced attorneys is always recommended because the time and money spent early can save huge amounts later.

The S Corporation

In an effort to help small businesses, Congress has provided for subchapter S corporations, which are named after the subchapter of the Internal Revenue Code that permits their existence. These corporations are now called S corporations. The tax code allows the earnings of these small corporations to be taxed as partnership income to stockholders. In this way, the double taxation on dividends is avoided,

To exercise this tax option, the S corporation must meet a number of conditions, Two of the most important, based on the latest legislative changes, are that it can have no more than 100 stockholders and no more than 25 percent of the corporate income can come from such passive investments as dividends, rent, and capital gains.

An S corporation has other advantages. The full explanation of the impact and value of this option for a small corporation is best left to the firm's accountant or an outside certified public accountant. The option is available, and it should be considered. However, it is neither a tax dodge nor a panacea for tax problems. This is obvious, in that only 20 percent of small business corporations have chosen the S corporation option. Its specific advantages are simply not of value to every small corporation.[9]

The legal system has developed the S corporation as a legal "person," separate from its owners, to encourage risk-taking and faster economic development. Incorporation remains one of the linchpins of liability protection, and for business owners it remains the necessary first step in minimizing their exposure to personal liability.

However, incorporation is no panacea. There are at least ten categories of circumstances or conduct that can lead to a business owner's personal liability:[10]

1. Failure to actually operate as a legal corporation
2. Business assets owned outside the corporation
3. Personal guarantees of corporate obligations
4. Receipt of excessive corporate distributions
5. Personal faith (responsibility) for negligence
6. Piercing the "corporate veil"
7. Payment of past unpaid wages
8. Pension and profit-sharing plans and other ERISA plans
9. Shareholder liability for taxes
10. Environmental laws

The Limited Liability Company

An increasing number of states have authorized a new form of business organization called the *limited liability company (LLC)*. The LLC is a hybrid form of business enterprise that offers the limited liability of the corporation but the tax advantages of a partnership.

Today, all states have enacted LLC statutes. The various state LLC statutes are far from uniform, with variations based on the corporate and partnership laws of whatever state is enacting the LLC statute. A major advantage of the LLC is that, like the partnership and the S corporation, the LLC does not pay taxes as an entity; rather, profits are "passed through" the LLC and paid personally by the company members. Another advantage is that the liability of members is limited to the amount of their investments. In an LLC, members are allowed to participate fully in management activities, and under at least one state's statute, the firm's managers need not even be members of the LLC. Yet another advantage is that corporations and partnerships, as well as foreign investors, can be LLC members, whereas these entities cannot be shareholders in S corporations. Also, in contrast to S corporations, no limit is placed on the number of shareholder members of the LLC.

The disadvantages of the LLC are relatively few. Perhaps the greatest disadvantage is that LLC statutes differ from state to state, and thus any firm engaged in multistate operations may face difficulties. In an attempt to promote some uniformity among the states with respect to LLC statutes, the National Conference of Commissioners on Uniform State Laws drafted a uniform limited liability company statute for submission to the states to consider for adoption. Until all the states have adopted the uniform law, however, an LLC in one state will have to check the rules in the other states where the firm does business to ensure that it retains its limited liability.[11] See Table 5.1 for a complete comparison chart of the legal forms of organization.

Table 5.1 General Characteristics of Forms of Business

	Sole Proprietorship	Partnership	Limited Liability Partnership	Limited Partnership	Limited Liability Limited Partnership	Corporation	S Corporation	Limited Liability Company
Formation	When one person owns a business without forming a corporation or LLC	By agreement of owners or by default when two or more owners conduct business together without forming a limited partnership, an LLC, or a corporation	By agreement of owners; must comply with limited liability partnership statute	By agreement of owners; must comply with limited partnership statute	By agreement of owners; must comply with limited liability limited partnership statute	By agreement of owners; must comply with corporation statute	By agreement of owners; must comply with corporation state; must elect S corporation status under subchapter S of Internal Revenue Code	By agreement of owners; must comply with limited liability company statute
Duration	Terminates on death or withdrawal of sole proprietor	Usually unaffected by death or withdrawal of partner	Unaffected by death or withdrawal of partner	Unaffected by death or withdrawal of partner unless sole general partner dissociates	Unaffected by death or withdrawal of partner unless sole general partner dissociates	Unaffected by death or withdrawal of shareholder	Unaffected by death or withdrawal of shareholder	Usually unaffected by death or withdrawal of member
Management	By sole proprietor	By partners	By partners	By general partners	By general partners	By board of directors	By board of directors	By managers or members

(Continued)

Table 5.1 Continued

	Sole Proprietorship	*Partnership*	*Limited Liability Partnership*	*Limited Partnership*	*Limited Liability Limited Partnership*	*Corporation*	*S Corporation*	*Limited Liability Company*
Owner Liability	Unlimited	Unlimited	Mostly limited to capital contribution	Unlimited for general partners; limited to capital contribution for limited partners	Limited to capital contribution	Limited to capital contribution	Limited to capital contribution	Limited to capital contribution
Transfer Ability of Owners' Interest	None	None	None	None unless agreed otherwise	None unless agreed otherwise	Freely transferable, although shareholders may agree otherwise	Freely transferable, although shareholders usually agree otherwise	None unless agreed otherwise
Federal Income Taxation	Only sole proprietor taxed	Only partners taxed	Usually only partners taxed; may elect to be taxed like a corporation	Usually only partners taxed; may elect to be taxed like a corporation	Usually only partners taxed; may elect to be taxed like a corporation	Corporation taxed; shareholders taxed on dividends (double tax)	Only shareholders taxed	Usually only members taxed; may elect to be taxed like a corporation

Source: Adapted from Jane P. Mallor, A. James Barnes, Thomas Bowers, Arlen W. Langvardt, Jamie Darin Prenkert, and Martin A. McCrory, *Business Law: The Ethical, Global, and E-Commerce Environment*, 16th ed., New York, McGraw-Hill Irwin, 2016, p. 995.

L3C for Social Ventures

An L3C is a low-profit, limited liability company that can provide a structure that facilitates investments in socially beneficial, for-profit ventures. In 2008, Vermont became the first state to recognize the L3C as a legal corporate structure; however, similar legislation has been introduced in a number of states. Currently, the L3C is legal for activity all across the United States because it is designed to attract private investments and philanthropic capital in ventures designed to provide a social benefit. Unlike a standard LLC, the L3C has an explicit primary charitable mission and only a secondary profit concern. But unlike a charity, the L3C is free to distribute the profits, after taxes, to owners or investors. A principal advantage of the L3C is its qualification as a program-related investment (PRI). This means it is an investment with a socially beneficial purpose that is consistent with a foundation's mission. Because foundations can only directly invest in for-profit ventures qualified as PRIs, the L3C's operating agreement specifically outlines its respective PRI-qualified purpose in being formed, making it easier for foundations to identify social purpose businesses as well as helping to ensure that their tax exemptions remain secure. L3Cs could attract a greater amount of private capital from various sources to serve their charitable or education goals.

Summary

A sole proprietorship is owned and controlled by one person. It is currently the most common form of business ownership in the United States. Some of the advantages it offers are certain financial advantages, lack of restrictions, secrecy, and personal satisfaction. Its disadvantages include unlimited liability, limited size, and limited life.

A partnership is an association of two or more persons to carry on as co-owners of a business for profit. The two major types of partners are general and limited, but several less common types exist as well. General partners have unlimited liability. Limited partners' financial responsibility is restricted to their investment. Other partners tend to have limited liability. However, this can change if they represent themselves to the public as general partners and, as a result of their action, cause the partnership some financial loss. The advantages of the partnership include greater capital and credit, improved decision-making potential, improved chances for expansion and growth, and definite legal status. The drawbacks include unlimited liability, continuity problems, management problems, and size limitations.

Most large businesses in this country are corporations. As an entrepreneurial venture increases in size, this legal form of organization warrants attention. Although permission from the state is necessary for a corporation to start up, this structure provides some very important advantages, including limited liability, indefinite life, growth potential, managerial efficiency, and transfer of ownership. The disadvantages associated with the corporate form of ownership include heavy taxation, high organizing expenses, government restrictions, and lack of secrecy. Additionally, the owner should have a certified public accountant examine the company's books and help it decide whether to convert to an S corporation or a limited liability company

(LLC). Finally, a new form of ownership known as the L3C now exists for companies that have an explicit primary charitable mission. An L3C is a low-profit, limited liability company that can provide a structure that facilitates investments in socially beneficial, for-profit ventures.[12]

A Global Perspective

"'Local Businesses Aren't Local Anymore"

The increasingly global nature of the world economy means that businesses that operate within only a single country need to consider the global market trends that could impact their business. Globalization of the world economy has created increased opportunities for new companies. In terms of creating access to business resources and capabilities, the internet has made available global resources that would traditionally have been unavailable to new businesses. These include rare or hard to find production materials from around the world, affordable manufacturing capacity for low-margin products, and software development capabilities in countries with more talent than local opportunities. The internet has also expanded the availability of markets for sales since international marketplaces such as eBay, Amazon, and Alibaba allow buyers in foreign markets to purchase items from across the world with the click of a button.

However, the increased globalization of the world economy has also created a myriad of challenges, including legal and regulatory challenges for businesses, even if a business operates in a single country. A major challenge for businesses in the United States that sell manufactured products through marketplaces such as Amazon is online competitors selling counterfeit versions of products whose designs are protected under U.S. patent law. The majority of counterfeit items come into the U.S. market from China and Hong Kong, despite commitments from the Chinese government to protect intellectual property rights. Protecting intellectual property from counterfeit products can be particularly challenging for startups and small businesses that may not have the time, money, or legal resources to pursue claims against multiple counterfeit products. In some cases, the patent system can even work against businesses since granted patents include public information that can be used by counterfeiters to try to patent the design in their own country.

An additional challenge can come from the marketplace platforms themselves. Amazon has been accused of working hard to recruit sellers in China, some of which have sold counterfeit items or advertised their products using false or misleading advertising, to the detriment of U.S.-based manufacturers and sellers. At times, U.S. consumers are put at risk since some of the foreign-sourced products contain lead, cadmium, and other unsafe materials.

Increasingly, every business, including startups, needs to see itself as a global business and be aware of the potential legal challenges within its markets.

Source: Adapted from Spencer Kimball, "US Small Businesses Are Fighting an Uphill Battle Against Counterfeiters in China: 'It's Like Whack-a-Mole,'" CNBC, October 6, 2019, www.cnbc.com/2019/10/06/how-us-small-businesses-are-fighting-counterfeiting-in-china.html; and Jon Emont, "Amazon's Heavy Recruitment of Chinese Sellers Puts Consumers at Risk," *The Wall Street Journal*, November 11, 2019, www.wsj.com/articles/amazons-heavy-recruitment-of-chinese-sellers-puts-consumers-at-risk-11573489075.

Review and Discussion Questions

1. What is a sole proprietorship?
2. What are some of the advantages and disadvantages of a sole proprietorship? List and describe three of each.
3. In contrast to sole proprietorships, how popular are partnerships? Explain.
4. How does a general partner differ from a limited partner?
5. What is a silent partner, a secret partner, a dormant partner, a nominal partner?
6. What is a limited liability partnership (LLP)?
7. What are some of the advantages and disadvantages of a partnership? List and describe three of each.
8. What are some of the advantages and disadvantages of incorporating? Discuss four of each.
9. Why would a small business choose the S corporation or the limited liability company? Explain.
10. What is the L3C and why would a small venture seek that form of organization?

The Venture Consultant

Time to Incorporate?

Mitch, Ralph, and Nick Bachewicz started their own climbing equipment store and structured it as a partnership, split 33 percent apiece, in 2014. The brothers never had thoughts of growing the business too large, as their primary enjoyment stemmed from their expertise in the equipment they sold to their local community. However, their passion for climbing gear shone through to customers on the financial statements too. The company posted $2 million in revenue in 2015, just two years after inception.

Although the promising start was commendable, a key supplier went out of business, causing a decline in sales to $1,050,000 in 2016. While this was troubling news, the Bachewicz brothers were able to stay afloat by offering steep discounts to reacquire customer interest. A year later, the Bachewicz brothers were back to $1.5 million in revenue and looking to expand. To finance the expansion, the Bachewicz brothers needed $2 million.

Luckily for them, Donald, a savvy investor who had spent a career growing outdoor climbing businesses, had been tracking their progress and was interested in investing. Confident, Donald offered the Bachewicz brothers the $2 million they asked for in exchange for 25 percent of the company, contingent on the brothers incorporating the business. Tapping into his industry expertise, Donald knew that to sustain the expected growth in the future, the company would need to raise money again in a few years. He had seen multiple climbing businesses suffer from suppressed growth after an initial investment because they did not have enough cash to sustain the growth operations. As a corporation, it would be much easier to raise funds and support higher growth.

The Bachewicz brothers were initially concerned about company control, but Donald assured them they would be able to keep at least 50 percent of the company if they were to incorporate. This was exciting news but did not quell all of their fears. The brothers were also troubled by three other facts:

1. The tax rate as a corporation would be higher than in their current partnership.
2. Going public created more government restrictions and oversight.
3. Incorporating was costly, and the business would endure large organizing expenses.

Your Consultation

You are the sole advisor for the Bachewicz brothers and are tasked with making the best decision for the company. What are the advantages and disadvantages of incorporating? Pick three and explain. How serious are the drawbacks of incorporating? Would it possibly behoove the Bachewicz brothers to negotiate the incorporation clause with Donald? All things considered, is incorporating the climbing business a wise move? Why or why not?

Notes

1   See Constance E. Bagley and Craig E. Dauchy, *The Entrepreneur's Guide to Business Law*, 4th ed. Mason, OH: Cengage/South-Western, 2012.
2   David S. Hulse and Thomas R. Pope, "The Effect of Income Taxes on the Preference of Organizational Form for Small Businesses in the United States," *Journal of Small Business Management*, 1996, 34 (1): 24–35. See also Sandra Malach, Peter Robinson, and Tannis Radcliffe, "Differentiating Legal Issues by Business Type," *Journal of Small Business Management*, 2006, 44 (4): 563–576; and Mina Baliamoune-Lutz and Pierre Garello, "Tax Structure and Entrepreneurship," *Small Business Economics*, 2014, 42 (1): 165–190.
3   For further discussion on the legal aspects of sole proprietorships, see Kenneth W. Clarkson, Roger LeRoy Miller, and Frank B. Cross, *Business Law*, 13th ed. Mason, OH: Cengage/South-Western,

2015, pp. 706–708; see also Jean Murray, "All About Sole Proprietorships and Sole Proprietors," accessed on March 17, 2020 at www.thebalancesmb.com/sole-proprietorship-398896.

4 For the complete Revised Uniform Partnership Act, see Jane P. Mallor, A. James Barnes, Thomas Bowers, Arlen W. Langvardt, Jamie Darin Prenkert, and Martin A. McCrory, *Business Law: The Ethical, Global, and E-Commerce Environment*, 16th ed. New York: McGraw-Hill/Irwin Publishers, 2016.

5 For further discussion on the legal aspects of LLPs, see Clarkson, Miller, and Cross, *Business Law*, 13th ed., pp. 733–737.

6 For an excellent overview of partnerships, see Ibid., pp. 720–732.

7 For a detailed discussion of corporate laws and regulations, see Mallor, Barnes, Bowers, Langvardt, Prenkert, and McCrory, *Business Law*, 16th ed., pp. 1223–1417.

8 See Hulse and Pope, "The Effect of Income Taxes on the Preference of Organizational Form for Small Businesses in the United States."; see also Baliamoune-Lutz and Garello, "Tax Structure and Entrepreneurship."

9 See Bagley and Dauchy, *The Entrepreneur's Guide to Business Law*; and Clarkson, Miller, and Cross, *Business Law*, 13th ed., pp. 764–765.

10 Kenneth P. Brier, "A Dirty Dozen of Liability," *Family Business*, Winter 1994, 45–48.

11 See Clarkson, Miller, and Cross, *Business Law*, 13th ed., pp. 740–748; and Bagley and Dauchy, *The Entrepreneur's Guide to Business Law*.

12 Gene Takagi, "L3C—Low Profit Limited Liability Company," *Non Profit Law Blog*, accessed on July 11, 2016 at www.nonprofitlawblog.com/home/2008/07/l3c.html.

6   Strategic Pricing

The Hook

Introduction: Pricing Considerations

The pricing challenge is a major challenge for all entrepreneurial ventures. There are a number of basic considerations that must be understood by entrepreneurs when developing a pricing strategy. The new venture's primary consideration when pricing must be cost. No one can afford to sell below the cost level—at least not for very long. In other words, the entrepreneur must always be in search of a profit through pricing. However, since this point is obvious, we will not spend much time on it here. Rather, let us turn to other pricing considerations. These include the following:

1. The nature of the product
2. The competition
3. The marketing strategy
4. The customer and value perception
5. General business conditions

The Nature of the Product

The demand for some products seems to be little affected by a change in price. For example, whether the price of salt is raised or lowered has little effect on the quantity sold. However, the demand for many products does respond to price, and this demand can be stimulated with price changes in two ways. First, some goods will sell better if the price is *lowered*—that is, if demand increases. However, the opposite approach is to *raise* the price and manage to maintain approximately the same demand as before. If this occurs, it must be because buyers believe the product or service is still a good value at the higher price. In general, entrepreneurs are advised to set prices to compete on quality or innovation and not directly on price. Competing on price directly can be harmful because larger competitors can usually create more efficiencies and can undercut your price.

The Competition

A second pricing consideration is the competition. The way competing firms price similar goods affects what the new venture owner-manager can charge. This is particularly so when customers cannot distinguish the product one store sells from that another sells. For example, for most people, milk is milk, so it really does not matter where you buy it as long as the store is located conveniently. As a result, if two stores are across the street from each other and the price of milk is 10¢ a gallon less at one of them, customers will flock to that store. The same is true for bread, shoelaces, socks, and gasoline.

Few products are bought *solely* on the basis of price; however, many times people will pay more money for a particular good because it has a quality image. Television sets are an example. If a set has problems, the average consumer will not know how to repair it. Therefore, when that person buys, quality will be a major criterion, and price will rank farther down the list. Of course, the new venture owner-manager cannot guarantee quality in televisions, appliances, or similar goods, but the person can try to secure franchise agreements from well-known major manufacturers so that he or she can carry their products. This will provide a competitive edge over other stores.

Finally, regardless of quality, most goods eventually wear out or break down. Sooner or later, a car needs an engine repair or a computer has a hard drive that crashes, requiring replacement. This is where service comes in. Few new ventures can compete with large companies on a head-to-head price basis. However, they can distinguish their goods and services from those of the competition through personal customer service. For example, many people who go to a service station for car maintenance will return if the service is satisfactory. They also buy their gasoline and other auto-related products there. Similarly, services such as haircuts, dental work, and health care are all influenced greatly by their quality. Thus, price in and of itself will not always determine demand. In fact, businesses that offer high quality can often raise their prices without suffering any decline in demand.

The Marketing Strategy

A third pricing consideration is marketing strategy. Some new ventures prefer to be price leaders even if this means lower overall volume. Others prefer simply to meet the competition and price their merchandise between the highest and lowest prices of other sellers. Still others like to price low and make their money through increased volume.

The owner must decide whether he or she wants to make a lot of profit in the short run or aim for long-run profit in the form of repeat business. If the owner sells fad items, prices will probably be high because the person knows that the store has little chance of repeat business for any particular line. Additionally, if the fad suddenly fades, the owner may wind up with a lot of unsalable inventory. To prevent this, the owner will want to recover the investment as soon as possible. By contrast, many new ventures sell the same types of goods and services all the time. If they are high quality, the owner will probably have high prices and will develop a reputation for being "expensive but good." Conversely, owners who sell items of average quality usually price them competitively and work on securing repeat business.

Marketing strategy helps the public identify a firm. When people want to buy something at the lowest possible price, they go to companies they have come to know as discounters. But when they want to buy something of high quality that, if not satisfactory, can be returned, they go to stores that have a reputation for handling these kinds of transactions. In short, marketing strategy helps the business establish an *image*.

The Customer and Value Perception

There is no question that in today's environment a new venture entrepreneur must consider the targeted customer in the pricing strategy decision. In this vein, the customer's perception of value in the product or service is the ultimate judge of a fair price. So, entrepreneurs must be conscious of the value perception being created by their product or service. In addition, entrepreneurs must be willing to enhance their venture's image of value, as that will eventually impact the price that customers will pay.

General Business Conditions

Most ventures are affected by general business conditions. This is particularly true for newer enterprises. When economic conditions are poor, it is common for them to keep inventories at a minimum and price goods to move fast. The impact of the economic environment is most noticeable at the wholesale level because wholesalers tend to sell large quantities of goods on a very narrow profit margin. Changes in their cost of doing business often must be passed along immediately to protect this narrow margin. At the retail level, price changes occur more slowly because most stores price their goods high enough to absorb minor variations in the cost of doing business. Nevertheless, all costs are eventually passed along to the consumer.[1]

Remember, price is not just *what* the entrepreneur charges but *how* he or she charges. Hence, eBay could charge by the auction, or they could sell memberships and allow members to engage in as many auctions as they want for one price, or they could charge only the seller or only the buyer a commission based on the dollar value of the transaction. Let's begin by examining some of the key factors in pricing.

Key Pricing Factors

All pricing methods begin with understanding costs and what kind of price is necessary to break even on an item. New venture owner-managers may reduce the price and try to cut losses on a particular line; however, that would only happen as a result of careful analysis of certain key factors. We present three basic factors to consider when setting a price:

1. The cost of goods
2. Competitive prices
3. Market demand

The Cost of Goods

The primary objective of pricing for profit is to set a price that is high enough to cover the cost of the goods and the expenses incurred in selling them to generate some profit. A simple formula for this is as follows:

Selling Price = Purchase Price + Operating Expenses + Profit

In this formula, operating expenses fall into two categories: Production costs (materials and labor) and overhead (rent for the building, utility bills, and other general costs not covered directly when production costs are determined). Profit is then a percentage of the total. The profit percentage is impacted by the industry, type of product, or actions of competitors.

Competitive Prices

We have already discussed competitive prices in some depth. Most new venture owner-managers keep an eye on what their competitors are charging for similar goods and services. Unless new ventures have some good reason not to, most price with the competition.

Market Demand

Although demand has also been examined in some detail, we need to consider profit versus volume. Research reveals that many sellers try to hold the line on price to maintain market share. Sometimes, however, demand is so strong the owner will raise the price as high as market conditions allow. This usually can be done only when a new product or service is in short supply, coupled with a strong market demand. Additionally, it is important to remember that an "ideal" price may exist. This can be illustrated with a demand schedule, a graph that plots varying prices against antici-pated demand for each price (Figure 6.1). Note that four points are designated on this schedule. Computing the total revenue at each point, we get the following:

2,500 units @ $45 each = $112,500
5,000 units @ $35 each = $175,000
7,500 units @ $25 each = $187,500
10,000 units @ $15 each = $150,000

In this case, the owner should price at $25 since revenue would be maximized at that point. Anything higher or lower than $25 will result in less revenue. Accord-ing to the schedule, if the owner is willing to give up $37,500, he or she could sell another 2,500 units by pricing at $15. Typically, however, the owner prices for profit, so the $25 price would be preferred over the $15 price.[2]

Pricing Strategies

New ventures employ a wide variety of pricing strategies. However, these all have two common objectives: (1) to earn a profit for the firm and (2) to garner and main-tain market demand for the product.

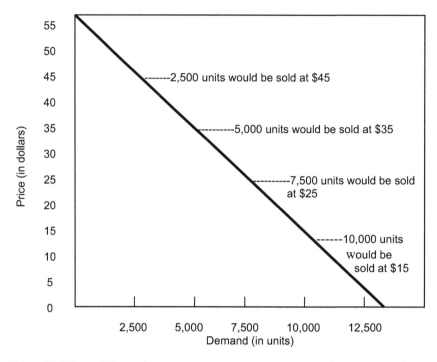

Figure 6.1 Price and Demand

The specific pricing strategy will be dictated by a number of considerations. For example, some companies tie their pricing to the product life cycle of the good. When the product is first introduced, they use one type of pricing strategy. When the product begins to mature, they employ another pricing strategy. As the good begins moving into the declining phase, they implement a third strategy. Regardless of whether this strategy is used, a host of pricing techniques typically serve as the basis for pricing decisions.[3] The following examines some of the most common.

Skimming pricing is the technique of selling at a high price to skim off the strongest demand in the marketplace. This strategy particularly helps a new venture generate high profit per unit. However, the strategy is often maintained for only a short time because the conditions that allow for skimming usually do not last very long. A common example is when a new venture has a product that is in strong demand, such as a clothing store with the latest and hottest clothing line. The store will often price this product at a high markup because the owner knows that anyone who wants to buy the latest fashions will pay a premium to get them early. When other clothing stores begin carrying similar lines of clothing, the owner will then drop the price down to its usual level because customers will no longer pay a premium price for a product they can obtain more cheaply elsewhere. This is also very common with technological products like the Apple iPhone. When a new iPhone hits the market, it is priced high with high profit margins. As other competitor products enter the market, the price is then reduced to compete with the competitors' products.

In some cases, skimming is an ongoing strategy because market conditions support this approach. A good example is high-end electronics stores where customers expect to pay high prices and often equate price with quality. A beauty salon that charges $50 for a haircut may not attract many customers, but if it is located in a fashionable part of the city and appeals to upscale clientele, the business is likely to do quite well with a skimming strategy. Moreover, if the salon decides to lower its prices to increase the number of customers, the owner will likely find that the new strategy has hurt the company's reputation and has resulted in a substantial decline of both revenue and profits. Skimming is also used when customers are willing to pay a premium for services they cannot, or will not, perform themselves. Lawn sprinkler installation companies often find they can charge high prices because homeowners do not know how to put in a sprinkler system, so they are willing to pay a premium price for the service. Although some competitors will try to capture the market share by offering lower installation prices, this strategy is often unsuccessful because the customer equates price with quality. As a result, the individual is afraid that a low-priced sprinkler system will continually break down or need an inordinate amount of periodic maintenance. The psychological effect helps installation companies maintain their skimming strategy.

Skimming is also used profitably when customers perceive a major difference between a high-priced good or service and lower-priced ones. For example, many patients prefer to stay with their current dentist rather than go to a university dental clinic or large dental facility located in a shopping center despite the fact that their current dentist often charges higher prices. These patients are convinced the dental care they receive from their dentist is superior to what they would get in a shopping center. Whether or not this is true, it helps explain why dentists in small offices are able to attract and maintain clientele in the face of lower-priced competition.

Penetration pricing is the strategy of employing a low price that is competitive and designed both to stimulate demand and to discourage competition. Penetration pricing most typically is used for low-priced goods where the firm's objective is to trade profit per unit for gross sales. Many new ventures, for example, have found that at a high price for an item, say $2.99, they will sell 100 units a month, but at $2.49 they will sell 500 units a month. If the cost of the unit is $2, the business will make a total profit of $99 at the high price and $245 at the lower price.

Another benefit of penetration pricing is that it discourages new competitors because the profit per item is low, and these firms are often unwilling to compete vigorously for the necessary market share. (This is in contrast to a skimming strategy, which often attracts competitors, who see the opportunity for large profit per unit.) Penetration pricing also helps a new venture build an image as a place where merchandise can be purchased at reasonable prices.

Another term used here is *parity pricing*, where the entrepreneur will charge at or near what competitors are charging. Marketing researchers Kotler and Armstrong[4] claim that the choice of strategy affects the competition the entrepreneur might face. A strategy with high margins may draw in others who would also like to take advantage. However, a low margin strategy may drive competitors out. To decide what to do, ask the following questions:

- How does the company's product or service compare to the competition?
- How strong are current competitors?
- How does the competitive landscape influence customer price sensitivity?

Many new ventures use penetration or parity pricing because they are better able to control their costs than are larger competitors. Thus, they can afford to take lower profit per unit and still remain viable. However, penetration pricing must be closely coordinated with inventory ordering to ensure that the business neither runs out of merchandise nor overstocks. Many companies feel this is a small price to pay for the potentially large profit they can generate with penetration pricing.

Sliding price strategy is a method of moving prices in relation to demand. This strategy involves a combination of skimming and penetration pricing. In most cases, the goods are priced high and demand at this level is skimmed off. Then, as demand weakens, the firm will lower its price and continue to generate demand. The move into penetration pricing will continue until the company drops the product line or freezes the price at the lowest level it can go.

In some cases, a sliding price strategy involves fluctuations both up and down. For example, when auto dealers receive a shipment of new cars, they try to sell the cars for as close to sticker price as possible. The dealers know that customers who want a new car will pay a premium price during the early months of the year. So, when new cars reach the market in September or October, it is common to find auto dealers using a skimming strategy. As the sales year wears on, however, demand will slacken, and during January and February it is common to find dealers more willing to bargain and take lower prices. Some buyers prefer to buy new cars at the tail end of the sales year (July, August, and September) because they know the dealer wants to clear out the year's models to make way for new models. This scenario shows how dealers use a skimming strategy followed by penetration pricing. However, this is not the only sales strategy pattern they employ.

If a new car is selling very well, the dealer will not resort to penetration pricing. The dealer will instead employ a skimming strategy throughout the entire year. Conversely, if the dealer knows that a monthly demand exists for 15–17 of this year's new trucks and the company received 24 trucks last month, the dealership will turn to penetration pricing to entice sales. However, if the business received only nine of these vehicles from the manufacturer this month, the car dealer will use a skimming strategy because they know that demand is greater than the supply on hand. So, under a sliding price strategy, prices can slide down *or* up depending on the business's reading of customer demand. This means that companies that sell a number of different products or product lines will use a sliding price strategy that results in a variety of price changes.

In most cases, however, a sliding price strategy follows a skimming and then penetration pattern, with progressively lower prices. One of the main reasons for this pattern is competition from new product offerings. For example, the price of microcomputers has continued to fall, with machines that cost $2,200 ten years ago now being purchased with more advanced systems for less than half that price today. As technology causes old products to become outmoded, sellers must lower their prices to maintain demand. New venture owners who sell these units know that the longer they have these units on hand, the greater the likelihood they will have to lower prices to create the necessary demand. Then the pricing emphasis is more on penetration than skimming.

Odd pricing is the setting of a price just below a round number. Examples include pricing a good at $1.99 rather than $2.00 or $299 rather than $300.[5] This strategy is based on the belief that customers perceive the odd price as much lower than the round number price. Obviously, the price is not significantly lower, as perceived, but the phenomenon helps account for why odd pricing is often referred to as *psychological pricing*. The major question for new venture owners is how much of an impact on sales will an odd price generate? The answer depends on the price. For example, razor blades selling at $2.99 are often more attractive than similar offerings at $3.00, but few people would be influenced to buy a refrigerator for $999.99 rather than $1,000 because the penny difference is not regarded as a sufficient savings. Recent research shows that odd pricing tactics can be helpful to new venture owners, but the approach has to vary depending on price level. Here are four guidelines that have been recommended:

1. *Products selling for under $1:* Prices for these goods should end in nine because this is psychologically attractive and generates higher profits for the firm. For example, a product selling at 59¢ will sell just as well as one priced at 54¢, so it is advisable to round the price up to 59¢ and maximize profits.
2. *Products selling for $1–$10:* The two best numbers in this price category are nine and five. So if a new venture feels it must price a product below $5, a selling price of $4.99 is often an attractive one. If the company feels too many of its products are priced 1¢ below the next dollar, then $4.95 is a good choice. If we compare the market appeal of prices for a good in the mid $8 range, for example, $7.49 is preferable to $7.50, and $7.45 is better than $7.44. Additionally, in the $1–$10 range, a price such as $6.41 or $9.52, a penny or two above a round number, is no better at attracting sales than a price of $6.49 or $9.55. By sticking to the nine and five options, new venture owners can generate more sales and profits in the $1–$10 range.
3. *Products selling above $10 and up to $100:* At these higher levels, the effect of prices ending in nine diminishes significantly. People cannot perceive the difference between $10.99 and $11.00 as important. Instead, new venture owners should use prices ending in 25¢, 50¢, or 75¢. For example, $10.75 is more attractive than $10.99, and $99.50 is more attractive than $99.99. At higher-level prices, the 25¢ difference is easier to evaluate.
4. *Products selling above $100:* At this level, only whole-dollar prices should be used. A television set selling for $699.99 will not generate any more demand than one selling for $700, so cents should be dropped from the price label. Additionally, it is important not to use decimal points after the dollar price. For example, $700 is preferable to $700.00 because the zeros after the decimal point make the price look greater. Working with these basic guidelines,

a new venture owner can then go back to the use of nine and five. For example, a refrigerator selling for $999 will be more attractive than one selling for $1,000. If the owner wants to nudge the price a little lower, $995 is another good choice. However, $992 or $991 will be no more effective than $995 in generating demand.

Odd pricing works only when it has a psychological benefit. The objective of the strategy is to make the price more attractive without giving away very much profit. One recent research study found that people perceive odd prices as being much lower than even prices. Participants in the study said they would buy significantly fewer items if even pricing was utilized even though the price was 0.3 percent different. This result was found for pricing at four different pricing levels.[6] For this reason, odd pricing tends to be used with competitive products and is more likely to supplement penetration pricing than a skimming strategy.

Leader pricing is the marking down of a popular product to attract more customers. The objective of this pricing strategy is to build customer traffic. One of the most popular forms of leader pricing has been the use of *loss leaders*, which are products sold *below* cost in an effort to generate increased overall sales for all products in a store. In many states, loss leaders have been outlawed because they are viewed as unfair competition. However, the basic idea of attracting customers through lower than usual prices continues to be a mainstay of most new venture pricing strategies. The logic behind leader pricing is that customers may come to buy one extremely low-priced product but end up buying normally priced products as well. The objective of the strategy is to increase the number of people coming into the business.

A store often uses leader pricing on a product known to be in demand to attract business. At other times, this strategy is employed to help cut large inventory levels. A good example is grocery stores that will advertise weekly leader priced specials to draw customers into their stores. While they may not make any profit—and in many cases may lose money—on the sale of these leader priced items, customers will also by many items that are more profitable and make up for the loss leader priced items.

Price lining is the process of offering merchandise in several different price ranges. Some experts call this *price flexibility* and relate it to the decision to apply the same price to all segments or differentiating based on different customers or regions.[7] One-price policies are best in mass selling markets, and variable pricing is usually applied when individual bargaining is involved.

Quite often a range of low, medium, and high prices are used. A good example of this strategy is a pizzeria that offers three different types of pies: Regular, additional, and grand. A regular pizza costs $8.95; a pizza with two additional toppings costs $11.95; and a grand pizza, which contains a wide assortment of toppings, costs $14.95. When customers place their orders, the individual totaling the bill knows that only three prices exist, regardless of what the individual wants on the pizza. As a result, price lining makes it easy to keep track of prices.

Businesses that use price lining try to cater to a variety of consumer tastes. The pizza example involves three price market niches. Some firms will have as few as two prices, while others will have four or more price ranges. As the number of product lines increases, however, it is common to find only two or three ranges per line because of the desire to simplify the buying, pricing, and stocking of merchandise.

Price lining most commonly is used when it is possible to distinguish among grades or levels of goods and services. Car washes, for example, often have a variety of service levels, ranging from a basic car wash (the least expensive service) to a special deluxe wash (the most expensive service). Beauty salons, coffee shops, auto parts stores, and many other new ventures use price lining strategies. The most important benefits of this technique are that it allows the company to offer a variety of prices for its goods and services and helps it cater to a series of different market niches.

Price bundling is a type of pricing where customers acquire a "host of goods or services" along with the products they purchase.[8] A good example of bundled pricing is the purchase of a cell phone and a calling plan. To get the special price on a desired cell phone you must also sign up for a calling plan that bundles minutes, weekend calling, email, text messaging, insurance, etc.—all at one cost.

Geographic pricing is a technique of charging customers based on where they live. Simply stated, this pricing strategy passes the cost of transporting goods to buyers. In some cases, this is handled merely by charging customers the cost of the product "plus shipping." If the company is located in New Jersey, the product's final cost will be greater for customers in San Francisco than for those in Philadelphia.

New ventures that sell locally seldom charge for transportation unless it is a standard practice in the industry or the cost of delivering goods or services is a large percentage of the overall bill. For example, if a dry cleaner charges $2.50 per shirt, the store will not deliver two shirts to a customer who lives 20 miles away without adding a delivery charge. At a cost of 50¢ per mile for the company vehicle, it would cost $20 round trip. The business would lose money on free delivery to the customer. To overcome resistance to geographic pricing, some companies divide the local area into zones and let customers know the additional charge for delivery to their zone. Other businesses simply have a fixed delivery charge, such as $5 per order. They then will group the orders and make a series of deliveries to customers, thus reducing the out-of-pocket expense per order and in many cases making a profit on the delivery. This technique often is accepted without question by customers even though, on close analysis, some people are paying more than they should for the service. For example, a person who lives only a few miles away will be charged the same transportation fee as someone who lives a great distance from the company.

In determining a geographic pricing strategy, companies also consider hourly employee costs. Many firms resolve this situation by using part-time help to handle delivery and by paying these people minimum wage. If a number of deliveries are to be made per hour, employees will take this job because they are counting on tips from clients. In this way, a person paid minimum wage who makes three deliveries in this period may end up with a total of $16 or more per hour. As a result, the firm never has to worry about hiring delivery people, and the transportation charge per order more than covers the hourly wage and cost of operating the vehicle.

A *discount* is a reduction in the list price. Many new ventures find they can profitably boost sales by deviating from a fixed-price strategy. In some cases, this is a result of selling experience; in other cases, it is mandated by competitive practices, and the business has no alternative but to grant discounts. An article in the *Harvard Business Review* suggests that a firm ask itself several questions when deciding to offer a discount:

• Are discount dollars being invested in the market segment that offers the best strategic value for the company?
• Do discount levels vary widely, and if so, what is the basis for this variation?
• Are discounts consistent over time or do they increase at the end of a quarter?
• Is widespread discounting a uniform problem across the company?

Some experts suggest that a company monitor their discount practices and ensure that pricing fits the firm's competitive place in the market and overall marketing strategy.[9] New ventures commonly use a number of different types of discounts. These types of discounts are discussed in the following paragraphs.

A *seasonal discount* is a price reduction given during particular times of the year. These types of discounts typically occur before or after peak buying periods. For example, swimsuit manufacturers offer discounts to retailers in the Midwest who buy before peak summer months. Since most bathing suits are sold between May and August, these discounts are given in March and April. Manufacturers use discounting to help increase sales as well as to minimize the cost of warehousing inventory. Retailers, in turn, offer seasonal discounts in the late summer and early fall in an effort to sell merchandise that soon will have no market demand and will have to be warehoused.

Another good example of new venture discounting involves post-holiday products, such as Valentine's Day candy, which is marked down on February 15, and holiday decorations, cards, and wrapping paper, which are heavily discounted during the last week of December. In an effort to generate even higher sales, some retailers now have begun changing these holiday sales periods and offering discounts *before* the holiday. Christmas sales on the Friday and Saturday after Thanksgiving are now quite common. One of the primary reasons for the change in this price strategy is that new ventures are realizing they must discount their products before large competitors do because the latter typically win these head-to-head price wars.

Another common strategy is *special group discounting*, such as 25 percent off list price for all senior citizens. This strategy has been very helpful in recent years in building and maintaining a loyal customer base among seniors, who are often retired and are careful about how they spend their money. Other groups often targeted include educators, students, veterans, and first responders.

A third type of discount is the *quantity discount*, which offers a lower cost per unit as the volume of the order increases. For example, a store may charge $35 for one shirt, $60 for two shirts, $75 for three shirts, and $20 for each additional shirt. Another variation of the strategy is to offer shirts for $35 each or three for $90. In this case, the company encourages people to buy three rather than trying to entice them up the sales ladder one shirt at a time.

A fourth variation of this strategy is the *cash discount*. Although this can take a variety of forms, one of the most important among new ventures is to offer a price reduction of three to five percent on purchases if the individual will pay with cash or a check rather than a credit card. Simply stated, the storeowner offers to pass the fee the credit card company charges the store back to the customer as an added inducement to buy. This discount tactic is legal and has gai ned some popularity because of current competitive retailing practices that emphasize discount buying. However, keep in mind that the world is continually moving toward a more cash-free exchange, so this strategy may have only limited benefit in the future.

Table 6.1 Pricing for the Product Life Cycle

Product Life Cycle Stage	Pricing Strategy	Reasons/Effects
Customer demand and sales volume will vary with the development of a product. Thus, pricing for products needs to be adjusted at each stage of their life cycle. The following outline provides some suggested pricing methods that relate to the different stages in the product life cycle.		
Introductory Stage Unique product	*Skimming*—deliberately setting a high price to maximize short-term profits	Initial price set high to establish a quality image, to provide capital to offset development costs, and to allow for future price reductions to handle competition
Nonunique Product	*Penetration*—setting prices at such a low level that products are sold at a loss	Allows quick gains in market share by setting a price below competitors' prices
Growth Stage	*Consumer pricing*— combining penetration and competitive pricing to gain market share; depends on consumer's perceived value of product	Demands on number of potential competitors, size of total market, and distribution of that market
Maturity Stage	*Demand-oriented pricing*—a flexible strategy that bases pricing decisions on the level of demand for the product	Sales growth declines; customers very price sensitive
Decline Stage	*Loss leader pricing*—pricing the product below cost in an attempt to attract customers to other products	Product possesses little or no attraction to customers; idea is to have low prices bring customers to newer product lines

Combination Strategies

The pricing strategies outlined so far are common among new ventures. Some are relied on more than others, but in most cases firms employ a combination of these. For example, whether the business is using a skimming or a penetration strategy, the owner will often consider a cash discount in lieu of a credit card. And regardless of pricing techniques, the company is likely to select target markets and offer special deals to these groups. Simply put, pricing strategies are often package deals that answer the question, what do we have to do to get this person's (or group's) business?

Of course, this does not mean new venture owners are always willing to discount heavily, to absorb all transportation charges, or to make other types of special deals. New venture owners should always be aware of the consequences of a "low price war."[10] If they find prices continuously being discounted, it may be a dangerous strategy to follow. (See "Avoiding a Price War!" in the New Venture Issues box.) If prices were discounted to the extreme, it could lead to complete failure of the new venture due to lack of any profit margin.

New Venture Issues

"Avoiding a Price War!"

Smaller ventures must apply consistent, direct, and responsive marketing and pricing strategies. Industries like the airlines and companies like Amazon and Walmart must stay in touch with customer needs and wants, place orders in quantity, and utilize modern inventory and logistics systems. Any retail firm should know a customer's minimum expectations for each element of its strategy (i.e., pricing strategy, store hours, product selection, and customer services) and work to be dominant in at least one aspect. For firms looking to build sustainable competitive advantage, dominance in multiple aspects is necessary. As it relates to pricing strategies, attempting to be the low-price leader can push small ventures into a price war that they cannot survive. Small business owners must act tactfully and intentionally to avoid price wars with larger companies that have more resources to deploy. The following strategies are examples of how small business managers can avoid price wars.

Understand the Diagnostics

For managers to better understand when to avoid or participate in a price war, they should research the impact of changing prices on demand for the product or service. Understanding the diagnostics of a price war helps managers communicate with customers and retain business in the long run.

Communicate With Competitors

As best you can, communicate with all stakeholders—including competitors. Revealing strategic intentions to competitors, while sometimes risky, can help communicate the importance of competing on attributes other than price.

Respond Creatively

Managers need to adequately respond to competitors' price cuts. In-depth customer segmentation research can lead to a better understanding of different customers and their respective price sensitivities; such an understanding allows managers to respond creatively to price cuts with actions like adding quality or features to products.

Employ Segmented Strategies

This allows managers to selectively employ strategies on segments of the customer population that are under competitive threat. Multi-part pricing, bundling, quantity discounts, and time-of-use pricing are examples of strategies that allow managers to sidestep a full-blown price war while maintaining competitive strategies.

Appeal With Full Service

Try to maintain an upscale appeal to full-service, status-conscious consumers. Further understanding the customer and creating a more exclusive product or service will cultivate customer loyalty and insulate against pricing competition. This relates to the marketing strategy as well as the product or service itself.

Enhance Customer Connections

Build relationships with customers that span beyond the simple transaction of a product or service. Ensuring robust and strong customer connections will build reliance and make "switching" costs for customers even higher, regardless of price.

Manage Customer Satisfaction

Work to appeal to people frustrated by the decline in retail service. Oftentimes, bigger companies fail to address the importance of customer contact and managing satisfaction. This can be a major differentiator for small businesses looking to avoid pricing wars.

Source: Adapted from Akshay R. Rao, Mark E. Bergen & Scott Davis, "How to Avoid a Price War," *Harvard Business Review*, March–April 2000, https://hbr.org/2000/03/how-to-fight-a-price-war (accessed March 19, 2020); and James Garvin, "How to Avoid Price Wars," Gaebler Resources for Entrepreneurs, March 20, 2020, www.gaebler.com/How-to-Avoid-Price-Wars.htm (accessed March 19, 2020).

Two other areas that must be considered to understand pricing strategies are market conditions and image. If market conditions are favorable because the company has a unique product or service, the new venture owner does not have to accommodate every buyer. The firm will be selective and sell to those willing to pay a premium price. Automobile companies such as BMW utilize this strategy. BMW limits supply and holds its dealers to a strict price level. Conversely, if demand is weak, the new venture owner is likely to make very attractive offers to generate demand. At the same time, it is important to remember that new ventures must maintain their image. If the business has a reputation for attracting upscale clientele, pricing strategies will focus on supporting and sustaining high prices because this is the firm's target market. By contrast, if the company has created an image as a low price competitor, it will continually try to maintain this reputation by keeping down costs and passing these savings along to the customer.

Both types of firms will also go out of their way to reinforce their price image through advertising and other forms of promotion. A good example is Walmart when it was a small but rapidly growing retailer in the South. The firm advertised itself as having everyday low prices and standing behind its merchandise. One day a man drove back to a Walmart store and told the manager he did not like the tires he had purchased at the store. They did not give him the ride he wanted. The manager told the customer to go to a tire dealer, buy another set of tires, and bring the others back for a full refund. The man did this and was pleased with Walmart's approach. What the store manager did not tell the man was that he could not have bought the tires at Walmart because, at the time, the company did not sell tires. However, the manager took them and gave the refund because he wanted to make the buyer a customer for life. This story has been told and retold at Walmart in an effort to get personnel to understand the company's philosophy of retailing. In the process, the story has helped build the Walmart image, a critical factor in every pricing strategy.

How New Ventures Set Prices

We now examine how prices are set by new ventures in each of the following categories: Wholesalers, retailers, service enterprises, and manufacturers.

Wholesalers

Wholesale prices are generally based on an established markup or gross profit for each line. At the wholesale level, price is very important because most retailers base their purchase decisions very heavily on price. If the wholesaler is not competitive, retailers will buy from a different wholesaler. Additionally, since wholesalers purchase in large quantities and cannot always pass along price increases immediately, they can lose money if prices fluctuate greatly. In particular, the wholesaler can get squeezed between the manufacturer and the retailer. If the manufacturer raises prices and the retailer resists increased costs, the wholesaler may have to absorb a large reduction in profit or even a loss. Since wholesalers have small profit margins, they monitor price movements carefully.

One way they monitor prices is by keeping abreast of competitors' prices. A second is by charging different retailers different prices for the same merchandise. This price differentiation is determined by factors such as the size of the order (larger orders get lower prices per unit), the individual retailer's bargaining ability, and services—such as credit and delivery—extended to a retailer. Wholesalers commonly use a discount or price schedule for each group of goods or services, with maximum and minimum prices for different quantities.

Retailers

Retailers offer the most interesting example of new venture pricing.[11] Except when the company uses manufacturers' suggested prices, the owner needs to be concerned with many of the concepts we have already discussed, including the nature of the product, competition, and general business conditions. Of these, the nature of the product is usually the most significant because different types of products are priced in different ways.

Staple convenience goods, such as candy bars, chewing gum, newspapers, or magazines that are standardized, tend to carry customary prices or the going market price. These goods usually have low prices, and any price cutting will be met quickly by the competition.

Fashion goods tend to be priced high and, if they do not sell, then marked down. Novelty or specialty goods also carry a high markup, and once the novelty wears off or the selling season is over, the price is lowered.

Groceries, on average, tend to be purchased in terms of the best buys. Many supermarkets have adopted unit pricing to help in this process. In fact, many states require it by law. *Unit pricing* calls for the listing of the product's price in terms of some unit of measurement, such as an ounce, pint, or yard. For example, with the price per ounce of sugar listed, consumers are able to comparison shop and determine which product offers the most for the money. Competitive pressures likely will force the small, independent grocer to do the same eventually.

A recent study on pricing strategy suggests that retailers should focus on six issues when developing a price strategy:

1. Identify key determinants of local store pricing. These key determinants include competition, brand, and customer.
2. Segment pricing based on store format and cluster of competitors.
3. Neutralize price as a competitive factor. It is suggested that the retailer set competitive pricing on "known value items" and feature them so that pricing on all other items is not emphasized.
4. Manage promotion intensity and avoid head-to-head competition on non-value items.
5. Create distinctive categories. Coordinate pricing based on category. Identify those items with high price promotion intensity and price differently than other categories.
6. Tailor prices based on market, category, brand, competition, and customer. Some products and brands are more price consistent.[12]

How do retailers, in particular, determine prices? Except when this decision is made for them, as with manufacturers' suggested retail prices, they tend to use systems of *markup* and *mark-on*.

Markup is the difference between the selling price of a good and its cost to the business. Sometimes the term *gross margin* is used, but it means the same thing. Some business owners mark up each item individually, but an average markup for various lines of goods carried is more common. For example, watches may be marked up 100 percent, television sets 35 percent, and dairy products 16 percent. With this approach, the time devoted to marking up goods can be reduced greatly.

Retailers have two basic ways of marking up goods. One is to use a *percentage of the retail selling price*. The other is to use a *percentage of the cost of the good*. For example, if a pair of socks costs $2.00 and is sold for $3.00, the markup ($1.00) on the retail selling price is 33 percent ($1.00/$3.00), while the markup on cost is 50 percent ($1.00/$2.00). The markup on the selling price is *always a smaller percentage* because the denominator in the calculation is larger. Today, most businesses base their markup percentage on the retail price because this tells them how much of their sales dollar can be used to pay bills and how much will be left over for profit.

The computation of markups is not difficult, especially if the owner has a markup table such as the one show in Table 6.2. A markup table allows the businessperson to quickly determine the retail price. The following examples illustrate how this is done.

Table 6.2 A Markup Table

Markup as Percentage of Retail Price	Markup as Percentage of Cost	Markup as Percentage of Retail Price	Markup as Percentage of Cost
10	11.11	31	44.93
11	12.36	32	47.06
12	13.64	33	49.25
13	14.94	34	51.52
14	16.28	35	53.85
15	17.65	36	56.25
16	19.05	37	58.73
17	20.48	38	61.29
18	21.95	39	63.93
19	23.46	40	66.67
20	25.00	41	69.49
21	26.58	42	72.41
22	28.21	43	75.44
23	29.87	44	78.57
24	31.58	45	81.82
25	33.33	46	85.19
26	35.14	47	88.68
27	36.99	48	92.31
28	38.89	49	96.08

Markup as Percentage of Retail Price	Markup as Percentage of Cost	Markup as Percentage of Retail Price	Markup as Percentage of Cost
29	40.85	50	100.00
30	42.86		

Example 1:

A retailer who sells electronics uses a standard 50 percent markup on retail on all flat-screen TVs. How much should a retailer charge for a small TV that costs $500? To answer this question, five steps should be taken:

1. Determine the cost of the good, which in this case is $500.
2. Find the required gross profit figure (50 percent) in the Markup as Percentage of Retail Price column in Table 6.2.
3. Find the corresponding figure opposite 50 percent in the Markup as Percentage of Cost column in Table 6.2, which is 100 percent.
4. Multiply the cost of the good ($500) by that figure to get the dollars-and-cents markup on cost—in this case, $500 × 1.00 = $500.
5. Add the markup-on-cost result ($500) to the cost of the good ($500) to arrive at the selling price: $500 + $500 = $1,000 selling price.

The solution can be checked by determining the results of selling 100 TVs.

Sales revenue (100 TVs × $1000) $100,000

Less : Cost of goods (100 TVs × $500)   50,000

Gross profit $50,000

Gross profit as a percent of sales :

$$\frac{50.000}{100,000} \times 100\% = 50\%$$

Thus, a markup of 100 percent on the cost of goods will produce a 50 percent gross profit (markup on retail).

Example 2:

A college bookstore is about to receive the books it has ordered for the fall semester. A quick scan of the sales reports shows that many of the hardcover business texts cost the store $80. The markup on retail is 25 percent. How much does the owner need to charge to attain this markup? To answer this question, the same five steps are used.

1. Determine the cost of the good, which in this case is $80.
2. Find the required gross profit figure (25 percent) in the Markup as Percentage of Retail Price column in Table 6.2.

3. Find the corresponding figure opposite 25 percent in the Markup as Percentage of Cost column in Table 6.2, which is 33.33 percent.
4. Multiply the cost of the good ($80) by that figure to get the dollars-and-cents markup on cost—in this case, $80 × 0.33 = $26.40.
5. Add the markup-on-cost result ($26.40) to the cost of the good ($80) to arrive at the selling price: $80 + $26.40 = $106.40 selling price.

The solution can be checked by determining the results of selling 100 books.

Sales revenue $(100 \ \text{texts} \times \$106.4)$	$10,640
Less : Cost of goods $(100 \ \text{books} \times \$80)$	8,000
Gross profit	$2,640

Gross profit as a percent of sales :

$$\frac{2,640}{10,640} = 25\%$$

Thus, a markup of 33.33 percent on the cost of goods will produce a 25 percent gross profit (markup on retail).

In these two examples, the selling prices after markup were $1,000 and $106.40, respectively. However, the selling price is usually adjusted up or down to make the price more appealing, especially for electronics, which the consumer does not *have* to buy. The student, of course, may feel that he or she cannot get through the course without the textbook. In any event, instead of charging $1,000 for the TV, the retailer may price it at $999.00 or $995.00. The bookstore may do the same, opting for a final price of $105.75. This *psychological pricing* attracts people better than a price rounded to the nearest dollar. Also, the business should compare its proposed price to its competition to make sure it is competing appropriately.

In addition to the initial markup, many retailers compute a *mark-on*. Simply stated, a mark-on is an increase above the initial markup on goods that will be reduced in price later or on goods that can be damaged or stolen easily. For example, high fashion goods tend to have a limited market. Therefore, although a shirt may be priced at $29.75 initially, if it does not sell, it may be marked down to $24.75 and then to $19.75. Realizing the unpredictability of the market, the retailer will add a sufficient mark-on to ensure that, after markdowns, the desired gross margin is maintained.

As an example, consider a retailer that estimates that, of the 300 shirts purchased last week, it will be possible to sell 100 at $29.75, another 100 at $24.75, and the last 100 at $19.75. Additionally, assume the owner wants a gross margin on sales of 40 percent and that the cost of each shirt is $15. From Table 6.2, it is obvious that a 40 percent markup on retail price requires the owner to add 66.67 percent to the cost. This results in a retail price of $25 ($15 × 0.667 = $10 markup plus the original cost of $15). Thus, the retailer must sell each shirt at an *average* price of $25. The retailer must add a mark-on to this price so that it can be reduced later. Without our showing the specific mathematical computations, the owner will average (just about) $25 if the three prices—$29.75, $24.75, and $19.75—are used and 100 shirts are sold at each price level. This is illustrated in the following table:

Price	Shirts Sold	Total
$29.75	100	$2,975.00
$24.75	100	$2,475.00
$19.75	100	$1,975.00
		$7,425.00

Dividing $7,425 by 300 gives an average selling price of $24.75

Service Enterprises

The many types of service enterprises vary widely in their pricing methods. In most cases, however, these firms employ one of two strategies: (1) they charge what everyone else is charging or (2) they set their own prices and try to justify the decision by differentiating the service and presenting it in a unique or creative way. Each of these approaches has benefits and drawbacks.

Charging Competitively

When a service enterprise charges the same as the competition, it implies a number of assumptions. One is that the competition knows its own costs and is pricing for profit. If this is not the case, many firms pricing at this level will lose money. A second assumption is that each firm's service cannot be distinguished from that of the competition, so a common price is justified for this generic offering. A third assumption is that oligopolistic market conditions exist so that any firms that raise their price will lose substantial market share and any that lower their price will find all of the competition following suit. Thus, the only logical strategy is to price at the same level as everyone else.

The primary benefit of pricing with the competition is that no market resistance occurs regarding this price. Customers do not complain by noting, "We can get this same service cheaper from other companies." Another benefit is that it saves the new venture time and money because a cost analysis is not needed to arrive at a price. The firm simply follows the competition.

The primary drawback to this pricing strategy is that the company does not analyze its costs, so the owner has no way of knowing for sure whether the firm is pricing for profit. The company actually may be losing money at this price level. A second drawback is that the firm is a market follower. It does nothing different in comparison to the competition. As a result, the company's profit is limited sharply, and the strategy typically is directed at providing more and more service, rather than better service, because quantity (giving as much service as possible at this predetermined rate) is given precedence over quality (giving distinctive service at rates determined by market conditions).

Despite the drawbacks to a strategy of following the leader when setting price, many small service enterprises use this approach. As long as they understand their cost structure and know that they are making an acceptable profit at this price, this strategy is viable. However, if they are able to differentiate themselves, they often can increase profit by raising their price and maintaining (and often increasing) market share.

Differentiating the Service

As noted, the problem with a follow-the-leader pricing strategy is that it fails to address the unique service offerings of the company. To the extent the new venture provides better service than the competition, more profitable strategies exist. However, these strategies are all based on the assumption the customer will pay more for better service. In determining whether this is true, new ventures can alter their prices and evaluate the elasticity of demand.

Elasticity of demand determines the effect of price increases on sales revenue. If demand is elastic, decreases in price will result in greater revenue and profit. Conversely, if demand is inelastic, then price increases will create more revenue and profit. Of course, some customers may refuse to pay the higher price, but a sufficient number of them will, and thus the price increase will generate higher revenue. Here is an example of a service company that raised its price by 20 percent and lost only ten percent of its customers:

	Before *Price Rise*	*After* *Price Rise*
Number of customers	$700	$630
Revenue per customer	$1,000	$1,200
Total revenue	$700,000	$756,000
Profit (20 percent of revenue)	$140,000	$151,000
Benefit of raising price:		$11,200

This simple illustration shows the effect of a price increase under inelastic market demand conditions. Of course, if the demand were elastic, the company would have lost money because the increase in price would have been more than offset by the decline in demand. However, this is why it is necessary to test market demand by tinkering with price and seeing what will happen. If the market does not respond to increased service at a higher price, then the firm will maintain its current pricing levels. However, the key to the success of price increases is differentiated service.

Service firms attempt to differentiate themselves from the competition in a number of ways.[13] It is important to remember that effective differentiation is often a matter of perception. If a beauty salon purchases new high-tech computer software that helps clients visualize a new hairstyle, does this result in a better haircut? Probably not, but the client may feel that this new software is worth the additional $3 for a haircut. All of the other ways businesses differentiate have one aspect in common: They provide increased value that the buyer is prepared to pay for.

An example of this concept is home delivery. Many people buy pizza only from outlets that deliver. Is the quality of this pizza better than that of the competition? The answer is that the taste and quality are acceptable to the buyers, but it is delivery service that ensures the order. The cost of this service is often minimal since, as noted earlier, drivers typically work for minimum wage and tips, which can add up to a substantial hourly rate.

Another example of differentiation is payment convenience. Many new ventures grant credit to their customers and settle the bill at the end of the month. Although this strategy can result in a loss of some profits (people do not pay or pay late, and the company has to carry the debt on its books), it also helps boost sales and the profit accompanying these revenues.

Lower price also helps to differentiate one service from another. Many new ventures cannot afford to offer a variety of supplemental services, so they focus on cutting their costs to the bone and passing on these savings to the customer. A number of strategies are employed in this process, but they all have one aspect in common: Services that have little value to the customer are eliminated, while those that are important are given priority. A good example is provided by home improvement stores, where people go to buy residential materials and fixtures. These stores buy in large quantities so that they can obtain substantial discounts, but many do not provide delivery, and they do not use their salespeople to market the products vigorously. Instead, the stores train their people to help customers by listening to what the buyer needs, showing the individual where these materials are located in the store, and, in some cases, helping the person choose a specific fixture or appliance for the job. As a result of this service, these stores are now riding the crest of the home improvement craze sweeping the nation.

When differentiating service, new venture owners must answer three questions: What can be done to attract more business? How much is the cost of adding these services? What effect will this decision have on profit? Based on the answers, the owner can formulate a plan of action.

Pricing Techniques

Many service enterprises set their price based on the going rate or what they feel the market will bear. However, more analytical ways of determining price exist. One is to keep careful cost records so that the company knows the expenses associated with each job. For example, assume Neal is in the computer repair business. The average engineer working for Neal is paid $44 per hour, including benefits. To this price Neal must add a markup for operating expenses (electricity, telephone, depreciation of machinery, insurance, and other expenses) as well as profit. Assuming Neal has set a figure of 30 percent to cover expenses, the computation for service follows:

$$1.00$$
$$\text{Price per hour} = \$44 / \text{hour} \times 1.0 - .30$$
$$= \$44 \times 1.428$$
$$= \$62.83 \text{ per hour}$$

In all likelihood, Neal will round this number to $65 per hour. In addition, the buyer will have to pay for the cost of materials and supplies through a markup. So, even if Neal's estimate of expenses is low, he has enough room to ensure profit. This is particularly true given that many small operations set minimum charges for service. A job billed at one hour may be completed in 45 minutes, thus allowing the employee to move on to another task.

Although this method of pricing work is fairly simple, it is indicative of most small service firms. They do not employ sophisticated analysis in their profit pricing strategy. They use a system that is easily understandable and that can be modified without much effort. This process is similar to that used by small manufacturers.

Manufacturers

The primary basis for pricing by small manufacturers is usually some form of "cost plus," where the company charges a markup over its own expenses. As with service enterprises, however, this pricing strategy often requires a great deal more thought than simply adding a predetermined percentage on top of overall cost. In most cases, small manufacturers will use a combination of competitive rates and differentiation techniques.

Charging Competitively

The simplest approach to pricing for manufacturers is to charge the going rate. However, manufacturers try to improve this strategy by working to contain and, where possible, to drive down costs. They do this in a number of ways. One is to negotiate carefully with vendors, thus ensuring the lowest possible cost of raw materials and supplies. In turn, these savings can be passed on to buyers, and thus generate increased demand for the company's output. A second way to drive down costs is to reduce production bottlenecks and inefficiencies. One of the best techniques used is process mapping, in which the steps used to accomplish the job are reduced or combined in some way. The result is a time savings, which cuts the cost of the job and helps make the company more price competitive. A third way is to purchase new equipment that increases productivity and allows the firm to both lower prices and provide an increased number of products. Most small manufacturers focus heavily on price competitiveness, and in markets where it is difficult to differentiate between one product and another, this is often the best pricing strategy to employ.

Differentiating the Product

Depending on the type of manufactured good, it is often possible to differentiate the product and charge a premium price. This can be done on a number of bases. Before deciding which one (or more) of these is important, the small manufacturer will need to have a solid understanding of retail buyers' needs. For example, complex products that are difficult to repair tend to carry higher markups. The customer is willing to pay for high-quality original parts because the individual wants the assurance the product will not break down or need continuous servicing. By contrast, when the product (or its parts) is easy to replace and can be purchased from many different suppliers, it is difficult to differentiate the product, and the manufacturer will compete most heavily on the basis of price.

Three of the most common ways to differentiate manufactured goods are on the basis of quality, delivery, and reliability. Where quality is concerned, technological advances are extremely important. A small manufacturer that remains on the cutting edge of technology and either develops or purchases these advances for use in the company's products will find some customers willing to pay extra for these benefits.

Delivery is a second way manufacturers try to differentiate themselves. Today many companies do not want to carry a great deal of inventory. They want it delivered on an "as-needed" basis. This just-in-time inventory strategy means that manufacturers must now align their production plans with the purchase plans of buyers. New ventures willing to deliver what is needed, when it is needed, and in desired quantities find they are better able to secure and hold customers.

A third differentiation strategy is reliability encompassed in effective service. If something goes wrong with the product, the buyer wants the manufacturer to stand behind the sale, replace the unit, or repair it as quickly as possible. Firms willing to do this can differentiate themselves from the competition and garner buyer loyalty.

Pricing Techniques

Small manufacturers rely most heavily on three pricing techniques. The most common is to sell at the going rate. For example, small manufacturers that produce units according to specifications the buyer provides typically will charge a price similar to that of other firms. Moreover, since the buyer tends to shop for the contact by asking for bids from a number of small manufacturers, if the price is too high, the company either will not get the job or will be told the prices competitors have bid and will be asked to bring its price into line or to drop out of the bidding.

A second common pricing technique involves a multiplier applied to the direct costs of a job. For example, if a job has direct costs of $300 and the multiplier is 1.7, the company will price the job at $510 ($300 × 1.7). The 70 percent differential covers all nondirect costs as well as profit. Although this technique is simple to apply, the biggest shortcoming is that the price differential may be too high, driving away business, or too low, resulting in little, if any, profitability. The key to using a multiplier effectively is to know the relation between direct and indirect costs and profitability.

A third common pricing technique is cost plus, the same approach service industries use. The benefit of this approach is that a company that knows its costs cannot lose money on the job because it also has an add-on for profit. The drawback to this approach is that it can result in uncontrolled costs and a manufacturer pricing itself out of the market. For example, if a new motor costs $400 to manufacture and the company uses a multiple of 2, the buyer will pay $800. The competition may be selling for the same price. However, if the latter applies cost-saving techniques to its operation and drives down the cost to $345 per unit, it may drop its price to $690 and force everyone else to take lower profits or drop out of this particular market. So, a cost plus system is effective only when coupled with a vigorous cost containment program.

A Global Perspective

"The Price is Right for Whom?"

It is a truism of business that "price is what you pay, and value is what you get." Businesses work to match the price they charge customers for their product or service with the value they provide, with consideration of competitors' prices in the market. As businesses expand into international markets, it must be with the knowledge that perceptions of what is a "fair" price can vary greatly depending on the economic conditions of the country.

In the United States, when a company is able to legally offer consumers a lower price than its competitors for a similar product, it is usually recognized as a positive development for consumers. Amazon and Walmart were able to leverage their size and capabilities to offer consumers lower prices than their competitors and grow into leading U.S. companies that dominate the retail landscape. However, their approach was met with significant skepticism when both companies entered the retail market in India. Small local retailers in India accused the companies of predatory pricing, offering prices lower than the cost of the product with the goal of putting smaller competitors out of business.

The potential for companies like Walmart and Amazon to dominate the Indian retail market was likened to foreign colonial control, a powerfully negative metaphor in a country that lived under Western colonial rule for hundreds of years before achieving independence. The result was laws placed on large companies and their subsidiaries and partners designed to limit their market influence in India.

Beyond market dynamics in individual countries, international trade relationships can impact pricing decisions. In recent years, tariffs have been a tool increasingly used by the United States and other governments to address perceived unfair trade practices. Tariffs have the effect of artificially raising the price of foreign-made goods in a local market. This can be a benefit for local companies competing against foreign companies since tariffs are often passed along to consumers through increases in the foreign-made product's price.

However, local companies that may benefit in terms of pricing their product against competitors face challenges because input components necessary to produce the product may be sourced from abroad.

Source: Adapted from Ari Altstedter and Ari Bloomberg, "Amazon and Walmart Thought India Would Be Their Next Giant Market. India's Shopkeepers Would Like to Disagree," *Fortune*, December 2, 2019, fortune.com/2019/12/02/amazon-walmart-india-shopkeeper-protest-predatory-pricing/; Andrea Shalal, "Trump Threat of More China Tariffs Could Hit Consumer Goods Before Christmas," Reuters, November 13, 2019, www.reuters.com/article/us-usa-trade-china/trump-threat-of-more-china-tariffs-could-hit-consumer-goods-before-christmas-idUSKBN1XN2TE; and Scott Horsley, "His Company Makes Speakers. Now He's Speaking Out, Opposing Tariffs," NPR, December 2, 2019, www.npr.org/2019/12/02/783359225/his-company-makes-speakers-now-hes-speaking-out-opposing-tariffs.

Summary

In this chapter, pricing techniques and strategies were examined. The venture owner's primary consideration when pricing must be cost. The individual cannot afford to sell below the cost level. In addition, the owner must consider the nature of the product, the competition, marketing strategy, and general business conditions. Pricing for profit also requires an understanding of the cost of goods, competitive prices, and market demand. Drawing on such considerations, new venture owners will apply a variety of pricing techniques.

One of the most common techniques is skimming pricing, a strategy characterized by a high price designed to satisfy the market niche willing to pay a premium price. Another common technique is penetration pricing, which is characterized by a low competitive price designed both to stimulate demand and to discourage competition. A third common approach is a sliding price strategy, characterized by prices that move in relation to demand. Other typical pricing techniques include odd pricing, leader pricing, price lining, geographic pricing, and discounting. In most cases, the new venture will use two or more of these techniques, employing what is commonly called a combination pricing strategy.

Competition is often keen among wholesalers, and retailers will buy elsewhere if prices are too high. As a result, the wholesaler sometimes cannot readily pass along manufacturers' price increases to the retailer. For this reason, the owner-manager spends a good deal of time watching wholesale prices to ensure the business is not caught in a price squeeze.

Retailers often price on the basis of a predetermined markup. For example, on certain goods, it is typical to add 50 percent. The markups provided in Table 6.2 illustrate how these price additions can be computed, both as a percentage of cost and as a percentage of retail price. In addition to the initial markup, many retailers compute a mark-on.

Service enterprises sometimes charge competitively, but they often try to differentiate their offerings so that they can increase their overall profit. Some of the bases for a differentiation strategy include home delivery, convenience, and lower price. Common pricing techniques include following the competition and adding a markup to operating expenses.

Manufacturers set their prices in accordance with the cost of production. If they produce more than one product, they use some method for allocating costs. Then a margin of profit is determined and a final selling price is set. Common pricing techniques for small manufacturers include following the competition, using a multiplier, and calculating cost plus.

Review and Discussion Questions

1. Explain what an owner-manager should know about the following price considerations: Nature of the product, competition, marketing strategy, and general business conditions.
2. Explain how the following factors influence the owner-manager's objective of pricing for profit: Cost of goods, competitive prices, and market demand.
3. Explain how the following pricing techniques work: Skimming, penetration, sliding price, odd pricing, leader pricing, price lining, geographic pricing, discounts, and combination pricing.
4. Why do most new ventures use a combination pricing strategy?
5. How do wholesalers set their prices? Do they charge these prices frequently? Explain.
6. One of the most important retail pricing concepts is markup. How does a markup work? Incorporate these terms in your answer: *cost, markup as a percentage of retail selling price, markup as a percentage of cost*, and *selling price*.
7. When would a retailer use a mark-on? Give an example, being sure to define the term *mark-on*.
8. How do service organizations set prices? Use two examples in your answer.
9. Explain how manufacturers set their prices. Use an example in your answer.

The Venture Consultant

Games for Sale

The Toy Store is a retail outlet that caters to adults as well as children and teenagers. The store carries the types of items found in most other toy stores plus unique games that appeal to teenagers and adults. Included in the latter category are the ever-popular computer games of skill. The Toy Store has an agreement with a large manufacturer by which it serves as the only retail outlet for the manufacturer's games within a 50-mile radius. Because of patent rights, the manufacturer is the only firm currently producing these games.

The store's typical toys are priced in line with the competition. The unique games, however, are not. In fact, the owner of the store, who has total control over the pricing of games, is determined to charge what the market will bear. Unfortunately, he does not know how to set the best price because he does not have any guidelines to follow. He has looked for similar games in some of the large department stores in the hope that he could charge 20 percent over this amount. However, he has found nothing.

One pricing method he has been considering lately is putting a 50 percent markup on games, in contrast to the 33 percent he gets on toys. With a 33 percent markup on games, he is unable to keep enough in stock. Demand is so high that he continually runs out. However, he is concerned about pricing too high and losing customers.

One of his friends has told him that a number of factors must be taken into consideration when pricing. Some of these are the nature of the product, the type of competition, the marketing strategy the business has typically used, and the state of the economy. However, the owner is unsure how these particular factors affect a pricing decision.

Actually, what the owner wants to do is determine an ideal markup for the goods, price them at this level, and be done with the matter. He wishes he knew more about pricing. Not having had any real training in setting prices, however, he believes the best thing he can do now is price games extremely high, and if they do not sell, start reducing the price downward to the point where supply and demand balance out. He realizes this is a trial-and-error approach, but it is the best he can come up with under the circumstances.

Additionally, the owner does not know very much about advertising. He tends to run the same basic newspaper ad week after week. It shows a picture of a couple of the store's toys and one of the games and relates the price of each. The purpose of the ad is to attract people to the store. Although the store is doing quite well, the owner believes his ads could be improved. The problem is that he lacks the inspiration for improving them. He simply writes the ads on the basis of instinct.

Your Consultation

Assume the owner is a personal friend of yours and has related this information to you. As best you can, give him your recommendations regarding the pricing of the unique computer games. Also, explain to him how he can charge prices to maximize his profits without losing customers. Be as specific as possible.

Notes

1 See Tessa Christina Flatten, Andreas Engelen, Timo Möller, and Malte Brettel, "How Entrepreneurial Firms Profit from Pricing Capabilities: An Examination of Technology-Based Ventures," *Entrepreneurship Theory & Practice*, 2015, 39 (5): 1111–1136.

2 See Eric Mitchell, "How Not to Raise Prices," *Small Business Reports*, November 1990, 64–67.

3 Aylin Aydinli, Marco Bertini, and Anja Lambrecht, "Price Promotion for Emotional Impact," *Journal of Marketing*, 2014, 78 (4): 80–96.

4 Philip Kotler and Gary Armstrong, *Principles of Marketing*, 16th ed. Upper Saddle River, NJ: Pearson/ Prentice Hall, 2016.
5 Fred Luthans and Richard M. Hodgetts, *Business*, 2nd ed. Fort Worth, TX: The Dryden Press, 1993, p. 407.
6 George Y. Bizer and Richard E. Petty, "An Implicit Measure of Price Perception: Exploring the Odd-Pricing Effect," *Advances in Consumer Research*, 2002, 29: 220–221.
7 Louis E. Boone and David L. Kurtz, *Contemporary Marketing*, 17th ed. Mason, OH: Cengage/South-Western, 2016.
8 Ibid.
9 Jim Geisman and John Maruskin. "A Case for Discount Discipline," *Harvard Business Review*, November 2006, p. 84.
10 Akshay R. Rao, Mark E. Bergen, and Scott Davis, "How to Fight a Price War," *Harvard Business Review*, March–April 2000, pp. 107–116; see also Chun-Hung Chiu, Tsan-Ming Choi and Duan Li, "Price Wall or War: The Pricing Strategies for Retailers," *IEEE Transactions*, 2009, 39 (2): 719–728.
11 Jie Zhang, Paul W. Farris, John W. Irvin, Tarun Kushwaha, Thomas J. Steenburgh, Barton A. Weitz, "Crafting Integrated Multichannel Retailing Strategies," *Journal of Interactive Marketing*, 2010, 24 (2): 168–180.
12 Ruth N. Bolton, Detra Y. Montoya, and Venkatesh Shankar. "Beyond EDLP and HiLo: A New Customized Approach to Retail Pricing," *European Retail Digest*, Spring 2006, 49: 7–10
13 For more on this topic, see Michael E. Porter, *Competitive Advantage*. New York: The Free Press, 1985, pp. 119–163; see also Richard L. Priem, "A Consumer Perspective on Value Creation," *Academy of Management Review*, 2007, 32 (1): 219–235.

Part III

New Venture Finances

7 Startup Capital

The Injection

Introduction: Basic Types of Capital

Generally new ventures are started by "bootstrapping."[1] In other words, entrepreneurs try to initiate the venture using marginal financial resources from personal savings, family, and friends. Studies have investigated the various sources of capital preferred by entrepreneurs. These sources range from debt (banks, credit cards, finance companies) to equity (angel investors, venture capital, crowdfunding) depending upon the type of financing that is arranged. Entrepreneurs have a number of sources of capital as their venture develops. Remember that the level of risk and the stage of the firm's development impact the appropriate source financing for the entrepreneurial ventures.

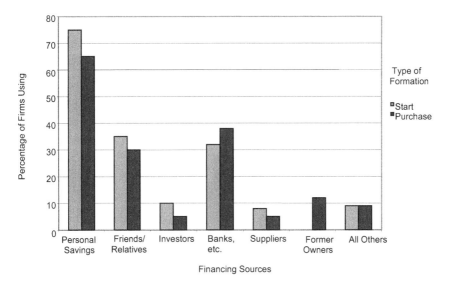

Figure 7.1 Sources of Small Business Startup Capital

Keep in mind that venture financing comes from two basic sources: Debt and ownership equity. *Debt* is borrowed money that must be repaid at some predetermined date in the future. *Ownership equity*, however, represents the owners' investment in the company, money they have personally put into the firm without any specific date for repayment. As owners, they recover their investment by withdrawing money from the company or by selling part or all of their interest in the firm. (See Table 7.1 for a new venture owner's financial glossary.)

Table 7.1 A Financial Glossary for New Venture Owners

Accrual system of accounting: A method of recording and allocating income and costs for the period in which each is involved, regardless of the date of payment or collection. For example, if you were paid $100 in April for goods you sold in March, the $100 would be income for March under an accrual system. (Accrual is the opposite of the cash system of accounting.)

Asset: Anything of value that is owned by you or your business.

Balance sheet: An itemized statement listing the total assets and liabilities of your business at a given moment. This is also called a *statement of condition*.

Capital: (1) the amount invested in a business by the proprietor(s) or stockholders and (2) the money available for investment or money invested.

Cash flow: The schedule of your cash receipts and disbursements.

Cash system of accounting: A method of accounting whereby revenue and expenses are recorded when received and paid, respectively, without regard for the period to which they apply.

Collateral: Property you own that you pledge to the lender as security on a loan until the loan is repaid. Collateral can be a car, home, stocks, bonds, or equipment.

Cost of goods sold: This is determined by subtracting the value of the ending inventory from the sum of the beginning inventory and purchases made during the period. Gross sales less costs of goods sold gives you gross profit.

Current assets: Cash and assets that can be easily converted to cash, such as accounts receivable and inventory. Current assets should exceed current liabilities.

Current liabilities: Debts you must pay within a year (also called short-term liabilities).

Depreciation: Lost usefulness, expired utility, diminution of service yield from a fixed asset, or fixed asset group that cannot or will not be restored by repairs or by replacement of parts.

Equity: An interest in property or in a business, subject to prior creditors. An owner's equity in his or her business is the difference between the value of the company's assets and the debt owed by the company. For example, if you borrow $30,000 to purchase assets for which you pay a total of $50,000, your equity is $20,000.

Expense: An expired cost; any item or class of costs of (or loss from) carrying on an activity; a present or past expenditure defraying a present operating cost or representing an irrecoverable cost or loss; an item of capital expenditure written down or off; or a term often used with some qualifying expression denoting function, organization, or time, such as selling expense, factory expense, or monthly expense.

Financial statement: A report summarizing the financial condition of a business. This normally includes a balance sheet and an income statement.

Gross profit: Sales less the cost of goods sold. For example, if you sell $100,000 worth of merchandise for which you paid $80,000, your gross profit would be $20,000. To get net profit, however, you would have to deduct other expenses incurred during the period in which the sales were made, such as rent, insurance, and sales staff salaries.

Interest: The cost of borrowing money. This is paid to the lender and usually expressed as an annual percentage of the loan. That is, if you borrow $100 at 12 percent, you pay one percent ($0.01 \times \$100 = \$1$) interest per month. Interest is an expense of doing business.

Income statement: Also called a profit and loss statement, this is a statement summarizing the income of a business during a specific period.

Liability: Money you owe to your creditors. Liabilities can be in the form of a bank loan, accounts payable, etc. They represent a claim against your assets.

Loss: When a business's total expenses for the period are greater than the income.

Net profit: Total income for the period less total expenses for the period (see *Gross profit*).

Net worth: The same as equity.

Personal financial statement: A report summarizing your personal financial condition. Normally this includes a listing of your assets, liabilities, large monthly expenses, and sources of income.

Profit: (See *Net profit* and *Gross profit.*) *Profit* usually refers to net profit.

Profit and loss statement: Same as income statement.

Variable costs: Costs that vary with the level of production in sales, such as direct labor, material, and sales commissions.

Working capital: The excess of current assets over current liabilities.

Source: Donald F. Kuratko, *Entrepreneurship: Theory, Process & Practice*, 11th ed., Cengage/Southwestern Publishing, 2020, pp. 258–259.

Debt capital is divided into three categories: (1) current or short term, (2) intermediate term, and (3) long term. Short-term liabilities (debt) include borrowed money that must be repaid within the next 12 months, intermediate term refers to loan payback periods from one to ten years, and long-term debt comes due and payable some time beyond ten years, depending on the loan terms.

Debt Capital

Short-term loans: A short-term loan is one that is scheduled to be repaid within a period of one year. The most common forms of short-term loans are trade credit—created when the seller allows the buyer to take the merchandise immediately and pay for it later—and short-term bank loans. Short-term loans are particularly helpful when a temporary need for more capital exists, such as when retailers build up a seasonal inventory and pay for it when it is sold. For example, it is typical to find businesses that sell swimwear increasing their inventory during the late spring, while those that sell skiwear will begin building up their inventory in the early fall. Without trade credit or a short-term bank loan, the owner would have to have a large amount of capital on hand to handle peak buying periods. Most trade credit and short-term bank loans are *self-liquidating*; that is, the money obtained from the sale of the inventory is used to pay off the loan. Most bank-financed loans are unsecured, which means they are not backed by collateral. However, if the business does not have a good credit rating or a lot of money is involved, the bank will insist that the loan be secured by some of the business's assets.[2]

Intermediate-term loans: Intermediate-term loans provide capital for periods from one to ten years. Such loans are usually paid back in a series of installments. Intermediate-term loans fill the gap in the financial requirements of many small- and moderate-sized businesses. They make capital available for other than temporary needs, helping the owner who needs funds but who lacks the capital resources to expand the operation. Thanks to this type of loan, owners are able to purchase machinery, equipment, and other fixed assets immediately and pay for them over the life of the loan.

In return, most banks and other lenders impose certain conditions. Primary among them are usually the right of the lender to control major expenditures during the life of the loan and the requirement that the borrower furnish the lender with annual financial statements. In this way the business is prevented from doing anything that might seriously endanger its chances of repaying the loan. Furthermore, it is common for the loan to be backed by collateral, such as the plant and equipment the business has purchased with the loan proceeds.

Long-term loans: Long-term loans have a duration of ten or more years. Only businesses that have been in existence for an extended period can get loans of this duration. Thus, they are usually reserved for large, stable corporations. Additionally, it is common for the lender to insist on collateral. When collateral is given in the form of a mortgage, however, long-term loans can also be secured by small- and intermediate-sized businesses. After all, if the business goes bankrupt, the bank can always step in, take the property, and sell it, thereby recovering at least part of the loan. Aside from this method of securing long-term funds, however, the new venture must often turn to equity capital to meet its needs. (See Table 7.2 for reasons entrepreneurs have their loan rejected.)

Equity Capital

Equity capital is an investment in the business and requires no promise from the borrowing firm to repay this capital. The investment, which usually comes about through the sale of common stock, is a permanent part of the firm's capital structure. This structure can be increased either by investing profits back into the business or by selling additional stock to investors.[3]

In many cases, equity capital is the only way a new venture can increase its capital base. Banks and other financial institutions may not be willing to assume the risk associated with lending the firm money, or the company may have borrowed so much already that the bank is unwilling to go any further. In financial terms, the company is *overextended*; it has nothing more to borrow against. When this happens, the business must sell stock, reinvest earnings, or pass up growth opportunities because no additional sources of capital exist to tap for taking advantage of these opportunities.

Table 7.2 Entrepreneurs' Ratings of Reasons for Loan Rejection[a]

Reason for Rejection	Mean Rating	Males	Females
Bad timing	4.22	3.89	4.52
Insufficient collateral	4.14	4.23	4.13
Inability to develop good chemistry	3.96	4.00	4.05
Excessive loan request	3.88	3.77	3.89
Lack of demonstration of critical management skills	3.82	3.97	3.65
Insufficient market research	3.69	3.69	3.70
Incomplete business plan	3.68	3.77	3.59
Loan officer failed to appreciate the entrepreneur's business experience	3.59	3.83	3.39
Lack of demonstration of critical entrepreneurial skills	3.38	3.71	3.05
Gender bias	2.96	2.78	3.14

[a]Rating scale: 1 = not at all important to 6 = very important
Source: E. Holly Buttner and Benson Rosen, "Rejection in the Loan Application Process: Male and Female Entrepreneurs' Perceptions and Subsequent Intentions," *Journal of Small Business Management*, January 1992, p. 62; and Rieva Lesonsky, "8 Reasons Your Small Business Loan Was Rejected," Fundbox Blog, July 24, 2018.

Sources of Capital

Choosing a source of capital is not an easy decision. Numerous alternatives exist, depending on the business, how much funding is needed, the firm's credit rating, prior sales records, and the economy in general.[4] The following sections examine some of the major capital sources available to the new venture firm and their relative merits and drawbacks.[5]

Personal Savings

It is important that a new venture owner have some personal assets in the business. Indeed, a main source of ownership equity for a beginning business typically comes from personal savings.

A study conducted by the National Federation of Independent Business found that *personal savings* are most frequently used for financing. Figure 7.1 illustrates that 74 percent of the entrepreneurs in the study used personal savings when they purchased or started a business from scratch.

Personal savings invested in the business eliminate the requirement of fixed interest charges and a definite repayment date. If profits fail to materialize exactly as expected, the business is not strapped with an immediate drain on capital.

Friends and Relatives

At times, loans from friends or relatives may be the only available source of new venture financing. Friends and relatives often can be a shortcut to financing.

However, friends and relatives who provide business loans sometimes feel they have the right to interfere in the management of the business. Be careful because financial troubles may also strain the bonds of friendship and family relationships.

Venture Capitalists

A growing source of equity for high-growth new ventures is through experienced professional firms providing a full range of financial services. New venture owners should recognize that these professional firms are specialized in particular industries, and they are looking for a large investment payback. Even though there is more venture capital available today, the trend is toward concentration of the funds under the control of larger venture capital firms.[6]

Keep in mind that it takes a long time to raise venture capital. On average, it could take six to eight weeks from the initial contact to raise venture capital. If the entrepreneur has a well-prepared business plan, the investor will be able to raise money in that time frame. A venture capitalist will see from 50 to 100 proposals a month. Of that number, ten will be of some interest. Of those ten, two or three will receive a fair amount of analysis, negotiation, and investigation. Of the two or three, one may be funded. This funneling process of selecting one out of 100 takes a great deal of time. Once the venture capitalist has found that one, he or she will spend a significant amount of time investigating possible outcomes before funding it.

One group of researchers outlined several suggestions on maximizing the value of the entrepreneur–venture capitalist relationship during the pre-investment, post-investment, and exit phases. A summarized list of these suggestions is provided below.[7]

Pre-Investment

- Getting venture capital
  - o Secure a good referral
  - o Have a good business plan
  - o Be honest
  - o Have patience
- Get the right venture capitalist
  - o Identify complementary skills
  - o Look for commitment
  - o Establish a trusting relationship
- Obtain the right amount of money
- Obtain a fair deal

Post-Investment

- Respect the VC
  - o Legal authority
  - o Power of money

- Respect yourself
- Communicate with the VC
- Be trustworthy
- Remain objective

Exit Phase

- Avoid a premature exit
- Exit harmoniously

Dealing with Venture Capitalists

Keep in mind that venture capitalists are extremely busy, and they are constantly inundated with business plans and pitch decks. As just mentioned, some firms will see over 100 business plans per month, and the eventual choices will be few. If chosen, there are some key tips to keep in mind when negotiating venture capital investments.

1. Make sure the venture capital firm has an interest and experience in the industry of your venture.
2. Know the exact value proposition of your venture, as that is most important.
3. Examine the size of your venture's potential in the next four years so that it meets the venture capitalist's expectations on timing of returns.
4. Know the exact amount of investment you are seeking and how much equity you are willing to provide the venture capitalist.
5. Prepare all materials (pitch deck and business plan) in advance.
6. Do not expect an immediate decision, as an interested venture capitalist will want to conduct due diligence on you and the venture before deciding.
7. Avoid embellishing facts or projections.
8. Never adopt the magic one percent rule for your target market, as real in-depth market research must be provided.
9. Check out the background of the venture capital fund to see the usual invested amounts.
10. Be prepared to pitch other venture capitalists to gain a perspective on your deal.

   Every entrepreneur should be honest about whether the venture capitalist option for funding is the right approach. It may be that seeking a more informal investor is a better source of potential funding. Let's examine that option.

Informal Investors

Many private individuals invest in entrepreneurial ventures, including persons who have moderate to significant business experience and affluent professionals. This source of financing has come to be known as *informal capital*, in that no formal marketplace exists where these individuals invest in companies. Appropriately, these investors have acquired the name *business angels*.[8]

The traditional path to locating angels is through contact with business associates, accountants, and lawyers. A more recent approach involves formal angel networks or "clubs." One example is the Venture Club in Indianapolis, Indiana. This group meets once a month with entrepreneurs giving presentations concerning their financial needs. The idea is to bring potential informal investors together as a network for entrepreneurs. These networks can increase the odds of finding an investor. Other entrepreneurs continue to be the best source of help in identifying prospective informal or private investors. Table 7.3 illustrates the five key questions every financing source asks.

Internal Funds

One of the most basic sources of capital, and one often overlooked by new ventures, is internal funds. These are monies kept in the firm in the form of retained earnings. Of course, few business people forget what they have earned in profits the previous year and have reinvested in the business, but many of them fail to consider that what they will make this year can be invested in the business to help meet expansion needs. Instead, they rush outside looking for bank loans. *The first place to look for funding is within the business itself.* With careful budgeting, many small firms can raise part or all of the money they need.

Table 7.3 Five Key Questions Every Financing Source Asks

---

1. How much money do you need? (Give the exact amount.)
2. What do you plan to use it for? (Working capital or specific assets?)
3. How will this money improve the business? (Provide actual projections.)
4. How are you going to pay it back or provide a return on the money? (Demonstrate cash flow projections.)
5. Do you have an alternative plan in case of a critical problem? (Provide a contingency plan.)

Trade Credit

Another commonly overlooked capital source is *trade credit*, by which suppliers, in effect, help finance operations. For example, most credit transactions have terms of 30, 60, or 90 days. The most common trade credit terms are *2/10, net 30* (*two ten, net thirty*): If the buyer pays the bill within ten days, the seller gives a two percent discount, and regardless of the buyer's position on payment schedules, the entire bill must be paid within 30 days.

Consider the effects of this approach on a business that buys $10,000 in merchandise on the first day of every month. If the merchandise is paid for on delivery instead of within ten days, the owner needs to have $10,000 available. Like most owners of new ventures, however, this one does not have this much on hand, so the owner arranges for a bank loan. Borrowing the money on the 1st of every month and repaying it by the 30th, for all practical purposes, results in the business having a $10,000 loan outstanding at all times. Assuming a ten percent interest rate, the annual loan cost is $1,000.

Instead, trade credit can be used to finance the inventory. By taking delivery on the 1st of the month and not paying until the 10th, the new venture owner will need a loan for only 20 days per month, so the interest paid for the year will be only $667 ($10,000 × 0.1 × 20/30). Furthermore, the owner gets the two percent discount, or $200 per month, off the bill. In a year's time, the use of trade credit is saving the business $2,400. After subtracting the loan cost of $667, the owner is ahead $1,733. Thus, trade discounts can be very profitable.

Another way of using trade credit is to get the supplier to provide the goods on consignment. Under this type of arrangement, the buyer does not pay for the goods until they are sold. Auto dealers, large-appliance retailers, and farm equipment dealers, for example, often pay for goods only after they are sold.

Banks

Banks offer many types of loan services. Some of the most common are lines of credit, straight commercial loans, term loans, accounts receivable loans, warehouse receipt loans, and collateral loans. The following sections examine each.

LINES OF CREDIT

A *line of credit* is an informal agreement or understanding between the borrower and the bank as to the maximum amount of credit the bank will provide the borrower at any one time. However, under this type of agreement, the bank is under no legal obligation to provide the stated capital. A similar arrangement that does legally commit the bank is a *revolving credit agreement*. The entrepreneur should arrange for a line of credit in advance of the actual need because banks extend credit only in situations they are well informed about.

STRAIGHT COMMERCIAL LOANS

Straight commercial loans are usually made for a period of 30–90 days. They are generally based on the financial statements of the borrower and are self-liquidating. It is common to use these loans for seasonal financing and for building up inventories.

TERM LOANS

Term loans have a maturity of between one and ten years. Most have shorter terms (one to four years) and are unsecured. Longer-term loans, however, are generally backed by some of the firm's assets. In either event, small loan repayments are made throughout the life of the loan monthly, quarterly, biannually, or annually. Depending on the specific terms of the agreement, it is not uncommon to make a large payment at the end of the loan. This is referred to as a *balloon loan*, when the periodic repayments are rather small and the large bulk of the loan is paid off at the end of the term. This, of course, can be very beneficial to a new venture because it means that on a loan of $25,000 for five years, perhaps as much as $20,000 can be paid at the end. This gives the company time to build up its business before having to make the large final payment. Furthermore, today's dollars will be inflated in five years, so the business is able to borrow "hard" dollars now and repay the loan with "soft" dollars later on.

ACCOUNTS RECEIVABLE LOANS

Accounts receivable loans are made by many large banks. In this case, the loan is made against the company's outstanding receivables; when they are collected, the bank is repaid. In some instances, the bank becomes actively involved by notifying the business's customers to make payments on their accounts directly to the bank. These collections are then credited to the borrower's account, after service and interest charges are deducted, of course. In other instances, the bank does not get involved directly, and the new venture simply collects the receivables and sends the proceeds to the bank to repay the loan. The disadvantages of this type of loan arrangement are that the cost is high and considerable record-keeping is required. As a result, a business must have a large amount of accounts receivable to make this method of raising capital feasible.

WAREHOUSE RECEIPT LOANS

For *warehouse receipt loans*, inventory is stored in warehouses, and a receipt for the inventory is given to the bank as security for a loan to pay off the supplier. As the business sells the merchandise, the business owner buys back portions of the loan. This kind of borrowing enables the business to operate with a small investment in working capital. However, warehouse receipt loans are used only for nonperishable items that are readily marketable. Thus, if the business owner cannot sell the goods, the bank can assume ownership and seek a buyer of its own. Such an approach ensures that the bank will, at worst, suffer only a partial loss of the loan.

COLLATERAL LOANS

Banks make *collateral loans* on the basis of such security as real estate mortgages, life insurance policies (the cash surrender value), stocks, and bonds. The borrower puts up the collateral, and the bank advances the money. As the loan is repaid the collateral is returned to the borrower.

New Venture Issues

"The Risks for Investors in Crowdfunding"

There is an expectation that the crowdfunding market will reach $1 trillion by 2025. However, the U.S. Securities and Exchange Commission (SEC) has issued some careful points for investors to be aware of as the crowdfunding opportunity increases. While crowdfunding offers investors an opportunity to participate in an early-stage venture, they should be aware that early-stage investments may involve very high risks, and they should research thoroughly any offering before making an investment decision. An investor should read and fully understand the information about the company and the risks that are disclosed before making any investment.

The following are some risks to consider before making a crowdfunding investment:

- **1. Speculative.** Investments in startups and early-stage ventures are speculative, and these enterprises often fail. Unlike an investment in a mature business, where there is a track record of revenue and income, the success of a startup or early-stage venture often relies on the development of a new product or service that may or may not find a market. An investor should be able to afford and be prepared to lose their entire investment.
- **2. Illiquidity.** An investor will be limited in his/her ability to resell the investment for the first year and may need to hold that investment for an indefinite period of time. Unlike investing in companies listed on a stock exchange, where one can quickly and easily trade securities on a market, an investor may have to locate an interested buyer when seeking to resell a crowdfunded investment.
- **3. Cancellation restrictions.** Once you make an investment commitment for a crowdfunding offering, an investor will be committed to make that investment (unless the investor cancels the commitment within a specified period of time).
- **4. Valuation and capitalization.** A crowdfunding investment may purchase an equity stake in a startup. Unlike listed companies that are valued publicly through market-driven stock prices, the valuation of private companies, especially startups, is difficult, and an investor may risk overpaying for the equity stake received. In addition, there may be additional classes of equity with rights that are superior to the class of equity being sold through crowdfunding.
- **5. Limited disclosure.** The company must disclose information about the business, its business plan, the offering, and its anticipated use of proceeds, among other things. An early-stage company may be able to provide only limited information about its business plan and operations because it does not have fully developed operations or a long history to provide more disclosure. The company is also only obligated to file information annually regarding its business, including financial statements.
- **6. Investment in the person.** An early-stage investment is also an investment in the entrepreneur of the venture. Being able to execute on the business plan is often an important factor in whether the business is viable and successful. An investor should be aware that a portion of the investment may fund the compensation of the company's employees, including the

entrepreneur. An investor should carefully review any disclosure regarding the company's use of proceeds.

- **7. Possibility of fraud.** In light of the relative ease with which early-stage companies can raise funds through crowdfunding, it may be the case that certain opportunities turn out to be money-losing, fraudulent schemes. As with other investments, there is no guarantee that crowdfunding investments will be immune from fraud.
- **8. Understanding of the investment.** There are different types of crowdfunding investments available depending on the crowdfunding website and funding strategy. Some websites, such as Kiva, focus on debt investments, while others, such as Wefunder, focus on equity investments. Still others, such as Kickstarter, offer investors only an award for investing. This reward could range from anything such as a free product to just a thank-you note, depending on the startup.

Source: Adapted from Regulation Crowdfunding, May 4, 2017, www.sec.gov/small-business/exemptofferings/regcrowdfunding; G. Detweiler, "Which Type of Crowdfunding Is Best for Your Small Business?," *Forbes*, January 9, 2020, www.forbes.com/sites/allbusiness/2020/01/09/small-business-crowdfunding/#16e62404600e.

Other Private Sources of Capital

In addition to the capital sources discussed in the preceding sections, other private sources of capital exist. The following sections examine some of them.

INSURANCE COMPANIES

Insurance companies collect billions of dollars every year. Some of these funds are used to pay claims, but a large portion is invested. This is particularly true for life insurance. Few people who buy a life insurance policy will die this year; however, the insurance company has to invest the monies paid for premiums to pay the face value of the policy when the policyholder does die. One of the primary ways the company accrues money is by investing in real estate loans or mortgages, particularly in new construction. Therefore, insurance companies may be especially interested in lending money to the new venture owner who has a construction firm. Also, if the owner has an insurance policy that has built up some cash surrender value, he or she can borrow that money at a relatively low interest rate. For example, although most banks today charge ten percent annual interest for loans, the typical insurance policy allows the policyholder to borrow the cash surrender value at five to six percent.

FINANCE COMPANIES

Some finance companies specialize in lending money to businesses. These firms are not to be confused with personal finance companies, which loan small sums to individual consumers. These finance companies deal mostly in secured loans, usually with interest rates much higher than those banks charge. Such companies often provide loans after a bank has reviewed the situation and has decided against granting the business a loan. Since the potential risk to the finance company is higher, the interest and origination fees are also higher.

FACTORS

Another source of capital, especially short-term funds, is *accounts receivable factoring*. Factors (which are similar to brokers) advance companies money on the basis of accounts receivable. They differ from other financial sources in that they *buy* the accounts receivable. This means they purchase them without recourse—if a person who *owes* an account receivable does not pay, the factor is the one who loses money. By contrast, when a bank finances accounts receivable, the business that borrowed the funds must make good on a failure to pay. Since the factor takes a greater risk, the cost of factoring is much higher than for accounts receivable financing. Additionally, the factor is unlikely to buy all of a business's accounts receivable. Rather, it will determine which ones offer the best chance for payment and will buy their accounts. The remainder will be left for the business to collect. Some business people object to the high cost of factoring and to the factor dealing directly with their customers. However, when a new venture needs money, factoring may be the only possible way to raise the necessary capital.

U.S. Small Business Administration Funding for Small Ventures

The Small Business Administration (SBA) is an independent agency of the U.S. government. It was established by Congress for the purpose of advising and assisting the nation's small businesses. One of the primary areas in which it helps small firms is by guaranteeing loans. These loans, known as 7(a) loans, are negotiated by the new venture owner and the bank, with repayment guaranteed by the SBA.

SBA 7(a) loans have a maximum loan amount of $5 million, and there is no minimum loan amount. During 2018, the SBA funded more than 66,000 loans through the 7(a) and 504 programs. These loans provided over $30 billion to small businesses throughout the United States. The actual interest rate for a 7(a) loan guaranteed by the SBA is negotiated between the applicant and lender and subject to SBA maximums. Both fixed and variable interest rate structures are available. The SBA can guarantee as much as 85 percent on loans of up to $150,000 and 75 percent on loans of more than $150,000. The SBA's maximum exposure amount is $3,750,000. Thus, if a business receives an SBA-guaranteed loan for $5 million, the maximum guarantee to the lender will be $3,750,000, or 75 percent. SBA Express loans have a maximum guarantee set at 50 percent.

Once you have decided to apply for a loan guaranteed by the SBA, you will need to collect the appropriate documents for your application. The SBA does not provide direct loans. The process starts with your local lender, working within SBA guidelines. Use the following SBA 7(a) Loan Application Checklist to ensure you have everything the lender will ask for to complete your application. Once your loan package is complete, your lender will submit it to the SBA.

1. *SBA loan application:* To begin the process, you will need to complete an SBA loan application form.
2. *Personal background and financial statement:* To assess your eligibility, the SBA also requires you complete a personal background that includes your financial information.
3. *Business financial statements:* To support your application and demonstrate your ability to repay the loan, prepare and include the following financial statements:

   • Profit and loss (P&L) statement: This must be current within 180 days of your application. Also include supplementary schedules from the last three fiscal years.
   • Projected financial statements: Include a detailed one-year projection of income and finances and attach a written explanation as to how you expect to achieve this projection.

4. *Ownership and affiliations:* Include a list of names and addresses of any subsidiaries and affiliates, including concerns in which you hold a controlling interest and other concerns that may be affiliated with you by stock ownership, franchise, proposed merger, or otherwise.
5. *Business certificate/license:* Your original business license or certificate of doing business. If your business is a corporation, stamp your corporate seal on the SBA loan application form.
6. *Loan application history:* Include records of any loans you may have applied for in the past.
7. *Income tax returns:* Include signed personal and business federal income tax returns of your business's principals for the previous three years.
8. *Résumés:* Include personal résumés for each principal.
9. *Business overview and history:* Provide a brief history of the business and its challenges. Include an explanation of why the SBA loan is needed and how it will help the business.
10. *Business lease:* Include a copy of your business lease or note from your landlord, giving terms of the proposed lease.
11. *If you are purchasing an existing business:* The following information is needed for purchasing an existing business:

    • Current balance sheet and P&L statement of business to be purchased
    • Previous two years of federal income tax returns for the business
    • Proposed Bill of Sale, including Terms of Sale
    • Asking price with schedule of inventory, machinery, equipment, furniture, and fixtures[9]

Small Business Investment Companies

Another avenue for securing funding is through Small Business Investment Companies (SBICs), which are privately managed for-profit investment funds that use privately raised capital and guaranteed SBA loans to provide long-term loans and equity investments to qualifying small businesses. Because SBICs seek attractive net returns for their private investors, SBICs use their own investment criteria and processes to make investment decisions. The SBA has no influence over SBIC investment decisions.

SBICs can only invest in small businesses, defined as businesses with tangible net worth of less than $18 million and an average of $6 million in net income or less over the previous two years at the time of investment. A business may also be deemed "small" based on its industry. SBICs cannot finance foreign activities. Such activities include investments to support foreign operations or businesses with more than 49 percent of their employees or tangible assets outside the United States. Although SBICs invest in many different industries, SBICs are prohibited from financing any of the following: Re-lenders or re-investors, passive businesses, most real estate businesses, farmland, project financings, or businesses contrary to the public interest.

You should research SBICs to identify those funds whose investment profiles best fit your business needs. Consider the stage of the companies in which they have invested, the size of the investments and any geographic or industry concentration they maintain. You should also be sure to verify that the SBIC is actively investing. Most SBICs stop making new investments in small businesses roughly five years after they obtain an SBIC license. Entrepreneurs have three sources to search for active SBICs:

- The SBIC Directory: A directory of active SBICs organized by state.
- The Small Business Investor Alliance (link is external): An association of private equity funds and investors that target the lower middle market.
- National Association of Investment Companies (NAIC) (link is external): An association dedicated to promoting investment in an ethnically diverse marketplace.

Most SBICs have a website where you can find out more information on their investment profile and some of their existing portfolio companies.

SBICs typically require a business plan to help them evaluate whether they should provide your company with financing. Like most private equity and venture capital funds, they receive hundreds of business plans from entrepreneurs every year. Simply emailing your business plan or calling their offices is unlikely to yield results. Entrepreneurs seeking capital from an SBIC will benefit most from a qualified introduction to the fund managers. Talk to accountants, attorneys, executives in your industry and other business colleagues to establish a connection with the SBIC. If one of these business professionals can introduce you to the fund, your business plan will have a much greater chance of being considered.[10]

Small Business Research Funding: SBIR and STTR Programs

Small Business Innovative Research (SBIR) and Small Business Technology Transfer (STTR) are highly competitive programs that encourage small businesses to explore their technological potential and provide the incentive to profit from commercialization opportunities. By including qualified small businesses in the nation's R&D arena, high-tech innovation is stimulated and the United States gains entrepreneurial spirit as it meets its specific research and development needs.

These two programs target the entrepreneurial sector because that is where most innovation and innovators thrive. However, the risk and expense of conducting serious R&D efforts are often beyond the means of many small businesses. By reserving a specific percentage of federal R&D funds for small business, SBIR and STTR protect the small business and enable it to compete on the same level as larger businesses. These programs fund the critical startup and development stages and encourage commercialization of the technology, product, or service, which in turn stimulates the U.S. economy.

Since their enactment in 1982 as part of the Small Business Innovation Development ment Act, these programs have helped thousands of small businesses compete for federal research and development awards. Their contributions have enhanced the nation's defense, protected our environment, advanced health care, and improved our ability to manage information and manipulate data.

The SBIR and STTR programs are structured in three phases:

1. *Phase I:* The objective of Phase I is to establish the technical merit, feasibility, and commercial potential of the proposed R/R&D efforts and to determine the quality of performance of the small business awardee organization prior to providing further federal support in Phase II. SBIR Phase I awards normally do not exceed $150,000 in total costs for six months.
2. *Phase II:* The objective of Phase II is to continue the R/R&D efforts initiated in Phase I. Funding is based on the results achieved in Phase I and the scientific and technical merit and commercial potential of the project proposed in Phase II. Only Phase I awardees are eligible for a Phase II award. SBIR Phase II awards normally do not exceed $1,000,000 in total costs for two years.
3. *Phase III:* The objective of Phase III, where appropriate, is for the small business to pursue commercialization objectives resulting from the Phase I/II R/R&D activities. The SBIR program does not fund Phase III. In some federal agencies, Phase III may involve follow-on non-SBIR funded R&D or production contracts for products, processes, or services intended for use by the U.S. government.[11]

The Rise of Crowdfunding

Crowdfunding seeks funding for a new venture by raising monetary contributions from a large number of people in the general public via the internet. The crowdfunding model has three principal parts: The entrepreneur who proposes the idea and/or venture to be funded, individuals or groups who support the idea, and a moderating organization (the "platform") that brings the parties together to launch the idea.[12]

It has been predicted that there will soon be over 2,000 crowdfunding platforms (Kickstarter and Indiegogo are the most well known), as the industry has grown to over $89 billion worldwide. It is estimated that crowdfunding now raises over $2 million per day, with some predictions of 100 percent growth each year. The World Bank says that the global crowdfunding market could reach $1 trillion by 2025—far greater than the global venture capital industry today.

In spite of these promising numbers and predictions, there are numerous critics of crowdfunding. One skeptic warns that equity crowdfunding may be just hype and that it will fail to significantly improve the supply of investment capital or improve the investment return of investors. The fear of future regulations is still a reality to some as well as the image of only desperate ventures seeking investors through crowdfunding. Therefore, it is wise for any entrepreneur to be aware of the potential concerns that still exist with crowdfunding.[13]

However, be assured that this new form of equity financing is here to stay, and with predictions of huge growth, crowdfunding may serve as a viable vehicle for raising those early seed stage dollars. As with any potential funding mechanism, entrepreneurs must be diligent in their pursuit of complete understanding of the regulations and drawbacks involved with the investments.

For a successful crowdfunding campaign, experts recommend keeping in mind a few tips:

1. Set a clear funding goal for your project. Break your goals into small contributions and calculate the number of backers you are looking for at each contribution level.
2. Target confirming 30 percent of your goal amount even before the campaign goes live. This could be from your personal network, friends, or family. No one likes to contribute to a campaign sitting on zero.
3. Promote your campaign consistently through social media. Crowdfunding is a lot about story telling. If your story is interesting and convincing, it will get shared and definitely have a higher chance of success.
4. Actively manage your campaign by regularly updating your email list about its progress. Encourage contributors to share the campaign among their network.
5. Express genuine gratitude to all the people who have contributed. Always try to bond with your contributors to form a strong, healthy relationship.[14]

A Global Perspective

"Capital Activity Hubs"

According to The World Bank, the United States leads the world in terms of venture capital availability; however, it may be difficult for entrepreneurs to find venture capital for risky projects. Certain regions or "hubs" have arisen, including Northern Europe, South Asia, and East Asia, where venture capital has been available for entrepreneurs with ideas for new businesses.

With the growth of opportunity for startups in artificial intelligence (AI), robotics, and other technologies that have the ability to disrupt existing markets and create outsized returns for investors, there is an increasing need for workers with specialized skills and an educational pipeline to deliver new workers into the labor market. Large urban areas, with their high population density, amenities, and systems for higher education, offer opportunities for development of a concentrated workforce that technology startups need to be successful. The high concentration of companies within one area also creates opportunities for collaboration and diffusion of innovative ideas.

Though the United States is still a world leader in entrepreneurship, numerous cities in dense urban areas globally, from Tel Aviv to Mumbai, are becoming hubs for innovation and new businesses. Des Moines, Iowa, and Bozeman, Montana, were the only U.S. cities in the top 20 globally for venture capital growth between 2010 and 2017. In 2019, venture capital investment stood at $52.7 billion. With increasing competition for venture capital globally, how can an entrepreneur put themselves in the best position to compete for funding?

One option is to take part in a business accelerator. Generally, in exchange for an average six percent equity stake in the company, accelerators offer startups a small investment, along with guidance, professional services, workspace, and exposure to larger venture funds to help the startups grow. Ranked in 2014 by researchers at the MIT Sloan School of Management, the University of Richmond, the University of Virginia's Darden School of Business, Y Combinator, Techstars, and AngelPad were judged to be the best performing accelerators. Y Combinator has helped launch companies such as Airbnb, Dropbox, DoorDash, and Instacart.

Successfully achieving investment from a top accelerator can be very challenging; however, there are increasing opportunities for entrepreneurs, as organizations as diverse as non-profit organizations, companies, and cities are looking to take advantage of this growing trend by setting up their own accelerator programs. In some cases, accelerators are focused on helping companies within a certain region or industry. Startup founders need to consider carefully if the opportunity offered by an accelerator is worth the equity to participate.

Source: Adapted from "Venture Capital Availability, 1–7 (Best)," The World Bank, tcdata360.worldbank.org/indicators/cap.avail?country=BRA&indicator=529&viz=line_chart&years=2007,2017; Leigh Buchanan, "Study: U.S. Businesses No Longer Dominate in Venture Capital Funding," *Inc.*, October 5, 2018, www.inc.com/leigh-buchanan/american-businesses-no-longer-dominate-venture-capital.html; Jason D. Rowley, "Q4 2018 Closes Out a Record Year for the Global VC Market," Crunchbase, January 7, 2019, news.crunchbase.com/news/q4–2018-closes-out-a-record-year-for-the-global-vc-market/; Jennifer Samuel, "Global Venture Capital Funding Holds Strong in Q2 '19," KPMG, July 11, 2019, home.kpmg/xx/en/home/media/press-releases/2019/07/enterprise-venture-pulse-report-q2.html; and Jonathan Shieber, "[Updated] These Are the 15 Best Accelerators in the U.S.," TechCrunch, March 10, 2014, techcrunch.com/2014/03/10/these-are-the-15-best-accelerators-in-the-u-s/.

Summary

One of the first questions a prospective new venture owner must be able to answer is, What kind of capital do I need, and where can it be obtained? Basically, *four* types of capital exist: Short-term loans, intermediate-term loans, long-term loans, and equity capital. Each was discussed in this chapter.

After determining the type of capital needed, the prospective entrepreneur must follow through and determine the source of this type of capital. Of the large number of capital sources available, those discussed in this chapter are internal funds, trade credit, equity sources, banks, other private sources of capital, the Small Business Administration, small business investment companies, the SBIR and STTR programs, and crowdfunding. In each instance, we examined the types of capital and services typically provided. Some of these capital sources are more valuable to one kind of business than another. For example, factoring would be used by a business that has a large amount of accounts receivable but not by a business that deals basically in cash.

In the latter part of the chapter, we examined the role of the SBA in helping the new venture owner obtain capital despite being turned down by his or her local bank. Regardless of the type of business, capital sources exist that can help the owner raise the all-important initial funding. Despite the potential risk to the investor, the business may even find a venture capitalist who feels the firm is promising and will return a large profit.

We then concluded with a look at crowdfunding as a source of startup funds. This new method of reaching out to the general public through the internet with a campaign to raise funds has gained great momentum, with predictions of huge growth in the next ten years. However, as with all forms of equity capital, the most important task for the new venture is to investigate these capital sources before plunging headlong into the venture.

Review and Discussion Questions

1. What are the two most common forms of short-term loans? Explain them.
2. What are intermediate-term loans, and when do new ventures use them? What about long-term loans?
3. What is equity capital?
4. Explain how new ventures use the following capital sources: Internal funds, trade credit, and equity sources.
5. What kinds of loan services do banks provide for new ventures? Describe four of them.
6. Discuss how the following can be of value to new ventures that want to raise capital: Insurance companies, finance companies, and factors.
7. In what way(s) does the SBA help new ventures raise capital? Be specific.
8. Explain crowdfunding and how it would assist smaller ventures seeking startup capital.

The Venture Consultant

The Power of the Crowd

Margot Iatarola has lived in Washington for the last ten years. She grew up an avid skier and had her eyes set on competing in the Olympics for the United States. In 2016, Margot had an unfortunate injury that now prevents her from skiing at the Olympic level. To continue her passion for skiing, Margot decided that she wanted to own a ski resort.

After moving back to Washington, Margot purchased a piece of land that was ideal for starting a ski resort. To officially launch the business, Margot needs chairlift equipment. After just two weeks of searching the market, Margot found an adequate set of equipment for her resort. It retails for $500,000 and has a personal guarantee from the manufacturer to last for at least ten years. Having just $110,000 of her own startup funds to put into the business, Margot needs additional funding for the purchase. Knowing $500,000 is likely the best price she can attain the equipment for, she began asking banks for a loan.

Margot was disappointed early and often in her search for a loan. She visited three banks, and none of them was willing to loan the capital. The bankers said Margot's plan had a lot of potential, and they were interested, although the timing wasn't the best. They also mentioned the loan was not "cookie cutter" enough and was too small for their general loan issuance policy. These issues permeated each of her meetings with the bankers. While these initial funding efforts were discouraging, Margot was not going to give up on her search for funding.

After speaking with more members of the financing industry, Margot heard about an equity crowdfunding platform called MicroVentures. MicroVentures specializes in helping small companies access capital from accredited and non-accredited investors in exchange for a small percentage of equity. She has heard many stories of entrepreneurs raising funds on this platform. The success stories cite the benefits of quick access to capital and the ability of the platform to hedge risk for the investor and entrepreneur.

However, she has heard about some sites offering crowdfunding only in exchange for large amounts of equity. This does not appeal to Margot because she hopes to retain as much ownership of the business as possible. Additionally, she has no idea how much she would have to give up in the crowdfunding scenario. Understanding this could still be a great opportunity, Margot begins perusing various crowdfunding sites to gauge their feasibility.

Your Consultation

Margot is skeptical that financing the business through crowdfunding is her best option. Discuss two advantages and two disadvantages of raising money through a crowdfunding platform. Then consider whether Margot should continue to speak with banks. What about their traditional funding techniques is appealing to Margot? Finally, make a recommendation on which technique you would advise Margot choose.

Notes

1 Jay Ebben and Alec Johnson, "Bootstrapping in Small Firms: An Empirical Analysis of Change over Time," *Journal of Business Venturing*, 2006, 21 (6): 851–865; see also Wing Lam, "Funding Gap, What Funding Gap? Financial Bootstrapping: Supply, Demand and Creation of Entrepreneurial Finance," *International Journal of Entrepreneurial Behavior & Research*, 2010, 16 (4): 268–295.

2 Brian T. Gregory, Matthew W. Rutherford, Sharon Oswald, and Lorraine Gardiner, "An Empirical Investigation of the Growth Cycle Theory of Small Firm Financing," *Journal of Small Business Management*, 2005, 43 (4): 382–392; and Liang Han, Stuart Fraser, and David J. Storey, "The Role of Collateral in Entrepreneurial Finance," *Journal of Business Finance & Accounting*, 2009, 36 (3–4): 424–455.

3 Larry D. Wall, "On Investing in the Equity of Small Firms," *Journal of Small Business Management*, 2007, 45 (1): 89–93; Andrew Winton and Vijay Yerramilli, "Entrepreneurial Finance: Banks versus Venture Capital," *Journal of Financial Economics*, 2008, 88 (1): 51–79.

4 Stuart Fraser, Sumon Kumar Bhaumik, and Mike Wright, "What Do We Know about Entrepreneurial Finance and Its Relationship with Growth?," *International Small Business Journal*, 2015, 33 (1): 70–88.

5 For a good analysis of sources of finance for entrepreneurs, see Thomas J. Chemmanur and Paolo Fulghieri, "Entrepreneurial Finance and Innovation: An Introduction and Agenda for Future Research," *The Review of Financial Studies*, 2014, 27 (1): 1–19.

6 Gary Dushnitsky and Zur Shapira, "Entrepreneurial Finance Meets Organizational Reality: Comparing Investment Practices and Performance of Corporate and Independent Venture Capitalists," *Strategic Management Journal*, 2010, 31 (9): 990–1017; Will Drover, Matthew S. Wood, and G. Tyge Payne, "The Effects of Perceived Control on Venture Capitalist Investment Decisions: A Configurational Perspective," *Entrepreneurship Theory & Practice*, 2014, 38 (4): 833–861.

7 Dirk De Clercq, Vance H. Fried, Oskari Lehtonen, and Harry J. Sapienza, "An Entrepreneur's Guide to the Venture Capital Galaxy," *Academy of Management Perspectives*, 2006, 20: 90–112; see also Yixi Ning, Wei Wang, and Bo Yu, "The Driving Forces of Venture Capital Investments," *Small Business Economics*, 2015, 44 (2): 315–344.

8 Annaleena Parhankangas and Michael Ehrlich, "How Entrepreneurs Seduce Business Angels: An Impression Management Approach," *Journal of Business Venturing*, 2014, 29 (4): 543–564; Veroniek Collewaert and Harry J. Sapienza, "How Does Angel Investor–Entrepreneur Conflict Affect Venture Innovation? It Depends," *Entrepreneurship Theory & Practice*, 2016, 40 (3): 573–597.

9 See Boyce D. Watkins, "On Governance Programs That Increase Small Firms' Access to Capital," *Journal of Small Business Management*, 2007, 45 (1): 133–136; and Ben R. Craig, William E. Jackson, and James B. Thomson, "Small Firm Finance, Credit Rationing, and the Impact of SBA-Guaranteed Lending on Local Economic Growth," *Journal of Small Business Management*, 2007, 45 (1): 116–132.

10 *SBA Loan Programs*, Washington, DC: U.S. Small Business Administration, 2016, www.sba.gov.

11 See SBIR and STTR programs at www.sbir.gov/.

12 Ethan Mollick, "The Dynamics of Crowdfunding: An Exploratory Study," *Journal of Business Venturing*, 2014, 29 (1): 1–16; and John Prpić, Prashant P. Shukla, Jan H. Kietzmann, and Ian P. McCarthy, "How to Work a Crowd: Developing Crowd Capital through Crowdsourcing," *Business Horizons*, 2015, 58 (1): 77–85.

13 Daniel Isenberg, "The Road to Crowdfunding Hell," *Harvard Business Review*, April 23, 2012.

14 See Carol Tice, "The Myth of Magical Crowdfunding—And What Actually Works," *Forbes*, October 10, 2014.

8 Financial Statements

The Scorecard

Introduction: Financial Statements

Financial statements are powerful tools owners can use to manage their ventures.[1] The basic financial statements an owner-manager needs to be familiar with are the balance sheet and the income statement. The following sections examine each of these in depth, providing a foundation for understanding the financial records that are needed.

The Balance Sheet

A balance sheet is a financial statement that reports a business's financial position at a specific time. Many accountants like to think of it as a picture taken at the close of business on a particular day, such as December 31. The closing date is usually the one that marks the end of the business year for the organization.

The balance sheet is divided into two parts: The financial resources owned by the firm and the claims against these resources. Traditionally, claims against the resources come from two groups: Creditors who have a claim to the firm's assets and can sue the company if these obligations are not paid and owners who have rights to anything left over after the creditors' claims have been paid.

The financial resources the firm owns are called *assets*. The claims creditors have against the company are called *liabilities*. The residual interest of the firm's owners is known as *owners' equity*. When all three are placed on the balance sheet, the assets are listed on the left, and the liabilities and owners' equity are listed on the right.

Assets	*Liabilities and Owners' Equity*

An asset is something of value the business owns. To determine the value of an asset, the owner-manager must do the following:

1.   Identify the resource.
2.   Provide a monetary measurement value of that resource's value.
3.   Establish the degree of ownership in the resource.

Most assets can be identified easily. They are tangible, such as cash, land, and equipment. However, *intangible assets* also exist. These are assets that cannot be seen; examples include copyrights and patents.

Liabilities are the debts of the business. These may be incurred either through normal operations or through the process of obtaining funds to finance operations. A common liability is a short-term account payable in which the business orders some merchandise, receives it, and has not yet paid for it. This often occurs when a company receives merchandise during the third week of the month and does not pay for it until it pays all of its bills on the first day of the next month. If the balance sheet was constructed as of the end of the month, the account would still be payable at that time.

Liabilities are divided into two categories: Short term and long term. *Short-term liabilities* are those that must be paid during the coming 12 months. *Long-term liabilities* are those that are not due and payable within the next 12 months, such as a mortgage on a building or a five-year bank loan.

Owners' equity is what remains after the firm's liabilities are subtracted from its assets. It is the claim the owners have against the firm's assets. If the business loses money, its owners' equity will decline. This will become clearer when we explain why a balance sheet always balances.[2]

Understanding the Balance Sheet

To fully explain the balance sheet, it is necessary to examine a typical one and determine what each entry means. Table 8.1 provides an illustration. Note that it has three sections: Assets, liabilities, and owners' equity. Within each of these classifications are various types of accounts. The following sections examine each type of account presented in the table.

Current Assets

Current assets consist of cash and other assets that are reasonably expected to be turned into cash, sold, or used up during a normal operating cycle. The most common types of current assets are those shown in Table 8.1.

Cash refers to coins, currency, and checks on hand. It also includes money the business has in its checking account and savings account.

Accounts receivable are claims of the business against its customers for unpaid balances from the sale of merchandise or the performance of services. For example, many firms sell on credit and expect their customers to pay by the end of the month. In many of these cases, they send customers a bill at the end of the month and ask for payment within ten days.

The *allowance for uncollectible accounts* refers to accounts receivable judged to be uncollectible. How does a business know when receivables are not collectible? This question can be difficult to answer. However, assume the business asks all of its customers to pay within the first ten days of the month following the purchase. Furthermore, an aging of the accounts receivable shows that the following amounts are due the firm:

Number of Days Outstanding	2021 Amount of Receivables
1–10	$325,000
11–20	$25,000
21–30	$20,000
31–60	$5,000
61–90	$7,500
97+	$17,500

In this case, the firm might believe that anything more than 60 days old will not be paid and will write it off as uncollectible. Note in Table 8.1 that the allowance for uncollectible accounts is $25,000, the amount that has been outstanding more than 60 days.

Inventory is merchandise held by the company for resale to customers. Current inventory in our example is $150,000, but this is not the entire inventory the firm had on hand all year. Naturally, the company started the year with some inventory and purchased more as sales were made. This balance sheet figure is what was left at the end of the fiscal year.

Prepaid expenses are expenses the firm has already paid but that have not yet been used. For example, insurance paid on the company car every six months is a prepaid expense entry because it will be six months before the entire premium has been used. As a result, the accountant would reduce this prepaid amount by one-sixth each month. Sometimes supplies, services, and rent are also prepaid, in which case the same approach is followed.

Table 8.1 EntreX Corporation Balance Sheet for the Year Ended December 31, 2021

Assets		
Current Assets		
Cash		$200,000
Accounts receivable	$375,000	
Less: Allowance for uncollectible accounts	$25,000	$350,000
Inventory		$150,000
Prepaid expenses		$35,000
Total current assets		$735,000

Fixed Assets		
Land		$330,000
Building	$315,000	
Less: Accumulated depreciation of building	$80,000	
Equipment	$410,000	
Less: Accumulated depreciation of equipment	$60,000	
Total fixed assets		$915,000
Total assets		$1,650,000
Liabilities		
Current Liabilities		
Accounts payable	$150,000	
Notes payable	$25,000	
Taxes payable	$75,000	
Loan payable	$50,000	
Total current liabilities		$300,000
Bank loan		$200,000
Total liabilities		$500,000
Owners' Equity		
Contributed Capital		
Common stock, $10 par, 40,000 shares	$400,000	
Preferred stock, $100 par, 500 shares		
Authorized, none sold	---------	
Retained earnings	$750,000	
Total owners' equity		$1,150,000
Total liabilities and owners' equity		$1,650,000

Fixed Assets

Fixed assets consist of land, building, equipment, and other assets expected to remain with the firm for an extended period. They are not totally used up in the production of the firm's goods and services. Some of the most common types are shown in Table 8.1.

Land is property used in the operation of the firm. This is not land that has been purchased for expansion or speculation; that would be listed as an investment rather than a fixed asset. Land is listed on the balance sheet at cost, and its value is usually changed only periodically. For example, every five years the value of the land might be recalculated so that its value on the balance sheet and its resale value are the same.

Building consists of the structures that house the business. If the firm has more than one building, the total cost of all the structures is listed.

Accumulated depreciation of building refers to the amount of the building that has been written off the books due to wear and tear. For example, referring to Table 8.1, the original cost of the building was $315,000, but accumulated depreciation is $80,000, leaving a net value of $235,000. The amount of depreciation charged each year is determined by the company accountant after checking with the Internal Revenue Service rules. However, a standard depreciation is five percent per year for new buildings, although an accelerated method is sometimes used. In any event, the amount written off is a tax-deductible expense. Depreciation therefore reduces the amount of taxable income to the firm and helps lower the tax liability. In this way, the business gets the opportunity to recover part of its investment.

Equipment is the machinery the business uses to produce goods. This is placed on the books at cost and then depreciated and listed as the *accumulated depreciation of equipment*. In our example, it is $60,000. The logic behind equipment depreciation and its effect on the firm's income taxes is the same as that for accumulated depreciation on the building.

Current Liabilities

Current liabilities are obligations that will become due and payable during the next year or within the operating cycle. The most common current liabilities are listed in Table 8.1.

Accounts payable are liabilities incurred when goods or supplies are purchased on credit. For example, if the business buys on a basis of net 30 days, during those 30 days the bill for the goods will constitute an account payable.

A *note payable* is a promissory note given as tangible recognition of a supplier's claim or a note given in connection with an acquisition of funds, such as for a bank loan. Some suppliers require that a note be given when a company buys merchandise and is unable to pay for it immediately.

Taxes payable are liabilities owed to the government—federal, state, and local. Most businesses pay their federal and state income taxes on a quarterly basis. Typically, payments are made on April 15, June 15, and September 15 of the current year and January 15 of the following year. Then the business closes its books, determines whether it still owes any taxes, and makes the required payments by April 15. Other taxes payable are sales taxes. For example, most states and some cities levy a sales tax. Each merchant must collect the taxes and remit them to the appropriate agency.

A *loan payable* is the current installment on a long-term debt that must be paid this year. As a result, it becomes a part of the current liabilities. The remainder is carried as a long-term debt. Note in the table that $50,000 of this debt was paid in 2021 by EntreX Corporation.

Long-Term Liabilities

As we have said, long-term liabilities consist of obligations that will not become due or payable for at least one year or not within the current operating cycle. The most common long-term liabilities are bank loans.

A *bank loan* is a long-term liability due to a loan from a lending institution. Although it is unclear from the balance sheet in the table how large the bank loan originally was, it is being paid down at the rate of $50,000 annually. Thus, it will take four more years to pay off the loan.

Contributed Capital

EntreX Corporation is owned by individuals who have purchased stock in the business. Various kinds of stock can be sold by a corporation, the most typical being common stock and preferred stock. Only common stock has been sold by this company.

Common stock is the most basic form of corporate ownership. This ownership gives the individual the right to vote for the board of directors. Usually, for every share of common stock held, the individual is entitled to one vote. As shown in Table 8.1, the corporation has issued 40,000 shares of $10 *par* common stock, raising $400,000. Although the term *par value* may have little meaning to most stockholders, it has legal implications: It determines the legal capital of the corporation. This legal capital constitutes an amount that total stockholders' equity cannot be reduced below except under certain circumstances (the most common is a series of net losses). For legal reasons, the total par value of the stock is maintained in the accounting records. However, it has no effect on the *market value* of the stock.

Preferred stock differs from common stock in that its holders have preference over the assets of the firm in case of dissolution. This means that after the creditors are paid, preferred stockholders have the next claim on whatever assets are left. The common stockholders' claims come last. The table shows 500 shares of preferred stock were issued, each worth a par value of $100, but none has been sold.

Retained Earnings

Retained earnings are the accumulated net income over the life of the corporation to date. In the table, the retained earnings are shown as $750,000. Every year this amount increases by the profit the firm makes and keeps within the company. If dividends are declared on the stock, they, of course, are paid from the total net earnings. Retained earnings are what remain after that.

Why the Balance Sheet Always Balances

By definition, the balance sheet *always* balances.[3] If something happens on one side of the balance sheet, it is offset by something on the other side. Hence, the balance sheet remains in balance. Before examining some illustrations, let us restate the balance sheet equation:

$$Assets = Liabilities + Owners'\ Equity$$

With this in mind, let us look at some typical examples of business transactions and their effect on the balance sheet.

182 New Venture Finances

A Credit Transaction

EntreX Corporation calls one of its suppliers and asks for delivery of $10,000 in materials. The materials arrive the next day, and the company takes possession of them. The bill is to be paid within 30 days. How is the balance sheet affected? *Inventory* goes up by $10,000, and *Accounts payable* rises by $10,000. The increase in current assets is offset by an increase in current liabilities. Continuing this illustration, what happens when the bill is paid? The company issues a check for $10,000, and *Cash* declines by this amount. At the same time, *Accounts payable* decreases by $10,000. Again, these are offsetting transactions, and the balance sheet remains in balance.

A Bank Loan

Table 8.1 shows that EntreX Corporation had an outstanding bank loan of $200,000 in 2021. Assume the company increases this loan by $100,000 in 2022. How is the balance sheet affected? *Cash* goes up by $100,000 and *Bank loan* increases by the same amount. Again, balance is achieved. However, what if the firm uses this $100,000 to buy new machinery? In this case, *Cash* decreases by $100,000 and *Equipment* increases by a like amount. Again, a balance exists. Finally, what if EntreX decides to pay off its bank loan? In this case, the first situation is reversed: *Cash* and *Bank loan* (long-term liabilities) decrease in equal amounts.

Company Sells Stock

Suppose the company issues and sells another 40,000 shares of $10 par *common stock*. How does this action affect the balance sheet? (This answer is rather simple.) *Common stock* increases by $400,000 and so does *Cash*. Once more, a balance exists.

With these examples in mind, it should be obvious why the balance sheet *always* balances. Every entry has an equal and offsetting entry to maintain this equation:

Assets = Liabilities + Owners' Equity

Keep in mind that in accounting language, the terms *debit* and *credit* denote increases and decreases in assets, liabilities, and owners' equity. This table relates debits and credits to increases and decreases.

Category	A Transaction Increasing the Amount	A Transaction Decreasing the Amount
Asset	Debit	Credit
Liability	Credit	Debit
Owners' equity	Credit	Debit

Applying this idea to the preceding examples results in the following:

	Debit	*Credit*
Credit Transaction		
Inventory	$10,000	
Accounts payable		$10,000
Bank Loan		
Cash	$100,000	
Bank Loan		$100,000
Stock Sale		
Cash	$400,000	
Common Stock		$400,000
	$510,000	$510,000

The Income Statement

An income statement is a financial statement that shows the change that has occurred in a firm's position as a result of its operations over a specific period. This is in contrast to the balance sheet, which reflects the company's position at a particular point in time.

The income statement reports the success (or failure) of the business during the period. In essence, it shows whether revenues were greater than or less than expenses. These *revenues* are the monies the venture has received from the sale of its goods and services. The *expenses* are the costs of the resources used to obtain the revenues. These costs range from the cost of materials used in the products the firm makes to the salaries it pays its employees.

Most income statements cover a one-year interval, but it is not uncommon to find monthly, quarterly, or semiannual income statements. All of the revenues and expenses accumulated during this time are determined, and the net income for the period is identified. Many firms prepare quarterly income statements but construct a balance sheet only once a year. This is because they are interested far more in their profits and losses than in examining their asset, liability, and owners' equity positions. However, it should be noted that the income statement drawn up at the end of the year will coincide with the firm's fiscal year, just as the balance sheet does. As a result, at the end of the business year, the organization will have both a balance sheet and an income statement. In this way, they can be considered together and the interrelationship between them can be studied. We will consider this in greater depth in Chapter 9 when we look at some of the financial ratios that simultaneously analyze balance sheet data and income statement data.

A number of different types of income and expenses are reported on the income statement. However, for purposes of simplicity, the income statement can be reduced to three primary categories:

1. Revenues
2. Expenses
3. Net income

Revenues are the gross sales the business made during the particular period under review. Revenue often consists of the money actually received from sales, but this need not be the case. For example, sales made on account are still recognized as revenue, as when a furniture store sells $500 of furniture today, delivers it tomorrow, and will receive payment two weeks from now. From the moment the goods are delivered, the company can claim an increase in revenue.

Expenses are the costs associated with producing goods or services. For the furniture store situation just cited, the expenses associated with the sale would include the costs of acquiring, selling, and delivering the merchandise. Sometimes these are expenses that will be paid later. For example, the people who deliver the furniture may be paid every two weeks, so the actual outflow of expense money in the form of salaries will not occur at the same time the work is performed. Nevertheless, it is treated as an expense.

Net income is the excess of revenue over expenses during the particular period under discussion. If revenues exceed expenses, the result is a *net profit*. If the reverse is true, the firm suffers a *net loss*. At the end of the accounting period, all of the revenues and expenses associated with all of the sales of goods and services are added together, and then the expenses are subtracted from the revenues. In this way, the firm knows whether it made an overall profit or suffered an overall loss.[4]

Understanding the Income Statement

To explain the income statement fully, it is necessary to examine one and determine what each account is. Table 8.2 illustrates a typical income statement. It has five major sections:

1. Sales revenue
2. Cost of goods sold
3. Operating expenses
4. Financial expenses
5. Estimated income taxes

Table 8.2 EntreX Corporation Income Statement for the Year Ended December 31, 2021

Sales Revenue	$1,750,000	
Less: Sales returns and allowances	$50,000	
Net sales		$1,700,000
Cost of Goods Sold		
Inventory, January 2018	$150,000	
Purchases	$1,050,000	

Sales Revenue	$1,750,000	
Goods available for sale	$1,200,000	
Less: Inventory, December 2018	$200,000	
Cost of goods sold		$1,000,000
Gross margin		$700,000
Operating Expenses		
Selling expenses	$150,000	
Administrative expenses	$100,000	
Total operating expenses		$250,000
Operating income		$450,000
Financial Expenses		$20,000
Income before income taxes		$430,000
Estimated income taxes		$172,000
Net profit		$258,000

Revenue

Every time a business sells a product or performs a service, it obtains revenue. This is often referred to as *gross revenue* or *sales revenue*. However, it is usually an overstated figure because the company finds that some of its goods are returned or some customers take advantage of prompt payment discounts.

In Table 8.2, sales revenue is $1,750,000. However, the firm also has returns and allowances of $50,000. These returns are common for companies that operate on a "satisfaction or your money back" policy. In any event, a new venture should keep tabs on these returns and allowances to see if the total is high in relation to the total sales revenue. If so, the firm will know something is wrong with what it is selling and it can take action to correct the situation.

Deducting the sales returns and allowances from the sales revenue, the company finds its *net sales*. This amount must be great enough to offset the accompanying expenses to ensure a profit.

Cost of Goods Sold

As the term implies, the cost of goods sold section reports the cost of merchandise sold during the accounting period. Simply put, the cost of goods for a given period equals the beginning inventory plus any purchases the firm makes minus the inventory on hand at the end of the period. Note in Table 8.2 that the beginning inventory was $150,000 and the purchases totaled $1,050,000. This gave EntreX goods available for sale of $1,200,000. The ending inventory for the period was $200,000, so the cost of goods sold was $1,000,000. This is what it cost the company to buy the inventory it sold. When this cost of goods sold is subtracted from net sales, the result is the *gross margin*. The gross margin is the amount available to meet expenses and to provide some net income for the firm's owners.

Operating Expenses

The major expenses, exclusive of costs of goods sold, are classified as *operating expenses*. These represent the resources expended, except for inventory purchases, in generating the revenue for the period. Expenses are often divided into two broad subclassifications: Selling expenses and administrative expenses.

Selling expenses result from activities such as displaying, selling, delivering, and installing a product or performing a service. Expenses for displaying a product include rent for storage space, depreciation on fixtures and furniture, property insurance, and utility and tax expenses. Sales expenses, salaries, commissions, and advertising also fall into this category. Costs associated with getting the product from the store to the customer are also considered selling expenses. Finally, if the firm installs the product for the customer, all costs, including the parts used in the job, are considered in this total. Taken as a whole, these are the selling expenses.

Administrative expenses is a catchall term for operating expenses not directly related to selling or borrowing. In broad terms, these expenses include the costs associated with running the firm. They include salaries of the managers, expenses associated with operating the office, general expenses that cannot be related directly to buying or selling activities, and expenses that arise from delinquent or uncollectible accounts.

When these selling and administrative expenses are added together, the result is *total operating expenses*. Subtracting total operating expenses from gross margin gives the firm its *operating income*. Note in Table 8.2 that selling expenses are $150,000, administrative expenses are $100,000, and total operating expenses are $250,000. When subtracted from the gross margin of $700,000, the operating income is $450,000.

Financial Expenses

Financial expenses are comprised of the interest expense on long-term loans. As seen in Table 8.2, this expense is $20,000. Additionally, many companies include their interest expense on short-term obligations as part of their financial expenses.

Estimated Income Taxes

As noted earlier, corporations pay estimated income taxes, and then, at some predetermined time (for example, December 31), the books are closed, actual taxes are determined, and any additional payments are made (or refunds claimed). When these taxes are subtracted from the income before income taxes, the result is the *net profit*. In our example, EntreX Corporation made $258,000.

Keeping Proper Records

The balance sheet and income statement are important financial statements. However, the new venture also needs to keep adequate accounting records for control purposes.[5] The two most basic record books are the Sales and Cash Receipts Journal and the Cash Disbursement, Purchases, and Expense Journal.

Sales and Cash Receipts Journal

The Sales and Cash Receipts Journal records daily income to the business. Table 8.3 provides an example. Note that total sales on March 15 amounted to $520, and this was credited to the account. Of this amount, $210 was charged, resulting in $310 in cash taken in. Additionally, $150 in accounts receivable was collected. However, $10 was lost due to change errors by the employee running the cash register. The business deposited $450 in the bank.

Note that Table 8.3 distinguishes debits (DR) and credits (CR). In *income accounts*, credit is an increase to the account and a debit is a decrease. In *expense accounts*, a debit is an increase and a credit is a decrease. The total of debits and credits should be equal. When they are not, an error exists in the entries. In addition, the total of the total sales column tells the firm how much has been sold during the period; this is the total used in the income statement.

Table 8.3 Sales and Cash Receipts Journal

					Misc. Income and Expenses		
Date	Description and/or Account	Total Sales (DR)	Credit Sales (DR)	Collected on Accounts (CR)	Income (CR)	Expense (DR)	Bank Deposit (DR)
3/15	Daily summary	$520.00	$210.00	$150.00			$450.00
	Cash short					$10.00	
3/16	Daily summary	$635.00	$300.00	$210.00			$550.00
	Cash over				$5.00		
3/17	Daily summary	$410.00	$225.00	$175.00			$345.00
	Cash short					$15.00	

Cash Disbursement, Purchases, and Expense Journal

The Cash Disbursement, Purchases, and Expense Journal is a record of expenditures of funds by the new venture. Table 8.4 illustrates a page from this journal. Note that the debits and credits balance. If they do not, an error exists, and the bookkeeper needs to check the figures to find it. With this journal and the Sales and Cash Receipts Journal, revenues, expenses, and changes in balance sheet accounts can be determined and financial statements drawn up

Managing the Books

A number of options for maintaining the books are available to the new venture owner-manager.[6] One is to turn the job over to an accountant who will come in once a month and take care of everything. However, since this is often expensive, it is the least popular method.

Table 8.4 Cash Disbursement, Purchases, and Expense Journal

Date	Payee and/ or Account	Check Number	Amount of Check (CR)	Merchandise Purchased (DR)	Gross Salaries (DR)	Payroll Deductions		Misc. Income and Expenses	
						Income Tax (CR)	Social Security (CR)	Income (CR)	Expenses (DR)
3/15	Acme Office Supplies	511	$75.00	$75.00					
3/15	Jackson Properties (rent)	512	$425.00						$425.00
3/16	Judson Materials, Inc.	513	$175.00	$175.00					
3/16	Anderson Materials Company	514	$100.00	$100.00					
3/17	Complete Furniture Rental	515	$90.00						$90.00
3/17	Payroll	516	$1,100.00		$814.00	$220.00	$66.00		

Another option is to have a full- or part-time employee keep the books. For example, many businesses hire a retired person or have one of their employees learn how to keep the books. Still others use a freelance bookkeeper who also keeps books for a number of other firms. Working on a contract basis, the person spends a few hours each week maintaining each company's books. This arrangement is often no more expensive than a part-time employee bookkeeper.

Finally, the owner-manager can maintain the books personally. The advantage of this is that the individual is constantly aware of his or her firm's financial situation. On the negative side, this takes time away from other management duties. As a result, most new ventures use part-time or freelance bookkeepers.

Computers, Software, and Financial Preparation

In recent years, a variety of software programs and software service programs have been developed to handle such needs as bookkeeping, billing, and financial control.[7] Prices vary for software from "free" to fairly expensive depending on what the requirements entail.

Many new ventures find that they cannot afford the luxury of a major accounting firm and a bookkeeper is potentially all they need. Their accountant periodically reviews the books and brings them up to date. At the end of the year, the accountant closes the books, prepares the income tax forms, and gets everything in order for the owner to send to the IRS. However, more and more entrepreneurs are finding that software service packages do pay off. The level of technology and functionality, along with the ease of use, has increased tremendously.[8] One other advantage to having the financials prepared in-house by the venture owner is that he or she learns to understand the numbers and gains a good understanding of how well the business is performing.

New Venture Issues

"Financial Software for Your Business?"

When a person decides to go into business, there are a large number of possibilities when it comes to financial management. An entrepreneur could spend a lot of time evaluating the best choices for accounting and financial management software. Some of the more popular options are discussed in the following sections.

Best Accounting Software for Small Business Overall

Intuit QuickBooks offers a wide range of features for all types of small businesses. This includes consultants, online merchants, store and restaurant owners, and service providers. For new venture startups or expansion of an existing business, QuickBooks is packed with basic and advanced features to meet your accounting needs. It offers easy navigation integrating more than 150 business apps, and it is used by accountants. It offers various plans starting at $8.00 per month.

Best Free Accounting Software for Small Business

Wave Accounting offers free cloud-based accounting software specifically designed for small businesses. Unlike other free accounting software programs that limit capabilities, Wave Accounting offers a comprehensive set of accounting features without the monthly price tag. It is completely free (with ads visible); however, customer service costs extra, and additional features come with the paid service.

Best Accounting Software for Really Small Business

Zoho Books offers really small businesses very simple accounting software that includes all the basic features microbusinesses need as well as advanced tools that grow with the business. Furthermore, compared with other accounting software for really small businesses, Zoho Books has the best price, for all of its capabilities, at $29 per month. It also connects with popular online payment gateways so the venture can get paid faster

Best Accounting Mobile App for Small Business

FreshBooks is a mobile app that offers ease of use, excellent customer service, and all of the features small businesses need to manage their finances on the go. The app is simple, with an intuitive user interface, and features a comprehensive set of tools for on-the-go accounting and plans starting at $7.50 per month.

The choice of software package seems to be based on the needs of the venture. With minimum investment, the venture owner can maintain an accurate account of financial information. All of the popular packages reviewed have proven capacities and acceptable levels of user satisfaction. If the firm can afford it, it may be advised to purchase a higher end software service that integrates more financial management functions. As the venture grows, this software will be ready to handle the increased financial documentation necessary to manage the business.

Source: Adapted from L. Fairbanks, Best Accounting Software and Invoice Generators of 2020, Business News Daily, December 30, 2019, www.businessnewsdaily.com/7543-best-accounting-software.html.

Early Warning Signs of Financial Trouble

The importance of financial statements for new ventures cannot be overemphasized. To keep careful track of a new firm's health, the manager must understand the balance sheet, income statement, and cash flow statement as well as sales journals and purchasing journals. If these statements are understood, managers can recognize the signs of financial problems before they ruin the business. The following list illustrates many of the early warning signs of financial trouble that new venture owner-managers need to be aware of:

- declining profits despite increased sales
- decreasing gross margin
- dwindling cash flow
- shrinking market share
- receding sales volume
- increasing interest expenses in relation to sales
- swelling overhead expenses
- irregular, inaccurate, or untimely internally prepared financial reports
- repeated failure to meet overly optimistic sales forecasts
- continual stretching of accounts receivable
- growing write-offs of uncollectible receivables
- increasing payables in relation to revenues
- credit limits nearing exhausting
- increased pressure from creditors to pay
- continual need to float checks due to bank overdrafts
- declining debt-to-worth ratio
- lack of control over purchasing and personnel
- slow-turning or out-of-balance inventories

A Global Perspective

"International Accounting Standards"

Globally, there are varying rules and requirements that govern accounting standards and that companies are required to follow. In the United States, financial reporting and accounting standards are governed by the Financial Accounting Standards Board (FASB), which puts forward Generally Accepted Accounting Principles, commonly known as GAAP. Outside of the United States, 100 countries have adopted common standards known as International Financial Reporting Standards (IFRS), which are put forward by the International Accounting Standards Board (IASB).

IFRS and GAAP are broadly similar in their requirements in terms of financial reporting, as outlined in this chapter, but there are important differences. GAAP is rule-based, specifying specific actions companies must take to be compliant, while IFRS is principle-based, meaning that it provides more broadly written guidelines that companies must follow. This potentially allows for broader interpretation of what actions companies need to take under IFRS.

Since the early 2000s, there have been periodic efforts to work toward convergence of the accounting standards, but the more nuanced differences in the accounting standards in terms of accounting for inventory and varying interpretations of guidelines across the countries that have adopted IFRS can result in potentially significant differences in the figures reported between the two standards.

It is up to each entrepreneur to investigate local accounting standards and ensure compliance with local requirements. Some rules may apply only to publicly traded companies, but it is important to know that even if a business is not required to follow specific reporting requirements, outside interests that interact with the company, such as banks, may have expectations that accounting standards are followed.

Source: Adapted from Sean Ross, "The Difference Between GAAP and IFRS," *Investopedia*, May 5, 2019, www.investopedia.com/ask/answers/011315/what-difference-between-gaap-and-ifrs.asp; and David H. Sherma and David Young, "Where Financial Reporting Still Falls Short," *Harvard Business Review*, 2016, hbr.org/2016/07/where-financial-reporting-still-falls-short.

Summary

The new venture owner-manager needs to be familiar with two basic financial statements: The balance sheet and the income statement. The balance sheet reports a business's financial position at a specific time. This statement is divided into two parts: The firm's financial resources and claims against these resources. Resources, which consist of assets, are equal to creditor claims and owners' equity combined. This results in the accounting equation of assets equal liabilities plus owners' equity.

A complete description of the balance sheet was presented, and accounts commonly found in each of the three sections of this financial statement were described. A balance sheet always balances because any change in assets is offset by an equal change in either liabilities or owners' equity or by an equal and opposite change in assets.

The income statement is a financial statement that shows the changes that have occurred in a firm's position as a result of its operations over a specific period. The five sections of the income statement are sales revenue, cost of goods sold, operating expenses, financial expenses, and tax expenses.

The two most basic record books are the Sales and Cash Receipts Journal and the Cash Disbursement, Purchases, and Expense Journal. The first records daily income to the business. The second records the firm's disbursement of funds.

For managing the books, the new venture owner-manager has a number of options. The most common approach is to use an in-house or freelance bookkeeper in conjunction with an accountant, who periodically balances the books, sees that the books are closed properly at the end of the fiscal year, prepares tax forms, and verifies that everything is in order for the new year. For keeping their books, billing, and maintaining financial control, new ventures today are turning to software services in the financial software industry. Before doing so, however, the owner-manager should compare the various software packages that deal with financial management to ensure the expenditure will be used effectively. (See "Financial Software for Your Business?" in the New Venture Issues box.)

Review and Discussion Questions

1. What is a balance sheet?
2. Define these terms: *assets*, *liabilities*, and *owners' equity*.
3. Describe the major sections of the balance sheet. What are the major accounts in each? Be specific.
4. Why does the balance sheet always balance?
5. What is an income statement?
6. Describe in detail the five major sections of the income statement.
7. How does the Sales and Cash Receipts Journal work? What types of information does it contain?
8. What is the Cash Disbursement, Purchases, and Expense Journal? What kind of information does it contain?
9. Explain why the two journals mentioned in questions 7 and 8 are the most basic record books for an owner of a new venture.
10. List the owner-manager's options for managing the company's books. Which option do you favor? Why?
11. When seeking software for handling financial control needs, what software or software service packages may be the most beneficial? Use the New Venture Issues story in the chapter to support your explanation.

The Venture Consultant

Does Business Success Align With the Income Statement?

Ellie Benson owns and operates Ellie's Soccer Kingdom. Ellie opened the shop three years ago and has done very well due to her expertise in soccer equipment. Additionally, Ellie entered the market at a time when more young adults and children were joining soccer teams. This combination propelled Ellie to running the most successful soccer shop within 100 miles, leaving her no direct competitors and steady revenue growth.

To this point, Ellie has needed a tremendous amount of willpower, time, and effort to service all her customers. Finally taking some free time for herself, Ellie reflected on her shop's history and how she had been so successful. She understood she was profitable because she sold her goods for more than it cost her to put them there. Outside of this fact, Ellie didn't understand much about financials and knew she needed to know more.

Ellie contacted her personal accountant, Suzanne, to discuss her firm's historical finances. Particularly, Ellie wanted to understand how the financials depicted her shop's performance in terms of financial statement items. Suzanne began by describing the business as performing excellently. However, Ellie desired further explanation and had to remind Suzanne that her expertise was in soccer, not financial statements.

Ellie's Soccer Kingdom		
Income Statement, End of Year 2021		
Sales Revenue	$700,000	
Less sales returns	$100,000	
Less sales allowances	$25,000	
Net sales		$665,000
Cost of Goods Sold		
Inventory, January 1, 2021	$35,000	
Purchases	$350,000	
Goods available for sale	$385,000	
Less inventory, December 31, 2021	$25,000	
Cost of goods sold		$360,000
Gross margin		$305,000
Operating Expenses		
Selling expenses	$20,000	
General and administrative expenses	$80,000	
Total operating expenses		$100,000

Ellie's Soccer Kingdom	
Operating income	$205,000
Financial Expenses	$20,000
Income before income taxes	$195,000
Estimated Income Taxes (20%)	$39,000
Net income	$156,000

Your Consultation

You are assuming the role of Ellie's personal accountant, Suzanne. What aspects of the income statement indicate Ellie's strong financial performance? Consider her sales revenue, cost of goods sold, operating expenses, and net profit. Also, what does Ellie's gross margin illustrate about her business? Explain each of your answers.

Notes

1 Kenneth M. Macur and Lyal Gustafson, "Financial Statements as a Management Tool," *Small Business Forum*, Fall 1992, 23–34. See also Robert Dove, "Financial Statements," *Accountancy*, January 2000, 7; and Michael Minnis, "The Value of Financial Statement Verification in Debt Financing: Evidence from Private U.S. Firms," *Journal of Accounting Research*, 2011, 49 (2): 457–506.
2 See Carl S. Warren, James M. Reeve, and Jonathan Duchac, *Accounting*, 26th ed. Mason, OH: Cengage/South-Western Publishers, 2016.
3 See Gary A. Porter and Curtis L. Norton, *Financial Accounting: The Impact on Decision Makers*, 10th ed. Mason, OH: Cengage/South-Western Publishers, 2017.
4 See "Financial Reporting Standard for Smaller Entities," *Accountancy*, January 1998, 81–109; and James M. Wahlen, Jefferson P. Jones, and Donald P. Pagach, *Intermediate Accounting: Reporting and Analysis*, 2nd ed. Mason, OH: Cengage/South-Western Publishers, 2016.
5 See Ervin Black, "Usefulness of Financial Statement Components in Valuation: An Examination of Start-Up and Growth Firms," *Venture Capital: An International Journal of Entrepreneurial Finance*, 2003, 5 (1): 47–69; and Mary E. Barth, "Including Estimates of the Future in Today's Financial Statements," *Accounting Horizons*, 2006, 20 (3): 271–285.
6 Jennifer Francis, "Have Financial Statements Lost Their Relevance?," *Journal of Accounting Research*, Autumn 1999, 37 (2): 319–353; see also John R. M. Hand, "The Value Relevance of Financial Statements in the Venture Capital Market," *The Accounting Review*, 2005, 80 (2): 613–648.
7 Daniel J. Power and Ramesh Sharda, "Model-Driven Decision Support Systems: Concepts and Research Directions," *Decision Support Systems*, 2007, 43 (3): 1044–1061; F. Robert Jacobs and F. C. Ted Weston, Jr., "Enterprise Resource Planning (ERP)—A Brief History," *Journal of Operations Management*, 2007, 25 (2): 357–363.
8 Muthu Ramachandran and Victor Chang, "Financial Software as a Service—A Paradigm for Risk Modelling and Analytics," *International Journal of Organizational and Collective Intelligence*, 2014, 4 (3): 65–89.

9 Financial Analysis

The Gauges

Introduction: Financial Statement Analysis

Analysis of financial statements involves the comparison of a business's performance with that of other businesses in the same industry.[1] This assists the new venture owner in identifying deficiencies and taking appropriate actions to improve performance. Financial statement analysis is useful both as a way to anticipate future conditions and, more importantly, as a starting point for planning actions that will influence the future course of events. The goal of any business is to correct its weaknesses and capitalize on its strengths. Financial statement analysis is a tool for accomplishing that goal from a financial perspective.[2]

The most effective way to examine financial statements is by *ratio analysis*. A ratio expresses a mathematical relationship between one item and another. In financial statement analysis, ratios are computed between various financial items. These ratios are merely indicators; any judgment regarding whether they are good or bad must be based on an understanding of what other firms in the industry are doing and how they are performing.[3] We will examine key ratios derived from the balance sheet and the income statement.

Balance Sheet Analysis

In Chapter 8, we examined the component parts of the balance sheet. In this chapter, we undertake an analysis of this financial statement. To do so, it is necessary to compare a company's balance sheets for at least two periods. We will use EntreX Corporation's balance sheets for 2020 and 2021 (Table 9.1). Their data are placed side by side in Table 9.1.

Many comparative methods are used to analyze balance sheets. However, since new venture owner-managers seldom need to use sophisticated techniques, we concentrate on two types of ratios useful for analyzing the balance sheet: Those reflecting the firm's current position and those reflecting its long-run position.

Current Position Ratios

A liquidity ratio indicates how easily an asset can be turned into cash (or is already in the form of cash). A business with a high liquidity ratio is referred to as "highly liquid." However, keep in mind that high or low liquidity is not by itself good or bad. Before judging how good a ratio is, we must look at the industry and see what is considered good for that particular type of business.

The company's current position is most commonly measured by three liquidity ratios:

1. Working capital
2. Current ratio
3. Acid test ratio

Table 9.1 EntreX Corporation Balance Sheet for the Years Ended December 31, 2020, and December 31, 2021

Assets	2020		2021	
Current Assets				
Cash		$125,000		$200,000
Accounts receivable	$400,000		$375,000	
Less: Allowance for uncollectible accounts	$40,000	$360,000	$25,000	$350,000
Inventory		$135,000		$150,000
Prepaid expenses		$50,000		$35,000
Total current assets		$670,000		$735,000
Fixed Assets				
Land		$315,000		$330,000
Building	$315,000		$315,000	
Less: Accumulated depreciation, building	$65,000	$250,000	$80,000	$235,000
Equipment	$420,000		$410,000	
Less: Accumulated depreciation, equipment	$30,000	$390,000	$60,000	$350,000
Total fixed assets		$955,000		$915,000
Total assets		$1,625,000		$1,650,000
Liabilities	2020		2021	
Current Liabilities				
Accounts payable		$245,000		$150,000
Notes payable		$50,000		$25,000

Liabilities	2020		2021	
Taxes payable	$100,000		$75,000	
Loan payable	$50,000		$50,000	
Total current liabilities		$445,000		$300,000
Long-Term Liabilities				
Bank loan		$250,000		$200,000
Total liabilities		$695,000		$500,000
Owners' Equity				
Contributed Capital				
Common stock, $10 par, 40,000 shares	$400,000		$400,000	
Preferred stock, $100 par, 500 shares authorized, none sold	--------		------	
Retained Earnings	$530,000		$750,000	
Total owners' equity		$930,000		$1,150,000
Total liabilities and owners' equity		$1,625,000		$1,650,000

Working Capital

A company's working capital is actually not a ratio, but it is a very important measure of current financial position. The calculation of working capital is as follows:

Current Assets–Current Liabilities

For EntreX Corporation (Table 9.1), here is the calculation:

	2020	2021
Total Current Assets	$670,000	$735,000
Total Current Liabilities	–445,000	–300,000
Working Capital	$225,000	$435,000

The company had $225,000 in working capital last year and $435,000 this year. This calculation shows that the firm has more than adequate capital to pay its short-term obligations. As a result, the business should have no trouble paying its bills as they come due.

Computing working capital is especially useful for determining a firm's short-term financial strength. Obviously, the company must have sufficient working capital to do business on a day-to-day basis. Inadequate working capital is often the first sign of financial difficulty for a firm.[4]

Current Ratio

The current ratio is simply the relationship between current assets and current liabilities. It is one of the best known and most commonly employed financial ratios. For EntreX Corporation, the ratio is computed this way:

	2020	2021
Total Current Assets	$670,000	$735,000
Total Current Liabilities	$445,000	$300,000
Current Ratio	**1.51**	**2.45**

The computation shows a substantial increase in the current ratio from 1.51:1 to 2.45:1. Is this good or bad? No hard and fast rules exist. However, a rule of thumb in recent years is that anything above 1.0:1 is satisfactory. But 2.0:1 or more is generally considered satisfactory for a manufacturing firm. For EntreX Corporation, the ratio has risen above the 2.0:1 level, so the ratio is much better than before. Keep in mind, however, that a current ratio can be too high. For example, if industry comparisons show that most firms in EntreX Corporation's industry have current ratios in the neighborhood of 2.2:1, then a 5:1 ratio would be excessive.

Acid Test Ratio

The acid test ratio, often referred to as the "quick ratio," is a measure of the firm's ability to convert its current assets quickly to cash for the purpose of meeting its current liabilities. To calculate the acid test ratio, it is first necessary to determine which assets are most rapidly convertible to cash. Aside from cash itself, accounts receivable (after allowing for uncollectible accounts) are included because they can usually be sold quickly to banks and finance companies. Noticeably absent, however, are inventory and prepaid expenses; neither of these is convertible to cash in the short run. The quick ratio for EntreX (Table 9.1) is calculated as follows:

	2020	2021
Current Assets (Less Inventory and Prepaid Expenses)	$485,000	$550,000
Current Liabilities	$445,000	$300,000
Acid Test Ratio	**1.09**	**1.83**

The trend from 2020 to 2021 is favorable. In fact, an acid test ratio of 1.0 is considered satisfactory because it indicates a company can easily pay all current liabilities within a short period.

Long-Run Position Ratios

Although owner-managers are always interested in their firms' short-run position, it is important to consider long-run stability.[5] Three balance sheet ratios reflect a company's long-run position:

1. Debt/asset ratio
2. Equity/asset ratio
3. Debt/equity ratio

Debt/Asset Ratio

The debt/asset ratio expresses the relationship between a company's total debt (liabilities) and total assets. This ratio tells the owner-manager how much of the firm's assets have been financed by debt and provides creditors with an indication of how much protection they have. If the ratio is very high, the firm does not have much equity: Most of the company's assets are provided by debt. In such a case, creditors might be wise to refuse the company any more credit. Remember, when a firm goes out of business, it usually cannot sell its assets for the dollar amount shown on the balance sheet. As a result, the total amount the creditors and owners receive is less than the amount of their claims on the balance sheet. However, the creditors have first claim to the assets, and sometimes nothing is left for the stockholders. The creditors' question is, does the firm have enough equity to prevent our having to settle for less than what is truly owed us? The lower the debt/equity ratio, the more likely the creditors will get their money back. For EntreX Corporation, here is the debt/equity ratio:

	2020	2021
Total Liabilities	$695,000	$500,000
Total Assets	$1,625,000	$1,625,000
Debt/Asset Ratio	**42.8%**	**30.3%**

As shown, the ratio has been reduced from 42.8 to 30.3 percent between 2020 and 2021. The creditors of the corporation have a greater degree of protection than before.

Equity/Asset Ratio

The equity/asset ratio is computed by dividing the owners' equity by the total assets. It is the complement of the debt/asset ratio; that is, if the debt/asset ratio were 45 percent, the equity/asset ratio would be 55 percent. The equity/asset ratio is of particular interest to investors because it indicates the percentage of total assets the owners can claim. A very low equity/asset ratio is an indication that in the event of financial difficulties, the owners may receive little, if any, of their original investment. For example, if an equity/asset ratio is ten percent, it means that ten percent of the assets are owners' equity and 90 percent is due to debt. In case of dissolution, creditors would be entitled to so much of the firm's assets that nothing would be left for the owners after the debt was paid. Theoretically, then, the higher the equity/asset ratio, the more advantageous it is for the owners (and for the creditors).

The equity/asset ratio for EntreX Corporation is as follows:

	2020	2021
Total Owners' Equity	$930,000	$1,150,000
Total Assets	$1,615,000	$1,650,000
Equity/Asset Ratio	**57.2%**	**69.7%**

Before we continue, one point merits our attention. It is *not* always advantageous to the firm to have the highest equity/asset ratio. Many times, it is good business for the firm to borrow some money. This is particularly true when the rate of interest is less than the return the owners can generate with the funds. For example, if it costs 15 percent to borrow money from the bank, but the business can make 28 percent on this money, then borrowing is indeed wise. The important point is not to borrow *too much*. If the business does make 28 percent, it can put some of the profits back into the firm. The natural inclination is to make money on someone else's funds and not tie up one's own funds. However, sooner or later the business may grow large and accumulate so much debt that a slowdown in the economy could drastically affect its ability to meet debt obligations. For this reason, debts must be undertaken prudently. Too little debt may deny the firm a source of funds for increasing profits. Too much debt can be overburdening. By consulting industry statistics, the company can get an idea of a desirable ballpark equity/asset ratio.

Debt/Equity Ratio

This ratio expresses the relationship between liabilities and owners' equity. A very high debt/equity ratio indicates to creditors they are financing most of the business's operations. It also indicates to the owners their claim in the business is small.

For EntreX Corporation, the debt/equity ratio is calculated as follows:

	2020	2021
Total Liabilities	$695,000	$500,000
Total Owners' Equity	$930,000	$1,150,000
Debt/Equity Ratio	**74.7%**	**43.5%**

This comparison indicates that debt, as a percentage of equity, is declining. The firm's operations are increasingly financed through owners' equity. This, of course, is a direct result of plowing net profits back into retained earnings. In 2021, the net profit was $258,000, as noted in Table 9.2. As shown in the preceding calculation, owners' equity increased by this amount, while total liabilities decreased. This trend should be viewed positively by both the owners of EntreX and its creditors.

Income Statement Analysis

As with the balance sheet, financial ratios can be used to analyze the income statement. Some of these use data from the income statement exclusively. Others, known as combination ratios, draw on data from the balance sheet and the income statement. Both types of ratio analyses are useful for evaluating a new venture's income and profitability performance. To best interpret financial ratios, it is good to research what the industry standards are for your type of business. In general, research has shown that there are no significant differences in liquidity ratios between large and small firms.[6] We will use EntreX Corporation's income statements for 2020 and 2021 in our analysis (Table 9.2).

Table 9.2 EntreX Corporation Income Statement for the Years Ended December 31, 2020, and December 31, 2021

	2020		*2021*	
Sales Revenue	$1,565.000		$1,750,000	
Less: Sales returns and allowances	$65,000		$50,000	
Net sales		$1,500,000		$1,700,000
Cost of Goods Sold				
Less inventory, January 1	$135,000	$150,000		
Purchases	$1,000,000		$1,050,000	
Goods available for sale	$1,135,000		$1,200,000	
Less inventory, December 31	$150,000		$200,000	
Cost of goods sold		$985,000		$1,000,000
Gross margin		$515,000		$700,000
Operating Expenses				
Selling expenses	$125,000		$150,000	
Administrative expenses	$95,000		$100,000	
Total operating expenses		$220,000		$250,000
Operating income		$295,000		$450,000
Financial Expenses		$20,000		$20,000
Income before income taxes		$275,000		$430,000
Estimated Income Taxes		$125,000		$172,000
Net profit		$150,000		$258,000

Income Statement Ratios

Balance sheet ratios provide indicators of short-run and long-run financial stability. Income statement ratios provide information on current operating performance and efficiency. Two of the most important are the operating expense ratio and the number of times interest earned ratio.

Operating Expense Ratio

Operating expenses are expenses incurred in the normal day-to-day running of the business. They include selling and administrative expenses but not interest expenses or income tax expenses. The operating expense ratio is calculated by dividing total operating expenses by net sales.

In 2020 and 2021, EntreX Corporation's operating expense ratio is calculated this way:

	2020	2021
Total Operating Expenses	$220,000	$250,000
Net Sales	$1,500,000	$1,700,000
Operating Expense Ratio	**14.7%**	**14.7%**

The ratio has remained the same for both years. Selling and administrative expenses are up almost 14 percent, but so are net sales. This is a good sign; it shows the firm is keeping operating expenses under control.

Number of Times Interest Earned Ratio

A second indicator of financial stability is the number of times interest is earned on long-term debt. This appears on the income statement as a financial expense. If a firm can just barely meet this expense, it may be in financial difficulty. Conversely, a business that can meet this financial expense easily is probably in sound financial condition. The number of times interest earned ratio is computed by dividing *operating income* (income before financial expenses and income taxes) by annual financial expenses.

For EntreX Corporation, that calculation is as follows:

	2020	2021
Operating Income	$295,000	$450,000
Annual Financial Expenses	$20,000	$20,000
Number of Times Interest Earned	**14.7 ×**	**22.5 ×**

The ratio is very high for both 2020 and 2021. The firm should have no trouble paying its interest on the bank loan.

If EntreX Corporation wanted to be more conservative, as some owner-managers do, it could deduct income tax from operating income before dividing by annual financial expenses. In this case, the calculation would be as follows:

	2020	2021
Operating Income	$170,000	$278,000
Annual Financial Expenses	$20,000	$20,000
Number of Times Interest Earned	**8.5 ×**	**13.9 ×**

The number of times interest is earned is now lower, but it is still more than adequate. What really counts, however, is the trend from year to year. In the preceding calculations, the trend is upward. As long as the ratio does not drop drastically, EntreX should be able to more than meet its interest payments.

Combination Ratios

As mentioned earlier, some ratios show the relationship between items on the income statement and the balance sheet, four of the most common of which are:

1. Inventory turnover
2. Accounts receivable turnover
3. Rate of return on total assets
4. Rate of return on equity

Inventory Turnover

Inventory turnover, simply put, is the number of times, on average, inventory is replaced during the year. A low inventory turnover indicates that goods are not selling very well; they are remaining on the shelf in the warehouse for extended periods. If already paid for, inventory represents tied-up money that is not providing any return to the business. If inventory was obtained on consignment, the firm can send back whatever it does not sell, but it must pay the storage bill as long as the goods are on hand. Of course, a very high turnover also may not be good, for it can indicate the firm is continually running out of items and having to turn customers away. As a result, most companies want a turnover that is neither too low nor too high.

To compute turnover, cost of goods sold is divided by the average inventory. Ideally, average inventory is computed by adding the beginning inventory of each month, from January of one year through January of the next, and dividing by 13. This assures no bias occurs due to the traditionally lower inventory figures at the end of the calendar year. However, it is much easier to simply take the beginning inventory for the year, add it to the ending inventory, and divide by two. This gives an average that is satisfactory for most purposes. In addition, once the turnover is determined, it is possible to calculate the average number of days to turn over, thereby providing the manager with a detailed view of the inventory picture.

For EntreX Corporation, the place to start is with a computation of the average inventory for both 2020 and 2021 (Table 9.2). The calculations look like this:

$$\text{Average Inventory} = \frac{\text{Beginning Inventory} + \text{Ending Inventory}}{2}$$

$$\text{For } 2020: \frac{\$135,000 + \$150,000}{2} = \$142,500$$

$$\text{For } 2021: \frac{\$150,000 + \$200,000}{2} = \$175,000$$

The number of times the inventory turned over is then calculated using these values. The average number of days to turn over is obtained by dividing the number of days in a year by inventory turnover. These calculations look like this:

	2020	2021
Cost of Goods Sold	$985,000	$1,000,000
Average Inventory	$142,000	$175,000
Days in a Year	365 days	365 days
Inventory Turnover	6.91	5.71
Average Number of Days to Turn Over	**53 days**	**64 days**

These calculations indicate an unfavorable trend. In 2020, EntreX's inventory turnover was 6.91, while in 2021 it dropped off to 5.71. Additionally, in 2020 it took 53 days to turn over the inventory, while in 2021 it took 64 days. The time needed to turn over the inventory is lengthening.

What accounts for this increase? The calculations do not, in and of themselves, provide the answer. Perhaps, to increase its sales, the firm has been forced to carry more slow-moving items. That would increase inventory and result in a lower turnover. In such an instance, the decrease in turnover would not be a very negative factor. However, if the firm simply has been buying more goods in anticipation of higher sales, it should now reduce purchases and maintain lower inventories.

Accounts Receivable Turnover

The analysis of accounts receivable is similar to that of inventory turnover. It is a measure of how rapidly accounts receivable are collected. In general terms, the higher this turnover, the better. A low turnover is usually regarded as unfavorable for two reasons: The interest expense in maintaining receivables is increasing and an abnormally high number of these receivables may become uncollectible.

The accounts receivable turnover is computed by dividing net sales on credit by average accounts receivable. Since we have no data for EntreX Corporation for 2019, we will use the accounts receivable for 2020 (Table 9.1) and assume that the beginning and ending receivables were the same. This gives us an average of $360,000. In addition, for 2021 (Table 9.1), the average receivables are figured this way:

$$\frac{\$360,000 + \$350,000}{2} = \$355,000$$

The calculations from here are as follows:

	2020	2021
Net Sales	$1,500,000	$1,700,000
Average Accounts Receivable	$360,000	$355,000
Days in a Year	365 days	365 days
Accounts Receivable Turnover	4.2	4.8
Average Age of Accounts Receivable	**86.9 days**	**76.0 days**

Overall, the trend for EntreX Corporation is favorable. Turnover has risen from 4.2 to 4.8 times, and the average number of days from sale to collection has declined from 86.9 to 76.

Many times, as a company's sales increase, its accounts receivable also increase, but the turnover of the receivables declines. This is often occasioned by a lenient credit policy that allows poor-risk customers to buy on credit. Such customers tend to purchase up to their credit limit and then fall behind in their payments. As a result, although sales are up, so are receivables, and the chance of collecting all of these accounts is very small. More and more must be written off as uncollectible. At EntreX Corporation, this has not happened.

Rate of Operating Return on Total Assets

In addition to knowing the net income of the company, the owner-manager needs to know the rate of return the business is earning on its assets. The greater the amount of assets, the more income the firm should earn. In short, by comparing operating income and average assets, owner-managers can find out how well the firm has performed with its available resources. This ratio is known as the *rate of return on total assets* and is computed by dividing operating income by average assets.

Table 9.1 shows that EntreX's average assets for 2021 were $1,637,500 [($1,625,000 + $1,650,000)/2]. We do not know its average assets for 2020 because we do not have 2019 figures. However, assume the assets between 2019 and 2020 have remained the same, giving an average of $1,625,000. The rate of return on total assets can then be computed as follows:

	2020	2021
Operating Income	$295,000	$450,000
Average Assets	$1,625,000	$1,650,000
Rate of Return on Total Assets	**18.2%**	**27.3%**

This return is very good: 18.2 percent is far higher than what could have been obtained if the money had been invested in a bank note or simply left in a savings account. It is also a higher return than the ten percent the firm is currently paying on its bank loan. In short, the company is making a fine return. In 2021, this return was 50 percent higher than in 2020, which indicates even better performance.

Rate of Return on Equity

Although the rate of return on total assets discloses how well management is performing with the resources available, the new venture owner is also interested in how this translates in terms of his or her own investment. This can be determined by a simple calculation of the rate of return on (common stockholders') equity: The net income is divided by the owners' equity.

This computation for EntreX Corporation is as follows:

	2020	2021
Net Income	$150,000	$258,000
Common Stockholders' Equity	$400,000	$400,000
Rate of Return on Equity	**37.5%**	**64.5%**

EntreX's rate of return on equity is extremely high. The owners earned a return of 37.5 percent in 2020 and 64.5 percent in 2021. Of course, it is important to analyze why EntreX has performed so remarkably. If everyone else in the industry did as well, the conclusion would have to be tempered accordingly. If everyone else did poorly, then the owner-manager would want to investigate what makes EntreX so successful. In either event, an industry comparison would be very helpful.

New Venture Issues

"The Z-Score"

Edward I. Altman, author and professor at New York University, was the first to suggest using statistics as indicators for business failure. Almost 40 years ago, Altman developed Z-score analysis as a technique to help determine the likelihood of a company's going bankrupt. The tool was devised and refined after studying 66 companies: 33 control firms and 33 experiment firms. The test can be used internally to assess financial health and externally by investors to judge the stability of on investment. Since its original introduction, Dr. Altman has introduced the "Z-Score Plus." The original Z-score was focused on U.S.-based manufacturing firms, while the Z-Score Plus can be used with both U.S.-based and internationally based firms, along with both non-manufacturing and manufacturing firms, among other improvements.

Plugging numbers from the financial statements into the five formulas and then multiplying by the predetermined weight factor will result in a ratio. When the five ratios are added, a number between −4 and +8 will indicate the company's "fiscal fitness."

Ratio	Formula	Weight Factor	Weighted Ratio
Return on Total Assets	Earnings Before Interest and Taxes/Total Assets	× 3.3	
Sales to Total Assets	Net Sales/Total Assets	× 0.999	
Equity to Debt	Market Value of Equity/Total Liabilities	× 0.6	
Working Capital to Total Assets	Working Capital/Total Assets	× 1.2	

Ratio	Formula	Weight Factor	Weighted Ratio
Retained Earnings to Total Assets	Retained Earnings/Total Assets	× 1.4	
		Z-score	

Z-score above 2.99—you're in good shape
Between 2.99 and 1.81—warning sign
Below 1.81—could be heading toward bankruptcy

Source: Adapted from: Z-Score Calculator. Gateway Commercial Finance, https://gatewaycfs.com/bff/z-score-calculator; Experience Stern: Faculty & Research, January 24, 2012, www.stern.nyu.edu/experience-stern/faculty-research/altman-launches-zscore-plus; and Altman Z-Score Mobile App: Bond Rating Equivalent: PD: Credit Rating Web App, https://altmanzscoreplus.com/primer.

Limitations of Financial Statement Analysis

Until now, we have been concerned with the various ways of analyzing financial statements. However, we need to moderate our remarks with some comments on the limitations of financial statement analysis for comparing companies.[7] Accounting experts have stated such limitations this way:

1. Companies may have differing year ends, which could cause a different composition of assets, particularly current assets. For example, one company may choose to operate on a fiscal year that comes at a low point in its production. This causes its inventory to be at an exceptionally low level, while its cash, marketable securities, and accounts receivable are unusually high. Another company, selecting a point for its fiscal year when accounts receivable are low, finds its inventory and cash positions at a high point. Of course, these problems, although confounding comparisons among companies, are of no importance when the ratios for a company are compared against themselves over a period because the firm will always be at either a low inventory level or a low receivable level at that time of year.

2. Companies may have acquired their property, plant, and equipment in differing years. Because the accountant follows a stable dollar approach to financial reporting, periods of inflation between the times two companies acquire assets may result in vast dollar differences between the amounts shown for two assets that serve the same purpose. Again, comparisons of one company's results over time are affected only mildly by this condition.

3. Companies may account for the same items using alternative accounting methods.

4. Industry patterns cause significant differences among companies in terms of the amount and the relationship of a particular item to the total. For example, a company that takes more than a year to manufacture a particular machine, such

as a printing press, tends to have a large inventory balance when compared to a company merely selling purchased items, such as a grocery store selling produce.

These limitations illustrate that, whereas the owner-manager can compare his or her own firm's financial statements from one year to the next to determine improvements or problems, care must be exercised in making comparisons with other firms. It is necessary to ensure that the firms chosen for comparison are indeed similar; that is, they should sell the same types of goods and services, be about the same financial size, and operate under similar economic conditions.[8]

Financial Budgeting

Budgets are plans as well as control tools. As plans, they pinpoint objectives the new venture wants to attain in areas such as sales, product line growth, number of personnel, and expenses. In each case, the owner-manager sets a target, such as sales of $230,000, 11 percent growth of product line A, and increasing the number of personnel by two employees. The individual can then incorporate these objectives into the financial budgeting process by asking what the firm must do to attain them. One answer might be that it must increase sales by 25 percent. If the business can do that, the other objectives will be attained in the process.

However, without covering a long list of the objectives a new venture might have, let us look at the two most valuable types of financial budgeting: Sales budgets and cash budgets. Then we will examine some other budgetary considerations.

Sales Budget

The sales budget is the primary budget for the new venture; once it is worked out, all of the other budgets flow from it. For example, if the owner-manager believes sales next year will be $400,000, the business will want to stock inventory, hire personnel, and put together a marketing strategy based on this objective. Of course, the owner-manager needs more information than just the total sales figure. It is necessary to break down the dollar amount by month or quarter so that all of the other budgets can be tied to the particular time of year. For example, if half the sales are expected during the first three months of the year, half of the production should be finished and ready for shipping during (or soon after) that period. Likewise, greater cash and personnel demands on the business will occur during that quarter of the year than during any other.

By linking the other budgets to sales, the owner-manager can adjust expenditures up or down depending on the status of operations. If sales are greater than expected, production can be raised and the number of personnel can be increased. Conversely, if sales are slower, production can be halted temporarily and some employees can be released.

How closely should everything be tied to sales? This depends on the size of the business. If the organization has sufficient capital to ride out a sluggish six months, the owner-manager need not be as concerned as if the firm were living hand to mouth and could not afford any financial setback. Depending on how closely operations must be monitored, the firm can control them on a weekly or biweekly basis or let them go as long as three to six months.

Cash Budget

Cash budgeting is vital to new venture survival.[9] At the heart of the cash budgeting process is *cash planning*. Cash planning requirements for a new venture are of two types: The daily and weekly cash needs for the normal operation of the business and the maintenance expenses of the organization during this period. The first relates to cash on hand for day-to-day operations. Usually, the business estimates its needs for a 30- to 60-day period and then determines how much money it is likely to collect during this time. If a cash shortage is anticipated after comparing the inflows and outflows, then a line of credit or a short-term loan can be arranged.

The maintenance part of this budget takes into account expenses such as insurance, rent, payroll, purchases, services, and taxes. This long-run view of operations provides the firm the opportunity to balance its annual cash needs. Figure 9.1 provides a sample cash budget form that can be used to accomplish both operational and maintenance objectives.

The first four lines in Figure 9.1 help determine the amount of cash that will be collected over the next three months. The *collection on accounts receivable* (line 2) is especially important and warrants discussion. Remember that many new ventures sell on credit. And although these obligations may be due within 30 days, some people wait 60 to 90 days, and others never pay. How much will be collected each month? In answering this question, the owner-manager needs to examine past collections. For the purposes of this discussion, however, assume the business's records show that half of all sales are made for cash and the other half are paid within 90 days. Of this latter amount, 70 percent are collected the first month, 20 percent the second, and eight percent the third, and the remaining two percent are written off as uncollectible. Additionally, assume sales were $8,000 in October, $10,000 in November, and $16,000 in December, so 50 percent of these sales will be estimated as cash sales for January through March. Using these data, the owner-manager can determine both cash and accounts receivable collections. Table 9.3 shows these calculations.

Lines 5 through 12 in Figure 9.1 take into account items for which the firm pays cash. Some of these outflows, such as administrative expense and repayment of loans, will remain basically the same. Others will rise or fall depending on the activity level. For example, as production goes up, payroll and raw material expenses will go up; the reverse is also true.

Lines 14 through 19 of Figure 9.1 involve balancing the cash account, along with a determination of any short-term loans that will be needed and the amount of cash, if any, that will be available for dividends and short-term investments. Lines 21 and 22 help the firm compare desired cash with actual cash to see how much is available for capital investment.

CASH BUDGET
(for 3 months ending March 31, 2021)

	January		February		March	
	Budget	Actual	Budget	Actual	Budget	Actual
EXPECTED CASH RECEIPTS						
1. Cash sales						
2. Collection on accounts receivable						
3. Other income						
4. Total cash receipts						
EXPECTED CASH PAYMENTS						
5. Raw materials						
6. Payroll						
7. Other factory expenses (including maintenance)						
8. Advertising						
9. Selling expense						
10. Administration expense (including salary of owner-management)						
11. New plant and equipment						
12. Other payments (taxes, including estimated income tax, repayment of loans, and interest						
13. Total cash payments						
14. Expected cash balance at beginning of the month						
15. Cash increase or decrease (item 4 minus item 13)						
16. Expected cash balance at end of month (item 14 plus item 15)						
17. Desired working cash balance						
18. Short-term loans needed (item 17 minus item 16, if item 17 is larger than item 16)						
19. Cash available for dividends, capital cash expenditures, and/or short-term investments (item 16 minus item 17, if item 16 is larger than item 17)						
CAPITAL CASH						
20. Cash available (item 19 after deducting dividends, etc.)						
21. Desired capital cash (item 11, new plant and equipment)						
22. Long-term loans needed (item 21 minus item 20, if item 21 is larger than item 20)						

Figure 9.1 Cash Budget Form

Source: J.H. Feller, Jr. Small Business Administration, *Is your Cash Supply Adequate?* (Washington, DC: U.S. Government Printing Office).
Management Aids, No. 174

Other Budgetary Considerations

Sales and cash budgets are not the only ones a new venture needs for controlling its operations. Others are actually spin-offs of items on the cash budget form (Figure 9.1), including payroll, advertising, selling expense, and new plant and equipment budgets.[10] Depending on the size of the firm, these budgetary categories will be handled through the cash budget or broken out and given special consideration. For example, a manufacturing operation may have a manufacturing and purchasing budget, while a sales business may have a selling expense budget. However, since the new venture will not want to overburden itself with budgets, it should have as few as possible.

Table 9.3 Cash and Accounts Receivable Collection Calculations

Month	Cash Sales	70% of Receivables 30 Days Old +	20% of Receivables 60 Days Old +	8% of Receivables 90 Days Old =	Total Collected on Accounts Receivable
January	$4,000	$5,600	$1,000	$320	$6,920
February	$5,000	$2,600	$1,600	$400	$4,800
March	$6,000	$2,800	$800	$640	$4,940

Note: The accounts receivable collection constitutes a flow of cash into the firm. By tracking its flow on a monthly basis, the owner can determine the amount of cash the business will have for operations.

As a result, the astute owner-manager uses the exception principle of control for handling budgetary problems. This principle holds that the owner-manager should be concerned with results that are extremely good or extremely bad, not with operations that go as expected. If sales for January are forecasted at $8,000 and instead are $8,200, the firm has little need for concern. However, if they are $15,000, the owner-manager should be concerned about filling the orders (if it is a manufacturing firm) or purchasing more materials or products (if it is a retail or wholesale operation). Likewise, sales of only $4,000 would be a sufficient deviation to warrant making some changes in the next month's budget by curtailing purchases, laying off some people, or taking other actions.

The most important fact to remember is that budgetary controls must be kept in their proper perspective. They are tools that help the business set goals and evaluate performance. If problems occur, budgets should help the owner-manager pinpoint where and why they arose. For this reason, every budget should possess two characteristics: Economy and timeliness. If the budget is too cumbersome or detailed, it may take $1 of effort to pinpoint a 50¢ problem. The budget must be worth its cost. Also, the budget should be timely; it should allow the owner-manager to collect, analyze, and interpret information in time to take required action.

If the company runs on a fixed three-month budget but is subject to widely varying sales fluctuations, it may be out of cash before the budget period is over. In this case, the firm needs to budget for shorter periods—that is, a month at a time. Finally, remember that in most cases the owner-manager can rely on one or two budgets, such as the sales and cash budgets, and can assume that if these are in line, then everything else is okay. Generally, the owner-manager will be right.

A Global Perspective

"Budgeting for International Expansion"

International expansion creates the risk of additional expenses that need to be considered when making budgeting decisions.

Depending on the nature of the business and how it conducts transactions, fluctuating exchange rates have the potential to impact the value of transactions. Exchange rates change on a continual basis on open exchange markets, and depending on the economic stability of the countries involved, the exchange rate can be volatile. Between the United States and the European Union, in 2018, the rate of exchange for U.S. dollars to euros included a high of 1.25 U.S. dollars for 1 euro and a low of 1.18 U.S. dollars for 1 euro, a fall of 5.6 percent. That would make a U.S.-based business's products more expensive relative to local competitors for a customer based in the EU if the EU customer is paying for the product in U.S. dollars. However, the value of Indian rupees increased in value over 17 percent relative to the U.S. dollar over a period in 2018, making items bought by Indian customers in U.S. dollars less expensive relative to local competitors.

Another area of financial risk is taxation. Tax laws vary from country to country and place a variety of requirements on businesses operating internationally. Even if a business is based in one country, providing products or services abroad could create a taxable presence in a foreign country. Consulting a tax professional is a good first step to understanding local legal requirements.

Other sources of potential financial risk may be less obvious. Differing laws internationally related to termination of employees can create obligations for businesses when managing their international workforces. In one case, misunderstanding French labor law cost a U.S. company 180,000 U.S. dollars in damages for not following all the appropriate steps to terminate an employee accused of misconduct.

Unexpected expenses are an inevitable part of expanding a business internationally. The key to success is understanding the sources of financial risk and budgeting for them appropriately.

Source: Adapted from Linsey Knerl, "Budgeting for International Expansion," Master Card, August 5, 2019, www.mastercardbiz.com/2019/08/05/knowing-the-costs-budgeting-for-international-expansion/; Market Turmoil Cascades Through Currencies. *The Wall Street Journal*, https://www.wsj.com/articles/market-turmoil-cascades-through-currencies-11583739387; and Larry Harding, "Uncovering the Hidden Costs of Global Expansion," *Forbes*, March 4, 2015, www.forbes.com/sites/groupthink/2015/03/04/uncovering-the-hidden-costs-of-global-expansion/#5a3a409837d3.

Summary

One of the most effective control techniques for new ventures is financial analysis. The balance sheet provides the owner-manager with the opportunity to examine the current state of the firm's assets and liabilities and the owners' equity. Some of the most useful ratios in this examination are working capital, current ratio, acid test ratio, debt/asset ratio, equity/asset ratio, and debt/equity ratio.

The income statement can also be examined using ratio analysis. Two of the most common metrics are the operating expense ratio and the number of times interest earned ratio.

Some useful combination ratios draw on data from both the balance sheet and the income statement. Four of the most common ratios are inventory turnover, accounts receivable turnover, rate of return on total assets, and rate of return on equity.

The budget is another useful financial analysis tool. New ventures must be careful not to have too many budgets, for the paperwork is time-consuming. By relying on a couple—such as the sales budget and cash budget—the new venture can maintain effective budgetary control. For handling budgetary problems, the astute owner-manager uses the exception principle of control. In this way, he or she concentrates on major developments and not on minor problems.

Review and Discussion Questions

1. How does a business compute its working capital? Give an example.
2. What does the current ratio tell the owner-manager? Also, what is a *good* current ratio?
3. Explain how the acid test ratio differs from the current ratio.
4. Why would the owner-manager be interested in the debt/asset ratio? Equity/asset ratio? Be sure to explain in your answer what each ratio tells the owner-manager.
5. Which ratio is of greater interest to the owner-manager, the operating expense or the number of times interest earned? Support your answer.
6. How is inventory turnover computed? What does it tell the owner-manager?
7. How is accounts receivable turnover computed? What does this calculation tell the owner-manager?
8. Which ratio is of greater interest to the owner-manager, the rate of return on total assets or the rate of return on equity? Support your answer.
9. List and explain three of the limitations of financial analysis.
10. How does a sales budget work?
11. How does the cash budget help the owner-manager control operations? Include a description of this budget in your answer.
12. Explain the value of the exception principle of control to the owner-manager.

The Venture Consultant

"A Case of Liquidity"

Mark Orland, Kizdar Brewing Company Chief Financial Officer, prepared a balance sheet that compared the operating years of 2020 and 2021 and gave it to Jeff Kizdar, the Chief Executive Officer (see balance sheet below).

Mark and Jeff had been in business together for seven years and would meet at year end about the strength of the company's financial statements. As it was December 31, the two executives mingled jovially about the balance sheet's improved composition at the end of 2021. Overhearing the positive conversation and knowing about Mark and Jeff's annual meeting, Chief Operating Officer Anne Marie entered the room and commented, "I'm guessing the year went well?"

Jeff motioned Anne Marie into the room and began showing her the balance sheet. He pointed out that the company's liquidity had improved substantially, equity ownership had risen, and the company was able to pay off a substantial part of its debt—all encouraging events. However, Jeff could see Anne Marie was perplexed by parts of the conversation and wanted to help. He motioned to Mark, saying, "Mark, would you mind explaining to Anne Marie why and how our balance sheet improved so much in 2019? I would start by explaining the financial ratios." Mark agreed to give Anne Marie a brief introduction to balance sheet ratios.

Your Consultation

Using the following statements, what ratios should Mark explain to Anne Marie? Highlight three important ratios and explain why they are important. How has Kizdar Brewing Company's liquidity changed from 2020 to 2021? Explain the importance of liquidity ratios and how the change has affected the company's balance sheet. Be specific in your evaluation.

Kizdar Brewing Company
Balance Sheet Ending December 31, 2020 and December 31, 2021

Assets		2020		2021
Current Assets				
Cash		$45,000		$60,000
	$150,00		$180,00	
Accounts Receivable	0		0	
Less: Allowance for uncollectable				
accounts	10,000	140,000	12,000	168,000
Inventory		35,000		25,000
Prepaid expenses		7,000		6,000
Total current assets		$227,000		$259,000
Fixed Assets				
Gross Plant, Property and				
Equipment	150,000		160,000	
Less: Accumulated Depreciation	45,000	105,000	51,000	109,000
Total Assets		332,000		368,000

Liabilities	2020	2021
Current Liabilities		
Accounts Payable	$51,000	$25,000
Notes Payable	10,000	15,000
Taxes Payable	5,000	0
Loan Payable	15,000	10,000
Total Current Liabilities	81,000	50,000
Long Term Liabilities		
Bank Loans	125,000	95,000
Total Liabilities	206,000	145,000

Shareholders' Equity	2020	2021
Common Stock: 25,000 shares @ $2 Par		
value	50,000	50,000
Retained earnings	76,000	183,000
Total owners' equity	126,000	223,000
Total Liabilities and equity	332,000	368,000

Notes

1 James M. Whalen, Stephen P. Baginski, and Mark Bradshaw, *Financial Reporting, Financial Statement Analysis and Valuation*, 8th ed. Mason, OH: Cengage/South-Western Publishing, 2015.
2 Christine Post-Duncan, "The Manager's Guide to Financial Statement Analysis," *The National Public Accountant*, November 1999, 30; see also Doron Nissim and Stephen H. Penman, "Financial Statement Analysis of Leverage and How It Informs about Profitability and Price-to-Book Ratios," *Review of Accounting Studies*, 2003, 8 (4): 531–560.
3 See Doron Nissim and Stephen H. Penman, "Ratio Analysis and Equity Valuation: From Research to Practice," *Review of Accounting Studies*, 2001, 6 (1): 109–154.
4 See Patricia Lee Huff, "Are There Differences in Liquidity and Solvency Measures Based on Company Size?," *American Business Review*, June 1999, 96–107; see also Ram Mudambi and Monica Zimmerman Treichel, "Cash Crisis in Newly Public Internet-Based Firms: An Empirical Analysis," *Journal of Business Venturing*, July 2005, 20 (4): 543–571.
5 See Robert Hitchings, "Ratio Analysis as a Tool in Credit Assessment," *Commercial Lending Review*, Summer 1999, 45–49; see also Nissim and Penman, "Financial Statement Analysis of Leverage and How It Informs about Profitability and Price-to-Book Ratios."
6 J. Constand Osteryoung, Richard L. Constand, and Donald Nast, "Financial Ratios in Large Public and Small Private Firms," *Journal of Small Business Management*, July 1992, 35–46; see also Patricia M. Fairfield and Teri Lombardi Yohn, "Using Asset Turnover and Profit Margin to Forecast Changes in Profitability," *Review of Accounting Studies*, 2001, 6 (4): 371–385.
7 For example, see Eugene E. Comiskey, "Analyzing Small Company Financial Statements: Some Guidance for Lenders," *Commercial Lending Review*, Summer 1998, 30–43; and E. H. Feroz, S. Kim, and R. L. Raab, "Financial Statement Analysis: A Data Envelopment Analysis Approach," *Journal of the Operational Research Society*, 2003, 54 (1): 48–58.
8 For an interesting discussion, see Patricia Lee Huff, "Should You Consider Company Size When Making Ratio Comparisons?," *National Public Accountant*, February/March 2000, 8–12.
9 See Whalen, Baginski, and Bradshaw, *Financial Reporting*.
10 See, for example, Christine Post-Duncan, "The Manager's Guide to Financial Statement Analysis," *National Public Accountant*, November 1999, 30; and Michael Minnis, 2011. The Value of Financial Statement Verification in Debt Financing: Evidence from Private U.S. Firms, Journal of Accounting Research, 49 (2): 457–506.

Part IV

New Venture Growth

10 HR and the Development of Teams

The People

Introduction: The Challenge of Managing Human Resources

Diversity, globalization, deregulation, technological advancements, and the "millennial" nature of the younger segment of the workforce are changing the nature of jobs and work.[1] For instance, a pronounced shift from manufacturing jobs to service jobs has occurred in both North America and Western Europe. Today more than two-thirds of the U.S. workforce is employed in producing and delivering services, not products. At the end of 2019, 99 percent of all businesses were small businesses (under 500 employees) and accounted for 47.3 percent of the private sector workforce.[2] The majority of these jobs (approximately 80 percent) were in the service sector. These service jobs, in turn, require new types of "knowledge" workers, new human resource management methods to manage them, and a new focus on human resources.[3] It is important to note that the COVID-19 pandemic will impact these numbers, causing an initial decrease in the number of small businesses that have been severely impacted by forced closures and disruptions in business operations. Additionally, this disruption will also impact human resource management practices, especially as more employees work remotely, people with disabilities are more greatly impacted, and increased safety precautions are required.

Smaller firms also generate nearly 65 percent of the new jobs in the private sector and employ 43 percent of high-tech workers.[4] However, most of the research and literature in human resource management have tended to focus on larger, more established companies. Most human resource management books assume that a firm has at least one human resource professional in place who has the expertise and competence to understand and carry out the practices they describe in their publications. While most new firms and smaller ventures aspire to grow into larger firms, focus is needed to provide guidance on effectively dealing with human resource issues as they emerge, whether it is a fledgling company or one that must deal with challenges presented by larger employee groups. In support of this argument, a study of young entrepreneurs found that HR topics ranked highest among areas for needed learning.[5] Also, another research study of 323 smaller firms showed that superior human resource decisions based on a "family-like" work environment lead to higher organizational performance.[6] Similar results have been found in Australia and the UK.[7]

These rapid changes in the work environment have major implications for human resource management, including a need for more awareness and appreciation of differing cultural backgrounds in recruitment, selection, and promotion.[8] Also, the low supply of skilled and experienced labor directly affects small business survival. Small business owners must rise to this challenge. Employees in smaller firms are sometimes the difference between success and failure. Human resource responsibilities for smaller businesses are just as great as they are for larger firms, but duties are not delegated as easily. Table 10.1 illustrates the positions and responsibilities for human resource management in smaller firms versus larger corporations.

Table 10.1 Responsibilities for Human Resource Management in a Small Company Versus a Large Corporation

Small Company		Large Corporation	
Position	*Responsibilities*	*Position*	*Responsibilities*
Human Resources Director	Grievances Human resource planning Labor relations Managerial/ professional compensation Recruiting	Vice President, Human Resources	Executive committee Human resource planning Organization planning Policy development
Assistant Human Resources Director	Interviewing Orientation Reassignments Recruiting Safety and health Special programs Terminations Training Wage and salary administration	Director, Recruitment and Employment Director, Compensation and Benefits	Interviewing Placement Recruiting Terminations Testing Bonuses, profit sharing plans Compensation administration Employee benefits Job analyses and evaluation Performance appraisals Surveys
Personnel Assistant	Employee benefits Employee services Interviewing Job descriptions Job evaluation Suggestion plan Testing Training	Director, Labor Relations	Arbitration Cafeteria Contract administration Grievance procedure Health and safety Medical plans Negotiations

Small Company		Large Corporation	
Position	*Responsibilities*	*Position*	*Responsibilities*
Administrative Assistant	Interviewing Records Secretary to staff Word processing	Director, Training and Development	Career planning and development Exit interviews Management development Orientation Quality circles Training
		Director, Employee Relations	Contract compliance Employee counseling Equal Employment Opportunity (EEO) relations Outplacement Staff assistance program

Source: Wendell L. French, *Human Resources Management*, 6th ed., Boston, Houghton Mifflin, 2007, p. 15. Copyright © 2007 by Houghton Mifflin Co. Adapted with permission.

Increasing Regulatory Concerns

Governmental regulations targeted toward the workplace are clearly focused on human resources. Generally, these regulations apply to all categories of employees, including supervisors, professionals, and executives, who work for employers with 15 or more employees. However, similar state laws and regulations may affect even smaller organizations. Table 10.2 describes the various key laws that affect human resource management. As shown, numerous regulations affect business owners. Although it is not our intent to cover the specific details of all these regulations, five acts and a Supreme Court decision that have profound effects on small firms warrant attention.[9]

Table 10.2 Major Governmental Laws Affecting Human Resource Management

Governmental Regulation	Effect on Human Resource Management
Fair Labor Standards Act (FLSA)	Prescribes standards for minimum wage, overtime pay, and child labor. Non-exempt employees must make the federal minimum wage and make one and a half times the normal rate of pay for hours worked in excess of 40 hours in a seven-day work week. Employees between the ages of 14 and 16 work restricted hours and employees between the ages of 14 and 17 cannot work in dangerous environments.
Equal Pay Act, 1963	Prohibits discrimination on the basis of sex in wage payments for jobs that require equal skill, effort, and responsibilities under similar working conditions in the same establishment.

Governmental Regulation	*Effect on Human Resource Management*
Civil Rights Act, 1964	Title VII prohibits employment or membership discrimination by employers, employment agencies, and unions based on race, color, religion, sex, or national origin; the act creates the Equal Employment Opportunity Commission (EEOC).
Age Discrimination in Employment Act (ADEA), 1967	Prohibits discrimination against persons aged 40–65 in such matters as hiring, job retention, compensation, and other terms, conditions, and privileges of employment.
Occupational Safety and Health Act (OSHA), 1970	Authorizes the Secretary of Labor to establish mandatory safety and health standards.
Equal Employment Opportunity Act, 1972	Amendments to the Civil Rights Act permit the EEOC to bring enforcement actions in federal courts.
Vocational Rehabilitation Act, 1973	Requires federal contractors to take affirmative action to employ and promote qualified persons with disabilities.
Employee Retirement Income Security Act (ERISA), 1974	Prescribes eligibility rules, vesting standards, and an insurance program for private pension plans.
Vietnam Era Veterans' Readjustment Assistance Act, 1974	Protects the employment rights of all disabled veterans and sets forth obligations of employers to military reservists and National Guard members called to active duty.
Amendments to Age Discrimination in Employment Act, 1978	Extends protection until age 70 for most workers and is without an upper limit in federal employment.
Pregnancy Discrimination Act, 1978	Requires employers to give pregnant workers the same group health insurance or disability benefits given to other workers and makes it illegal to fire or refuse to employ a woman because of pregnancy.
Immigration Reform and Control Act, 1986	Makes it illegal for employers to hire illegal immigrants; requires proof of legal authorization to work from all employees hired after November 6, 1986; imposes record-keeping requirements on employers; and provides stiff fines for hiring undocumented workers and for paperwork violations.
Amendments to Age Discrimination in Employment Act, 1986	Bars most mandatory retirement programs.
Employee Polygraph Protection Act, 1988	Bars most private employers from using polygraph tests when screening applicants and from testing current employees unless they have a reasonable suspicion of theft.
Drug-Free Workplace Act, 1988	Requires employers with federal contracts to establish policies and procedures to create a drug-free workplace and to make a good faith effort to maintain a drug-free workplace.
Older Workers Benefit Protection Act, 1990	Requires that waivers of ADEA rights be "knowing and voluntary" and codifies the "equal benefit or equal cost" principle.

Governmental Regulation	Effect on Human Resource Management
Americans With Disabilities Act (ADA), 1990	Makes it illegal to discriminate in human resource procedures against individuals with known physical or mental limitations who can perform the essential functions of the job; requires employers to make "reasonable accommodation" for applicants and employees with disabilities.
Family and Medical Leave Act (FMLA), 1993	Requires large employers to give workers unpaid leave up to 12 weeks for family or medical emergencies.
Health Insurance Portability and Accountability Act (HIPAA), 1996	Protects health insurance coverage for workers and their families when they change or lose their jobs.
Affordable Care Act (ACA), 2010	Key provisions in the ACA are to increase access to insurance, increase consumer protections, emphasize prevention and wellness, improve quality and system performance, and possibly control rising health care costs.

The first act is the Fair Labor Standards Act (FLSA). The FLSA prescribes standards for minimum wage, overtime pay, and child labor. Non-exempt employees must make the federal minimum wage and make one and a half times the normal rate of pay for hours worked in excess of 40 hours in a seven-day work week. Additionally, employees between the ages of 14 and 16 must work in nonhazardous work environments and can work only eight hours per day in a non-school week and three hours a day, outside of school hours, in a school week. Employees between the ages of 16 and 17 cannot work in dangerous environments. The term *exempt employee* refers to an employee performing work that is not considered administrative, executive, professional, or outside sales. These employees are exempt from the overtime provision of the FLSA. Additionally, late 2016 updates to the law require all employees who make under $47,476 in a full year to be considered non-exempt. This change in salary requirement can negatively impact many new ventures and small businesses because it requires them to pay overtime to a much larger percentage of their workforce. See Table 10.3 for a summary description of the major provisions of the FLSA.

Table 10.3 Key Elements of the Fair Labor Standards Act

FLSA minimum wage: Effective July 24, 2009, the federal minimum wage is $7.25 per hour. Many states also have minimum wage laws. In cases where an employee is subject to both state and federal minimum wage laws, the employee is entitled to the higher minimum wage. Additionally, many states have minimum wage laws that are higher than the federal level. Also, employees who make over $30 a week in tips can be considered tip employees who can be paid $2.13 an hour; however, if their weekly pay does not add up to the weekly minimum wage ($7.25 × 40), the employer is required to make up the difference to ensure the tip employee receives the legally required minimum wage.

(Continued)

Table 10.3 Continued

FLSA overtime: Covered non-exempt employees must receive overtime pay for hours worked over 40 per work week (any fixed and regularly recurring period of 168 hours—seven consecutive 24-hour periods) at a rate not less than one and a half times the regular rate of pay. There is no limit on the number of hours employees 16 years or older may work in any work week. The FLSA does not require overtime pay for work on weekends, holidays, or regular days of rest unless overtime is worked on such days.

Hours worked: Hours worked ordinarily include all the time during which an employee is required to be on the employer's premises, on duty, or at a prescribed workplace.

Record-keeping: Employers must display an official poster outlining the requirements of the FLSA. Employers must also keep employee time and pay records. These records are subject to audit by a Department of Labor investigator and can require that back wages and penalties be paid.

Child labor: These provisions are designed to protect the educational opportunities of minors and prohibit their employment in jobs and under conditions detrimental to their health or well-being.

Source: Adapted from U.S. Department of Labor, www.dol.gov/agencies/whd/flsa (accessed June 1, 2020).

The second act is the 1964 Civil Rights Act (CRA). This is one of the major laws regulating employers on the selection of employees. Title VII of the 1964 CRA prohibits employers, unions, and employment agencies with 15 or more employees or members from discriminating with regard to any employment decision (i.e., selection, compensation, firing, and other benefits of employment) against an employee on the basis of sex, race, color, religion, or national origin. In addition, this act created the Equal Employment Opportunity Commission (EEOC). The EEOC was given the power to investigate and challenge any person or company that is allegedly participating in unlawful employment procedures identified in Title VII. The EEOC was originally established to investigate discrimination based on race, color, religion, sex, or national origin. Now, however, it also investigates charges of pay, age, and handicap discrimination.

The third act is the Americans With Disabilities Act (ADA), which was passed July 26, 1990. This act covers all employers with 15 or more employees. The general premise of the ADA is that employers may not discriminate against a qualified person in hiring, advancement, discharging, compensation, training, and other terms, conditions, and privileges of employment because of a disability. A qualified individual with a disability is defined as "an individual who, with or without reasonable accommodation, can perform the essential functions of the position that he desires or holds." The "essential functions" are job tasks that are fundamental and not marginal. The ADA requires employers to provide reasonable accommodation to persons with disabilities unless it would result in an "undue hardship" on the operation of the business. The ADA defines "reasonable accommodation" as making existing facilities employees use readily accessible to and usable by persons with disabilities; restructuring jobs; creating part-time or modified work schedules; reassigning qualified personnel with disabilities to vacant positions; acquiring or modifying equipment or devices; adjusting or modifying examinations, training materials, or policies; and providing qualified readers or interpreters.

The fourth act affecting human resource management is the Family and Medical Leave Act (FMLA), which took effect August 5, 1993, and entitles eligible employees to take up to 12 weeks of unpaid, job-protected leave each year (or 12-month period) for specified family-related and medical reasons. The FMLA applies to all public agencies, including state, local, and federal employers; local educational agencies (schools); and private sector employers that employ 50 or more employees in 20 or more work weeks in the current or preceding calendar year. The FMLA and the related regulations issued by the U.S. Department of Labor June 4, 1993, are extremely complex and impose a variety of requirements on employers. Covered employers must display the FMLA poster in conspicuous places in their work sites, develop a company policy on FMLA to be included in the employee handbook, prepare a notice describing the employee's and employer's obligations to be given to all employees requesting FMLA leave, and set up the required FMLA record-keeping system.

Finally, the fifth act is the Affordable Care Act passed in 2010. The key provisions in the ACA are to increase access to insurance, increase consumer protections, emphasize prevention and wellness, improve quality and system performance, and possibly control rising health care costs. Some of the major requirements include:

- providing tax credits to small businesses that cover employee health insurance costs
- requiring individuals to have insurance (some exceptions include financial hardship and religious belief)
- requiring creation of state-based (or multi-state) insurance exchanges
- requiring insurance plans to cover young adults on parent insurance policies

While the mandates in the ACA will generally increase the cost of employees, the ACA also provides an opportunity for young entrepreneurs to start a business since they do not have to worry about insurance coverage until they reach the age of 26. It is important to note that many of the provisions concerning the ACA requirements for providing health insurance have been changed or cancelled.

In addition to the laws passed in the 1990s, the U.S. Supreme Court increased the burden on businesses by requiring them to prevent sexual harassment in the workplace. Sexual harassment is viewed by the courts as a form of sexual discrimination protected by Title VII of the 1964 Civil Rights Act. Specifically, unwanted, unwelcomed, and repeated behavior of a sex-based nature is prohibited. In 1998, the Supreme Court ruled that a business must have a policy defining the firm's stance on sexual harassment, a training program on what behavior is prohibited, a procedure for making a complaint, and an appeals procedure if an employee is unhappy with a decision. The employer must take immediate corrective action when a complaint is filed. This responsibility includes separating the parties, confidentially investigating the issues, and taking the appropriate steps to prevent future incidents. Supervisors should be instructed to stop any sexual harassment when they observe it, even if the victim does not file a complaint. Also, for the person doing the harassing, there must be a "tangible job detriment." In other words, the punishment must fit the offense.[10]

As these five laws and court decision demonstrate, new venture owners need to perform human resource management functions carefully to attract, train, develop, and retain a quality workforce and not violate federal laws regarding discrimination and employee treatment. Additionally, managers should be aware of their state and local laws covering the management of human resources. In the following sections, we will examine many of the critical functions involved with human resource management, especially in the areas of staffing and performance management.

Staffing

One of the most important parts of the human resource management process is staffing. The identification of employees who have the necessary knowledge, skills, abilities, and other characteristics (KSAOs) for performing a job is critical at all stages of company development. However, the need to find good employees who function well in new, fast-paced, growth-oriented firms increases the need to carry out the staffing function in a systematic fashion.[11] We will examine each of these areas and will then present some staffing principles for small business owners.

Assessing Staffing Needs

The first step in staffing is to determine how many new employees will be needed over the next six to 12 months. The owner-manager begins this task by examining current operations and foreseeable work requirements and by predicting the probable turnover rate. The individual should be able to answer the following key questions:

- Will any additional workers be needed, or can the present workforce do all the work?
- Can any jobs be eliminated, thereby freeing people for other work?
- If more people are needed, should they be full-time, part-time, or contractual?
- Can I hire temporary help to help with seasonal demands?

On the basis of the answers to these questions, the owner-manager can begin recruiting necessary human resources. Generally, newer and smaller businesses should investigate the use of temporary labor sources, including part-time hiring and outsourcing, before they hire full-time, benefits-eligible employees. Only when the need for more employees is seen as sustainable should the decision to hire full-time employees be made. In new and growing ventures, employee costs generally make up the greatest part of the overhead. Every new hiring situation should be scrutinized and a staffing plan developed that looks at company growth, financial impact, and future goals before hiring is initiated.

Human Resource Recruiting

In recruiting human resources, owners should take four steps:

1. Assess short-run and long-run needs.

2. Learn federal, state, and local governmental regulations regarding discrimination in employment.
3. Write a job description and specifications for each vacancy.
4. Organize a recruiting campaign.

With these steps in mind, the owner-manager can begin formal recruiting. Several personnel sources are available for recruiting in smaller ventures. These sources are described in the following paragraphs.

Present Employees

Is a new person really needed, or would a current employee fit the bill? If the latter is the case, recruit this person. Remember, promotion is good for employee morale. Generally, this practice results in cost savings if you train new hires effectively and recruit from within for promotions and externally for entry-level positions and when there is a true need to bring in outside talent (e.g., special skills required, fill gaps).

Employee Referrals

Current and good past employees serve as a valuable source of recommendations for new hires. Generally, high-performing employees recommend individuals that they believe will also be high-performing. However, if you have diversity issues related to the employment of minorities, you need to be careful not to perpetuate this problem by hiring individuals similar to your current workforce demographics.

Former Employees

Sometimes past employees who have left of their own accord can be rehired. However, before someone is rehired, the owner-manager should look at *why* the person left. Regardless of how well the individual performed in the past, the owner should be wary of hiring someone who tends to move from job to job.

Commercial Employment Agencies

A reliable employment agency can be very helpful in locating applicants. These agencies, if used properly, will do the initial screening of candidates and will send over only those who appear to have the qualifications the owner-manager set. Such agencies charge fees for their services. These agencies are also very good for hiring seasonal help or replacements for employees on various types of leave. Another benefit is these employees are primarily the referral agency's employees, so they will be responsible for background checks, processing, and communicating separations. However, if there is an employment law violation, both the employer and the employment agency are potentially liable.

Classified Advertisements

While on the decline with the decline of newspaper readership, classified newspaper ads are a common way a business attracts recruits. Many people who are out of work look in the help wanted section of the newspaper. In the ad, the owner-manager can give a short description of the job, needed qualifications, and starting salary. In some cases, however, it is preferable to give a salary range or simply to say that salary is "competitive." This practice would apply to certain managerial or technical positions. Generally, classified ads are utilized for lower to mid-level positions. In many cases, classified ads may not be cost-effective because they tend to be very expensive in the face of declining readership.

The Internet

The internet has become the most common method for recruiting employees. Several websites, such as Monster, CareerBuilder, and LinkedIn, offer posting services where applicants can electronically post their resume for employers to see. Applicants can also identify companies who have paid to have their job openings posted and have their resume forwarded directly to them. Many more progressive companies utilize their own websites to attract recruits. They list current job openings and provide a direct link for applicants to email their resume to the company. Additionally, many firms have an open position link on their company website. This facilitates quick application and review of potential employees.

Schools and Professors

Many trade schools, business schools, and universities have employment or career services for their students and alumni. By spending an afternoon interviewing at one of these schools, a business may be able to recruit some qualified applicants. As the business taps the available labor supply, it may find more applicants are available than positions. At this point, the owner must decide whom to select.

New Venture Issues

"Professional Employer Organizations"

Being a new venture owner or entrepreneur is not a full-time job. It's three or four full-time jobs. The roles the person must play are numerous and of course require extensive knowledge of all aspects of running a growing, profitable, and compliant business. Corporations regularly outsource the tasks they choose not to handle in-house. New ventures, however, are not always so financially fortunate. Instead, entrepreneurs are usually stuck with mastering a task themselves or hiring a high-salary employee to handle it. Duties that can be outsourced include accounting, payroll, health care and wellness planning, background checks, and other various human resource functions that require time-consuming paperwork and legal compliance hassles.

The professional employer organization (PEO) industry dates back to the early 1980s and is worth between $136 and $156 billion, as measured in gross revenues. The industry provides services to 175,000 small and mid-sized businesses employing 3.7 million people. There are approximately 900 PEOs currently operating in the United States. The PEO industry has grown significantly, with an annual compound growth rate of 8.3 percent between 2008 and 2017. In addition, analysis from 2015 indicates that in each of the last 30 years, the industry has added, on average, roughly 100,000 worksite employees and 6,000 new clients. PEOs operate in all 50 U.S. states. Similar services are described in Sweden and Germany. International PEO services are now being offered, although the translation of applicable rules and regulations varies from country to country. PEO companies are able to deliver services in over 160 countries. This trend is attributed not only to the growing number of business owners but also to the fact that current owners are realizing the true value of using PEOs. Spending dollars on the "co-employer" is justified by the time the owner-entrepreneur is able to save up funds so as to focus on operations and generating more revenue. Also, given the competition among startups to find the best employees, PEOs offer another plus. By taking advantage of their large member numbers, PEOs are able to use leverage to obtain discounts on human resource benefit rates and pass them on to customers.

PEOs were established to offer basic services such as payroll processing, tax payments, and health insurance. Due to rising demand in the outsourcing market, many started offering retirement plans, workers' compensation insurance, and regulatory compliance monitoring as well. (Larger organizations offer an even broader menu of services, but they usually service corporations that can afford the high price tag.)

Some businesses remain skeptical about using PEOs because their legal status is not uniform across the country. Each state in the United States has differing regulations for workers' compensation insurance and state unemployment insurance, so PEOs are typically regulated at the state level.

Source: Adapted from National Association of Professional Employer Organizations, "Latest PEO Pulse Survey Shows Continued PEO Industry Growth," MarketWatch, April 25, 2018; and Laurie Bassi and Dan McMurrer, "An Economic Analysis: The PEO Industry Footprint," McBassi & Company, September 2015.

Screening Potential Employees

When screening job applicants, the place to start is with an employment *application form*. This provides information on the person's background and training. Is the business looking for a salesperson? If so, someone with selling experience may be preferable to someone without it. Is a mechanic being sought? If so, the person should have some certified training and experience in this area. The application form helps screen out those who are least likely to be successful in the job. It is advised that employers tailor the application to solicit the information needed to properly screen applicants. Remember, information should be job-related, as identified in the job description.

In addition, the applicant should be *interviewed*. Much can be learned about a person in the interview. Does the individual have the right temperament and personality for the job? Has the person written anything on the application form that warrants special consideration or discussion? Do any questions that were not on the application form need to be answered? In general, most firms, especially newer, smaller firms, do not understand the problems associated with using an interview for selection. When employees who conduct the interview are not trained, issues such as illegal discrimination can arise. Also, without sufficient practice and planning, the interview is an unreliable method for obtaining information about applicants.

The solution to most of the problems just cited is to develop and conduct a structured or planned interview. A structured interview involves a set of job-related questions, based on a job analysis, that are consistently asked of each applicant for a specific job.[12] In addition, interviewers should have a predetermined set of criteria on which to base their judgments regarding each candidate's performance so that they refrain from comparing job applicants with each other and commit the contrast effect. The contrast effect evaluates candidates on the basis of prior candidates. For example, if the individuals who interviewed before you were excellent you may not be rated as highly by the interviewer as your performance would objectively indicate. Conversely, if the individuals interviewed before you were absolutely unacceptable, you would more likely be rated higher than your objective performance level.

In some cases, a *test* is in order. For example, if the person will be required to carry heavy material, the individual should be asked to demonstrate this ability. If the employer has some questions about the applicant's physical health in regard to the job's tasks, a medical exam should be required. However, this request can only be made post offer, and you must still comply with the Americans With Disabilities Act and make reasonable accommodations if necessary. In addition, if the person will be typing or operating a machine, these skills should be evaluated. Is the individual sufficiently fast and accurate? Keep in mind, however, that the test must measure skills actually used on the job. If the company gives a math test, but the job requires no math, the business can be accused of discrimination or of using an improper testing instrument. In short, tie the test to the job, and if this is not possible, do not use tests to screen applicants.

Reference checking is also a common method of applicant screening. Many states have passed legislation to protect employers when conducting good faith reference checking.[13] However, more and more employers are refusing to give out information due to the risk of being sued for possible discrimination or defamation. Many employers will simply provide information related to the type of job held and duration of employment.

Selecting and Orienting Employees

If the screening process is carried out properly, the owner-manager should be in a position to select applicants who are most fit for the job. In making the final cut, the owner-manager should direct attention toward applicants' *references*; they should be checked for both accuracy and input. Has the individual actually worked as an engineer for this other company? Why did the person leave the job? Does the applicant have any shortcomings that have not yet been identified but could be determined in a phone call to the previous employer?[14] Would you rehire this person if he or she were available?

If the individual checks out and is hired, the next step is job orientation. The person should be made to feel at home in the organization. Many new employees feel lost or nervous during their first few days on the job. To help them overcome this, managers should show them around, introduce them to people they will be working with, and show how their job fits into the overall mission of the enterprise. LinkedIn, a very popular professional social networking website, utilizes seven critical elements for a successful orientation program:[15]

1. Introductions and overview of the company
2. Company tour
3. Employee investment—a review of compensation and benefits programs
4. Exec Q&A—key executives and managers present and answer questions
5. Unpack your perks—additional benefits like day care, gym, and wellness programs
6. Tech support—utilizing company networks, hardware, software, and use etiquette.
7. Continued education—training and development opportunities for employees

Principles of Effective Staffing

Owner-managers should be aware of a number of staffing principles. Among the most important are these:

- *Staffing objective:* Owner-managers should fill all positions with personnel who are both willing and able to occupy them.
- *Staffing:* The more adequately owner-managers define the jobs to be done, the personnel requirements for these jobs, and the kinds of training and development required, the more likely workers will be competent in their jobs.
- *Job definition:* The more clearly each job is defined, the more likely personnel will know what is expected of them.
- *Open competition:* Owner-managers who fill job openings on the basis of the "best available candidate" are more likely to hire effective people than those who recruit on the basis of friendship or expediency.
- *Employee appraisal:* If job requirements are spelled out clearly and used as a basis for evaluating personnel, motivation will remain high, and tardiness, absenteeism, and turnover will be minimized.
- *Employee training:* The more effectively personnel are trained, the better job they will do.
- *Owner-manager training:* As owner-managers obtain on-the-job training and attend outside workshops and clinics designed to improve their performance, overall company efficiency and profit should increase.

In addition to the general recommendations for staffing just described, smaller firms must consider issues related to recruiting innovative employees with an entrepreneurial mindset and ability to work in teams. One article[16] suggests several rules of thumb the author believes help build effective cross-disciplinary innovation teams:

- You need people who fill in the gaps that you have in your own skill set and those of other existing team members as you build up competence in your specialty.
- Test for both breadth of literacy and deep competence. You do not need "jacks-of-all-trades."
- Identify the core competencies needed for a team. List them on a bunch of Post-it notes and have each person on the team write the name of the "go-to" person on the team who has the most depth in that area. If you lack depth in any specified core competency you should work to find people who can fill the gap.
- You need to hire I-shaped individuals who can think both pragmatically and abstractly.
- Hire people who do not require predictability and stability to be effective. Individuals who can continually reconfigure will be more effective in innovative environments.
- Hire people with strong interpersonal skills. Communication and conflict resolution skills are critical in innovation team environments.

Performance Management

Planned programs of employee improvement are critical if an organization wants to survive and compete in a global marketplace. Also, newer firms with growth-oriented strategies must continuously focus on assessing the strengths and weaknesses of the current workforce so that weaknesses can be eliminated through additional training or replacing workers with individuals who have the requisite skills and abilities to perform the work. This section focuses on the key performance management activities that assist in developing employees: Training; performance appraisal; compensation; and employee discipline, coaching, and corrective action.

Training

To get the greatest efficiency from employees, it is helpful to develop a training program. Such a program should be based on careful planning that includes the following:

1. Establishing training needs and goals
2. Choosing the most practical training methods
3. Evaluating the results[17]

In a very small business operation, the owner-manager usually does the training. In a slightly larger operation, it is possible to get the supervisor to train production and maintenance people, the office manager to train clerical workers, and the sales manager to perform this function with salespeople. Equipment manufacturers may also provide workshops and seminars to train employees on key aspects of equipment utilization. In cases where no one has the requisite expertise, a smaller company may want to pay outside trainers to conduct the training. The method of training will depend greatly on the type of job and its skill requirements. However, in broad terms, five training methods are available:

1. *Conference or structured discussion:* This usually involves a leader and is an excellent method for training supervisors. It is a guided discussion of important ideas. For example, human relations training is typically handled this way.
2. *Lecture:* This is ideal for providing basic policy and procedural information to trainees.
3. *Role playing:* This consists of acting out particular scenarios. It is particularly useful when trying to teach salespeople how to sell or supervisors how to discipline subordinates. It is learning by seeing and doing.
4. *Programmed instruction:* This consists of a "canned" presentation in which the individual learns at his or her own pace. These programs can be used to support the training effort and do not cost very much.
5. *On-the-job training:* This is the most practical of all methods in small business. It is used for specific job training, such as showing someone how to run a machine.

On-the-job training is the most common training method in small business. The first step is to break down the job into its various parts. This can be done by composing a job breakdown sheet that is kept for future reference as a training aid. It is not advisable to try to do a job breakdown off the top of one's head: Even the most skilled trainers fail to remember each step in carrying out a job. In working out the various job steps that need to be explained to the trainee, many trainers actually like to do the job and write down each step as they complete it. They then know that they have a complete list for instructional purposes.

On-The-Job Training Steps

Although the foregoing discussion provides some general information and guidelines for training people, the owner-manager should also know a number of specific facts about training.[18] For example, on-the-job training, which may vary from a few hours to several full days, depending on the complexity of the work, has four distinct steps that should be followed:

1. Preparation
2. Demonstration
3. Application
4. Inspection

In the *preparation* step, the trainer should find out what the trainee already knows about the job. The trainer can then proceed to cover what the individual still needs to learn. In the *demonstration* step, the trainee should be shown how the job is done. As each step in this process is completed, the trainer should encourage the trainee to ask questions. If the trainee asks none, the trainer should take the initiative and ask some: "What have I just told you about how to do that step?" "What would you do if this particular problem developed?" "How would you handle the situation?" If questions alone are insufficient, the trainer can also ask the trainee to carry out the step: "Show me how you would do it." Next, the trainer should allow the trainee to perform the entire process. In this *application* step, the trainer should not oversee the operation too closely because this may make the trainee nervous. The trainer should stand off to one side and watch. When the trainee does something right, praise should be given. If the trainee runs into trouble, the trainer should step in and show how to correct the situation. Finally, the *inspection* step is where the trainer looks over what has been done and evaluates it. The evaluation should be a positive one. If the trainee has done the job wrong, it should be pointed out, and advice should be given as to how the error can be avoided. The trainer should close on a positive note, indicating support and confidence in the trainee.

According to *Training Journal*, future trends in training and development programs must include the following:[19]

1. *Bite-sized learning*—focusing on:
   - Rapid consumption of information
   - Developing manageable learning modules
   - Tailored training for a diverse workforce

2. *Mobile learning*—delivering training using several modalities, including seminars and online and hybrid approaches, to accommodate the increased number of employees working from home and using co-working spaces.

3. *Access to the world's best talent*—online and other innovative platforms can be utilized to bring top trainers and content to employees regardless of location around the world.

4. *Gamification*—to address the needs of millennials and others, training should emulate aspects of video games, especially as it applies to user experience. Specifically, training programs should be designed to include goal setting, the creation of a competitive atmosphere, and the giving of feedback and rewards.

5. *Language for business*—in the globalized businesses environment, competitiveness is highly dependent on accurate language skills to foster effective relationships.

Performance Appraisal

Performance appraisal is the formal, systematic assessment of how well employees are performing their jobs in relation to established standards and the communication of that assessment to employees. The purpose of performance appraisal is to provide both owner-managers and employees with feedback on how well the latter are doing. These appraisals help determine actions such as merit pay increases, promotions, training, transfer, and discharge. In large measure, performance appraisal is the primary process for evaluating and developing organizational personnel.[20]

A well-designed appraisal system has five basic characteristics:

1. It is tied directly to the job and measures the individual's ability to carry out successfully the requirements of the position.
2. It is comprehensive, measuring all the important aspects of the job, rather than just one or two.
3. It is objective, measuring task performance rather than the interpersonal relationship of the rater and ratee.
4. It is based on standards of desired performance that were explained to the employee in advance.
5. It is designed to pinpoint the strong points and shortcomings of a person and to provide a basis to explain why these shortcomings exist and what can be done about them.[21]

There are many ways a manager can design and implement a performance appraisal system so that it will have these characteristics. One of the most useful is to tie the appraisal closely to the goals and objectives of the position. Also, the business owner or manager must consider two key issues. The first is organizational considerations such as leadership style, culture/climate, and availability of appraisal training. The second is appropriateness for the job. The performance appraisal process and instrument must match the type and level of jobs in the company.[22]

Although a number of different techniques can be used to conduct performance appraisals and most organizations design their own techniques, the most popular is *graphic rating scales*. These scales are easy to fill out, and regardless of how they are constructed, it is common to find the category or factor listed on the left and varying degrees of the category or factor listed along a continuum to the right. The form often contains a description of each category. Quality of work, for example, may be defined as "the caliber of work produced or accomplished in comparison to accepted quality standards." If the evaluation results are to be used to compare people within the same unit or department, some sort of weight is usually given to each factor, such as a 1 for very poor, 2 for below average, 3 for average, 4 for above average, and 5 for excellent. Figure 10.1 is an example of an integrative performance appraisal instrument that utilizes graphic rating scales and goal setting.

Recently, many employers have turned to 360-degree feedback. In addition to supervisor feedback, information is obtained from co-workers, clients, vendors, and other parties. The goal of this process is to provide developmental feedback relevant to how the employee can change real job behaviors. One author insists that utilizing 360-degree feedback is effective, but it must be administered and followed up on properly. If not, more harm may be done than expected.[23]

Formal performance appraisals are valued in several ways. Effective managers believe appraisal systems can be a beneficial tool for improving employee

PART I: IDENTIFICATION

Name_____   Position_____

Rating Period From_____   To_____

Rater Name_____   Title_____

Number of months rater has directly observed job performance_____

_____

PART II: SCALES

_____

Please identify the important job duties performed by this employee and rate their performance using the following scale: 1=very poor, 2=below average, 3=average, 4=above average, and 5=excellent.

Job Duties	Rating	Comments
1.	1 2 3 4 5	
2.	1 2 3 4 5	
3.	1 2 3 4 5	
4.	1 2 3 4 5	
5.	1 2 3 4 5	
6.	1 2 3 4 5	
7.	1 2 3 4 5	

Figure 10.1 Illustration of a Performance Appraisal Instrument

8.	| 1 2 3 4 5 |
	| |
	| |
9.	| 1 2 3 4 5 |
	| |
	| |
10.	| 1 2 3 4 5 |
	| |
	| |
12.	| 1 2 3 4 5 |
	| |
	| |

PART III: GOAL ACCOMPLISHMENT

Please review the goals set for this appraisal period in terms of their accomplishment.

Organizational Goals

Goal #1:   Measure:

Performance Assessment   1 2 3 4 5

Goal #2:   Measure:

Performance Assessment   1 2 3 4 5

Goal #3:   Measure:

Performance Assessment   1 2 3 4 5

Goal #4:   Measure:

Performance Assessment   1 2 3 4 5

Figure 10.1 Continued

Please review the goals set for this appraisal period in terms of their accomplishment.

Organizational Goals

Goal #1:   Measure:

Performance Assessment   1 2 3 4 5

Goal #2:   Measure:

Performance Assessment   1 2 3 4 5

Goal #3:   Measure:

Performance Assessment   1 2 3 4 5

Goal #4:   Measure:

Performance Assessment   1 2 3 4 5

PART IV: DEVELOPMENTAL APPRAISAL SUMMARY
Please summarize the employee's strengths, weaknesses and your recommendations for improvement.

_____

_____

_____

_____

_____

_____

_____

_____

Figure 10.1 Continued

PART V: GOAL SETTING

(for the next review period)

During the performance appraisal feedback session set new goals for the next appraisal period. Make sure that there is agreement how each goal will be measured for accomplishment.

Organizational Goals

Goal #1   Measure:

Goal #2   Measure:

Goal #3   Measure:

Goal #4   Measure:

PART VI: SIGNATURES

This report is based on my observation and knowledge. My signature indicates that I have reviewed this appraisal of both employee and the job. It does not mean that I agree with the results.

_____   _____

Supervisor   Date   Employee   Date

Figure 10.1 Continued

performance, attendance behavior, and job satisfaction. More specifically, effective appraisal systems can serve the following purposes:

- personal development
- reward
- motivation
- personnel planning
- communication[24]

Performance Goal Setting

How can a smaller business systematically assess employees' performances? One way is through an integrative applied process of goal setting. The manager-employee goal setting process generally includes the following steps:

- The owner-manager identifies the business's goals. What are the sales and profit objectives? What would the owner like to accomplish?
- The owner-manager needs to look over the current organizational structure to see what everyone is doing. This helps the individual determine whether personnel activities are supporting achievement of the goals. Can the goals be attained if everyone keeps doing what they currently do? Or should work assignments be changed so that a better blending occurs between goals and activities?
- The owner-manager needs to sit down with each employee and review his or her goals and objectives for the year, limiting them to a manageable four or five. This need not be highly formal. However, the worker should know exactly what job(s) he or she is to perform. For a salesperson, this is usually quite simple. For example, the owner-manager and employee may agree that the latter will "sell $750,000 worth of merchandise this year." For the office worker, purchasing manager, or sales clerk, it is more difficult to set specific, measurable performance objectives. Nevertheless, some attempt should be made, for only in this way can the owner-manager help ensure that the biggest rewards go to the most productive workers. In any event, the employee and owner-manager must agree on what the employee is to do. In this way, work assignments are made clear, and the worker has input in the decision.
- The employee decides how the assigned objectives can be attained efficiently. What shortcuts can be used to improve productivity? How can sales be increased? What steps can be taken to become more efficient? In this stage of the process, the worker answers such key questions as What must be done? How will it be done? How will I know when I've done a good job?
- During the year, the owner-manager has a basis for evaluating each worker's performance. Additionally, he or she can identify and help workers who are having problems. Finally, results are measured against objectives. This is the last stage of the controlling process, and for many owner-managers it is an arbitrary evaluation in which he or she concludes that the employee has done a poor, average, or good job. A better way to carry out this evaluation, however, is to use a rating form that is simple and to the point.

Goal setting is very popular because it is both comprehensive and easy to understand. In particular, managers like it because it helps them identify important business objectives and the people who are responsible for attaining them. A second benefit is that, whenever possible, goals and objectives are quantified and a time dimension is applied. Thus, the worker knows what is expected and when particular objectives are to be attained. Third, goal setting helps the manager identify the organization's key objectives. The business can pursue many goals, but some are more important than others. These are the ones that merit consideration. Additionally, minor objectives are often accomplished in the attainment of major ones.

Compensation

Another important aspect of staffing is compensation, which takes two forms: Wages/salaries and benefits. The former is the money people are paid on a weekly, biweekly, or monthly basis, while the latter consists of retirement benefits, insurance programs, sick leave, and paid vacations.

WAGE AND SALARY SYSTEMS

Most smaller growing firms have essentially two choices when it comes to wage and salary compensation. Employees can be paid either on the basis of *time* (by the hour, day, week, or month) or on the basis of *output* (incentive plans). In either case, compensation must be within the guidelines of the Civil Rights Act and Equal Employment Opportunity regulations to avoid discriminatory inequalities. This means equal pay must be given for substantially equal work. Therefore, once a job has been established and a pay rate set, anyone who performs this job should be paid the same rate. There are a few exceptions, including if the person has been doing the job for a number of years and has received annual pay increases. In such a case, any new incoming employee need be paid only the current *starting* wage. Also, if someone possesses more training, education, or direct experience in the industry, he or she can be brought in at a higher wage.

Straight salary is a fairly clear-cut compensation method. Pay is based on hourly rate or a weekly or monthly amount. One basic consideration is compliance with minimum wage and overtime regulations. Employers especially need to make sure they correctly classify those who are non-exempt from the overtime provision.

Incentive compensation systems base an individual's pay on how much work is completed. For example, in some instances the worker is paid a straight piece rate: He or she receives money for each item produced or processed, such as 25¢ per item. In other cases, the person is given a guaranteed day rate, such as $25 per day, regardless of how much work is done, as well as an incentive per item, such as 10¢ per piece.

The experts do not universally agree as to which method of wage payment is best—straight salary or incentive.[25] However, generally speaking, incentive wages are both practical and effective *only* under the following conditions:

1. The units of output are measurable and readily distinguishable. In this way, it is possible to tell how much work the individual has actually done.

2. A clear relationship exists between output and the worker's effort. The individual should be rewarded directly for what he or she does.
3. Quality is less important than quantity (if the work is highly technical, the output with incentive wages is likely to be shoddy and to fail inspection).
4. Supervisors do not have sufficient time to devote much attention to individual performance. If the work requires a lot of supervision, it probably cannot be done quickly and easily, so the workers will not like the incentive payment plan.
5. Advance knowledge is available regarding the cost per unit. In this way, the owner-manager can estimate how high the incentive rate can go.

BENEFITS

Many types of employee benefits are currently provided by small businesses. Some are required by law, while others are voluntary. One required benefit is unemployment compensation, which is designed to provide subsistence payments for employees who are between jobs. The fund for these payments is supported by employer contributions. Depending on the state and the amount of unemployment the firm has had in recent years, these contributions will vary.

Another required benefit is Social Security. Most firms are required to contribute to this fund and, along with employee contributions, serve to finance the system. On retirement, workers are entitled to a monthly payout based on their income and years in the workforce.

A third required benefit is workers' compensation, which is designed to help employees who have job-related illnesses or injuries and cannot work. The employer pays the entire cost of workers' compensation. Usually this is done by participating in a private or state-run insurance plan.

Voluntary programs take many forms. Some of the most common include paid holidays, paid vacations, health insurance, life insurance, disability insurance, day care, educational programs, and recreational programs. The number of programs and degree of employer participation vary, depending on how financially successful the firm is, the types of benefits employees most desire, and other factors.

One employee benefit smaller businesses may develop is pension or retirement coverage. Less than 20 percent of employees in small firms have any type of pension compared with 80 percent of employees in large businesses. A simplified employee pension (SEP), which operates like an individual retirement account (IRA) and a corporate profit sharing plan, may be one solution for small business owners. The paperwork and administrative fees are minimal since any brokerage house or mutual fund company will set up a prototype SEP plan at no cost to the employer. The administrative fees are charged to the participating employees. Because SEP forms are standardized, all the business owner needs to provide is a list of qualified employees.

In an effort to examine the various types of compensation and benefit practices of new venture firms, researchers conducted a study of founders' compensation governance structure and performance.[26] Their results indicate that the compensation and benefit practices of small businesses are more sophisticated than generally believed. It is interesting to realize that small firms now use more sophisticated incentive plans, such as gain sharing, commissions, and bonuses. In addition, benefits such as health insurance, dental insurance, life insurance, and disability and pension plans are now offered by small businesses with more regularity than ever before.

Employee Discipline, Coaching, and Corrective Action

Employee discipline centers around two major activities: Enforcing work rules and policies and ensuring that workers meet performance expectations. Initially, the major goal of corrective action is to coach and/or counsel employees who have violated reasonable workplace expectations, including policy, work performance, and/or behavior. Early detection of problems can lead to positive interventions so that the employee can retain his or her job and the company does not have to hire replacements. Also, early intervention is beneficial to reduce the risk the employer has for any violation or performance problem. One author recommends 11 activities to mitigate risk and improve performance. These activities are summarized in Table 10.3.

The key essentials for effective discipline appear to be documentation of job requirements, documentation of work rules and policies in an employee handbook, training managers on counseling techniques, and early counseling concerning problems.[27]

The Employee Handbook: A Key Tool for Employee Accountability

Up to this point in this chapter, several employment-related issues have been discussed. These issues are critical to employee attraction, development, and retention. However, as a company grows and evolves, communication between employees and management seems to become less effective. Employees lose touch with the ongoing feedback they received when the firm was small and supervisors had more time to provide hands-on management. The formalization of rules and policies is commonly one of the first steps to formalizing a human resource function. As the company grows and adds more managers, consistency in performance management and policy enforcement becomes problematic and employees become frustrated and disgruntled over inconsistent application of rules and perceived favoritism. Moreover, many of the employment laws require formal communication of an employee's rights in a written document (e.g., family leave, sexual harassment, and dealing with disabilities). Also, documentation that employees have received and understand the company's policies makes it easier to take and sustain appropriate disciplinary actions when necessary.

In any organization, the employee handbook summarizes the important human resource policies that every employee needs to know. In this chapter, all the important functional areas of human resource management have been described (i.e., selection procedures, compensation, benefits, and performance appraisal). The goal of a handbook is to illustrate the relevant aspects of these functions to help orient new and existing employees to company practices. Essentially, the hand-book serves as a guidebook to all the dos and don'ts of a particular company or organization. It is an effective way to communicate important information, such as a company's rules, procedures, and goals, as well as more abstract things, like a company's expectations and philosophy, to the company's workers. Employee handbooks help explain how the organization functions to new employees. A good employee handbook will provide a reliable source to which employees can turn when questions arise. When workers know the company's philosophy, goals, and motivations, they are likely to feel as if they are a part of the organization. Also, since employee handbooks usually include disciplinary procedures, they can serve as an effective management tool for dealing with problem employees. According to the Society for Human Resource Management, the business venture should utilize several important steps when developing an employee handbook.[28] These steps are adapted and summarized as follows:

Step 1:   *Review and make required revisions to the current company policies.* Ensure that all policies are legally compliant and reflect the current business culture you are trying to develop and sustain.

Step 2:   *Create an outline of what to include in the employee handbook.* Generally, handbooks have the following sections: Welcome message, policies and procedures, benefits, employee and employer safety requirements, discipline process, acknowledgments, and signatures.

Step 3:   *Create summarized versions of each policy and procedure.* Ensure that the policies are easily understood and accurate.

Step 4:   *Provide finalized version to legal counsel for review.* It is important that employee rights are protected and that the employer does not utilize wording that may signal an unwanted employment contract. For example, you do not want to include wording in your opening welcome that says, "If you follow these policies you will remain in good standing with the company."

Step 5:   *Select a means of distribution and acknowledgment.* It is advised that you provide a paper copy to each employee and require a signed receipt signifying that the employee has had an opportunity to review the policies and ask questions.

Step 6:   *Distribute handbooks, review with employees, and obtain signatures acknowledging review of policies.* This is especially important when disciplinary steps need to be taken. The employee cannot use the excuse that they did not know there was a policy regarding a specific behavior.

Step 7:   *Update as necessary.* Annual review and updates are highly recommended to make sure the policies adapt to changes in your organization and reflect the current culture you are trying to develop and maintain.

Critical Issues for the Future

The entire function of effective human resource management is one that small business owners need to develop and improve as they expand and grow.[29] In many startups and small firms, the owner personally must handle all human resource practices; thus, inefficiencies may occur due to the amount of other activities the owner performs. This situation creates the danger that small business owners might fail to recognize or understand critical issues regarding human resources.

Regardless of the size of the small business, it is clear that owner-managers need to obtain and retain a quality workforce. The role of HR has changed dramatically along with the workforce and economy, and that evolution will continue as machines and technology replace tasks once performed by humans. But that does not make individuals—or the HR teams that work with them—any less important. Tomorrow's HR leaders will need to be bigger, broader thinkers, and they will have to be tech savvy and nimble enough to deal with an increasingly agile and restless workforce. Thus, it is apparent that small business owners recognize what issues must be continually improved on if a quality workforce is desired. (See Table 10.4 for a complete breakdown of these critical issues.)

Table 10.4 Important Elements for Employee Discipline

1.	*Create an effective hiring process.* Standardize job descriptions and applications to ensure only qualified candidates are considered. Personnel involved in hiring should be formally trained on effective interviewing techniques, and once candidates meet the initial criteria, conditional offers can be made. This allows an organization to check references, perform drug testing, and check criminal or financial records before hiring.
2.	*Secure the support of administration.* Get the buy-in of the organization's leadership. Supervisors who refuse to terminate or otherwise discipline rule violators will erode the validity of the system. Build support for the program by securing the input of senior management during the development phase.
3.	*Work with a labor attorney.* Secure the advice and ongoing counsel of an attorney specializing in local labor law. The attorney should review every aspect of the proposed discipline program and should advise on the wording of disciplinary documentation and the structure of an employee grievance process.
4.	*Publish an employee manual.* This document will take time to create—sometimes as long as eight months in a union environment—but it is worth the effort. The manual should include policies on proper and improper attire, offensive behaviors, use of fleet vehicles, internet and email usage, and tardiness and absences. It should also outline the counseling, disciplinary, and grievance processes. Once the manual is finalized, all employees should be required to provide written agreement to the terms outlined in the manual.
5.	*Train supervisors.* Supervisors must understand all of the behavioral policies and disciplinary procedures because they will be on the front lines of explaining and enforcing the program. More importantly, management should be trained on coaching and counseling practices that are designed to help employees avoid running afoul of the discipline system.
6.	*Always begin with counseling.* It may seem counterintuitive, but the goal of an employee discipline program should be to avoid disciplinary action. The purpose is to correct behaviors and fix small problems before they escalate. Most people respond well to an initial discussion and a definition of the conditions that would require further action. If the situation does progress, it should move to written acknowledgment of the verbal counseling.

Table 10.4 Continued

7.   *Establish an employee evaluation process.* Regular performance reviews are an important component of an employee discipline program but are not the venue for bringing up new problems. There should be no surprises in an evaluation. As a rule of thumb, positives should outweigh negatives by 5:1.

8.   *Offer an employee assistance program.* Frequently, discipline problems can be traced to extenuating circumstances such as alcohol and drug abuse, mental health issues, and family crises. Most health plans offer EAPs that can help employees get the support they need and prevent personal issues from affecting work.

9.   *Standardize documentation.* Create form letters that document when counseling has taken place and exactly what was discussed. This both accurately informs employees of an official offense and defends the organization if an employee later alleges that he or she was unaware of their detrimental conduct.

10. *Establish a grievance procedure.* Employees may not always agree with a supervisor's version of events and must be provided with a forum for disputing disciplinary actions. Consult with a labor attorney about systems that comply with state laws.

11. Effective employee discipline programs are often required to secure employment practices liability insurance coverage and other policies because they significantly reduce overall risk exposure. Additionally, organizations that correctly implement these programs actually end up with improved employee morale. As long as policies are clear and rules are consistently and fairly enforced, with an eye toward helping employees succeed within the program, company-wide acceptance is assured.

Source: Joseph C. Palermo, "Well-Crafted Worker Discipline Program Diminishes Risk," *Business Insurance*, 2007, Vol. 41, Issue 8.

Employee Morale

Even though human resource management issues are recognized and are being improved on, certain questions about employees must be addressed. Are workers doing what they should be doing? Is morale good? Are the personnel content? Do they feel they are being treated properly?

In answering these questions, owner-managers often find their attention turning toward such behavioral topics as communication, motivation, and leadership. These concerns fall within the control process because they affect a company's overall performance. The major reason for employee problems can often be traced to lack of job satisfaction.

Job satisfaction determines how employees view their work. When they view it favorably, the likelihood of high productivity is much greater, although the two are not directly related. For example, in some organizations, workers are very satisfied, but their output is no higher than that of firms where average satisfaction is reported. Nevertheless, by remaining alert for signs of dissatisfaction, the owner-manager can assess when job satisfaction is within acceptable bounds. Keeping in mind that "acceptable" varies depending on the type of business and industry, the following are indicators of job satisfaction levels:

•   *Labor turnover:* Is the number of people leaving the organization for jobs elsewhere increasing? If so, what is driving the increase?

- *Productivity:* Is the cost per unit rising because of worker inefficiency?
- *Waste and scrap:* Is the amount of material discarded higher than it should be?
- *Product quality:* Are customers returning goods because they have been made improperly or do not perform as expected?
- *Service quality:* Are customers complaining about the service they receive?
- *Tardiness and absenteeism:* Are employees corning to work late or staying home more frequently than before?
- *Accidents:* Have more accidents or injuries occurred in the workplace than usual?
- *Complaints or grievances:* Is the owner-manager hearing more worker complaints, especially about minor things?
- *Suggestions:* If a suggestion box exists, is the number of suggestions for improving morale or working conditions beginning to increase?
- *Exit interviews:* When individuals separating employment are asked why, do they indicate dissatisfaction with the work environment?

These are not the only indexes of employee morale, but they are some of the primary ones. When poor morale is indicated, the owner-manager needs to take appropriate action.

Improving Employee Performance

Two control-related areas warrant the owner-manager's special attention because they are related to employee morale. The first is the link between pay and performance. The second is the spirit of teamwork.

One of the most common causes of poor morale can be tied to the pay/performance link. Do those who do the best work receive the highest salaries? In many small businesses, the minimum wage is paid to beginning personnel and all salaries are kept secret. Only the owner and the respective employee know how much the employee makes.

Over time, however, raises are usually given to those who stay, and they are not uniform; some people get more money than others. This can create a morale problem when employees feel that raises are arbitrary and are not tied to performance. When this is the case, two things can happen. First, those who can make more money by going elsewhere will take advantage of such employment opportunities. Second, those who stay will do less work, reasoning that "I may not be paid what I'm worth, but I'm not putting forth as much effort as I used to either."

How should this problem be handled? First, the manager should try to tie raises to performance whenever possible (as discussed in the previous section on management by objectives). Not everyone's job is quantifiable. It may be easy to evaluate a salesperson's performance simply by looking at how much the person sold, but a stock clerk's performance may call for a highly subjective evaluation. This is why some kind of evaluation system should be used. Second, the owner-manager should remain alert to locally competitive salaries. What are other firms paying? Some businesses are unable to match the salaries of other employers, but they must come as close as possible or risk losing key personnel. Overall, however, few people leave their jobs just because of dissatisfaction with their pay. In many cases, that is just one of the reasons. Another is dissatisfaction with the work environment, as when it has no feeling of teamwork, so personnel simply do not like it there.

Teamwork occurs when everyone in the organization acts in a cooperative way. Individuals pitch in to help one another out, and any competition is of a friendly, constructive nature. Although some owner-managers believe they encourage teamwork, they actually promote competition. For example, the owner who goes overboard in praising and rewarding the best salesperson will soon find the other salespeople working to undermine that individual. The secretary may slow down processing paperwork for this star salesperson's orders. Other salespeople will probably stop passing leads to the person for fear they might increase his or her sales even more. The result is infighting among the personnel.

How can the owner-manager ensure that teamwork develops? The best way is to reward those who are team players and, most important of all, to reprimand (and in some cases fire) those who refuse to cooperate for the overall good.

Remember that money is an important work variable. No employee will continue to work for the small business owner-manager who pays low salaries when higher paying jobs are available. However, the work climate is also important. People want to be happy in their jobs. Research shows that attending to the psychological side of the work environment—including aspects such as a feeling of importance, creating an opportunity to do meaningful work, and the belief that workers are contributing to the business—is often more important to employees than salary and working conditions. When these good feelings are present, morale tends to be high and performance good.

The COVID-19 Pandemic: A Critical Challenge for Human Resource Management

The COVID-19 pandemic has caused a major disruption in how human resource management practices are implemented with regard to remote working, layoffs, terminations, staffing, etc. This is especially true in work monitoring, maintaining an effective business culture, recruitment and staffing, employee motivation, and legal compliance. A recent article highlighted five critical areas that need to be addressed.[30]

Remote Work Will Become a Permanent Platform for Many Organizations

To reduce the spread of the virus, most workers were moved to "working from home." Companies had to adjust their communication and technology infrastructures to enable the required connectivity among work teams/units and customers. Many employers found that this could be an effective way to work and could substantially reduce real estate overhead costs. This is especially important for new and growing businesses because minimizing fixed overhead costs is a lifeline for long-term sustainability. However, according to *HR Morning*, the following human resource questions need to be addressed when managing employees working from home.[31]

- How will managers translate existing policies, meeting schedules, and communications networks to a work from home platform?

- Who will pay for remote workers' technology needs, and how do you protect the security of your information systems?
- How will you handle performance evaluations and discipline?
- How must job descriptions and work roles change to accommodate remote work?
- How will you monitor and enforce attendance, especially for non-exempt workers?
- How do you maintain morale and motivation when employees are physically separated?

The article recommends having a strategy and contingency plans to adapt HR practices to a rapidly changing environment.

Developing a Strong Positive Culture Gets More Challenging

A positive and strong work culture is essential for the success of a business, especially a new and growing business. A strong culture drives the mission and vision of the organization; however, in times of great disruption, the identity employees derive from the culture can become fragmented if it is not addressed effectively. Intensive communication and feedback are critical elements for sustaining the culture during disruption or long-term work process changes. Six steps are recommended to reinforce your company's positive culture.[32]

1. *Start with a purpose:* What is the overall mission and vision for the company?
2. *Define a common language, values, and standards:* How will you communicate the important elements of your culture to your employees, especially in remote environments or in the face of disruption?
3. *Lead by example:* How will company leadership communicate effectively and motivate employees?
4. *Identify your (cultural) ambassadors:* Who in your organization can act as mentors and sounding boards for employees who have concerns or questions?
5. *Be truthful and always communicate:* Are you willing to intensify your communication so that employees working remotely and under some distress feel included and involved on a regular basis?
6. *Treat people right:* As a leader, are you willing to invest in your employees and empower them to be productive in their new normal state?

Recruiting and Retaining Talent Is Critical

The disruption of the COVID-19 pandemic resulted in layoffs, furloughs, and terminations due to the uncertain business climate. While limiting short-term expenses may be a necessary reaction to the disruptive challenges facing the business, it may hurt the company's ability to attract and retain top talent. Even if key employees are retained, they see the instability around them and start to look for other opportunities. Also, applicants you are very interested in see that your company may be unstable and will not seek employment with you. Some specific recommendations for moving forward after a major disruption like the pandemic are listed as follows:

- Identify and communicate with key talent within your company. Reassure them that while there are some necessary downsizing movements needed, they are valued. Also provide them a map for moving forward with the company.
- When your company begins to recover from the disruption and you need more employees, utilize contract and temporary employees when possible so you maintain workforce flexibility when moving forward.
- Continue to revise your staffing plan and recruitment efforts. Maintaining a pipeline of talented individuals will enable the company to quickly staff up with competent employees when the need arises.
- When downsizing, make sure your company follows all legal and policy guidelines. While you may have to act quickly to ensure your employment force is the right size, be sure to follow all local, state, and federal laws and confirm that all policies in your company handbook are followed.

Keeping Employees Engaged, Motivated, and Productive

Employee motivation and engagement are key challenges during a disruptive time, especially when employees are working remotely. Dealing with uncertainty enhances anxiety and other responses that could lead to disengagement and lower productivity. Activities to counteract these results are the responsibilities of managers but usually need to be directed by human resources. Besides intensifying communication among employees and reinforcing the positive corporate culture, team-based structures improve productivity. When working remotely, being connected to a team enhances and reinforces the feeling of connectedness and accountability that often diminishes when people work distantly.

Additionally, the Gallup Organization has identified the need for a "high development culture" in the company. A high development culture focuses on an environment where people can "see their impact on the organization and its customers through their work."[33] According to the Gallup Organization, a high development culture focuses on four themes:

1. High development cultures are leader-driven and need to be integrated and reinforced from the top down.
2. High development cultures need managers to move from "boss" to "coach."
3. High development cultures emphasize intense communication throughout the organization.
4. High development cultures hold managers accountable for sustaining the positive culture.

Research by the Gallup Organization shows that companies with a high development culture have happier employees who are motivated and productive.

Accommodation and Compliance

Finally, managing in the "new normal" after a major disruption must also include an adherence to the laws regarding the Americans With Disabilities Act (ADA),

Family and Medical Leave Act (FMLA), Fair Labor Standards Act (FSLA), Title VII, and other state and local laws and regulations. For example, if you require employees to work remotely, are you still providing them the reasonable accommodations necessary under the ADA?

Other Critical Challenges in a Changing World

As ventures scale and grow, there are newer challenges that confront the management of human resources due to the rapidly changing environment.[34] While there are numerous and continuous changes happening at an exponential rate, we present some of the most critical for which new venture managers should be vigilant.[35] Table 10.5 provides a more complete summary of these challenges.

Table 10.5 Critical Human Resource Management Issues for 2025

Technology and analytics: Millennials, now the largest generation in the workplace, are used to getting information right away through a computer or smartphone. Therefore, a wide range of employee experiences—from application to onboarding to checking benefits and paid time off—should be available online to accommodate the digital customer experience younger workers prefer, and HR should be managing that effort. HR professionals will need to embrace analytics and big data to become strategic leaders in their companies.

Strategic thinking by HR: HR leaders need to understand the strategic direction of the business and the economic and social environment in which the company operates. They need to anticipate and prepare for changes in work and the workforce. Only then can HR leaders effectively manage human capital and align HR initiatives with the organization's goals.

Remain focused on people: Embracing technology does not mean taking humans out of the equation. In fact, HR managers in 2025 will have more time to focus on individuals, enhancing both recruitment and retention. Technology will bring a level of intelligence to HR that really thrusts HR into a compelling consultancy role. HR professionals of tomorrow could become "talent brokers" and coaches who help guide the individual careers of everyone at the firm.

Rise of the new workforce: The 2025 workforce will include more transient workers, as millennials are open to continuously new job opportunities, which will give rise to gig workers who pop in and out of jobs on a daily basis. In addition, HR will need to help assess which tasks throughout the organization can be automated and then reskill those whose jobs are affected by automation.

Remote working: Remote work programs will not be the exception but the new normal. Without a doubt, HR will increasingly have to tackle the challenge of managing a remote workforce. HR will need to leverage employees where and when they are most productive and impactful—even if that means seven or ten time zones away—as globalization leads to an increasingly diverse workforce.

Newer benefits packages: Attracting and keeping talent will involve offering (and administering) newer benefits packages that appeal to the future worker. Given the demographics and importance of attracting talent, this includes parental leave, flextime, caregiver leave, expanded fertility benefits, gender reassignment and transformation assistance, financial wellness programs, and other benefits that support critical life events.

Compliance issues: Complying with tax regulations, laws like the federal Family and Medical Leave Act, and Form I-9 and E-Verify requirements will continue to be at the core of HR compliance. But as the workforce changes, HR will need to be agile enough to comply with laws related to the gig economy and remote workers. Additionally, changing state laws on marijuana use will force HR to deal with potential new policies (though federal law conflicts with the states that have approved recreational or medicinal marijuana use).

HR outsourcing will increase: A shift to smaller HR departments will be caused by new technologies and increased employee participation in HR processes. As regulations surrounding employment, and particularly benefits, become more and more complex, companies will need to turn to field experts to help navigate the landscape.

HR will become a marketer: Recruiting is going to need to identify specific micro-segments of either job seekers or job holders to target that talent for the firm. HR will evolve the internal marketing role to include social marketing coordination and brand ownership; that is, outside talent buying into the company brand to potentially work in the organization.

Source: Adapted from Susan Milligan, "HR 2025: 7 Critical Strategies to Prepare for the Future of HR," SHRM, October 29, 2018, www.shrm.org/hr-today/news/hr-magazine/1118/pages/7-critical-strategies-to-prepare-for-the-future-of-hr.aspx; and Brian Westfall, "6 Bold Predictions for HR Departments in 2020," Software Advice, August 25, 2019, www.softwareadvice.com/resources/the-hr-department-of-2020/ (accessed March 21, 2020).

Challenges of Changing Demographics

Due to better medical treatment and longer life spans, there is an older population of workers throughout the developed world that may seek to continue in the workforce. In other words, the commonly cited retirement age (65) may no longer be reasonable for this new generation, which raises the challenge of the workplace and conflicting generations. In addition, there are concerns that if individuals do retire at 65, the remaining working population will not be able to support the increased expenditures on elderly care and pensions.

Challenges of Workplace Diversity

Diversity has been on the rise in every business and industry with regard to gender, generation, and culture. However, now working arrangements with employees are changing rapidly. As just mentioned, longer life spans are likely to result in employees staying in the workplace until a later age, yet that may mean different working arrangements. Another challenge is the attraction and retention of millennials, who tend to be more mobile and have higher expectations for their job and work-life balance and thus become difficult to retain. Still another challenge focuses on the substantial proportion of women who seek temporary and part-time work, many of whom do not want to be physically present in the workplace (e.g., telecommuting). These new challenges in workplace diversity will necessitate a multi-layered, carefully thought out managerial approach as growing ventures seek to find the best talent in a highly competitive environment.

Challenges of Technology

All of the recent advances in communication technology have slowly diminished the proportion of employees working from a central company location. Remote working (telecommuting) is definitely on the rise, which will enable ventures to access a deeper pool of available talent. Today's technology allows ventures to maintain instant contact with clients in distant locations, thus allowing greater global expansion. However, technology that allows cross-cultural teams to work together sets up wholly new and complex managerial challenges, such as how to accommodate cultural differences and avoid potential conflicts to gain maximum team advantage. Recent technological advances have also automated many routine tasks formerly performed by mid-skilled workers, while the demand for technologically skilled positions will continue to rise. Thus, the need for properly trained workers in this new digital age will be a major challenge.

Challenges of Outsourcing

Ventures will continue to investigate where and how to outsource certain operations. While China may now be a less attractive destination for outsourcing due to the steep rise in wages, it is likely that India, Vietnam, and Indonesia will further establish a strong position for outsourcing over the next few years. Central and Eastern Europe may appeal as an outsourcing destination for highly skilled work. Thus, venture managers will need to find sufficiently reliable data and analytics about human capital issues in new potential markets to make sound strategic business decisions and minimize risk.

If new venture managers can approach these challenges successfully, the chances of having higher employee performance levels will be much greater. Human resources has and always will be one of the most difficult areas for new venture managers to confront. Yet it may prove to be the most beneficial when the venture seeks to scale.

Review and Discussion Questions

1. How would you describe some of the rapid changes confronting the American workplace?
2. List some recent regulatory legislation affecting human resources.
3. What are the key federal acts that relate to employment? Describe each.
4. What are some of the questions an owner-manager must ask to assess the firm's personnel needs?
5. How should the new venture owner recruit personnel? Include in your answer the four steps discussed in this chapter.
6. How should the owner-manager screen and select new employees? Explain.
7. What is performance appraisal? How do graphic rating scales work?
8. Define goal setting and describe how it works. What are its benefits?
9. List some of the current human resources practices that small firms in all size categories use.
10. How can the owner-manager tell when employee job satisfaction is declining?
11. What are some typical job satisfaction indicators? List and describe at least five.
12. Identify the critical human resource issues and challenges that new venture managers must face in today's world.

The Venture Consultant

"Raising Morale to Increase Profits"

IndMis Capital is an international investment firm run by three partners who have achieved average returns over the years of 2019, 2020, and 2021. The firm operates on a global scale, looking to take advantage of investment opportunities internationally and domestically. Recently, the company has felt pressure from its investors to achieve higher returns. The investors have 100 percent trust in the three partners, as they are considered by experts to be exceptional relative to industry peers, but do not fully understand why investment returns have been so average. Many believe it may have to do with IndMis's notorious work hours, high employee turnover, and low employee morale.

IndMis Capital employs 75 people, who work, on average, 90 hours a week. Outside of the firm partners, who often take Friday, Saturday, and Sunday off to vacation, IndMis Capital employees are expected to produce high-quality work for each of those 90 hours. In this high-stress environment, mistakes are not tolerated and can often lead to firings. Additionally, the employees are given only five excused sick days and five vacation days per year. While the pay is above average, employees are known to be unhappy with the people they work with, and many decide to move on after gaining experience for a year. The company, while having a tremendous reputation for talent, has become a stepping stone for young professionals.

The three partners have become aware that their firm culture may be the reason why profits have been suffering and people are leaving. They have incurred a lot of extra hiring and firing costs in recent years and believe there is a better way to motivate employees, consequently improving the firm's morale.

Your Consultation

Assume that the partners are correct that the firm's poor employee morale is the reason for mediocre profits. What human resource practices would you recommend the partners implement? Explain. How would these recommendations positively affect the business work environment at IndMis Capital? In what ways could the workers be incentivized to stay?

Notes

1 See Randall S. Schuler, Susan E. Jackson, and Ibraiz Tarique, "Global Talent Management and Global Talent Challenges: Strategic Opportunities for IHRM," *Journal of World Business*, 2011, 46 (4): 506–516.
2 United States Small Business Administration Office of Advocacy. https://advocacy.sba.gov/2019/09/24/whats-new-infographic-lets-you-see-the-answers-to-top-small-business-faqs/.
3 See Jeffrey S. Hornsby and Donald F. Kuratko, *Frontline HR*. Mason, OH: Thomson Publishing, 2005; Karen Roberts, Ellen Kossek, and Cynthia Ozeki, "Managing the Global Workforce:

Challenges and Strategies," *Academy of Management Executive*, November 1998, 12 (4): 93–106; see also Robert Gatewood, Hubert S. Field, and Murray Barrick, *Human Resource Selection*, 8th ed. Mason, OH: Cengage/South-Western Publishers, 2016; and Scott A. Snell, Shad S. Morris, and George W. Bohlander, *Managing Human Resources*, 17th ed. Mason, OH: Cengage/South-Western Publishers, 2016.

4 United States Small Business Administration Office of Advocacy. https://advocacy.sba. gov/2019/09/24/whats-new-infographic-lets-you-see-the-answers-to-top-small-business-faqs/.

5 R. L. Heneman, J. W. Tansky, and S. M. Camp, "Human Resource Management Practices in Small and Medium-Sized Enterprises: Unanswered Questions and Future Research Perspectives," *Entrepreneurship Theory and Practice*, 2000, 25: 11–26.

6 M. Davermann, "HR=Higher Revenues?," *Fortune Small Business*, July 2006, 16: 80–81.

7 B. Kotey and P. Slade, "Formal Human Resource Management Practices in Small Growing Firms," *Journal of Small Business Management*, 2005, 43 (1): 16–40.

8 Elaine Farndale, Hugh Scullion, and Paul Sparrow, "The Role of the Corporate HR Function in Global Talent Management," *Journal of World Business*, 2010, 45 (2): 161–168; and Schon Beechler and Ian C. Woodward, "The Global "War for Talent," *Journal of International Management*, 2009, 15 (3): 273–285.

9 Brian E. Becker and Mark A. Huselid, "Strategic Human Resources Management: Where Do We Go from Here?," *Journal of Management*, 2006, 32 (6): 898–925; and Hornsby and Kuratko, *Frontline HR*.

10 Sandy Lim and Lilia M. Cortina, "Interpersonal Mistreatment in the Workplace: The Interface and Impact of General Incivility and Sexual Harassment," *Journal of Applied Psychology*, 2005, 90 (3): 483–496; and Chelsea R. Willness, Piers Steel, and Kibeom Lee, "A Meta-Analysis of the Antecedents and Consequences of Workplace Sexual Harassment," *Personnel Psychology*, 2007, 60 (1): 127–162; also see Robert K. Robinson, William T. Jackson, Geralyn McClure Franklin, and Diana Hensley, "U.S. Sexual Harassment Law: Implications for Small Business," *Journal of Small Business Management*, April 1998, 1–12.

11 See Christopher J. Collins and Ken G. Smith, "Knowledge Exchange and Combination: The Role of Human Resource Practices in the Performance of High-Technology Firms," *Academy of Management Journal*, 2006, 49 (3): 544–560; Christopher J. Collins and Kevin D. Clark, "Strategic Human Resource Practices, Top Management Team Social Networks, and Firm Performance: The Role of Human Resource Practices in Creating Organizational Competitive Advantage," *Academy of Management Journal*, 2003, 46 (6): 740–751.

12 Mitchell G. Rothstein and Richard D. Goffin, "The Use of Personality Measures in Personnel Selection: What Does Current Research Support?," *Human Resource Management Review*, 2006, 16 (2): 155–180; and Frederick P. Morgeson, Michael A. Campion, Robert L. Dipboye, John R. Hollenbeck, Kevin Murphy, and Neill Schmitt, "Reconsidering the Use of Personality Tests in Personnel Selection Contexts," *Personnel Psychology*, 2007, 60 (3): 683–729.

13 "What Can Employers Say about Former Employees? How Much Information Employers Can Disclose about Employees," *About Careers*, June 22, 2016, http://jobsearch.about.com/od/backgroundcheck/f/whatemployerscansay.htm.

14 See Hornsby and Kuratko, *Frontline HR*.

15 Stephanie Bevegni, "7 Elements of a Good New Hire Orientation," *LinkedIn Talent Blog*, March 9, 2015.

16 B. Buxton, *BusinessWeek Online*, July 14, 2009, p. 9, www.businessweek.com/innovate/content/jul2009/id20090713%5f33

17 Antonios Panagiotakopoulos, "Barriers to Employee Training and Learning in Small and Medium-Sized Enterprises (SMEs)," *Development and Learning in Organizations: An International Journal*, 2011, 25 (3): 15–18; Herman Aguinis and Kurt Kraiger, "Benefits of Training and Development for Individuals and Teams, Organizations, and Society," *Annual Review of Psychology*, 2009, 60: 451–474.

18 See Dilani Jayawarna, Allan Macpherson, and Alison Wilson, "Training Commitment and Performance in Manufacturing SMEs: Incidence, Intensity and Approaches," *Journal of Small Business and Enterprise Development*, 2007, 14 (2): 321–338.

19 Adapted from Donavan Whyte, "Training Trends for 2016," *Training Journal*, January 4, 2016.

20   Angelo S. DeNisi and Robert D. Pritchard, "Performance Appraisal, Performance Management and Improving Individual Performance: A Motivational Framework," *Management and Organization Review*, 2006, 2 (2): 253–277.
21   June M. L. Poon, "Effects of Performance Appraisal Politics on Job Satisfaction and Turnover Intention," *Personnel Review*, 2004, 33 (3): 322–334; and Peter Prowse and Julie Prowse, "The Dilemma of Performance Appraisal," *Measuring Business Excellence*, 2009, 13 (4): 69–77.
22   Snell, Morris, and Bohlander, *Managing Human Resources*.
23   Harriet Edleson, "Do 360 Evaluations Work? Yes, But Too Often They Aren't Administered or Followed Up Properly. Here's How to Boost Their Value," *American Psychological Association*, 2012, 43 (10): 58.
24   Jon Werner and Mark Bolino, "Explaining U.S. Courts of Appeals' Decisions Involving Performance Appraisal: Accuracy, Fairness, and Validation," *Personnel Psychology*, 1997, 50: 1–24; and Michelle Brown, Douglas Hyatt, and John Benson, "Consequences of the Performance Appraisal Experience," *Personnel Review*, 2010, 39 (3): 375–396.
25   See Ian Larkin, Lamar Pierce and Francesca Gino, "The Psychological Costs of Pay-for-Performance: Implications for the Strategic Compensation of Employees," *Strategic Management Journal*, 2012, 33 (10): 1194–1214; and Dawn S. Carlson, Nancy Upton, and Samuel Seaman, "The Impact of Human Resource Practices and Compensation Design on Performance," *Journal of Small Business Management*, 2006, 44 (4), 531–543.
26   Lerong He, "Do Founders Matter? A Study of Executive Compensation, Governance Structure and Firm Performance," *Journal of Business Venturing*, 2008, 23 (3): 257–279.
27   Joseph C. Palermo, "Well-crafted Worker Discipline Program Diminishes Risk," *Business Insurance*, 2007, 41 (8).
28   Society for Human Resource Management, accessed on June 2, 2020 at www.shrm.org/resourcesandtools/tools-and-samples/how-to-guides/pages/developemployeehandbook.aspx.
29   Kotey and Slade, "Formal Human Resource Management Practices in Small Growing Firms"; and Jeffrey S. Hornsby and Donald F. Kuratko, "Human Resource Management in U.S. Small Businesses: A Replication & Extension," *Journal of Developmental Entrepreneurship*, 2003, 8 (1): 73–92.
30   HR Morning, "5 Ways the Covid-19 Crisis Will Transform HR's Role," accessed on June 2, 2020 at www.hrmorning.com/articles/covid-will-transform-hr/.
31   Ibid.
32   Adapted from *Entrepreneur*, "Six Steps to Building a Strong Company Culture," accessed on June 2, 2020 at www.entrepreneur.com/article/277727.
33   Adapted from *Gallup*, "4 Factors Driving Record-High Employee Engagement in U.S.," accessed on June 2, 2020 at www.gallup.com/workplace/284180/factors-driving-record-high-employee-engagement.aspx.
34   Becker and Huselid, "Strategic Human Resources Management."
35   See Mark J. Schmit, *Future Global HR Trends: Evolution of Work and the Worker*. Alexandria, VA: SHRM Foundation, 2014.

11 Successful Business Plans

The Compass

Introduction: The Nature of A Business Plan

Most people who want to start a new venture need to borrow money. Most investors, banks, and other financial institutions will not loan funds without a detailed *business plan* that shows the planned activities of the company, its management team, its projected expenses and earnings, and its plans for repaying the loan. Even those who do not need to borrow money can profit from preparing a plan.[1]

The major advantage of such a plan is that it forces the entrepreneur to answer these questions:

- Where am I going?
- How will I get there?
- What opportunities and problems will I run into along the way?
- How will I deal with them?

Ultimately, the business plan assesses the feasibility of an idea as a sustainable business. It is a *roadmap* for the would-be entrepreneur. Like all plans, much of it may not happen as expected. However, preparing the plan forces the individual to think about the conditions he or she will face. If the plan has to be changed, the person who prepared it can modify the plan to fit reality. The emphasis of the business plan should be final implementation of the venture. In other words, it is not enough to just write an effective plan; entrepreneurs must also see that the plan is executed in a way that will lead to a successful enterprise. The New Venture Issues box provides an interesting look at the value of business plans.

New Venture Issues

"The Great Debate—Business Plans or Business Models?"

Business schools and consultants have long believed that completing a formal business plan increases the chances of success for an entrepreneurial venture.

Entrepreneurs spend long hours working on business plans that can range from 20 to 30 pages and include market research and financial projections. There is general consensus that the most viable reason to write a business plan is to gain resources from venture capitalists, banks, or other outside investors such as angel investors. However, schools have recently begun to wonder whether business plans really *do* help a new venture succeed or whether the Business Model Canvas is enough to prepare for a new venture.

At the 2015 Global Consortium of Entrepreneurship Centers Conference, a great debate was staged between professors on two sides of the issue. One side argued for only a Business Model Canvas approach with the basic feasibility of the venture outlined, while the other side argued for the complete business plan.

In the debate, some scholars suggested that entrepreneurs who are not looking for outside startup financing need only a basic Business Model Canvas and cash flow projections. Then, with some market testing, they could rework the business model after starting the business—in other words, learn and adapt through experience. In a study completed by Babson College, businesses started by alumni were examined to compare the success of businesses that started with a business plan to those that did not. It concluded that the only reason you would be required to write a business plan is to raise outside capital from venture capitalists or business angels.

Other scholars argued that the Business Model Canvas was too brief and failed to delve deeper into the sophisticated preparation needed for a successful venture. In addition, they argued that viewing a business plan as only a capital raising document was shortsighted. A solid business plan should serve as a planning tool that helps guide the venture through the early years. It becomes a dynamic living document that is continually updated and adjusted as the entrepreneur learns more about the market, the operations, and the environment. Thus, a complete business plan becomes a valuable document beyond raising outside capital.

The winners? Both sides! It was agreed that the business plan and the business model are both important and both play critical roles. At the stage of an idea or concept, the model (either the Business Model Canvas or the other and often better frameworks available for the business model) can be quite useful. Students and teams that are moving to the point of taking a concept to a viable business that operates 365 days of the year, has employees, makes payroll, does real marketing and selling, and is actually dealing with suppliers and producing a product or delivering a service through a real-time operating model need the discipline of a business plan—and it imposes far more discipline than does the business model. As one scholar explained, the plan is the blast furnace in which the metal is formed and molded into a viable shape with regard to a wide range of issues not addressed in the business model. The business plan is not a straitjacket—it is a platform for adaptation, experimentation, and innovation. It provides strategic direction for venture launch and management, but it has a short shelf life—as encounters with reality force ongoing adaptation and continued learning—as the actual opportunity and a workable and sustainable business model emerge once the venture is launched.

Hence, the debate is over!

Source: The Great Debate at the 2015 Global Consortium of Entrepreneurship Centers, moderated by Donald F. Kuratko.

Importance of a Business Plan

Business planning forces entrepreneurs to analyze all aspects of their venture and to prepare an effective strategy to deal with the uncertainties that may arise. Thus, a business plan may help an entrepreneur avoid a project doomed to failure. As one researcher states,

> If your proposed venture is marginal at best, the business plan will show you why and may help you avoid paying the high tuition of business failure. It is far cheaper not to begin an ill-fated business than to learn by experience what your business plan could have taught you at a cost of several hours of concentrated work.[2]

Great ideas with high potential, while still benefiting from the planning process, may not necessarily need the extensive work required by a business plan. Perhaps the value of the business plan is highest for bad business ideas where the process shows glaring problems that must be dealt with before the entrepreneur uses his or her own funds or investments from others.

The need for entrepreneurs to prepare their own business plan extends to the entrepreneurial team as well. All of the key members should be involved in writing the plan. However, the lead entrepreneur must still understand each contribution to the team. In addition, consultants may be sought to help prepare a business plan, yet the entrepreneur must remain the driving force behind the plan. Seeking the advice and assistance of outside professionals is always wise, but entrepreneurs need to understand every aspect since they are the people whom the financial sources scrutinize. Thus, the business plan stands as the entrepreneur's description of and prediction for his or her venture, and it must be defended by the entrepreneur. Simply put, it is the entrepreneur's responsibility.

The business plan can provide a number of specific benefits for entrepreneurs who undertake the challenge of developing this formal document. Listed here are some of these benefits:

1. The time, effort, research, and discipline needed to create a formal business plan force entrepreneurs to view the venture critically, objectively, and holistically.
2. The competitive, economic, and financial analyses included in the business plan subject entrepreneurs to close scrutiny of their assumptions about the venture's success.

3. Because all aspects of the business venture must be addressed in the plan, entrepreneurs develop and examine operation strategies and expected results for outside evaluators.
4. The business plan quantifies goals and objectives, which provides measurable benchmarks for comparing forecasts with actual results.
5. The completed business plan provides entrepreneurs with a communication tool for outside financial sources as well as an operational tool for guiding the venture toward success.

What Is a Business Plan?

A *business plan* is the entrepreneur's roadmap for a successful enterprise. It is a written document that describes in detail a proposed venture, and its purpose is to illustrate the current status, expected needs, and projected results of a new or expanding business. Every characteristic of the project is described: Marketing, research and development, manufacturing or service provision, management, risks, financing, and a timetable for accomplishing clearly identified goals. Each of these components is necessary to show a clear picture of what the venture is, where it is going, and how the entrepreneur proposes to get it there.

As highlighted by the different scholars presented in the earlier New Venture Issues box, planning is essential to the success of any undertaking. Proper planning requires that an entrepreneur formulate the objectives and directions for the future. Business plans can serve the role of an effective planning device. However, several critical factors must be addressed. The business plan must have realistic goals that are specific, measurable, and set within time parameters. A commitment to success must be supported by everyone involved in the venture. Milestones must be established for continuous and timely evaluation of progress. Finally, the business plan must be flexible to allow for the anticipation of obstacles and the formulation of alternative strategies.

New ventures and business plans go together. The reason is obvious: New ventures require capital—often substantial amounts of capital. Providers of capital, whether they are lending institutions, major investors in securities, or venture capitalists, require a great amount of information about the enterprise, and anything less than a detailed business plan is insufficient for the task.

In summary, the business plan is the major tool for guiding the operation of the venture as well as the primary document for managing it. Its main thrust is to compile the strategic development of the project into a comprehensive document for outside investors to read and understand. It allows entrepreneurs entrance into the investment process. A secondary benefit is that it enables the enterprise to avoid common pitfalls that cause less organized efforts to fail.[3]

The Components of a Business Plan

Readers of a business plan expect it to have two important qualities: It must be organized and it must be complete. The entrepreneur should also consider who the intended audience is when the plan is presented for funding. Mason and Stark

(2004) suggest that most of the research on business plans ignores the needs of different types of funding sources.[4] Their research suggests that business plans should be customized based on the following:

- Bankers stress the financial aspects of the plan and place little emphasis on market, entrepreneur, or other issues.
- Equity investors, capital fund managers, venture capital fund managers, and business angels emphasize both market and financial components.[4]

With this in mind, the following list describes the 11 components that make up a complete and organized business plan.

1. *Executive summary:* A short description of the venture and its mission should be the first information the reader encounters. The executive summary should be written in an interesting way, with proper emphasis on the more important aspects of the plan, such as the unique characteristics of the venture, the major mission of the venture clearly articulated, the major marketing points, and the desired end result. Its purpose is to whet the reader's appetite for more information. A good summary will guarantee that the rest of the plan will be read.
2. *Descriptions of the business:* This section contains a more comprehensive account of the venture and the mission of the proposed business model. The description of the business should include a brief history of the company where applicable and some information about the overall industry. The product or service should be described in terms of its unique value to consumers. Finally, goals and milestones should be clarified.
3. *Marketing:* The marketing section is divided into two major parts. The first is research and analysis. The target market must be identified, with emphasis on who will buy the product or service. Market size and trends must be measured, and the market share must be estimated. In addition, the competition should be studied in considerable detail. The second part is the marketing plan. This is perhaps the most important part of the business plan. It must discuss marketing strategy, sales and distribution, pricing, advertising, promotion, and public relations. Some businesses make the mistake of preparing only a marketing plan, but by itself and outside the structure of a business plan, a marketing plan will not meet the needs of a new venture.
4. *Research, design, and development:* The research, design, and development sections include developmental research leading to the product or service's design, development, or delivery. Technical research results should be evaluated, and the cost structure of the newly designed product or service should be determined.
5. *Operations segment:* This section requires an investigation focused on identifying the optimal location for the venture. Proximity to suppliers, availability of transportation, and labor supply are of prime importance. If the venture requires highly skilled or educated labor, the entrepreneur should consider locating in areas where the supply of talent will allow them to successfully recruit and retain employees at reasonable costs. The requirements and costs

of production facilities and equipment must be determined in advance. Specific needs should be discussed in terms of the facilities required to handle the new venture (plant, warehouse storage, and offices) and the equipment that needs to be acquired (special tooling, machinery, computers, and vehicles). For internet-based businesses, the outline of operations is essential, as the customer base may be diverse and geographically dispersed. Finally, the cost data associated with any of the operation factors should be presented. The financial information used here can be applied later to the financial projections.

6. *Management:* The management team necessarily requires the presence of outstanding individuals to make the venture a success. Methods of compensation, such as salaries, employment agreements, stock purchase plans, and ownership levels, must be determined. The board of directors, advisors, and consultants are also part of the management team, and their selection should be based on their potential contribution to the enterprise.

7. *Critical risks:* Risks must often be analyzed to uncover potential problems before they materialize. Outside consultants can often be engaged to identify risks and to recommend alternative courses of action. The important concept is that risk can be anticipated and controlled. Doing so will result in a more successful venture.

8. *Financial forecasting:* Accountants can make a major contribution to this section. Obtaining financing has always depended on fair and reasonable budgeting and forecasting. From the sales budget and projected inventory, material and labor requirements can be determined. Variable overhead can be scheduled for various capacity levels, and when these are added to fixed overhead, the budget can be completed. A capital budget can then be prepared; when it is coupled with debt service requirements, cash flow needs can be identified. This information can be summarized in pro forma financial statements, such as forecasted statements of earnings, financial position, and cash flows. If the work is done well, these projected statements should represent the financial achievements expected from the business. They also provide a standard against which to measure the actual results of operating the enterprise. These financial projections will serve as valuable tools for managing and controlling the business in the first few years.

9. *Harvest strategy:* This segment projects a long-term plan for how the entrepreneur(s) will benefit from the success of the venture. Harvest strategies can include selling the business, going public and offering stock, or merging with another business. In the case of a family business venture, it could also include a business succession plan.

10. *Milestone schedule:* This segment of the business plan requires the determination of objectives and the timing of their accomplishment. Milestones and deadlines should be established and then monitored while the venture is in progress. Each milestone is related to all the others, and together they constitute a network of the entire project. Milestones should be objective and quantifiable so milestone achievement can be adequately measured.

11. *Appendix:* The appendix includes valuable information not contained in other sections. It may include names of references and advisors as well as drawings,

documents, agreements, or other materials that support the plan. If deemed desirable, a bibliography may be presented.

Preparing the Business Plan

Constructing a business plan is a challenge because of the great amount of work required to put together the 11 components just discussed. After the requisite information is compiled, the package must be assembled in good form. Remember that a business plan gives investors, suppliers, and potential employees their first impression of a company. Therefore, the plan should present a professional image. Form as well as content is important. The document should be free of spelling, grammatical, or typographical errors. Perfection should be the norm; anything less is unacceptable. Binding and printing should have a professional appearance. The written plan should not exceed 20 pages (excluding appendixes). The cover page should be attractive, and it should contain the company name and address. A title page should contain the same information as the front cover as well as the company's telephone number and the month and year the plan is presented.

The first two or three pages should contain the executive summary, which explains the company's current status, its products or services, the benefits to customers, financial forecast summarized in paragraph form, the venture's objectives in the next few years, the amount of financing needed, and the benefits to investors. This is a lot of information for two pages, but if it is done well, the investor will get a good impression of the venture and will be enticed to read the rest of the plan.

A table of contents should follow the executive summary. Each section of the plan should be listed with the page numbers on which it is found. Obviously, the remaining sections will follow the table of contents. If the last section, the appendix, is too lengthy, it may be necessary to present it is a separate binder to keep the plan within the recommended limit of 20 pages. Each of the sections should be written in a simple and straightforward manner. The purpose is to communicate, not dazzle.

Attractive appearance, proper length, an executive summary, a table of contents, and professionalism in grammar, spelling, and typing are important factors in a comprehensive business plan. Believe it or not, when reviewed by outside funding sources, these characteristics separate successful plans from failed ones. (See Table 11.1 for a description of online resources that are available for assistance when developing a business plan.)

Table 11.1 Online Resources for Business Plan Development

Numerous sources are available for assistance in developing a business plan, the internet being one of the cheapest, most easily accessible ones. The following list provides some source descriptions and current addresses.	www.gale.com
The Gale website has several resources that could be of use. It offers business plan examples and market research for different industries. The company maintains over 600 databases online, in print, and in eBook form.	http://fintel.us/

Continued

Table 11.1 Continued

Numerous sources are available for assistance in developing a business plan, the internet being one of the cheapest, most easily accessible ones. The following list provides some source descriptions and current addresses.	www.gale.com
Fintel is a resource that can be used to help with the financial issues of putting together a business plan. It has current industry reports, financial benchmarking, customized research options, and other resources available.	www.marketresearch.com/
MarketResearch.com is the world's largest collection of market research for different industries. This website can give you information such as product trends and analysis of a given market.	https://data.census.gov/cedsci/
The U.S. Census Bureau website is a great resource for information regarding population, housing, economic, business, industry, and geographic data.	http://entrepreneur.com/marketingideas/lowcostideas/archive115812.html
Smallbiztrends.com is a site that will provide you with updates on trends that affect small and medium-sized businesses. It features traditional websites containing small business data as well as a blog.	www.logoyes.com
LogoYes is a leading provider of do-it-yourself logos for small businesses. Here one can design a logo for one's business. To download the logo, it may cost some money.	https://segmentationsolutions.nielsen.com/consumeractivation/Default.jsp?ID=self-register
The Nielsen Segmentation and Market Solutions site will define the market for your business. It offers information on consumer segments and defined and described customer segmentation profiling. It can answer questions such as What are the customers like? Where can I find them? How can I reach them?	www.ebscohost.com/academic/business-source-premier
Business Source Premier is one of the best business research databases, providing the full text for more than 2,300 journals. It provides information on the following topics: Marketing, management, MIS, POM, accounting, finance, and economics.	http://referenceusa.com/Home/Home
ReferenceUSA is a database that offers access to information about millions of U.S. businesses and residents. It also offers information on a variety of business topics such as annual reports, SEC information, trade publications, and newspapers.	www.netadvantage.standardandpoors.com/NASApp/NetAdvantage/index.do
Standard and Poor's Net Advantage is a source of company, financial, and investment information. It also provides industry analysis from S&P's analysts.	

Remember, a well-written business plan is like a work of art: It is visually pleasing and makes a statement without saying a word. Unfortunately, the two are also alike in the sense that they are worth money/investment only if they are good. Following are ten key questions to consider when writing and revising an effective business plan.

1. *Is your plan organized so key facts leap out at the reader?* Appearances do count. Your plan is a representation of yourself, so do not expect an unorganized, less than acceptable plan to be your vehicle for obtaining funds.
2. *Is your product/service and business mission clear and simple?* Your mission should state very simply the value you will be providing to your customers. It should not take more than a paragraph.
3. *Where are you really? Are you focused on the right things?* Determine what phase of the business you are really in, focus on the right tasks, and use your resources appropriately.
4. *Who is your customer?* Does the plan describe the business's ideal customers and how you will reach them? Is your projected share of the market identified, reasonable, and supported?
5. *Why do (or will) your customers buy? How much better is your product/service?* Define the need for your product and provide references and testimonial support to enhance it. Try to be detailed in explaining the customer's benefit in buying your product.
6. *Do you have an unfair advantage over your competitors?* Focus on differences and any unique qualities. Proprietary processes/technology and patentable items/ideals are good things to highlight as competitive strengths.
7. *Do you have a favorable cost structure?* Proper gross margins are key. Does the break-even analysis take into consideration the dynamics of price and variable costs? Identify, if possible, any economies of scale that would be advantageous to the business.
8. *Can the management team build a business?* Take a second look at the management team to see whether they have relevant experience in small business and the industry. Acknowledge the fact that the team may need to evolve with the business.
9. *How much money do you need?* Financial statements, including the income statement, cash flow statement, and balance sheet, should be provided on a monthly basis for the first year and then on a quarterly basis for the following two or three years.
10. *How does your investor get a cash return?* Whether it is through a buyout or initial public offering, make sure your plan clearly outlines this important question regarding a harvest strategy.

These questions give entrepreneurs the benefit of self-evaluating each segment of their plan before presenting it to financial or professional sources. The following are some helpful hints for developing the business plan. While some of these hints may seem redundant based on the material already presented, they highlight in a bullet style the key points to remember.

Helpful Hints

Executive Summary

- Confine the summary to no more than three pages. This is the most crucial part of your plan because you must capture the reader's interest.

- Answer all fundamental questions. What, how, why, and where must be explained briefly.
- Complete the executive summary after you have a finished business plan.

Business Description Segment

- Identify your business by name.
- Provide a background of the industry along with a history of your company (if any exists).
- Clearly describe the potential of the new venture.
- Spell out any unique aspects of this venture.

Marketing Segment

- Convince investors that sales projections can be met and competition can be beaten.
- Use and disclose market studies.
- Identify the target market, market position, and market share.
- Evaluate all competition and specifically cover why and how you will be better than your competitors.
- Identify all market sources and assistance used for this segment.
- Demonstrate pricing strategy since your price must penetrate and maintain a market share to produce profits. (Thus, the lowest price is not necessarily the best price.)
- Identify your advertising plans and include cost estimates to validate the proposed strategy.

Research, Design, and Development Segment

- Cover the extent of and costs involved in needed research, testing, and development.
- Explain carefully what has already been accomplished (prototype, lab testing, early development).
- Mention any research or technical assistance provided for you.

Operations Segment

- Describe the advantages of your location (zoning, tax laws, wage rates).
- List the production needs in terms of facilities (plant, storage, office space) and equipment (machinery, furnishings, supplies).
- Describe the access to transportation (for shipping and receiving).
- Indicate the proximity to your suppliers.
- Mention the availability of labor in your location.
- Provide estimates of manufacturing costs. (Be careful; too many entrepreneurs underestimate their costs.)

Management Segment

- Supply resumes of all key people in the management of your venture.
- Carefully describe the legal structure of your venture (sole proprietorship, partnership, or corporation).
- Cover the added assistance (if any) of advisors, consultants, and directors.
- Give information on how and how much everyone is to be compensated.

Critical Risks Segment

- Discuss potential risks before investors point them out. Examples:

  o price cutting by competitors
  o any potentially unfavorable industry-wide trends
  o design or manufacturing costs in excess of estimates
  o sales projections not achieved
  o product development schedule not met
  o difficulties or long lead times encountered in the procurement of parts or raw materials
  o greater than expected innovation and development costs to stay competitive

- Provide some alternative courses of action.

Financial Segment

- Give actual estimated statements. Describe the needed sources of your funds and the uses you intend for the money.
- Develop and present a budget.
- Create stages of financing for purposes of allowing evaluation by investors at various points.

Milestone Schedule Segment

- Develop a timetable or chart to demonstrate when each phase of the venture is to be completed. This shows the relationship of events and provides a deadline for accomplishment.

Remember, the business plan has the following purposes:

- Leads to a sound venture structure.
- Includes a marketing plan.
- Clarifies and outlines financial needs.
- Identifies recognized obstacles and alternative solutions.
- Serves as a communication tool for all financial and professional sources.

Assessment of the Business Plan

The complete business plan assessment provided in Table 11.2 offers entrepreneurs an opportunity to self-evaluate the business plan as it is developed.[5] Each section is broken down into questions that examine the information needed in that particular segment of the business plan. The columns are then used to evaluate (1) whether the information is in the plan, (2) whether the previous answer is clear, and (3) whether the answer is complete.

Table 11.2 Complete Business Plan Assessment

A COMPLETE ASSESSMENT OF THE COMPONENTS

There are ten components of a business plan. As you develop your plan, you should assess each component. Be honest in your assessment since the main purpose is to improve your business plan and increase your chances of success.

Assessment

Directions: The brief description of each component will help you write that section of your plan. After completing your plan, use the scale provided to assess each component.

5 = Outstanding—thorough and complete in all areas

4 = Very Good—most areas covered but could use improvement in detail

3 = Good—some areas covered in detail but other areas missing

2 = Fair—a few areas covered but very little detail

1 = Poor–No written parts

The Ten Components of a Business Plan

1. Executive Summary–This is the most important section because it has to convince the reader that the business will succeed. In no more than three pages, you should summarize the highlights of the rest of the plan. This means that the key elements of the following components should be mentioned.

The executive summary must be able to stand on its own. It is not simply an introduction to the rest of the business plan. This section should discuss who purchases your product or service, what makes your business unique, and how you plan to grow in the future. Because this section summarizes the plan, it is often best to write this section last.

Rate this component:	Outstanding	Very Good	Good	Fair	Poor
	5	4	3	2	1

2. Description of the Business–This section should provide background information about your industry, a history of your company, a general description of your product or service, and your specific mission that you are trying to achieve. Your product or service should be described in terms of its unique qualities and value to the customer. Specific short-term and long-term objectives must be defined. You should clearly state what sales, market share, and profitability objectives you want your vbusiness to achieve.

Key Elements	Have you covered this in the plan?	Is the answer clear? (yes or no)	Is the answer complete? (yes or no)
a. What type of business will you have?			

---

b. What products or services will you sell?			
c. Why does it promise to be successful?			
d. What is the growth potential?			
e. How is it unique?			

Rate this component: **Outstanding** **Very Good** **Good** **Fair** **Poor**

                                        5   **4**   **3**   **2**   **1**

3. Marketing–There are two major parts to the marketing section. The first is research and analysis. Here, you should explain who buys the product or service—or, in other words, identify your target market. Measure your market size and trends, and estimate the market share you expect. Be sure to include support for your sales projections. For example, if your figures are based on published marketing research data, be sure to cite the source. Do your best to make realistic and credible projections. Describe your competition in considerable detail, identifying their strengths and weaknesses. Finally, explain how you will be better than your competitors.

The second part is your marketing plan. This critical section should include your market strategy, sales and distribution, pricing, advertising, promotion and public awareness. Demonstrate how your pricing strategy will result in a profit. Identify your advertising plans, and include cost estimates to validate your proposed strategy.

Key Elements	*Have you covered this in the plan?*	*Is the answer clear? (yes or no)*	*Is the answer complete? (yes or no)*
a. Who will be your customers? (Target Market)			
b. How big is the market? (Number of Customers)			
c. Who will be your competitors?			
d. How are their businesses prospering?			
e. How will you promote sales?			
f. What market share will you want?			
g. Do you have a pricing strategy?			
h. What advertising and promotional strategy will you use?			

Continued

Table 11.2 Continued

Rate this component:	Outstanding 5	Very Good 4	Good 3	Fair 2	Poor 1

4. Location–In this segment it is important to describe the actual location and outline its advantages. Zoning, taxes, access to transportation, and proximity to supplies should all be considered in this section.

Key lements	Have you covered this in the plan?	Is the answer clear? (yes or no)	Is the answer complete? (yes or no)
a. Have you identified a specific location?			
b. Have you outlined the advantages of this location?			
c. Any zoning regulations or tax considerations?			
d. Will there be access to transportation?			
e. Will your suppliers be conveniently located?			

Rate this component:	Outstanding 5	Very Good 4	Good 3	Fair 2	Poor 1

5. Management–Start by describing the management team, their unique qualifications, and how you compensate them (including salaries, employment agreements, stock purchase plans, levels of ownership and other considerations). Discuss how your organization is structured and consider including a diagram illustrating who reports to whom. Also include a discussion of the potential contribution of the board of directors, advisers or consultants.

Key Elements	Have you covered this in the plan?	Is the answer clear? (yes or no)	Is the answer complete? (yes or no)
a. Who will manage the business?			
b. What qualifications do you have?			
c. How many employees will you have?			
d. What will they do?			
e. How much will you pay your employees and what type of benefits will you offer them?			
f. What consultants or specialists will you use?			
h. What regulations will affect your business?			

Rate this component:	Outstanding	Very Good	Good	Fair	Poor
	5	4	3	2	1

6. Financial–Three key financial statements must be presented: a balance sheet, an income statement, and a cash flow statement. These statements typically cover a one-year period. Be sure you state any assumptions and projections you made when calculating the figures.

Determine the stages where your business will require external financing and identify the expected financing sources (both debt and equity sources). Also, clearly show what return on investment these sources will achieve by investing in your business. The final item to include is a break-even analysis. This analysis should show what level of sales will be required to cover all costs. If the work is done well, the financial statements should represent the actual financial achievements expected from your business plan. They also provide a standard by which to measure the actual results of operating your business. They are a very valuable tool to help you manage and control your business.

Key Elements	Have you covered this in the plan?	Is the answer clear? (yes or no)	Is the answer complete? (yes or no)
a. What is your total expected business income for the first year? Quarterly for the next two years? (Forecast)			
b. What is your expected monthly cash flow during the first year?			
c. Have you included a method of paying yourself?			
d. What sales volume will you need in order to make a profit during the three years?			
e. What will be the break-even point?			
f. What are your projected assets, liabilities, and net worth?			
g. What are your total financial needs?			
h. What are your funding sources?			

Rate this component:	Outstanding	Very Good	Good	Fair	Poor
	5	4	3	2	1

1. **Critical Risks**–Discuss potential risks before they happen. Here are some examples: price-cutting by competitors, potentially unfavorable industry-wide trends,

Continued

Table 11.2 Continued

design or manufacturing costs that could exceed estimates, sales projections that are not achieved. The idea is to recognize risks and identify alternative courses of action. Your main objective is to show that you can anticipate and control (to a reasonable degree) your risks.

Key Elements	Have you covered this in the plan?	Is the answer clear? (yes or no)	Is the answer complete? (yes or no)
a. What potential problems have you identified?			
b. Have you calculated the risks?			
c. What alternative courses of action are there?			

Rate this component:	**Outstanding**	**Very Good**	**Good**	**Fair**	**Poor**
	5	**4**	**3**	**2**	**1**

8. Harvest Strategy–Ensuring the survival of an internal venture is hard work. A founder's protective feelings for an idea built from scratch make it tough to grapple with such issues as management succession, organizational rivalries, and harvest strategies. With foresight, however, entrepreneurs can keep their dream alive, ensure the security of his/her venture, and usually strengthen their business in the process. Also, it is important to identify the potential harvest opportunities that may be available for this venture.

Key Elements	Have you covered this in the plan?	Is the answer clear? (yes or no)	Is the answer complete? (yes or no)
a. Have you planned for the orderly transfer of the venture assets if ownership of the business is passed to this corporation?			
b. Is there a strategy for identifying potential harvest opportunities?			

Rate this component:	**Outstanding**	**Very Good**	**Good**	**Fair**	**Poor**
	5	**4**	**3**	**2**	**1**

9. Milestone Schedule–This is an important segment of the business plan because it requires you to determine what tasks you need to accomplish in order to achieve your objectives. Milestones and deadlines should be established and monitored on an on-going basis. Each milestone is related to all the others and together they comprise a timely representation of how your objective is to be accomplished.

Key Elements	Have you covered this in the plan?	Is the answer clear? (yes or no)	Is the answer complete? (yes or no)
a. How have you set your objectives?			
b. Have you set deadlines for each stage of your growth?			

Rate this component: **Outstanding**   **Very Good**   **Good**   **Fair**   **Poor**

                               5   **4**   **3**   **2**   **1**

10. Appendix–This section includes important background information that was not included in the other sections. This is where you would put such items as: resumes of the management team, names of references and advisers, drawings, documents, licenses, agreements, and any materials that support the plan. You may also wish to add a bibliography of the sources from which you drew information.

Key Elements	Have you covered this in the plan?	Is the answer clear? (yes or no)	Is the answer complete? (yes or no)
a. Have you included any documents, drawings, agreements, or other materials needed to support the plan?			
b. Are there any names of references, advisers, or technical sources you should Include?			
c. Are there any other supporting documents?			

Rate this component: **Outstanding**   **Very Good**   **Good**   **Fair**   **Poor**

                               5   **4**   **3**   **2**   **1**

Summary: Your Plan

Directions: For each of the business plan sections that you assessed in The Components section, circle the assigned points on this review sheet and then total the circled points.

Components		Points			
1. Executive Summary	5	4	3	2	1
2. Description of the Business	5	4	3	2	1
3. Marketing	5	4	3	2	1
4. Location	5	4	3	2	1
5. Management	5	4	3	2	1
6. Financial	5	4	3	2	1

Continued

Table 11.2 Continued

7. Critical Risks	5	4	3	2	1
8. Harvest Strategy	5	4	3	2	1
9. Milestone Schedule	5	4	3	2	1
10. Appendix	5	4	3	2	1

Total Points: _____

Scoring:

50 pts.	—	**Outstanding! The ideal business plan. Solid!**
45–49 pts.	—	**Very Good.**
40–44 pts.	—	**Good. The plan is sound with a few areas that need to be polished.**
35–39 pts	—	**Average. The plan has some good areas but needs improvement before presentation.**
30–34 pts.	—	**Average. Some areas are covered in detail yet certain areas show weakness.**
20–29 pts.	—	**Below Average. Most areas need greater detail and improvement.**
Below 20 pts.	—	**Poor. Plan needs to be researched and documented much better.**

Updating Your Business Plan

The business plan should serve as a planning tool that helps guide the startup and execution of a new venture. Once the venture is started, the business plan is still a vital tool for planning continued growth and/or profitability. Experts suggest several reasons for updating the business plan:[6]

1. The start of a new financial period. Updating your plan on at least a yearly basis helps you project financials and plan for fiscal needs.
2. You need additional financing. The business plan must be up-to-date and reflect current business numbers and not the ones projected before the business was started.
3. There's been a significant change in your market. You must consider changes in your customer base and competition and how these changes affect your business.
4. Your company launches a new product or service. It is a valuable practice to assess the feasibility of any proposed new product or service to determine its viability. Engaging the business plan process is an essential method to assess this viability.
5. Change in management. A new management team should develop their own plan and not rely on past information. Eventually, new management also wants to initiate their own strategies for growth.
6. Your old plan does not seem to reflect reality. Many business plans are written with estimated numbers and projections that may not be accurate when the

business is started. Business plans should be updated to reflect the new reality as information becomes available. Also, pre-startup plans are often hastily written with less detail than is desired for an effective planning tool.

Practical Example

Although every new venture should have a plan, many entrepreneurs seeking to establish a new venture have no idea of the details required for a complete business plan. An example of an actual business plan prepared for funding competition is included in the appendix. Each of the parts of a business plan discussed earlier in the chapter is illustrated in this detailed example. By carefully reviewing this business plan, you will gain a much better perspective of the final appearance that an entrepreneur's plan must have.

A Global Perspective

"Planning for International Markets"

Modern technology allows even the smallest startup to instantly become a global company, selling products and services across the globe. However, this does not necessarily mean that the startup is an international company. There is a difference between building a product or service for a local market and finding that individuals beyond that market value your product or service and purposefully building a product or service for an international market.

The decision to expand to international markets by building products specifically for those markets requires careful assessment and planning. The first step is generally assessing the market, understanding how that market functions differently than your current market, and determining if there is a profitable opportunity for your product in the market. For example, perceptions about a particular brand may differ from country to country depending on the brand's history in the country and brand associations. An example is the Belgian beer Stella Artois. In Belgium, Stella Artois was extremely popular in the 1980s, but it lost favor over the years as it became associated with an older generation. This is contrasted with the popularity of the beer abroad, where marketing efforts have emphasized the beer's history and European heritage.

Beyond understanding how the brand may be viewed differently internationally, it is important to understand how your product may need to be modified to meet local tastes. McDonald's has thousands of restaurant locations across the world. They maintain many elements of their brand identity and product offerings across regions, including the iconic yellow arches, burgers, and fries. However, McDonald's also offers specific products to appeal to local tastes. In Singapore, McDonald's offers a Nasi Lemak burger, a take on a local rice dish cooked in coconut milk, along with a range of coconut-inspired desserts. In Japan, McDonald's offers a fizzy drink flavored with yuzu fruit and Mentai-Mayo fries.

The key to successful expansion is understanding the large and small cultural, social, and legal differences between the current market and the expansion market and how these factors affect business decisions.

Source: Adapted from David Marcelis, "Belgians Have a Term for People Who Drink Stella Artois—Tourists," *The Wall Street Journal,* September 16, 2016, www.wsj.com/articles/hey-stella-its-getting-really-hard-to-find-belgiums-most-famous-beerin-belgium-1474037470; Mark Matousek, "Here's What It's Like to Eat at McDonald's in 7 Countries Around the World," Business Insider, July 11, 2018, www.businessinsider.com/what-mcdonalds-is-like-around-the-world-2017-11#singapore-1; Steven Carpenter, "A Startup's Guide to International Expansion," TechCrunch, December 23, 2015, techcrunch.com/2015/12/23/a-startups-guide-to-international-expansion/; and "5 Things to Consider for International Expansion," *Entrepreneur,* April 28, 2016, www.entrepreneur.com/article/274815.

Summary

A business plan is a roadmap for the would-be entrepreneur. The plan contains objectives, forecasts, and a description of the business—that is, what it will do and how it will operate. Plans may vary in length. However, every plan must include detailed research that clearly illustrates the business concept, marketing element, management structure, critical risks involved, financial needs and projections, milestone objectives, and appendix material.

In each specific part of the plan, the prospective owner describes operations and then addresses major issues likely to be confronted. Many entrepreneurs find it most helpful to begin their initial plan by describing how they will get into business and will deal with startup problems. Both of these areas relate to the financial side of operations. After putting dollar amounts on projected sales revenues, expenses, and profit, the new owner is in a position to develop the management and marketing parts of the plan. These parts are easier to prepare when the financial calculations needed to support them have already been made.

No plan is complete and unchangeable. Additions or deletions are always needed. Some aspects will not work out as expected. Others will have gone unnoticed in the original plan and will have to be added later. In any event, the important point is that the plan provides initial direction for the owner. From there, the individual can modify material as necessary.

Review and Discussion Questions

1. What is the major advantage of a small business plan? Explain.
2. What is contained in the executive summary section of a small business plan? Be complete in your answer.

3. What are some of the startup problems that should be addressed in a small business plan? Identify and describe three.
4. Of what value is a projected income statement to a small business plan? What parts of the plan does it support?
5. What kinds of issues or considerations would you address in the part of the plan that deals with purchasing and inventory control? Insurance? Be complete in your answer.
6. The specific parts of a business plan will vary depending on the goods or services the firm is selling. Explain this statement.
7. Overall, what does a business plan look like? What are the main parts of such a plan? How would a plan for a small business manufacturing firm differ from one for a small retailing firm? Compare and contrast them.

The Venture Consultant

Planning for Sunny Days

Eldon and Marlene have sold sunglasses for the last ten years and have finally decided to start their own sunglasses business. In their previous jobs, both were regarded as extremely effective salespeople where they were tasked with engaging customers to buy sunglasses. Because of their combined experience in the business of selling sunglasses, they were eager to jump into starting the business. With just $70,000 in startup capital, Eldon and Marlene found a great location within a shopping mall just five minutes from their home and decided to launch their own store. Although they received some pushback from other family members and industry friends, Eldon and Marlene chose to ignore their warnings and open the business. Just three months after its inception, Eldon and Marlene looked to be proved right. They experienced gross profits of $40,000 in June, $50,000 in July, and $47,000 in August—exceeding even their own expectations. However, September through January was a much different story. Gross profit plummeted to $10,000 in September, where it leveled off until January, when gross profits were dead even. The change of season quickly applied more pressure to the business because selling, general, and administrative costs totaled $15,000 a month, bringing total pre-tax profits down ($15,000) in January. Consequently, Eldon and Marlene are now struggling to meet their rental payments. Also, with February and March profit expectations similar to January, Eldon and Marlene are bracing for two similarly poor performing months. In an attempt to turn profits, Eldon and Marlene know they need a loan to cover the business expenses, so they set up a meeting with a bank. In the meeting, Eldon and Marlene disclosed their monthly profit figures and expressed their astonishment with how the last few months had gone. To gauge the business better, the banker asked Eldon and Marlene for their most current business plan. They responded by saying because the first months started so well, they felt no need to expend the energy drawing one up.

Unsurprised, the banker questioned whether Eldon and Marlene considered that they were opening up their business during the most profitable portion of the year and should have planned for the downturn: "Thinking through the first few years of your business will help you make more accurate projections and foresee issues like seasonality."

Reassuringly, the banker expressed that Eldon and Marlene were by no means out of business, but before the bank could consider loaning them money, they would need an updated business plan and income statement of the next projected 12 months. The banker recommended that Eldon and Marlene meet with her friend Mary, who was an expert at creating business plans, and return the following week. Eager to try and save the business, Eldon and Marlene reached out to Mary to set up a meeting to complete the business plan.

Your Consultation

Pretend you are Mary. How would you advise Eldon and Marlene to create their business plan? What are three crucial aspects to include? How should seasonality of their business be reflected in their income statement for the next 12 months? Be thorough in your analysis.

Notes

1 For additional information on writing effective plans, see Jeffrey A. Timmons, Andrew Zacharakis, and Stephen Spinelli, *Business Plans that Work*. New York: McGraw-Hill, 2004; and Bruce R. Barringer, *Preparing Effective Business Plans: An Entrepreneurial Approach*, 2nd ed. Upper Saddle River, NJ: Pearson/Prentice Hall, 2015.

2 Joseph R. Mancuso, *How to Write a Winning Business Plan*. New York: Simon & Schuster, 1992, 44. See also Barringer, *Preparing Effective Business Plans*.

3 See Donald F. Kuratko, "Demystifying the Business Plan Process: An Introductory Guide," *Small Business Forum*, Winter 1991, 33–40.

4 Colin Mason and Matthew Stark, "What Do Investors Look for in a Business Plan?," *International Small Business Journal*, 2004, 22 (3), 227–248.

5 Donald F. Kuratko, *The Complete Entrepreneurial Planning Guide*. Bloomington, IN: Kelley School of Business, Indiana University, 2015.

6 For example, see "8 Reasons to Update Your Business Plan Right Now," *Yahoo Finance*, February 24, 2015, http://finance.yahoo.com/news/8-reasons-business-plan-now-153000306.html

12 Scaling Ventures

The Future

Introduction: Venture Growth

Scaling a venture for growth is seemingly what every entrepreneur desires. However, the challenges that come with scaling for growth can be overwhelming if the entrepreneur is not prepared. Thus, the "desire for growth" can be far different than the actual ability to "manage growth." Keep in mind that many entrepreneurial ventures have failed due to the entrepreneur's inability to manage growth. It is truly the entrepreneurial challenge of the 21st century.

Growing ventures differ in many ways from larger, more structured businesses. Several unique managerial challenges involve smaller ventures in particular. These challenges may seem insignificant to the operation of a large business, but they do become important to many owner-managers of smaller growing ventures.[1]

In addition, there are specific challenges associated with scaling on a global level. While most ventures have the ability to "go global" due to the interconnectedness of the internet, there still remain the issues involved with working on an international scale.[2]

Finally, every entrepreneur must keep in mind the ethical challenges that arise when scaling up. When a venture is quite small, the ethical issues seem obvious and easy to deal with; however, when growth is introduced it can bring about a myriad of ethical issues that are sometimes unexpected and difficult to resolve.[3]

Unique Challenges of Growing Ventures

The Distinction of Smaller Size

The distinction of *smallness* provides newer ventures certain disadvantages as well as advantages. From the disadvantage viewpoint, the limited market, for example, restricts venture growth. Because a new venture has fewer employees and other resources, it is limited in its ability to geographically extend throughout a region or state. Another disadvantage is the higher ordering costs that burden many newer ventures. Since they do not order large lots of inventory from suppliers, newer ventures usually do not receive quantity discounts and must pay higher prices. Finally, a smaller staff forces firms to accept less specialization of labor. Thus, employees and managers are expected to perform numerous functions.[4] One research study that reviewed case histories of smaller emerging firms found that newer and/or smaller ventures suffer from several impediments to growth. Specifically, the study cited the following:[5]

- lack of financing
- lack of the right mix of employee skills
- lack of market knowledge
- lack of innovation in new markets
- lack of innovation in new products
- lack of management expertise
- poor business systems
- technology constraints

Smaller ventures have some advantages that should be recognized and capitalized on. One advantage is greater flexibility. In smaller firms, decisions can be made and implemented immediately, without the input of committees and the delay of bureaucratic layers. Production, marketing, and service are all areas that can be adjusted quickly for a competitive advantage over larger businesses in the same field. A second advantage is constant communication with the community.[6] The owner of a smaller venture lives in the community and is personally involved in community affairs. The special insight of this involvement allows the owner to adjust products or services to suit the specific needs or desires of the particular community. This leads to the third and probably most important advantage of closeness to the customer: The ability to offer personal service. The personal service that an owner of a smaller venture can provide is one of the key elements of success today. Major corporations work feverishly to duplicate or imitate the idea of personal service. Since the opportunity to provide personal service is an advantage small firms possess by virtue of their size, it *must* be capitalized on.

The One-Person Band Syndrome

Smaller ventures are started by the entrepreneur alone or with a few family members or close associates. In effect, the business is the entrepreneur and the entrepreneur is the business.[7] However, a danger arises if the owner refuses to relinquish any authority as the smaller venture grows. Some owners fail to delegate responsibility to employees, thereby retaining *all* decision-making authority. One study revealed that most planning in smaller firms is done by the owner alone, as are other operational activities.[8] This "syndrome" is often derived from the same pattern of independence that helped start the business in the first place. However, the owner who continues to perform as a one-person band can restrict the growth of the firm because the owner's ability is limited. How can proper planning for the business be accomplished if the owner is immersed in daily operations? Thus, the owner of a smaller growing venture must recognize the importance of delegation. If the owner can break away from the natural tendency to do *everything*, then the business will benefit from a wider array of that person's abilities.

Time Management

Effective time management is not exclusively a smaller venture's challenge. However, limited size and staff force the entrepreneur to face this challenge most diligently. It has been said a person will never *find* time to do anything but must, in fact, *make* the time. In other words, owners of smaller growing ventures should learn to use time as a resource and not allow time to use them.[9] To perform daily managerial activities in the most time-efficient manner, owner-managers should follow four critical steps:

1. *Assessment:* The business owner should analyze his or her daily activities and rank them in order of importance. (A written list on a notepad is recommended.)
2. *Prioritization:* The owner should divide and categorize the day's activities based on his or her ability to devote the necessary time to the task that day. In other words, the owner should avoid procrastination of duties.
3. *Creation of procedures:* Repetitive daily activities can easily be handled by an employee if instructions are provided. This organizing of tasks can be a major time saver for the owner that would allow the fourth and last step to be put into effect.
4. *Delegation:* Delegation can be accomplished after the owner creates procedures for various jobs. As mentioned in the description of the one-person band syndrome, delegation is a critical skill smaller venture owners need to develop.

All of these steps in effective time management require self-discipline on the part of owners seeking to grow their ventures.

Community Obligations

Proximity to the community was mentioned earlier as a size advantage of smaller ventures. However, unlike major corporations with public relations departments, the owner of a smaller growing venture is involved with community activities directly. The community presents unique challenges to smaller ventures in three ways: Participation, leadership, and donations.

Each of these expectations from the community requires owners to plan and budget carefully. Many community members believe the owner has "excess" time since he or she owns the business. They also believe the owner has leadership abilities needed for various community activities. Although the latter may be true, the owner usually does not have excess time. Therefore, owners of growing firms need to plan carefully the activities they believe would be most beneficial. One consideration is the amount of advertising or recognition the business will receive for the owner's participation. When the owner can justify his or her community involvement, both the business and the community benefit.

Financial donations also require careful analysis and budgeting. Again, because consumers have access to the owner of a smaller venture (as opposed to the chief executive officer of a major corporation), he or she may be inundated with requests for donations to charitable and community organizations. Although each organization may have a worthy cause, the owner cannot support every one and remain financially healthy. Thus, the owner needs to decide which of the organizations to assist and budget a predetermined amount of money for annual donations. Any other solicitations for money must be placed in writing and submitted to the venture owner for consideration. This is the only way owners can avoid giving constant cash donations without careful budget consideration.

The critical fact to remember is that time and money are extremely valuable resources for a growing smaller venture. They should be budgeted in a meaningful way. Therefore, owners need to analyze their community involvement and continuously reassess the costs versus the benefits.[10]

Continuing Management Education

A final unique concern for the owner of a growing venture is continuation of management education. All of the previously mentioned concerns leave very little time left for owners to maintain or improve their managerial knowledge. However, the environment today has produced dramatic changes that can affect the procedures, processes, programs, philosophy, and even the product of a smaller venture. The ancient Greek philosopher Epictetus once said, "It is impossible for a man to learn what he thinks he already knows." This quote illustrates the need for smaller venture owners to dedicate time to learning new techniques and principles for their business. Trade associations, seminars, conferences, publications, and college courses all provide opportunities for smaller venture owners to continue their management education. Staying abreast of industry changes is another way for growing entrepreneurs to maintain a competitive edge.

New Venture Issues

"The Ultimate in Scale: Unicorns & Decacorns"

Unicorns is a term commonly used to identify venture-backed private companies founded after 2003 that have grown in valuev to at least $1 billion. The term *unicorn* conjures up images of something rare (not achieved very often) and magical, both of which apply to companies seeking this status. Another term that has gained popularity is *decacorn*, which refers to ventures that surpass the unicorn stage of $1 billion market value and grow to $10 billion market value.

Today, there are over 400 unicorns in existence, with valuations now exceeding $1.3 trillion in total. Being valued at $1 billion is not just a financial boost;

it is a psychological milestone indicating that the venture is a real force in the marketplace. It has a resounding effect on publicity, investors, and employees. As of 2020, the top nine unicorns were ByteDance, DiDi Chuxing, JUUL Labs, SpaceX, Stripe, Airbnb, Kuaishou, One97 Communications, and Epic Games. Each of these companies has in fact moved beyond being just a unicorn to being considered a decacorn—a venture-backed private company valued at over $10 billion.

Characteristics that have been noted in unicorns include:

Smaller size: Most unicorns have relatively small numbers of employees compared to traditional public companies. The small size of unicorns allows the top management teams to be directly and deeply involved in most of the strategic decisions, which are then implemented through a flat organization. This makes it easier to take decisions and put them into practice very swiftly.

Serial entrepreneur founders: Unicorns are often founded and led by serial entrepreneurs who have experienced business failures several times in their professional lives. The history of the founders and entrepreneurs behind unicorns is therefore rich in failures; this allows them to instill in their companies a culture that emphasizes the importance of anticipating the constraints in an innovative idea as fast as possible by testing its viability.

VC-backed: Uber raised more than $10 billion from VCs, Airbnb raised $2.3 billion, and Snapchat raised $1.2 billion. The strong presence of VCs creates enormous pressures to build successful new businesses very quickly and move toward a liquidity event for investors. It is unlikely that firms with different ownership structures, such as publicly listed companies, would be as fast as unicorns in creating their innovations and bringing them to market.

Aspirational: Unicorns want to revolutionize the world by tackling new problems on an enormous scale and building something that the world has never seen before. Uber's mission was not to build an app that got you a car; rather, it was about innovating the traditional taxi industry and providing consumers something better.

Platform leverage: By leveraging platforms like Facebook and Apple's App Store, the products or services of unicorns can acquire a high volume of users faster than ever before. Thus, for the first time it is possible for new ventures to scale up to tens of millions of users in a very short time.

Market focus: Using a sharp market focus on what they set out to do, the top management teams of unicorns stay directed on the specific strategic challenges in their market. Moreover, the innovations lying at the heart of unicorn success stories are digital innovations. By leveraging pervasive digital platforms and social networks as channels through which they enter the market and reach their target customers, digital innovations require smaller efforts and investments in marketing and commercialization than traditional products or services, and they can be diffused much faster.

Unicorns tend to get big fast and achieve very steep growth rates. However, in recent years there has been increasing skepticism of the strategy of some unicorns to spend freely to grow and acquire customers at the expense of profitable growth. A notable case is The We Company, the parent company of WeWork, an office space rental startup that used startup capital to grow quickly and build its brand, eventually garnering a $47 billion private valuation. However, when WeWork began the process of becoming a public company, it became clear that the revenue generated by the business and issues with the management team likely did not add up to such a lofty valuation. The company did not complete the process to become a public company. Over the course of several months, valuation of the company fell to $8 billion. Long-term success for unicorns is dependent on being able to make the transition from a high-growth, high-expense company to one that can generate sustainable revenue and effectively manage costs.

Source: Adapted from Alfredo DeMassis, Federico Frattini, and Franco Quillico, "What Big Companies Can Learn From the Success of the Unicorns," *Harvard Business Review*, March 16, 2016; Lydia Dishman, "More Unicorns but Fewer Deals: The Current State of Venture Capital Funding," *Fast Company*, July 19, 2016; Begum Erdogan, Rishi Kant, Allen Miller, and Kara Sprague, "Grow Fast or Die Slow: Why Unicorns Are Staying Private," McKinsey & Company, May 2016; The Global Unicorn Club, CB Insights, www.cbinsights.com/research-unicorn-companies (accessed March 22, 2020); and Maureen Farrell, Liz Hoffman, Eliot Brown, and David Benoit, "The Fall of WeWork: How a Startup Darling Became Unglued," *The Wall Street Journal*, October 24, 2019, www.wsj.com/articles/the-fall-of-wework-how-a-startup-darling-came-unglued-11571946003 (accessed March 22, 2020).

Other Issues in the Formative Years

Smaller ventures confront many other managerial issues in the formative years of the business. Growth can demand huge inputs of cash at a time when the venture is simply "cash strapped." The unique stress that this situation presents can be another managerial challenge for the entrepreneur. That is why we spent time in Chapter 9 outlining the important financial gauges that every entrepreneur needs to be aware of in a period of rapid growth. Table 12.1 provides a list of the ten most crucial issues identified by smaller venture managers. As shown in the table, these issues focus on internal problems that require traditional managerial skills. Marketing, human resource planning, finance, and legal concerns summarize the issues most often cited.

The unique managerial concerns of smaller ventures presented in this section directly impact the growth period through which many smaller ventures evolve. The next section examines some of the key elements of the growth stage.

Table 12.1 The Most Critical Problems Firms Encounter in Their Formative Years

1. Finding new customers
2. Obtaining financing
3. Recruiting and hiring new employees
4. Recruiting and hiring new managers
5. Dealing with current employee problems
6. Product pricing
7. Planning for market expansion
8. Handling legal problems
9. Determining and maintaining product quality
10. Dealing with various governmental agencies

Source: Adapted from Guvenc G. Alpander, Kent D. Carter, and Roderick A. Forsgren, "Managerial Issues and Problem-Solving in the Formative Years," *Journal of Small Business Management*, April 1990, p. 12.

Key Elements of Growth

Six key managerial actions come into play during the growth stage: Control, responsibility, effective delegation, tolerance of failure, change, and flexibility.

Control

Growth creates problems in command and control. To solve these problems, management must answer three critical questions: Does the control system imply trust between managers and employees? Does the resource allocation system imply trust? Is it easier for an employee to ask for permission than to ask for forgiveness? These questions reveal a great deal about the control of a venture. If they are answered with yes, the venture is moving toward a good blend of control and participation. If they are answered with no, the reasons for the negative response should be closely examined.

Responsibility

As the smaller venture grows, the distinction between authority and responsibility becomes more apparent. Authority can always be delegated, but it is also important to create a sense of worker responsibility. It is through responsibility that flexibility, innovation, and a supportive environment are established. Since people tend to look beyond the ordinary limits of their job if a sense of responsibility is developed, the growth stage is better served by the innovative activity and shared responsibility of all of the business's members.

Effective Delegation

In the operations of a new venture in a growth stage, effective delegation is a key component of success. This process entails three steps: (1) assigning specific duties, (2) granting authority to carry out these duties, and (3) creating the obligation of responsibility for necessary action. Why is delegation so essential to growth-oriented ventures? Because to continue growth and innovation, the entrepreneur needs to free up his or her time and rely on others in the enterprise to carry on the day-to-day activities.

Tolerance of Failure

Even if a venture has avoided the initial startup pitfalls and has expanded to the growth stage, it is still important to maintain a tolerance of failure. The level of failure the entrepreneur experienced and learned from at the start of the venture should be the same level expected, tolerated, and learned from in this stage. Although no business should seek failure, continual innovation and growth will require a degree of tolerance of, as opposed to punishment for, failure. Three forms of failure should be distinguished:

- *Moral failure:* A violation of internal trust. Since the firm is based on mutual expectations and trust, this violation can result in serious negative consequences.
- *Personal failure:* Brought about by a lack of skill or application. Usually, responsibility for this form of failure is shared by the firm and the individual. Normally, those involved attempt to remedy the situation in a mutually beneficial way.
- *Uncontrollable failure:* Caused by external factors and the most difficult to prepare for or deal with. Resource limitations, faulty strategic direction, and market changes are examples of forces outside the control of employees. Top management must carefully analyze the context of this form of failure and work to prevent its recurrence.

Change

Planning, operations, and implementation all are subject to continual changes as the venture moves through the growth stage and beyond. Retaining an innovative and opportunistic posture during growth requires variation from the norm. It should be realized, however, that change holds many implications for the enterprise in terms of resources, people, and structure. It is therefore important that flexibility regarding change be preserved during growth. This allows for faster managerial response to environmental conditions.

Flexibility

One of the most powerful assets a smaller venture possesses is flexibility. During the growth stage, the ability to access and accumulate resources is needed. Networking is a method of using external resources the smaller venture does not own.[11] Only through the ability to remain flexible can entrepreneurs establish the network of relationships they need for assistance during growth periods.

The Transition From Entrepreneurial to Managerial

The transitions between the various stages of a venture are complemented (or in some cases retarded) by the entrepreneur's ability to make a transition in style. Entrepreneurial style relates to the creativity, innovation, and risk-taking ability needed to start up a venture, whereas managerial style emphasizes the planning and organizational ability needed to operate the business. A key transition occurs during the growth stage, when the entrepreneur shifts into a managerial style. This is not easy to do. As noted by researchers Charles Hofer and Ram Charan,

> Among the different transitions that are possible, probably the most difficult to achieve and also perhaps the most important for organizational development is that of moving from a one-person, entrepreneurial managed firm to one run by a functionally organized, professional management team.[12]

A number of problems arise during this transition, especially if the enterprise is characterized by factors such as (1) a highly centralized decision-making system, (2) an overdependence on one or two key individuals, (3) an inadequate repertoire of managerial skills and training, and (4) a paternalistic atmosphere.[13] These characteristics, although often effective in the startup and survival of a new venture, pose a threat to the firm's development during the growth stage. Quite often, these characteristics inhibit the venture's development by detracting from the entrepreneur's ability to manage the growth stage successfully.

To bring about the necessary transition, the entrepreneur must plan carefully and gradually implement the transitional process. The following provides a suggested seven-step process:

1. The entrepreneur must want to make the change and must want it strongly enough to undertake major modifications in his or her own behavior.
2. The day-to-day decision-making procedures of the organization must be changed. Specifically, participation in this process must be expanded. Greater emphasis should also be placed on formal decision techniques.
3. The two or three key operating tasks that primarily are responsible for the organization's success must be institutionalized. This may involve the selection of new people to supplement or replace those "indispensable" individuals who have performed these tasks in the past.
4. Middle-level management must be developed. Specialists must learn to become functional managers, while functional managers must learn to become general managers.
5. The firm's strategy should be evaluated and modified, if necessary, to achieve growth.
6. The organizational structure and its management systems and procedures must be modified slowly to fit the company's new strategy and senior managers.
7. The firm must develop a professional board of directors.[14]

Transitioning the Focus

In managing the growth stage, owner-managers must remember two important points. First, an adaptive firm needs to retain certain entrepreneurial characteristics to encourage employee innovation and creativity while making a
transition toward a more managerial style.[15] This critical entrepreneur/man-
ager balance is extremely difficult to achieve. As Howard Stevenson and David
Gumpert have noted,

> Everybody wants to be innovative, flexible, and creative. But for every Apple,
> Google, and Domino's Pizza, there are thousands of new restaurants, clothing
> stores, and consulting firms that presumably have tried to be innovative, to grow,
> and to show other characteristics that are entrepreneurial in the dynamic sense—
> but have failed.[16]

The ability to remain entrepreneurial while adopting administrative traits is vital
to a venture's successful growth. Table 12.2 compares some of the entrepreneurial and managerial characteristics associated with five major factors: Orientation,
opportunity recognition, resource commitment, resource control, and organizational structure.

Table 12.2 The Entrepreneurial Focus Versus the Managerial Focus

Entrepreneurial Focus		*Managerial Focus*
Orientation	Driven by perception of opportunity	Driven by controlled resources
Opportunity Recognition	Revolutionary, with short duration	Evolutionary, with long duration
Resource Commitment	Many stages, with minimal exposure at each stage	A single stage, with complete commitment to the decision
Resource Control	Episodic use or rent of required resources	Ownership or employment of required resources
Organizational Structure	Flat, with multiple informal networks	Hierarchical

Source: Adapted from Donald F. Kuratko, Jeffrey S. Hornsby, and Laura M. Corso, "Building an Adaptive Firm," *Small Business Forum*, Spring 1996, pp. 41–48; and Howard H. Stevenson and David E.
Gumpert, "The Heart of Entrepreneurship," *Harvard Business Review*, March/April 1985, pp. 86–87.

Each of these five areas is critical to the balance needed for entrepreneurial
management. At the two ends of the continuum (from an entrepreneurial focus
to a managerial focus) are specific points of view. Key questions to consider
include:

THE ENTREPRENEURIAL FOCUS:	**THE MANAGERIAL FOCUS:**
• Where is the opportunity?	What opportunity is appropriate?
• What resources do I need?	What resources do I control?
• What structure is best?	What structure fits our market?

A recent study suggested that entrepreneurs practice "disciplined entrepreneurship." Even when the venture is up and running, the owner continuously faces the entrepreneurial challenge of dealing with risk and uncertainty when deciding on new products, markets, etc. Based on a review of the case histories of several entrepreneurial ventures, one author recommended an approach similar to the scientific method when pursuing entrepreneurial activities, using the analogy that entrepreneurial ideas are like experiments. Based on this analogy, the author of the study suggests the following three steps:[17]

Step 1. Formulate a Working Hypothesis

- Keep it "fluid" and change your hypothesis as the facts come in.
- Be sure you have the right to an opinion by gaining the appropriate expertise.
- Identify deal killers.

Step 2. Assemble Resources

- Raise enough financing for the "next round of experiments."
- Stabilize the business model before making "key" hires.
- Outsource functions that are distracting to your "experiments."

Step 3. Design and Run Experiments

- In the initial stages of the venture, conduct partial experiments by testing small parts of the business model.
- Conduct holistic experiments when several variables must be tested at once.
- Stage experiments where you invest in partial experiments before you participate in the more expensive holistic experiments.
- Avoid "experiment creep" by not letting the experiments drag on too long, exhausting your resources.

Outside Managerial Assistance

Since smaller ventures are limited in size and employees, assistance outside of the venture can be helpful. One study identified the impact of outside assistance on the performance of small firms.[18] The findings supported smaller ventures benefiting from outside assistance, especially in administration and operations.

Another suggested source of assistance is a board of advisors. "Quasi-boards" are composed of volunteers who serve in an advisory capacity to the owner.[19] This group can be made up of professionals, such as accountants, lawyers, or consultants, with whom the smaller venture owner is familiar. The board provides an outside view of the business and makes recommendations for the smaller venture owner. The quasi-board avoids some of the legal responsibilities associated with formal boards of directors.[20] However, as the venture grows it is advisable to formalize a structure with an actual board of directors.

The Challenges of Scaling Globally

For many years U.S. entrepreneurs shuddered at the thought of "going global" because it was just too big a step, too risky, and too uncertain. Over the past two decades foreign investment grew four times faster than world output and three times faster than world trade. Entrepreneurs rushed enthusiastically to those countries that were blighted by communism, state socialism, or authoritarian, isolationist governments. Prime targets included Japan, China, India, Russia, South America, and Latin America.[21]

Why Globalize for Growth?

Countries vary with respect to the quantity and proportion of resources they possess, which forms the basis for a competitive advantage of nations. *Resource-rich countries* (those having extractive assets) include the OPEC block nations and many parts of Africa. *Labor-rich*, rapidly developing countries include China, Sri Lanka, India, the Philippines, and South America. *Market-rich countries* such as Europe, Brazil, Mexico, and the United States have purchasing power, in contrast to some countries that possess large populations but suffer from lack of purchasing power. Each country has something that others need, thus forming the basis of an interdependent international trade system.

Internationalization can be viewed as the outcome of a sequential process of incremental adjustments to changing conditions of the firm and its environment. This process progresses step by step as risk and commitment increase and entrepreneurs acquire more knowledge through experience. The entrepreneur's impression of the risks and rewards of internationalizing can be determined by feasibility studies of the potential gains to be won.

An entrepreneur's willingness to move into international markets is also affected by whether he or she has studied a foreign language, has lived abroad long enough to have experienced culture shock, and is internationally oriented. Another factor is the entrepreneur's confidence in the company's competitive advantage in the form of price, technology, marketing, or financial superiority. This advantage might include an efficient distribution network, an innovative or patented product, or possession of exclusive information about the foreign market.

Deteriorating market conditions at home may propel entrepreneurs to seek foreign markets to help offset declining business, or a countercyclical market may be sought to balance the fluctuations of a single market subject to one set of local economic conditions. Some growing ventures internationalize immediately and do not wait to expand their horizons. Multinational from inception, these companies break the traditional expectation that a business must enter the international arena incrementally, becoming global only as it grows older and wiser. (See Table 12.3 for proactive and reactive reasons to globalize.)

Table 12.3 Major Reasons to Globalize a Growing Venture

Proactive Reasons	Reactive Reasons
Increased profit	Competitive pressures
Unique goods or services	Declining domestic demand
Technological advantage	Overcapacity
Exclusive market information	Proximity to customers
Owner-manager desire	Foreign competition counterattack
Tax benefits	
Economies of scale	

According to researchers Ben Oviatt and Patricia P. McDougal, seven character-istics of successful global startups are (1) global vision from inception, (2) inter-nationally experienced management, (3) a strong international business network, (4) preemptive technology or marketing, (5) a unique intangible asset, (6) a linked product or service, and (7) tight organizational coordination worldwide.[22]

As global opportunities expand, entrepreneurs are becoming more open-minded about internationalizing. The primary advantage of trading internationally is that a company's market is expanded significantly and growth prospects are greatly enhanced. Other advantages include utilizing idle capacity, minimizing cyclical or seasonal slumps, getting acquainted with manufacturing technology used in other countries, learning about products not sold in the United States, learning about other cultures, acquiring growth capital more easily in other countries, and having the opportunity to travel for business and pleasure.[23]

Researching the Global Market

Before entering a foreign market, it is important to study the *unique culture* of the potential customers. Different concepts regarding how the product is used, demo-graphics, psychographics, and legal and political norms are usually different from those in the United States. Therefore, it is necessary to conduct market research to identify these important parameters.

1. *Government regulations:* Must you conform to import regulations or patent, copyright, or trademark laws that would affect your product?
2. *Political climate:* Will the relationship between government and business or political events and public attitudes in a given country affect foreign business transactions, particularly with the United States?
3. *Infrastructure:* How will the packaging, shipping, and distribution system of your export product be affected by the local transportation system—for exam-ple, air or land?
4. *Distribution channels:* What are the generally accepted trade terms at both wholesale and retail levels? What are the normal commissions and service charges? What laws pertain to agency and distribution agreements?

5. *Competition:* How many competitors do you have and in what countries are they located? On a country-by-country basis, how much market share does each of your competitors have, and what prices do they charge? How do they promote their products?
6. *Market size:* How big is the market for your product? Is it stable? What is its size individually, country by country? In what countries are markets opening, expanding, maturing, or declining?
7. *Local customs and culture:* Is your product in violation of cultural taboos?

How can a growing venture learn about international cultures and thus know what is acceptable and what is not? A number of approaches can be employed. One of the most helpful is international business travel. This provides the individual with firsthand information regarding cultural dos and don'ts. Other useful methods include training programs, formal educational programs, and reading the current literature.

Global Threats and Risks

Capturing global markets is not as simple as it may seem. Dangers exist and must be monitored carefully. *Ignorance and uncertainty*, combined with *lack of experience* in problem-solving in a foreign country, top the list. *Lack of information* about resources to help solve problems contributes to the unfamiliarity. *Restrictions* imposed by the host country often contribute to the risk. Many host countries demand development of their exports and insist on training and development of their nationals. They can also demand that certain positions in management and technological areas be held by nationals. Many seek technologically based industry rather than extractive industry. In other instances, the host country may require that it own a controlling interest and/or limit the amount of profits or fees entrepreneurs are allowed to take out of the country.

Political risks include unstable governments, disruptions caused by territorial conflicts, wars, regionalism, illegal occupation, and political ideological differences. *Economic risks* that need to be monitored include changes in tax laws, rapid rises in costs, strikes, sudden decreases in raw materials, and cyclical/dramatic shifts in GNP. Social risks include antagonism among classes, religious conflict, unequal income distribution, union militancy, civil war, and riots. *Financial risks* include fluctuating exchange rates, repatriation of profits and capital, and seasonal cash flows. *Health-related risks* could also endanger a workforce or hamper any operations. The COVID-19 pandemic is a classic example, with the global panic that set into motion travel restrictions and suspended business operations.[24] While unprecedented, it highlights a new category of risk that was never considered too serious before this terrible onslaught happened.

Foreign government import regulations can affect a company's ability to export successfully. These regulations represent an attempt by foreign governments to control their markets to protect a domestic industry from excessive foreign competition, to limit health and environmental damage, or to restrict what they consider excessive or inappropriate cultural influences. Most countries have import regulations that are potential barriers to export products. Exporters need to be aware of import tariffs and consider them when pricing their product. While most countries have reduced their tariffs on imported goods, there are still other major restrictions to global trade, such as non-tariff barriers (NTBs). These include prohibitions, restrictions, conditions, or specific requirements that can make exporting products difficult and sometimes costly.

Most entrepreneurs avoid international trade because they believe it is too complicated and fraught with bureaucratic red tape. They also believe that international trade is only profitable for large companies that have more resources than smaller businesses. Some other perceived drawbacks of international trade include becoming too dependent on foreign markets; foreign government instability that could cause problems for domestic companies; tariffs and import duties that make it too expensive to trade in other countries; products manufactured in the United States that may need significant modification before they are accepted by people in other countries; and foreign cultures, customs, and languages that make it difficult for Americans to do business in some countries.[25]

International marketing research is critical to the success of a new venture's efforts to sell goods and services in overseas markets. Although venture owners can tap a host of sources to obtain the needed information, these efforts should be directed toward answering the following three questions:

1. *Why is the company interested in going global?* The answer to this question will help the firm set its international objectives and direct the marketing research effort. For example, if the entrepreneur wants to establish and cultivate an overseas market, then the firm will be interested in pinpointing geographic areas where future market potential is likely to be high. If the business owner wants to use the market to handle current overproduction, then the company will be interested in identifying markets that are most likely to want to make immediate purchases. Regardless, the firm will have established a focus for its marketing research efforts.

2. *What does the foreign market assessment reveal about the nature and functioning of the markets under investigation?* The answer to this question, which is often comprehensive in scope, helps identify market opportunities and provide insights regarding the specific activities of these individual markets. For example, if the firm identifies potential markets in Spain, Italy, and Mexico, the next step is to evaluate these opportunities. This can be done by gathering information related to the size of the markets, competition that exists in each, the respective government's attitude to foreign businesses, and steps that will have to be taken to do business in each location. Based on this information, a cost/benefit analysis can be conducted and a decision made regarding the market(s) to be pursued.

3. *What specific marketing strategy is needed to tap the potential of this market?* The answer to this question involves a careful consideration of the marketing mix: Product, price, place, and promotion. What product should the firm offer? What specific features should it contain? Does it need to be adapted for the overseas market, or can the firm sell the same product it sells domestically? At

what stage in the product life cycle will this product be? How much should the firm charge? Can the market be segmented so that a variety of prices can be used? How will the product be moved through the marketing channel? What type of promotional efforts will be needed? Advertising, sales promotion, personal selling, or a combination of these?

Once these questions have been answered, the owner of a growing venture will be in a position to begin implementing the global phase of the firm's strategy.

A Global Perspective

"The Opportunities and Challenges of Going International"

For a firm based in the United States or Europe looking for growth, international markets, especially developing markets, present an enticing opportunity. Between 2013 and 2030, it is projected that up to 97 percent of global population growth will be in developing countries, generating new market opportunities. GDP growth rates in developing countries are also higher than in developed countries. In 2018, the U.S. GDP growth rate was 2.9 percent, while India's GDP growth rate was 6.8 percent.

Despite these opportunities, many companies have tried and failed to find success in international markets. EBay pulled its operations out of China just two years after entering the country in 2006, and UK grocery chain Tesco closed operations in the United States six years after entering the country, incurring a large loss. Companies that have failed to successfully expand internationally often did not recognize the strength of local competition, did not adapt their operations and culture to the local environment, and falsely believed that their competitive advantages in their home country, such as a strong brand, would easily transfer to international markets.

Businesses can take steps to lower the risk that they find losses instead of success with international expansions. Hiring local talent who understand the market and empowering them with real decision-making authority within the business ensure that individuals with a local perspective are driving business decisions. It is easy to misinterpret situations from the outside looking in. Related to this is ensuring that the business is clear on what "local" means. Unfamiliar countries, and even whole regions, can seem homogeneous in many ways, when in fact there may be nuanced cultural, social, and economic differences within small geographic areas. Customized strategies need to be developed for each market entered, possibly down to the level of individual cities or smaller partitions, to ensure local conditions are accounted for.

The financial, logistical, and cultural challenges of international expansion mean that it may be a better secondary option pursued only after local opportunities are depleted. However, there are opportunities abroad for savvy businesses. Netflix was able to successfully expand to 190 countries in seven years. It was successful because it planned carefully and was responsive to the needs of local markets.

Source: Adapted from Katie Hope, "The Challenges of Going Global," BBC News, June 23, 2015, www.bbc.com/news/business-33224596; Nataly Kelly, "The Most Common Mistakes Companies Make With Global Marketing," *Harvard Business Review*, September 7, 2015, hbr.org/2015/09/the-most-common-mistakes-companies-make-with-global-marketing; Louis Brennan, "How Netflix Expanded to 190 Countries in 7 Years," *Harvard Business Review*, October 12, 2018, hbr.org/2018/10/how-netflix-expanded-to-190-countries-in-7-years; "97% of Population Growth to Be in Developing World," Consultancy.uk, June 24, 2015, www.consultancy.uk/news/2191/97-percent-of-population-growth-to-be-in-developing-world; and GDP Growth (Annual %), The World Bank, data.worldbank.org/indicator/NY.GDP.MKTP.KD.ZG?view=map.

The Ethical Challenges in Scaling the Venture

Innovation, risk-taking, and venture creation form the backbone of the free enterprise system. The qualities of individualism and competition that have emerged from this system have helped to create new jobs and generate enormous growth in new ventures. However, these same qualities have also produced complex trade-offs between economic profits and social welfare. On the one hand, the success rate is measured in profits, jobs, and efficiency. On the other hand, there is the quest for personal and social respect, honesty, and integrity. Ideally, society would provide one ethical norm to calculate the greatest good for the greatest number and would thus help resolve such ethical dilemmas. However, developing an *ethical code* that suits all people in all situations is nearly impossible. To illustrate, a study by researchers Justin Longenecker, Joseph McKinney, and Carlos Moore examined the ethical concern of entrepreneurs regarding specific business issues that needed strong ethical actions versus those that could be tolerated more.[26] There was little consensus on the issues, and the contradictory nature of their findings proves that ethical decision-making is a complex challenge due to the nature and personal perception of various issues.[27]

However, general public perception stereotypes *business ethics* as a contradiction in terms. It is a stereotype based on three principal misconceptions that dominate society. The first is that profit and morality are necessarily incompatible. In other words, the pursuit of wealth is a barometer of success, yet it is believed that wealth tends to corrupt individuals. The second is that all ethical problems have simple solutions: They always have a right and a wrong answer. This misconception is based on an assumption that an absolute standard exists for judging moral conduct. The third is that ethics is simply a matter of compliance with laws and regulations. Although laws and regulations often emerge from ethical concerns, they are not *always* considered ethical. In spite of these misconceptions, the fact remains that unethical behavior does take place. Why? A few explanations are possible:

- greed
- an inability to distinguish between activities at work and activities at home
- a lack of foundation in the study of ethics
- survivalist (bottom-line) thinking
- a reliance on other social institutions to convey and reinforce ethics

Ethical decision-making is a challenge faced by small and large businesses. The challenges are only compounded as the venture emerges.[28]

As an example, a popular term that has recently developed in Silicon Valley to describe aggressive scaling is *blitzscaling*, which prioritizes speed over efficiency in an environment of uncertainty. There are three distinct features of blitzscaling: Rapid growth, growth on a global scale, and scaling toward a first mover advantage.[29] As blitzscaling requires companies to prioritize speed over efficiency, companies that grow rapidly are often pressured to cut corners and sacrifice culture and ethics in pursuit of growth. One well-known example is Theranos, a venture that sought to revolutionize the health care industry through its disruptive technology in blood testing, which claimed it could perform hundreds of tests on only a few drops of blood. Started in 2004 with modest investments, Theranos used blitzscaling to grow, and by 2014 it achieved a valuation of $9 billion after receiving more than $600 million from investors. However, problems began to arise as the New York State Department of Health received a formal complaint in 2015 and *The Wall Street Journal* published an article questioning the company's technology, which prompted investigations by the FDA and the Centers for Medicare & Medicaid Services.[30] The investigations and rumors came to a dramatic head in March 2018, when the U.S. Securities and Exchange Commission charged Theranos as well its CEO, Elizabeth Holmes, and COO, Sunny Balwani, with massive fraud. Theranos officially closed its doors in September 2018. In the span of only four years, Theranos went from one of the top startups, valued at $9 billion, to an illegal and unethical venture that had to shut down.[31] Thus, rapid growth must be carefully monitored so that ethical conduct is followed at all times. One established method to employ are codes of conduct.

Ethical Codes of Conduct

In the broadest sense, ethics provides the basic rules or parameters for conducting any activity in an "acceptable" manner. More specifically, ethics represents a set of principles prescribing a behavioral code that explains what is good and right or bad and wrong; ethics may, in addition, outline moral duties and obligations.[32] The problem with most definitions of ethics is that they are static descriptions that imply that society agrees on certain universal principles. Because society operates in a dynamic and ever-changing environment, however, such a consensus does not exist. Continual conflict over the ethical nature of decisions is quite prevalent. Therefore, a code of conduct within a business is a statement of ethical practices or guidelines to which an enterprise adheres. A variety of such codes exist. Some relate to the industry at large, and others relate directly to corporate conduct. These codes cover a multitude of subjects, ranging from misuse of corporate assets, conflict of interest, and use of inside information to equal employment practices, falsification of books and records, and antitrust violations.

Two important points on codes of conduct should be kept in mind. First, codes of conduct are becoming more prevalent in all firms. Management is not just giving lip service to ethics and moral behavior; it is putting its ideas into writing and distributing these guidelines for everyone in the organization to read and follow. Second, in contrast to earlier codes, more recent ones are proving more meaningful in terms of external legal and social development, more comprehensive in terms of their coverage, and easier to implement in terms of the administrative procedures for enforcing them.[33]

New Venture Issues

Tips for Organizational Integrity

In establishing a culture of integrity within a growing organization, there are numerous elements that need to be considered. Researchers have been working with companies to figure out the most crucial elements for organizational leaders to develop. In one recent research article, certain elements were pointed out. Organizations that display true integrity display four characteristics:

1. *The language of ethical decision-making is used.* The employees will openly and confidently discuss the ethical implications of decisions and actions.
2. *Structural supports and procedures that facilitate ethical decision-making have been developed.* Employees have a clear channel to air and discuss problems or issues and explore the gray areas of compliance.
3. *A culture of openness, responsibility, and commitment to multiple business goals has been created and sustained.* Employees can articulate several business goals beyond the bottom line, such as the organization's responsibility to society, employees, the profession, or ideals.
4. *Employee development is valued.* Employees experience regular opportunities to learn and develop. This includes personal and career development opportunities within the organization. This commitment makes employees feel a valuable part of the organization and ties individual success to organizational success.

For organizations to build a culture of integrity there needs to be an understanding of deeply held assumptions. One example is a three-phased approach.

> Phase 1: *Understand the "why" of integrity.* Organizations need to educate employees on the importance of ethics and integrity in all aspects of the job. This helps everyone understand why integrity is crucial to the organization as a whole.
> Phase 2: *Understand the "why not" of integrity.* Clearly spelling out the rewards for ethical actions and the consequences of unethical actions is important for all employees. This is where employees commit to the processes and behaviors that are rewarded.
> Phase 3: *Understand the "practices" of integrity.* Provide employees with the knowledge and tools necessary to resist unethical actions and adopt appropriate behaviors. Coaching and intensive feedback are recommended.

Finally, all of these ideas can only be sustained through a concerted effort by the executive team of the venture. There must be a true *business integration* of all the espoused policies and desired actions. In addition, organizations need to *measure* progress and success in these areas. Moreover, the key component is for *executive support* to be a strategic priority.

Source: Adapted from D. Christopher Keyes, David Stirling, and Tjai M. Nielsen, "Building Organizational Integrity," *Business Horizons*, 2007, 50(1), pp. 61–70.

Ethical Leadership by Entrepreneurs

Even though ethics and social responsibility present complex challenges for owners of growing ventures, the entrepreneur-owner's *value system* is the key to establishing an ethical organization. An owner has the unique opportunity to display honesty, integrity, and ethics in all key decisions. The owner's behavior serves as a model for all employees to follow.

In one study of 282 smaller venture owners, four specific ethical concepts were examined: Business development/profit motive, money-related theft, administrative decision-making, and accession to company pressure. The researchers found underlying dimensions of these concepts that were broader than simple adherence to the law. The study refuted the stereotypes of "ethics equating only to law" or "the law is ethics' only guide." In other words, smaller venture owners rely on considerations beyond the legal parameters when making decisions. Their value systems were demonstrated to be a critical component in business decisions.[34]

In smaller ventures, the ethical influence of the owner is more powerful than in larger corporations because his or her leadership is not diffused through layers of management. Owners are identified easily and are observed constantly by employees in a smaller venture. Therefore, smaller venture owners possess a strong potential to establish high ethical standards for all business decisions.[35]

A recent 20-year longitudinal study on ethical attitudes in smaller firms and large corporations found that ethical decisions are improving across all organizations regardless of size. The researchers also found that leaders in smaller ventures seem to respond more ethically today than they did when the study began in 1985.[36]

New Ventures and the Future

As the pace of change escalates exponentially throughout the world today, it is difficult to imagine exactly what the future will hold for new ventures. Technology has become a driving force in almost every facet of life. This new age of technology will bring forth new ways to build and scale ventures, which means newer challenges may be on the horizon. Disruptive technologies will continue to displace the current methods of business and reshape the world we know today.[37] In a recent report from the Rand Corporation, it was stated that

> the revolution of information availability and utility will continue to profoundly affect the world in all these dimensions. Smart materials, agile manufacturing, and nanotechnology will change the way we produce devices while expanding their capabilities . . . the results could be astonishing. Effects may include significant improvements in human quality of life and life span, high rates of industrial turnover, lifetime worker training, continued globalization, reshuffling of wealth, cultural amalgamation or invasion with potential for increased tension and conflict, shifts in power from nation states to non-governmental organizations and individuals, mixed environmental effects, improvements in quality of life with accompanying prosperity and reduced tension, and the possibility of human eugenics and cloning.[38]

This definitely points to significant changes on the horizon for our world. New ventures will be at the core of fostering exponential change through innovation. Thus, entrepreneurs are the actual masters of the future because they turn ideas into reality.

Even with the uncertainty with regard to the future, we believe the foundational elements of new venture management presented in this book will stand the test of time and change. From inception of the idea to the eventual scaling of the venture, the methods and practices developed throughout this book will serve as an excellent basis for understanding not only the current challenges facing new ventures but also how future uncertainties will drive newer concepts.

Having an understanding of the chapter material will provide any entrepreneur a roadmap for the journey ahead. And that journey will entail creating the future!

Summary

A growing venture presents unique managerial challenges for owners to consider. Understanding the disadvantages as well as advantages of their smaller size helps the entrepreneur/venture manager gain a better focus on their strategies for success. The one-person band syndrome occurs when a smaller venture begins to grow, but the entrepreneur is still accustomed to doing everything alone. Learning to delegate and share responsibilities is essential for the venture to expand. Effective time management through assessment, prioritization, and delegation will help the venture owner avoid wasting valuable time on needless activities and concentrate more on critical areas. Community involvement by the entrepreneur is a distinctive advantage in one sense, but it must be handled carefully. Time—as well as money—is a valuable resource that must be meaningfully budgeted. Finally, continuation of management education is essential if the owner wants to remain current in both knowledge and abilities.

The key elements of the growth stage are control, responsibility, effective delegation, tolerance of failure, change, and flexibility. The entrepreneur's evolution during this stage requires a transition in style from that of an entrepreneur to that of a manager. Differences in focus can be understood by reviewing the five major factors in Table 12.2. Outside assistance is recommended for growing firms. "Quasi-boards" can be developed in which professionals volunteer to assist in an advisory capacity.

The global expansion challenge was explored. The chapter examined the reasons for "going global," the research needed to extend beyond domestic borders, and the threats that need to be understood.

The chapter described the challenges of ethics in newer and smaller ventures today. The complexity of ethical decisions was discussed along with the misconceptions society has in regard to business and ethics. Codes of conduct are statements of ethical practices or guidelines to which a business adheres. These codes of conduct are becoming more prevalent in businesses, and owners are emphasizing their importance to the business more than ever. Business owners can provide ethical leadership due to their personal involvement with the business. The owner's value system can permeate the business and become a standard of ethical performance.

Finally, we concluded the chapter with a look into the future, with all of its uncertainties, and showed that the foundations presented in this book will be a valuable resource for any entrepreneur.

Review and Discussion Questions

1. Identify five unique managerial concerns of smaller ventures.
2. What are some of the advantages and disadvantages associated with the distinction of small size?
3. Define the one-person band syndrome.
4. Describe the six key elements involved in the growth stage of a business.
5. Explain the transition a smaller venture owner must make from entrepreneur to manager.
6. How can a "quasi-board" help smaller ventures?
7. Why should growing ventures globalize their operations?
8. What are some of the major threats and risks associated with foreign markets?
9. Explain the misconception that society has regarding business and ethics.
10. What is a code of conduct and how can it assist ethical practices?
11. How can smaller venture owners assume an ethical business leadership position?
12. What does the future hold for entrepreneurs and their new ventures?

New Venture Consultant

A Case of Growing Pains

When he first opened his own business, Richard Jacobs loved it. He went to work early in the morning and did not leave until after 9:00 P.M. To spend time with his family, he would take off a few hours in the afternoon and then return to the store after supper, staying until closing time. While he was gone from the store in the late afternoon, part-time personnel handled the operation.

That was five years ago. Since then, Richard's business has grown tremendously. Now he employs eight full-time people and sells seven times as much as he did originally. With this increase in business, however, have come a lot of headaches. In particular, Richard has to make many more decisions than he did before. Additionally, although he wants to get his employees involved in the decision-making process and not do all the work himself, he feels he must do many tasks on his own. He does not believe he can delegate much authority. For example, Richard still makes all decisions regarding purchasing, pricing, advertising, hiring, firing, and merchandise display, and he still sells goods in the store.

Recently, Richard went to the doctor for his annual physical. The doctor told him he was working too hard and had to start slowing down. "You've been running that store single-handedly for as long as I can remember," the doctor said. "You've got lots of help in the store. Start relying on them to help you out."

Richard does not disagree. The doctor is offering good advice, and Richard knows he has to start delegating more authority and getting out of the actual hustle and bustle of daily activity. However, this worries him. A few months ago he tried turning over more work to his employees and staying in the background. During that time, he concerned himself with the overall operation of the store and left the minor day-to-day business to the staff. But Richard was bored with this side of the operation. He wants to be actively involved for two reasons. First, he believes the owner-manager's job is to play an active role in the business, not just to sit on the sidelines. Second, he wants to be in the forefront of the action, like he always has been.

Richard does not know how to resolve this dilemma. He would like to maintain his level of involvement at the shop but realizes that, for health reasons, this is inadvisable. However, being a manager in the true sense of the word seems boring to him.

Your Consultation

Help Richard by explaining the key aspects of growing a venture and how important delegation is for growth. Next, explain the key elements in the growth stage Richard should understand. Finally, recommend a way Richard can avoid the one-person band syndrome.

Notes

1 See Donald F. Kuratko, *Entrepreneurship: Theory, Process, & Practice*, 11th ed. Boston, MA: Cengage Publishing, 2017, pp. 391–393; and Zoltan J. Acs, David B. Audretsch, Pontus Braunerhjelm, and Bo Carlsson, "Growth and Entrepreneurship," *Small Business Economics*, 2012, 39 (2): 289–300.

2 Li Dai, Vladislav Maksimov, Brett Anitra Gilbert, and Stephanie A. Fernhaber, "Entrepreneurial Orientation and International Scope: The Differential Roles of Innovativeness, Proactiveness, and Risk-Taking," *Journal of Business Venturing*, 2014, 29 (4): 511–524.

3 Jared D. Harris, Harry J. Sapienza, and Norman E. Bowie, "Ethics and Entrepreneurship," *Journal of Business Venturing*, 2009, 24 (5): 407–418.

4 See Michael H. Morris, Nola N. Miyasaki, Craig R. Watters, and Susan M. Coombes, "The Dilemma of Growth: Understanding Venture Size Choices of Women Entrepreneurs," *Journal of Small Business Management*, 2006, 44 (2): 221–244.

5 Rob Sims, John Breen, and Shameem Ali, "Small Business Support: Dealing with the Impediments to Growth," *Journal of Enterprising Culture*, 2002, 10: 241–256.

6 See Jerry R. Cornwell, "The Entrepreneur as a Building Block for Community," *Journal of Developmental Entrepreneurship*, Fall/Winter 1998, 3 (2): 141–148; and Ana María Peredo and James J. Chrisman, "Toward a Theory of Community-based Enterprise," *Academy of Management Review*, 2006, 31 (2): 309–328.

7 David E. Gumpert and David P. Boyd, "The Loneliness of the Small Business Owner," *Harvard Business Review*, November/December 1984, 19–24.

8 Charles B. Shrader, Charles L. Mumford, and Virginia L. Blackburn, "Strategic and Operational Planning, Uncertainty, and Performance in Small Firms," *Journal of Small Business Management*, October 1989: 45–60; see also Patrice Perry-Rivers, "Stratification, Economic Adversity, and Entrepreneurial Launch: The Effect of Resource Position on Entrepreneurial Strategy," *Entrepreneurship Theory & Practice*, 2016, 40 (3): 685–712.

9 Charles R. Hobbs, "Time Power," *Small Business Reports*, January 1990, 46–55; Jack Falvey, "New and Improved Time Management," *Small Business Reports*, July 1990, 14–17; and B. Claessens, W. van Eerde, C. Rutte and R. Roe, "A Review of the Time Management Literature," *Personnel Review*, 2007, 36 (2), 255–276.

10 Terry L. Besser, "Community Involvement and the Perception of Success among Small Business Operators in Small Towns," *Journal of Small Business Management*, October 1999, 37 (4): 16–29; and Rhonda Walker Mack, "Event Sponsorship: An Exploratory Study of Small Business Objectives, Practices, and Perceptions," *Journal of Small Business Management*, July 1999, 37 (3): 25–30.

11 J. Carlos Jarillo, "Entrepreneurship and Growth: The Strategic Use of External Resources," *Journal of Business Venturing*, 1989, 4: 133–147; and Candida G. Brush, Dennis J. Ceru, and Robert Blackburn, "Pathways to Entrepreneurial Growth: The Influence of Management, Marketing, and Money," *Business Horizons*, 2009, 52 (5): 481–491.

12 Charles W. Hofer and Ram Charan, "The Transition to Professional Management: Mission Impossible?," *American Journal of Small Business*, Summer 1984, 9 (1): 3; see also Michael J. Roberts, "Managing Growth," in *New Business Ventures and the Entrepreneur*. New York: Irwin/McGraw-Hill, 1999, in *Annual Editions, Entrepreneurship (2001)*, pp. 170–172.

13 Hofer and Charan, "The Transition to Professional Management," 4.

14 Ibid., 6.

15 Donald F. Kuratko, Jeffrey S. Hornsby, and Laura M. Corso, "Building an Adaptive Firm," *Small Business Forum*, Spring 1996, 41–48; see also Saul Estrin, Julia Korosteleva, and Tomasz Mickiewicz, "Which Institutions Encourage Entrepreneurial Growth Aspirations?," *Journal of Business Venturing*, 2013, 28 (4): 564–580.

16 Howard H. Stevenson and David E. Gumpert, "The Heart of Entrepreneurship," *Harvard Business Review*, March/April 1985, 85.

17 Donald N. Sull, "Disciplined Entrepreneurship," *MIT Sloan Management Review*, Fall 2004, 71–77; see also Bill Aulet, *Disciplined Entrepreneurship*. Hoboken, NJ: John Wiley & Sons, 2013.

18 James J. Chrisman and John Leslie, "Strategic, Administrative, and Operating Problems: The Impact of Outsiders on Small Business Performance," *Entrepreneurship Theory and Practice*, Spring 1989, 13 (3): 37–49.

19 Harold W. Fox, "Quasi-Boards-Useful Small Business Confidants," *Harvard Business Review*, January/February 1982, 60: 64–72.
20 Fred A. Tillman, "Commentary on Legal Liability: Organizing the Advisory Council," *Family Business Review*, Fall 1988, 1 (3): 287–288.
21 See Donald F. Kuratko and Harold P. Welsch, *Strategic Entrepreneurial Growth*, 2nd ed. Mason, OH: Thomson/South-Western Publishing, 2004; see also Hiroyuki Okamuro and Nobuo Kobayashi, "The Impact of Regional Factors on the Startup Ratio in Japan," *Journal of Small Business Management*, 2006, 44 (2): 310–314; and Lucia Naldi and Per Davidsson, "Entrepreneurial Growth: The Role of International Knowledge Acquisition as Moderated by Firm Age," *Journal of Business Venturing*, 2014, 29 (5): 687–703.
22 Ben Oviatt and Patricia P. McDougall, "Global Start-ups," *Inc.*, June 1993, p. 23
23 Mike Peng, *Global Business*. Mason, OH: Cengage/South-western, 2017; see also Dianne H. B. Welsh, Ilan Alon, and Cecilia M. Falbe, "An Examination of International Retail Franchising in Emerging Markets," *Journal of Small Business Management*, 2006, 44 (1): 130–149.
24 Joe Miller, Martin Arnold, and Miles Johnson, "European Companies Face Coronavirus Hit to Supply Chains," *Financial Times*, February 26, 2020; and Shane Murphy, "The US Industries Hit Hardest by Coronavirus: The Growing Health Crisis Is Shaking Up How the U.S. and the World Do Business," *MoneyWise*, February 25, 2020.
25 Lance E. Brouthers and George Nakos, "The Role of Systematic International Market Selection on Small Firm's Export Performance," *Journal of Small Business Management*, 2005, 43 (4): 363–381; see also Leo Sleuwaegen and Jonas Onkelinx, "International Commitment, Post-Entry Growth and Survival of International New Ventures," *Journal of Business Venturing*, 2014, 29 (1): 106–120; and Hana Milanov and Stephanie A. Fernhaber, "When Do Domestic Alliances Help Ventures Abroad? Direct and Moderating Effects from a Learning Perspective," *Journal of Business Venturing*, 2014, 29 (3): 377–391.
26 Justin G. Longenecker, Joseph A. McKinney, and Carlos W. Moore, "Ethics in Small Business," *Journal of Small Business Management*, January 1989, 27–31.
27 Elisabeth J. Teal and Archie B. Carroll, "Moral Reasoning Skills: Are Entrepreneurs Different?" *Journal of Business Ethics*, April 1999, 19: 229–240; Shailendra Vyakarnman, Andy Baily, Andrew Myers, and Donna Burnett, "Towards an Understanding of Ethical Behavior in Small Firms," *Journal of Business Ethics*, November 1997, 16: 1625–1636; see also Sherry Hoskinson and Donald F. Kuratko (Eds.) *Advances in the Study of Entrepreneurship, Innovation, and Economic Growth; Volume 25: The Challenges of Ethics and Entrepreneurship in the Global Environment*. Bingley: Emerald Press, 2015.
28 George G. Brenkert, "Innovation, Rule Breaking and the Ethics of Entrepreneurship," *Journal of Business Venturing*, 2009, 24 (5): 448–464.
29 Reid Hoffman and Chris Yeh, *Blitzscaling*. New York: Random House, 2018.
30 J. Carreyrou, *Bad Blood: Secrets and Lies in a Silicon Valley Startup*. New York: Knopf, 2018; and Lydia Ramsey, "The Rise and Fall of Theranos, the Blood-Testing Startup That Went from Silicon Valley Darling to Facing Fraud Charges," *Business Insider*, April 11, 2019, accessed on March 22, 2020 at www.businessinsider.com/the-history-of-silicon-valley-unicorn-theranos-and-ceo-elizabeth-holmes-2018-5.
31 Donald F. Kuratko, Harrison Holt and Emily Neubert, "Blitzscaling: The Good, The Bad, and The Ugly," *Business Horizons*, 2020, 63 (1): 109–119.
32 M. Schwartz, "The Nature of the Relationship between Corporate Codes of Ethics and Behaviour," *Journal of Business Ethics*, 2001, 32 (3): 247–262.
33 For more on this topic, see Muel Kaptein and Mark S. Schwartz, "The Effectiveness of Business Codes: A Critical Examination of Existing Studies and the Development of an Integrated Research Model," *Journal of Business Ethics*, 2008, 77 (2): 111–127.
34 Jeffrey S. Hornsby, Donald F. Kuratko, Douglas W. Naffziger, William R. LaFollette, and Richard M. Hodgetts, "The Ethical Perceptions of Small Business Owners: A Factor Analytic Study," *Journal of Small Business Management*, October 1994, 32 (4): 9–16. See also Justin G. Longenecker, Carlos W. Moore, J. William Petty, Leslie E. Palich, and Joseph A. McKinney, "Ethical Attitudes in Small Businesses and Large Corporations: Theory and Empirical Findings from a Tracking Study Spanning Three Decades," *Journal of Small Business Management*, 2006, 44 (2), 167–183.
35 Neil Humphreys et al., "The Ethical Decision-Making Process of Small Business Owner/Managers and Their Customers," *Journal of Small Business Management*, July 1993, 31 (3): 9–22; see also Donald

F. Kuratko, Michael G. Goldsby, and Jeffrey S. Hornsby, "The Ethical Perspectives of Entrepreneurs: An Examination of Stakeholder Salience," *Journal of Applied Management and Entrepreneurship*, 2004, 9 (4): 19–42.

36 Longenecker, Moore, Petty, Palich, and McKinney, "Ethical Attitudes in Small Businesses and Large Corporations: Theory and Empirical Findings from a Tracking Study Spanning Three Decades"; and Terry L. Besser, "The Consequences of Social Responsibility for Small Business Owners in Small Towns," *Business Ethics: A European Review*, 2012, 21 (2): 129–139.

37 Salim Ismail, Michael S. Malone and Yuri van Geest, *Exponential Organizations: Why New Organizations Are Ten Times Better, Faster, Cheaper Than Yours (and What to Do About It)*. New York: Diversion Books, 2014.

38 Rand Corporation, "The Global Technology Revolution," 2015, www.rand.org/pubs/monograph_reports/MR1307/MR1307.sum.html

Appendix: Complete New Venture Plan

Executive Summary

Who Are We?

Liquivinyl LLC is an automotive enthusiast company created by two college students. We strive to produce the best value products with customer feedback in mind. Our foundation comes from years of experience in spray wrap—a paint solution that can peel off like a wrap. The idea wasn't scalable, and we were anxious to build on our potential. As we created a name and took on bigger tasks, we pivoted to aerodynamic parts after being frustrated with current offerings. Aftermarket aerodynamic parts allow enthusiasts to add functional styling cues to their vehicles. Our company makes components for the front, sides, and rear of the vehicle. Uncovering a new-to-market material, we targeted the current generation of Mustangs to test and validate our product.

What Are We Competing Against?

Aerodynamic parts are made from three materials: Plastic, metal, and carbon fiber. The plastic materials are cheap and flimsy; metal is not durable, as it must be cut thin for this application; and carbon fiber is far too expensive, priced at around $1,000.

Why Are We Unique?

The material we are bringing to market is a plastic and aluminum hybrid—an aluminum skin with a poly core. Metal surface strength to provide rigidness and a solid poly core to give the product durability while maintaining light weight. The end result? A practical product that can take a beating and look great while doing so at $225. We are in the provisional patent process.

Sales to Date

We officially released our test product line on January 1, 2019. At the end of quarter one (Q1), we had just surpassed $21,000 in sales, with no defective products or customer complaints. Since then, we've also surpassed our goals of 100 units sold and 100 orders.

Marketing Strategy

We are targeting enthusiasts who are looking to customize the appearance of their vehicles. Specifically, young males in states such as California, Texas, and Florida. By offering ambassador discounts and sponsorships for both individuals and groups, we can implement experiential word of mouth marketing to build brand equity and drive sales.

Management and Advisors

As our company grows, we plan to expand our reach by launching product lines for a new model of car quarterly. We believe feedback is a gift and push to do the best we can for every product, every customer, every time. There are two owners pushing the growth, both prospective Indiana University grads with degrees in finance, entrepreneurship, and informatics. Our board of advisors includes experts in automotive small business, manufacturing, and marketing.

Company Overview

Liquivinyl LLC was created out of a desire. The world of cars is very much pay to play—an expensive hobby that leaves you wanting more. Being a car enthusiast in college can be frustrating. Often we don't have our own tools, a safe space to work on our cars, or money for parts. Getting tired of hiding in parking garages to work on our cars, we aspired to build a brand for ourselves to help us afford these amenities and maximize our potential as enthusiasts. In 2018, we've made a major pivot to start manufacturing our own line of aerodynamic products under the name LVA (Liquivinyl Aerodynamics).

Liquid Wrap—What Is Liquivinyl?

Our first gig came from a friend who owned a used car dealership. He had been looking to outsource vinyl wrap work for his high-end vehicles. Vinyl wrap is a labor-intensive process in which workers conform adhesive vinyl sheeting to body panels on a car. Imagine a giant sticker applied with perfection on an entire vehicle. The wrap can be peeled at any time, allowing one to effectively change the color of their car. It is rather difficult to apply, doesn't behave like paint (cannot buff or wax), and is limited to pre-manufactured colors. This cost a lot in material but far more in labor hours.

Luckily, we had numerous years of experience in spray wrap—a competitor to vinyl wrap. A spray wrap is sprayed through a paint gun onto the vehicle. The solution can still be peeled off the car, and the top coat is a real automotive clear coat (it has an overdose of flex agent, allowing it to peel off with the base coats). It takes far less time to spray down a vehicle, and we were able to offer our customers the ability to mix any color of their choice using liquid formulas. Offering a superior product while pushing out eye-catching designs (such as arctic camo), we quickly built a name within our community.

Pivoting From Wrap to Aerodynamic Parts

The pivot point started with our first overhaul project. The same used car dealership provided us all the shop space and covered our utilities in exchange for discounted work. This project in particular required a part called a front splitter (shown in the graphic), an accessory that the owner of the dealer said was gaining interest and wanted us to display. We ordered a top of the line product from APR for roughly $500 out the door, but it was too heavy for our application. It would not adhere properly, even breaking off the vehicle and dragging on the road. We had a custom splitter made out of plastic at low cost (opposite end of the spectrum) for about $100. The quality was subpar at best. The surface was unfinished, and the product warped in the sunlight a few days after. In the process of ordering the cheaper unit, we began to realize how quick and easy the R&D for such a product was, as the two units were identical in shape—the flaw was in the materials. We validated our vision by reaching out to our personal car-related social media followings (combined 20,000 followers) and became amazed as we saw the interest and encouraging words flood through our messages. We set out to find our own solution for this problem. The end result is Liquivinyl Aerodynamics (LVA). A proprietary line of aero products with a new-to-market material that solves our needs—a stronger, lighter, better product.

Our Product

Not only are LVA products affordable, but our unique material also provides consumers with aerodynamic parts that are durable, functional, and lightweight. We design splitters, side skirts, diffusers, and canards for each submodel of a vehicle to ensure our customers have the best fitting, full coverage kits of the highest quality. The front splitter is the most popular product by far, taking over 80 percent of our sales.

Legality

Our company filed as an LLC on July 25, 2018. There are two owners at a 50/50 split. **LLC fees in the state of Indiana are $85 up front (E-file) and $30 every other year**. We have also purchased a **retail merchant's certificate for $25, which is a one-time cost** with free renewal. We are currently in the provisional patent process, which will be touched on in the intellectual property section.

Accomplishments to Date

We have both been surprised and anxious after seeing a successful Q1 in 2019. We beat our 100-unit goal, with 110 units sold. We broke $20,000 in sales while operating in one test market, with zero defective units. Overall, the feedback in Q1 gave us a boost in confidence and a stronger will to serve our customers.

Management

Brian Tao

Brian is a junior at Indiana University, studying finance and entrepreneurship. His current responsibilities are administrative. This means managing legal documents and compliances, handling accounting and tax filings, paying bills, ordering materials from suppliers, and following up on account management. He currently manages the social media accounts as well.

His leadership experience comes from a background at Culver Military Academy (class of 2016). In terms of automotive knowledge, Brian worked at a local Auto-Zone before transitioning to recon management at an exotic car dealership, managing over $1 million in vehicles at one time. He has interned with Quicken Loans in business analysis, law, and human resources.

Brenden Beshore

Brenden is a sophomore at Ball State, transferring to Indiana University fall of 2019. There he will be pursuing a degree in informatics. His current day-to-day operations include scheduling contractors, paying wages, overseeing material delivery, and overseeing package shipment. He also purchases some materials from local shops and supplies personally and is heavily involved in order fulfillment and quality control. He takes all product photos and creates promotional videos as well. Media is a hobby of his, and he is able to produce top quality content using his own equipment.

Brenden began offering automotive detailing services five years ago. He first started spray wrap three years ago under the brand name "Driven." In high school, he was competitive in DECA and placed third in his three years of experience at states, one year competing internationally.

Team Gaps

One of the biggest flaws in our team is not having manufacturing industry knowledge. We are eager to learn more about physical components, such as which manufacturing techniques are most suitable for what kinds of materials and what work flows in manufacturing are easier than others. We can further develop our proficiency by utilizing software that is standard to the industry. For example, efficiency in a CAD system would drastically improve our new product design work flow and ability to communicate designs with other firms. We can attempt to combat this by bringing on multiple advisors who have high industry knowledge. Additionally, CAD courses have been accounted for in expansion costs to help offset this knowledge gap. As young entrepreneurs, there is much to be learned about business in general. Neither of us has graduated college or held a full-time job (internships excluded). We are severely lacking in these experiences but are quickly learning from every mistake we make. We carry this saying through our everyday lives: "Only make new mistakes." If a mistake is new, it is worth the learning process in our eyes. We need guidance to offset our potentially emotionally charged decisions to place us in the best position for future growth. We've asked some relevant business owners to advise us.

Advisory Board Members

Jake Aruta, Marketing President at iHeart Media. He has over 15 years' experience in growth-focused marketing strategy. He also has an extensive background in building business teams that perform strongly.

Elanor Daily, Manager at Mitsubishi Electric Automation. She has 20+ years of experience managing a team that provides manufacturing solutions for automobile companies. She is highly knowledgeable on the different software, equipment, and process flows in modern-day automotive manufacturing.

Blake Hansley, Owner, Lackard Machine—one of the oldest and largest jobbing machine shops in the St. Louis area. Blake not only has industry expertise in machining and working with similar materials, but he is also an avid car enthusiast. We have the opportunity to meet with him in person often.

Tom Relaten, Owner and CEO, DipYourCar—the go to resource for removable paint solutions. Tom is a known innovator in the automotive styling space. Not only is he a great resource for trends and building connections, but he also has a business degree and recently left a successful career in consulting.

Rinagen & Associates, U.S. patent attorneys specializing in identifying, protecting, and preserving these assets, a requirement for success in today's highly competitive marketplace. Alex Rinagen has been great in offering free help in our patent process. He has offered to continue offering advice and overseeing our progress.

Dr. Regan Stevenson, Professor at Indiana University—a professor with strong experience in entrepreneurship and business strategy. Additionally, he will be key in providing insight on his expertise in distribution.

Dan Houser, CPA, H&L Associates P.C.—one of the most respected accountants in Bloomington. Dan is experienced and works with other businesses with similar functions in the area. Dan is a great resource for financial and accounting guidance.

Industry Analysis

Current Test Market

We consider the s550 generation (latest generation) Ford Mustang our test market. Brenden owns a highly modified Mustang (s550 generation), so it was very convenient to use his vehicle as an outlet to build brand reputation and gather feedback. We have also built aerodynamic kits for those who have worked for us, so we have listed those products on our website to portray to customers that we don't plan on being just a Mustang parts company.

Market Overview

Car enthusiasts have unique buying trends, just as in any other industry. Often, this is influenced by what's known as show season and tax season. Car enthusiasts habitually buy in the winter months, especially around the tax return period. Purchasing habits resurface in peak summer months at a lower rate, as car culture is more active in warmer months, leading to more word of mouth interaction. Enthusiasts like to "build" their cars throughout the winter to prep them for the summer season. In the summer, they are focused on attending events as well as working on their cars. The data are provided by Hedges & Company. Unfortunately, more relevant data were not available.

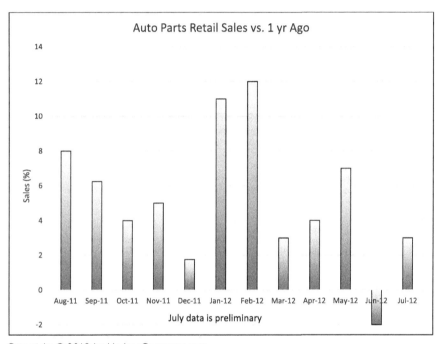

Auto Parts Retail Sales vs. 1 yr Ago

July data is preliminary

Relevant Market Size

The best resource to study this market is the **Specialty Equipment Market Association (SEMA)** of the automobile aftermarket. SEMA is the most credible body, encompassing all things automotive aftermarket. In their 2018 market report, SEMA estimates the size of the accessory and appearance products market at $23.05 billion. We can break down market sizing from a couple different statistics in the fender, hood, and body upgrades section. Thirty-four percent of users are purchasing online only, with no installation. Additionally, seven percent of consumers are purchasing directly from manufacturer, and 23 percent of the market is purchasing for a sports car or small car application. Finally, example parts in this section include fenders, body kits, bumpers, and hoods, of which our product would fit best under body kits.

We will divide the market into four parts to account for this segment. The total market size for the fender, hood, and body upgrades section is $1.78 billion.

Customer Analysis

Target Customers

Our ideal tip of the spear customer is a Mustang owner who lives in a warm climate (large car enthusiast populations) such as California, Florida, or Texas and is aged 20, male, and attends many shows and events. He has already shown an interest in car care or has modifications on his car. As we offer sponsorship opportunities and hunt for brand ambassadors, we have found a large majority of applicants fit these demographics.

Demographics and Validation

The aerodynamic trend caters to young car enthusiasts. SEMA provides these statistics:

AGE % OF TOTAL U.S. POPULATION			Source: 2016 SEMA Consumer Market Data
	TOTAL U.S. POPULATION	ACCESORIZERS	NON-ACCESORIZERS
18-29	21%	28%	19%
30-39	17%	27%	14%
40-49	17%	18%	17%
50-59	18%	15%	19%
60+	27%	12%	31%

The 18–29 age range is our largest market of "accessorizers." Our current Instagram followers show that 83 percent of our audience is between the ages of 18 and 34, which is perfectly in line with our target market. Of that age range, we **are targeting the 18- to 24-year-olds**. Additionally, most of our followers are male. Current data from Instagram analytics:

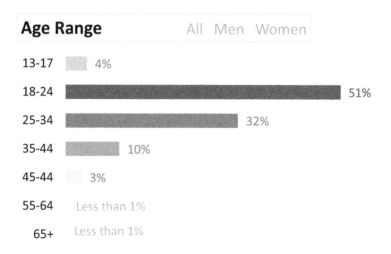

Age Range   All   Men   Women

13-17	4%
18-24	51%
25-34	32%
35-44	10%
45-44	3%
55-64	Less than 1%
65+	Less than 1%

Gender

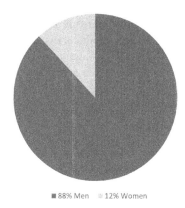

■ 88% Men   ▨ 12% Women

From our Squarespace analytics tool, we found that most of our website visits are from the previously listed states: California, Texas, and Florida. The next set of states to target would be the Midwest. There is a large population of car enthusiasts in Indianapolis, Chicago, and Detroit. Additionally, we can attend a lot of local events here with ease to further boost our reach.

Interactions With Customers

We attempt to set ourselves apart from our competitors by being active on social media and available to our audience. We believe that feedback is a gift, and there is no better way to gather feedback than directly from the consumer. Often, consumers have simple, clarifying questions. We can turn around with a fast, polite answer and offer a discount code. On many occasions, this has resulted in a sale. Additionally, we are often commended for our customer service in these types of interactions, which is great for our brand equity. Most importantly, customers let us know what they want to see in our current products. A customer of ours with a 2018 Mustang noticed that our product was partially covering brake ducts on the underside of the vehicle. After speaking with the customer numerous times over video chat, he helped us clearly understand the issue and derive a solution. Now, all of our 2018 model year products include two cutouts for better flow in the brake ducts. The customer shared all the measurements with us. In return, we offered him a discount on all future products and sent some promotional goodies (shirts and stickers). Since then, he has sent us numerous sales through word of mouth, and we commonly converse casually as well. These types of interactions align with the core of what we stand for as a brand. Aside from learning what customers are looking for in existing products, customers also let us know what cars they'd like to see us make product lines for. For example, we have received an overwhelming amount of requests for s197 Mustang and 5th generation Camaro products, so they are the next two product lines in our growth plan.

Customer Needs

In this automotive aftermarket enthusiast space, customers are always looking for the best quality at fair pricing. Customers are looking for firms that are personable, flexible, and able to give them products that are both unique in design and functional in purpose. With a great product comes great customer service. We make ourselves available on social media and reply to every customer within a few hours.

Competitive Analysis

There are three main classifications of aerodynamic products: Plastic, metal, and carbon fiber. We will break down each type of offering.

We are currently the only company that produces aerodynamic parts from a poly and aluminum hybrid material.

Direct Competitors

Plastic competitors sell lower tier products. Commonly, these firms use ABS plastic that is cheap and lightweight. This is a very popular solution (plastic), and firms can charge as little as $100 (before shipping). The downside to plastic is that it is flimsy and doesn't have high surface strength. Additionally, plastic becomes malleable with heat, and with cooling it retains its new shape. The end result can be a warped, wavy looking product.

Metal competitors are the middle tier. You can find product offerings in the $300–$400 range. Metal will provide a much higher surface strength and resistance to warping. The issue with metal is that, to keep weight down, the metal must be cut extremely thin. This leaves consumers with a brittle product that cracks easily. This is the least popular option.

Carbon fiber competitors are the highest tier. These materials are usually found in high end cars like Lamborghini, Ferrari, etc. The product offerings hover around the $1,000 range, with some exceptions. Carbon fiber is extremely strong and offers a great aesthetic bonus. However, even though carbon fiber is known to be a lightweight material, carbon products are still relatively heavy for this application. The material is not easy to work with either.

Our **main competitor is APR Performance**. They are the only firm that portrays the same level of quality and customer care that we strive to provide. Our lead time on products is one week. Most of our competitors take multiple weeks or even months to deliver the product. APR works with carbon fiber exclusively and takes two weeks' lead time. This is a much more expensive material due to its woven nature. Regardless of carbon fiber's popularity, our product can still provide a metal surface strength at less than 50 percent the weight of APR products. We were able to compare an APR splitter to ours and found that with the same dimensions, our product weighed seven pounds versus APR's 17 pounds. APR prices their products starting at $428. We price around $225, with more details in the pricing section in the marketing plan.

Indirect Competitors

Chin spoilers are the alternative competitor to front splitters. For all four of our product categories, full body kits can also be seen as a competitor. Both chin spoilers and body kits need to be painted, while traditional aero parts do not.

Chin spoilers are pieces that enhance purely the aesthetic of a vehicle's front bumper. They have little to no functional purpose. Splitters are 2D shapes (flat), while chin spoilers are 3D shapes that are molded. The splitter attaches to only the bottom of the bumper, while the chin spoiler uses its molded shape to fit only the outer edge of the bumper, including the front face of the bumper. The products are often plastic or fiberglass and are priced in the neighborhood of $250–$500.

Body kits change the look of a car. A body kit involves either replacing existing panels on a car or adhering major attachments to them. Most body kits needs to be installed by a professional body shop, which can be very expensive. This method is a far more complicated alternative. Shipping alone on a body kit costs more than a full kit from our product line. Full body kit costs after paint tend to be $7,000 or more, according to some estimates. However, it is still a route that some take to achieve a similar aesthetic effect.

Competitive Advantage

Our competitive advantage comes from our material. The material is constructed from a special core sandwiched between two thin aluminum skins, with a painted finish on top. The aluminum surface retains high strength and won't allow the product to warp. The solid poly core gives the product lightweight thickness, increasing durability. Our material itself is also fairly cheap—about the same price as our plastic competitor's materials. An LVA product is lightweight, strong, durable, and at an incredible price point, starting at $225.

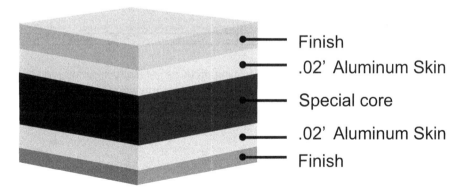

Finish
.02' Aluminum Skin
Special core
.02' Aluminum Skin
Finish

Intellectual Property

We are currently in the process of filing for a provisional patent. The patent work has been taken pro bono by law firm Faegre Baker Daniels. The material is new to this application, but the material itself is not a new invention. It has previously been used in other industries. Therefore, it was not obvious for use, as the material was invented many years prior to our use. There are no competitors using this material currently, and the use of this material gives our product a competitive advantage. We hope to secure the ability to use this type of material in exterior car parts overall. Our lawyers have given us an estimated time frame of mid-June. As pro bono clients, we need to pay only **the filing fees, at a maximum of $280**. In one year, we can expect to pay about **$8,000 for the patent**—an estimate provided by our advisor, Tim Thomas.

Brand and Product Positioning

We aim to position our brand as a firm that offers superior materials with superior service at budget pricing. Our materials enable us to charge low prices, yet the nature of the material outperforms anything else in its price range. Our customer service is fast and friendly. We want our customers to be our friends and feel that by messaging us they are asking a friend for help, not sitting in a queue for a commercial response.

Products and Services

Our current line of products is comprised of four components: Splitters, diffusers, side skirts, and canards. We will not be offering installation services, as this is a high liability for us that would not yield a high return for resources used. Here is how the products appear on our website:

Marketing Plan

Our pricing chart is as follows:

Unit	Splitter	Splitter +Rods	Splitters + Side Fins	Splitter +Rods + Side Fins	Diffuser Kit	Canards	Side Skirts
List Price	$225.00	$245.00	$255.00	$275.00	$140.00	$150.00	$140.00

Compared to other vehicles, the Mustang products are large, meaning products for other vehicles use significantly less material. Our pricing strategy should not increase, as material costs will not increase.

Promotional Strategy

According to a study by McKinsey, word of mouth drives 20–50 percent of sales, and this method is even more effective if it's a first time purchase or a relatively expensive purchase. We want to utilize experiential word of mouth by incentivizing early adopters who are strategically selected. We are currently promoting our business by sponsoring vehicles, going to events, partnering with clubs, and attending numerous shows to let consumers experience our product. To strictly boost sales platforms, we look to push Instagram advertisements, capitalize on abandoned carts, and integrate eBay sales.

Sponsorship Overview

We refer to sponsorships as partnerships or arrangements with individuals, clubs, and events. The term *sponsorship* is popular in the automotive enthusiast industry to describe any type of professional relationship. In the Discount Provided column, we dictate what discount percentage is provided. These sponsored parties use these discounts when buying products for their personal use. Additionally, we provide a discount code (ten percent or less) to provide to their followings. It is important to note that not all of these arrangements are full, 100 percent sponsorships, but partial sponsorships at discount. The following table details these relationships:

Sponsorships		
Discount Provided	Qualifications	Obligations
20%	Good social media following (2,000+), good social media interaction, high quality photos	None
30%	More than 5,000 followers and meets 20% requirements OR Military Status	None
50%	Media obligation sponsorship. We require high youtube following or the use of a professional cinematography team.	20% up front discount.The additional 30% is kicked back upon completion of this video.
50%	Be a test/template car or product photo car	Must bring car to us - have bumper removed for product fitting and allow for photo/video work afterwards
100%	Media obligation and discount code/sales sponsorship. Meet 50% requirements and receive a 10% kickback per sale. For very high profiles only (over 1M views on Youtube, 10,000+ followers, or comperable)	50% up front discount, second 50% kicked back upon reaching 5 sales (using propreitary discount code).
Club (10%)	Club must include at least one of our sponsored cars.	Grant access to club social media pages. List our business as an officail sponsor on pages.
EVENT (10%) + $100 voucher	Event must be tailored to our product line (ie. Event just for Mustangs)	Place our logo on all event fliers and ads, tag our Instagram on all posts.

Sponsored Cars/Brand Ambassadors

Sponsored cars act as our brand ambassadors. Some customers get on board with just a 20 percent discount for their products. Other arrangements involve free products in exchange for review videos, sales targets, etc. We are much more selective with regard to any of the sponsorships over 30 percent. These sponsored individuals can earn their money back through sales (tracked through use of their discount codes) and therefore will be much more motivated and active in talking about our company. This can hurt us if these individuals are not chosen wisely! We suspect that these sponsored individuals will be most effective in their first year. We will be allocating $1,000 per product line to drive traction in early stages.

Partnered Shops

A great way to help boost our sales and build relationships is by offering our product at a discount to local shops. We have already begun testing this with a local performance mechanic shop: Jericho Motorsport. We offer the product to the shop at a ten percent discount. The shop specializes in cars that we have products for. The shop also generates additional revenue by offering installation services. We have looped Jericho Motorsport into our sponsorship program as a partnered shop. These discounts are accounted for in our sales discounts variable expense.

Partnered Clubs

Clubs can help us narrow down a group of potential customers. For example, we can extend a club discount of five percent to a Mustang owners club. We can locate these clubs on Instagram, Facebook, and forums. These discounts are accounted for in our sales discounts variable expense.

Instagram

Our company utilizes an Instagram heavy strategy to better target customers. We have one person dedicated to answering Instagram messages and comments and have **received outstanding feedback on our service so far**. Currently, we like AND comment on ALL photos where we have been tagged or mentioned. We reply to every story mention and respond to every message within two to three hours. We **post three times a week** and consistently post stories to tease our audience with new products, informing them of things happening in our customer community, etc. We estimate spending on this space to be **$600 monthly**, costing $50 per post. Instagram's built-in tools will divert our ads to our selected market, with criteria such as age, region, and interest. We will focus these posts from sponsored vehicles on products that have reached their estimated one year effective life but will spread out spending over the estimated three-year duration of a significant volume from a new product line.

Research from Forrester demonstrates the capability and advantage of an Instagram-based marketing model. **Instagram's ability to engage and touch followers is far superior** to comparable marketing platforms.

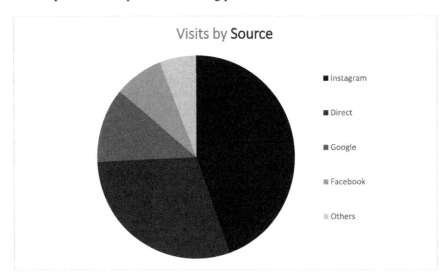

On the back end, Instagram is validated as a source of web traffic. To the left is a display of unique visitor figures from top sources this year. Almost half of our traffic is derived from Instagram.

Trade Shows and Events

Our strategy is to bring three display vehicles to every show. We will be driving two of our own vehicles and inviting a local sponsored car to fill the third spot. Below are some events we look to attend to expand our visibility.

The Performance Racing Industry (PRI) trade show is one of the 100 largest trade shows in the United States. The show is attended every December by over 1,100 exhibiting companies and racing pros from 72 countries. It is a fantastic place to meet new suppliers and vendors and make personal connections to find advisors and mentors. Attending last year, we were able to learn so much about new equipment and manufacturing processes! The PRI trade show is the largest show on our list, making it the most expensive. We will be purchasing their smallest size package. **It includes a 10 × 10-foot booth for $1,800**. No other expenses will be factored in, as the show is in our home state and less than one hour travel time. **Total cost to attend: $1,800**.

Atlantic City Enthusiast Summit (ACES) is a new-to-industry show starting this year (2019) in May. The ACES show is unique, as it is open to every category: Off road, old school, sports cars, etc. This show is possible due to the combined efforts of a plethora of East Coast automotive enthusiasts. A great incentive for us to attend ACES is to expand our reach in the Northeast market and take advantage of exclusive pricing. As we have a good relationship with one of the event coordinators, **we are able to secure a three-car booth with electricity for only $500**. We can estimate an additional $1,000 overhead cost to cover travel, hotel, and food for our team. **Total cost to attend: $1,500**.

Tuner Evolution is a traveling car show. Here is their description for the Chicago event: "Held at Schaumburg Convention Center on September 14th 2019 (Indoor/Outdoor Show Fields). Coming to Chicago for the 3rd time as a full automotive lifestyle event." Tuner Evolution is a great place to build social media presence and brand image with car culture, rather than industry. While other shows are more business-to-business-oriented, Tuner Evolution attracts younger enthusiasts who are looking to observe the latest trends. We would spend roughly $800 to secure adequate booth space and estimate an additional $600 to cover gas, hotels, and food for our team. **Total cost to attend: $1,400**.

Horsepower Lyfe–Florida Ride Out Dyno Day. This event is more of a functional event for enthusiasts. A dyno is a machine used to test power output on a vehicle, and these events are very popular with all car modification enthusiasts. Below is an ad by Horsepower Lyfe. You can see our logo among other top tuner brands, such as Corsa and Adams. Our cost of entry is providing gift vouchers as prizes. For 2019, we are providing a 1st place $100 voucher, two 2nd place $50 vouchers, and five 3rd place $20 vouchers. As this show is more functional/active and not about exhibition, we will not be attending in person. Our sponsored vehicles are attending on behalf of us. **Total cost to attend: $300 in vouchers**.

Assuming we attend each of these events annually, our total trade show and event cost comes to $5,000.

Distribution Channels

Currently, our main channel is our online sales platform powered by Squarespace. Driving continuous traffic to our website will help us take better advantage of all of the analytics and benefits through Squarespace's highest tier offerings. As we expand, we hope to push our products to eBay as well to gain more exposure.

Abandoned Cart

Our sales platforms built in analytics show that out of 62 percent of visitors, 14 percent add to cart, and 19 percent of those consumers then move on to make a purchase. **The end result is that 1.65 percent of our page visits currently result in a transaction**. By upgrading our Squarespace package, we gain access to the full set of features. This platform will help us tap into information on customers who have left behind abandoned carts.

Our estimates show that with abandoned cart data displays, we can recover over $20,000 in carts. According to Klaviyo's Ecommerce Industry Benchmark Report, firms selling products in the $100–$500 range can expect to recoup four percent of abandoned cart sales.

*The recoverable data charts are provided by our provider, Squarespace, as they began collecting this data in 2016.

The service can automatically send recovery emails to potential customers who have already shown a heightened interest by creating a customer profile for checkout. We are hoping to incentivize these customers by **providing alternative contact information (Instagram) and five percent discount codes**

The current cost for our web platform provider is $26 per month (prepaid annually). After upgrading to the highest package, which includes abandoned cart recovery, our **fees will increase to $40 per month**.

eBay

This sales platform is very popular in the car enthusiast market. Not only will it make our products easier to find, but we can also take advantage of all the payment options, financing programs, etc., that eBay has to offer. Almost all of our competitors have products on eBay. As consumers continue to search for products there, our brand will gain more exposure. An eBay user selling a direct competitor to our product has sold an average of seven units a month.

Growth and Expansion

According to SEMA's market report, the entire automotive aftermarket **industry is expected to grow at roughly four percent a year.**

Facility Expansion

The year 2019 is a year to test our market and build our brand equity. We want to observe one full year's performance before investing capital for expansion. Additionally, we can focus efforts in 2019 on building brand equity and giving each of our expansion choices due diligence. In August 2019, as both owners will be in Bloomington, the business will relocate from Muncie to a residential garage in Bloomington. In 2020, we anticipate outgrowing current facilities with the addition of new product lines. For cost analysis, we've included new monthly costs, annual costs, and fixed one-time costs for the full year. These cost structures will be broken down in the financial portion of this plan.

New Product Strategy

As we continue to pursue success in the s550 generation Mustang market, we can multiply our volume by introducing product lines for more cars. It is important to note that our test market, the s550 (2015+) Mustang, refers to just one generation of the Mustang; each generation can be referred to as a new market. Commonly, a generation is three to five years, with automakers usually refreshing styles every generation. To assess how each product line will affect our sales, we can use the size of the market to derive a growth multiple. Data are available from carsalesbase. com regarding how many units of that vehicle generation are sold in the United States (by year). By dividing the number of available vehicles by our baseline test market, we can attempt to gauge how much of an impact each new product line will have on our business.

In year four, we plan to further expand our product offerings based on the feedback of our customers. There are many potential applications for this material regarding automotive aftermarket parts. We plan to lead off with our test market in year four, deploying items such as fog light delete panels, rear seat delete panels, aluminum vents, and other products that are frequently requested by consumers. All of these products can be made with our flat material sheets, and the manufacturing process is very similar. **We're expecting to see a ten percent growth in sales as a result.**

Market Expansion to Canada

Speaking with our customers online, we've noticed an increased demand for products in Canada. Our UPS policies and rates cover Canada, Puerto Rico, and the U.S. Virgin Islands. We can use the same growth multiple strategy to assess growth results from entering Canada:

We can attribute an additional eight percent of growth to this expansion. This expansion will take place in year four, or 2022.

United States Sales		Canada Sales	
s550 Mustang		**s550 Mustang**	
2018	75,842	2018	8,055
2018	81,866	2017	8,348
2016	105,932	2016	7,655
2015	122,439	2015	6,787
Total Size	386,079	Total Size	30,845
Weight of Market	100.00%	Weight of Market	7.99%

Growth Schedule

We plan to release a new product line every quarter starting 2020. For 2019, the strategy is to release a new product line only in Q3 to allow for proper brand development and to build a strong foundation for future growth. Our growth schedule is purposefully staggered by alternating between high market share and low market share vehicles. This will help to act as a buffer for our business in case there are any quality control, volume, or fulfillment issues. Simultaneously, we can continue adding new product lines to build further brand equity for LVA. The graphic on the next page shows a potential year's growth schedule. The figures in yellow are the calculated growth multiples (new vehicle units sold/test market units sold).

7th Generation Charger = 183 percent
5th Generation Camaro = 125 percent
Subaru BRZ = ten percent
Kk2 Genesis Coupe = nine percent

Operations Plan

With our 2020 expansion plan, some costs will fluctuate as order quantities rise. All pricing data changes between 2019 and 2020 are directly from suppliers.

Key Functions

Currently, manufacturing and distribution are in-house processes. As we grow to new markets, we will outsource manufacturing to a local water jet company.

Production

After speaking with an industry expert on our board of advisors, we learned that the **best method for manufacturing our product is water jet**. Water jets are fairly expensive machines, with costs of the machine, transportation, installation, setup, and training totaling over $100,000. A water jet allows for clean cuts on the metal surface without compromising overheating issues in the plastic core (may occur with machines like C&C). At 2019 quantities, water jet will cost $22 per unit. In 2020, costs will be reduced to $20 per unit with higher quantities.

With current in-house manufacturing, we have to sand and clean our products after cutting. By outsourcing to water jet, no sanding is necessary. After sanding, the splitters need edge trim. **The trim process is for splitters and canards ONLY.** This is a rubberized material that adds a high end finish to the exposed product edge and hides any imperfections in the cutting process. The rubber lip wraps around both sides of the product and includes an adhesive on the inner edges.

Materials

LVA products are cut from 12-meter sheets. The material is supplied by Masters, Inc., a plastic fabrication company in Indianapolis, Indiana. **Each sheet of material can cut two splitters and a variety of smaller pieces.** The "drop" is the leftover material after a cut and can cut a large number of smaller products. The maximum lead time on materials is one week.

Each sheet is 8 × 4 feet and is ordered in quantities of ten. Alternatively, one sheet can also cut four sets of side skirts and a set of fins for each set. As side skirt cuts are long and tedious, we have them machine cut by the supplier.

To estimate costs, we will assume that one sheet cuts two splitters, two sets of side fins, and one rear diffuser kit. Delivery fee is our wage to our drivers. Below is the breakdown of material costs. The bolded figures show economies of scale adjustments taking place in 2020.

	Full Material Sheet Pricing			Precut Side Skirt Pricing	
	Unit Price 2019	Unit Price 2020+	Total	Unit	Total
Material Cost	$59.00	**$56.28**	$562.80	$7.58	$75.75
Tax	$4.13	**$3.94**	$39.40	$0.53	$5.30
Delivery	$4.55	**$1.00**	$50.00	$4.55	$50.00
Total Costs	$67.68	**$61.22**	$652.20	$12.65	$131.05

Material Cost Per Unit				
Unit	# Per Sheet	% of Material Sheet	Cost Per Unit 2019	**Cost Per Unit 2020+**
Splitter	2	18%	$11.84	$10.71
Side fins (Set)	2	3%	$1.69	$1.53
Diffuser (Kit)	1	10%	$6.77	$6.12
Canards (Set)	1	10%	$6.77	$6.12
Total Units	6	60%		

The edge trim is from a special supplier. The material is purchased from AutoZone at $12.99, and one roll can complete two units. The product is purchased at $10.52 after commercial discounts. **Cost is $5.26 per splitter. Additionally, cost is $2.63 per set of canards.**

Listed below are individual hardware pieces as well as the costs associated with each type of product offering. The hardware comes from a contracted company and has a maximum lead time of seven business days. The hardware is treated for resistance to the elements. The bolded figures show economies of scale adjustments taking place in 2020.

Hardward Prices With Economies of Scale		
Item	Unit Price 2019	Unit Price 2020
Button Head SCS BLK #6-32x12"	$0.08	$0.07
Finishing Cup Washer 1/4	$0.06	$0.05
Finishing Cup Washer BLK #6	$0.05	$0.05
Flat Washer SAE 1/4	$0.05	$0.04
MS Nuts Black #6-32	$0.08	$0.07
Nylon Lock Nut 1/4	$0.04	$0.03
SS Socket Cap Screw BLK 1/4-20x1"	$0.28	$0.27
Flat Washer BLK #6	$0.09	$0.08
Black Corner Braces	$1.08	$1.07

Hardware Costs		
Unit	$ Value 2019	$ Value 2020
Splitter	$5.16	$4.68
Side Fins (Set)	$6.72	$6.44
Diffuser Kit	$24.48	$23.60
Canards	$13.44	$12.88
Sikde Skirt	$6.88	$6.24

Splitters can also utilize an accessory known as a "rod," which is a support piece we saw on over 90 percent of sales. We purchase the rods from a noted supplier. We purchase the rods in quantities of 15 and drop ship rods to customers when we are out of stock. The lead time is roughly one week to receive in-house or three days to drop ship to customers. We offer multiple colors and sizes online. For the sake of analysis, we will average the cost of long and short. After building a relationship with the supplier, our rod prices are:

Rod Costs	
Unit	$ Value Per Unit
Long	$15.29
Short	$13.59
Drop Ship Long	$16.19
Drop Ship Short	$14.39
Average	$14.87

We will use the average cost of $14.87 for analysis.

For packaging, we use a variety of supplies. Plastic cling wrap, packaging tape, masking tape, filament tape, and warning tapes are used. We include a decal in every package. **We will assume the overhead cost on miscellaneous materials is $3 a package**. The cost of decals is negligible, as we have our own cutting machines, and material costs are extremely low. For the purpose of analysis, we will assume the cost for decals is $1 per unit. For boxes, we use two XL size, double corrugated boxes from U-Haul costing $2.37 per splitter. Accessory items are packaged with scraps from splitter boxes. We will neglect those costs for the purpose of analysis. **Box costs for splitters are $4.74. Total packaging material costs are $8.74.**

Labor

According to our quote from local water jet companies, we can expect to pay $22 per unit (minimum 20 pieces). With economies of scale, **the price will be reduced to $20 per unit in 2020**. The side fins are cut AND finished at $5 a set, and the diffusers are cut AND finished at $10 a unit. While the side skirt is cut by the supplier, we add an additional indent, which costs $5 a unit in labor. We pay a labor rate of $10 to sand and trim a splitter. Sanding may not be necessary with water jet, but we will include it for analysis, as we still have to pay the cost to trim the splitter. We pay a labor rate of $10 to package a splitter and side skirts (and accessory items included in the order). This rate is higher as these large items are harder to work with and require modifications to boxes. Side fins are an accessory item, so they are included with other packaging rates. The diffuser and canards are very small items. They use premade boxes (no modifications), so the labor rate is reduced.

	Cutting Costs		Labor Rates		
Unit	Cutting Labor Rates	Sand and Trim Labor Rates	Packaging Labor Rates	Total Labor Cost/Unit
Splitter	$22	$10	$10	$20
Side fins (Set)	$5			
Diffuser Kit	$5		$5	$5
Canards	$5	$5	$5	$5
Side Skirts	"precut"		$10	$10

Packaging and Fulfillment

Packaging and fulfillment involve a multi-step process. This includes selecting the right product, attaching a receipt, and including accessory items. After packaging, the orders are loaded up and dropped off at UPS once or twice a week.

Shipping

Our current shipping solution is UPS. We are UPS capital customers and get discounts on shipping rates. We are not legally allowed to disclose details on our shipping discounts/program, having signed a rate lock agreement with UPS. For analysis, **we can assume the average shipping cost is $35 a unit for splitters, $20 for side skirts, and $10 for other items**. These figures have been overestimated for analysis. In the event of shipping failure, we have purchased an insurance policy through UPS flex, which pays out over 95 percent of the time. The insurance cost is included in the earlier assumption.

New Product Development

All of these products are fairly similar in design language and application. As a result, developing new products is as easy as grabbing a template from a car. First, we analyze any potential issue. This could be any shapes (convex) on the car we have to cut around or any functional items that would be blocked by our product (such as an oil drain). To combat these issues, we simply mark on our blueprint the problem areas and cut those shapes out. For the future, we look to use CAD software to more efficiently and accurately design our products.

Insurance

Beyond the physical space, we need an insurance policy to cover any potential issues that may arise. This is called a **garage liability policy.** *Insurance Journal* **states,** "The intent of the policy is to cover bodily injury or property damage caused by an accident arising out of garage operations." Importantly for our application, it will cover any incidents that arise from our products. As provided by trustedchoice.com, "Products manufactured or sold by the shop that cause damage to a customer's vehicle."

The second policy is optional by law but a wise investment for any garage owner. This is **garage keeper's insurance**. It is defined by *Insurance Journal* as follows: "Garage keeper's coverage is an optional line offering protection to the garage business for loss to a customer's auto left in the insured's care, custody or control." The policy clarifies this by including the wording "while the insured is attending, servicing, repairing, parking or storing it in your garage operations."

Finally, we need to purchase workers' compensation to ensure the care of our employees. For the sake of analysis, we will overestimate this expense by using 2018 averages of auto repair shops provided by FitSmall Business:

Auto Repair Shop Insurance Costs at a Glance

Insurance Coverage Type	Average Cost of Annual Premium	Average Deductible
General Liability Insurance	$300 to $1,000	$1,000
Garagekeepers Insurance	$1,000 to $1,300	$250 to $500
Workers' Compensation	$1,400	None

For health insurance, we should expect to pay $4,702 per full-time employee (and per business owner, if applicable), as estimated by KFF (Kaiser Family Foundation).

Staffing

Using many part-time contractors, we will project staffing/labor costs as a unit variable cost. Beyond these variable costs, we will be looking to hire two additional general employees to take over some of the roles filled by the current owners. This includes customer service, commercial account management, social media, order fulfillment, shipping, safety, and compliance. These employees will have roles comparable to a secretary. They will be the only full-time employed staff (disregarding the owners' roles). **According to Payscale.com, average pay for this position is $31,041 annually.** In addition to their normal roles, they will be eligible to earn wages on per process labor, similar to our subcontractors, as listed later. **For the rest of our staffing, we will be utilizing part-time subcontractors.** A comparable business in the area revealed that this is an efficient way to staff labor, as many other jobs in the auto industry have part-time work or non-conventional scheduling. The result is a lot of workers who are already assimilated to the industry looking for part-time work.

Financial Plan

Our financial models will be based on Q1 sales in our test market. A shortened Q1 profit statement is as follows:

Total Income	**$21, 036.69**
Cost of Goods Sold	
Cost of Labor - COS	921.00
Freight & delivery - COS	2,045.16
Subcontractors - COS	505.00
Supplies & Materials -COGS	6,745.49
Total Cost of Goods Sold	**$10,216.65**
GROSS PROFIT	**$10,820.04**
Total Expenses	**$3,122.87**
NET OPERATING INCOME	**$7,697.17**
Other Income	
Reimbursements from Insurance	$283.05
Total Other Income	**$283.05**
NET OTHER INCOME	**$283.05**
NET INCOME	**$7,980.22**

We anticipate needing a $20,000 cash injection (via investment) to cover our expansion costs in January 2020.

Revenue and Costs

Our revenue comes from online sales. To better break down revenue and costs, we've compiled a table of our product combinations for the Ford Mustang and built out the appropriate variable costs for each. Direct labor is included as a percentage of sales as well. **The full table is available in the appendix (Figure 13.1).** To analyze how these revenues and costs will play out on a larger scale, we've taken a weighted average of revenue and each cost category for every product combination according to the trends we've seen in sales. Additionally, the Ford Mustang bumper size is abnormally large, so we don't expect any material costs to rise as we expand to new markets. Moreover, economies of scale factors have been compiled to produce a **new cost structure beginning in 2020**.

Weighted Average Variable Costs	2019	2020
List Price/Revenue	216.25	216.25
Material	5.29%	4.96%
Water Jet Cutting Costs	7%	6%
Edge Trim	3%	3%
Hardware	8%	8%
Labor	7%	7%
Packaging (Decals, Packaging Tape, Cardboard)	4%	4%
Shipping	13%	13%
Total CoGs	47.15%	45.67%
Sales Commissions	10%	10%
Sales Discounts	3%	3%
Sales Tax	7%	7%
Allowance for defective Products (1%)	1%	1%
Total Other Variable Expenses	21%	21%
Total Variable Expenses	68.15%	66.67%

2020 Expansion Costs

In 2020, we will accrue expansion costs that will heavily reduce our cash flows. We plan to use the $20,000 cash injection to mitigate these negative cash flows; the effects can be observed in the cash flow section. The expansion costs are as detailed later. Some of the costs will be depreciated over their respective time frames, while others will be expensed in January 2020.

Name	Cost		Method	2020 Expansion Expense	Annual Depreciation Expense
		Expansion Costs at Beginning of 2020			
Amenitites	$	5,800.91	Depreciate 10 yrs.		$ 580.09
Inventory Shelving	$	5,995.36	Depreciate 10 yrs.		$ 599.54
Lifts	$	9,100.00	Depreciate 10 yrs.		$ 910.00
Office Furniture	$	1,915.96	Depreciate 10 yrs.		$ 191.60
Workstations	$	3,584.00	Depreciate 10 yrs.		$ 358.40
Patent	$	8,000.00	Depreciate 20 yrs.		$ 400.00
Computers	$	3,279.96	Depreciate 5 yrs.		$ 655.99
Building upgrade to 220V power supply	$	4,000.00	Expense in 2020	$ 4,000.00	
CAD Training course	$	6,920.00	Expense in 2020	$ 6,920.00	
Safety	$	2,200.00	Expense in 2020	$ 2,200.00	
Security	$	751.99	Expense in 2020	$ 751.99	
Total	$	51,548.18		$ 13,871.99	$ 3,695.62

Each of these assumptions is broken down in more detail in the appendix (Figure 14.1). A full list of amenities is provided. The purpose is to fill the workspace with necessary items to improve the working experience. A 220-volt power supply is necessary to run most automotive tools. CAD training courses are for both owners and include two weekend seminars. Inventory shelving consists of eight cantilevered racks, which are more than capable of handling inventory. The racks are modular, so more shelves can be added with ease. Two lifts are required to easily pick up cars for new product development. A safety program to keep our workers secure and compliant will be purchased as well as baseline safety equipment, such as fire extinguishers and smoke alarms. Finally, we have accounted for furnishings and appliances for four office stations and eight work stations.

Monthly Costs

Fixed Expenses (Monthly)	May 2019	Aug 2019	Jan 2020
Insurance			$ 309.00
Internet and Phone Line			$ 117.00
Marketing (Instagram)	$ 600.00	$ 600.00	$ 600.00
Office Supplies		$ 50.00	$ 50.00
Rent and Utilities		$ 100.00	$ 1,671.72
Software and Phone			$ 248.00
Sponsorship/Partnership allowance		$ 333.33	$ 333.33
Truck (Lease, Insurance, Gas)		$ 1,081.00	$ 1,081.00
Wages			$ 11,840.17
Website		$ 40.00	$ 40.00
Total Fixed Expenses			$ 16,290.22

The previous chart shows the monthly cost structure throughout 2019 and a new structure following expansion in 2020. **More details are available in the appendix (Figure 15.1)**. For the remainder of 2019, we will deploy marketing costs in May to continue building brand equity. In August, the business is relocating from Muncie to Bloomington. We will be running the business temporarily out of a small garage attachment in a residential zone, so there will be a heavy decrease in costs. A new product line will be released that quarter, so sponsorship costs are included. As we move away from Muncie, we will also lose access to our currently borrowed vehicles, so we will start the truck lease then. In 2020, monthly costs will expand to reflect the large expansion of the company. Insurance covers liability of our product and any vehicles left on our premises. Marketing expenses account for Instagram promotions. Software includes G Suite, Grasshopper, QuickBooks, and AutoCAD. Our sponsorship allowance covers the $1,000 allowance per new product line (released quarterly). Starting 2020, both managers will be participating in the same labor as contractors and compensated equally. Their salaries will be $40,000 per year. Ten percent of revenue is distributed to owners as well (five percent each)

Annual Expenses

Fixed Expenses (Annual)	
Trade Shows and Events	$ 5,000.00
LLC Renewal Fee	$ 15.00
Health Insurance	$ 18,808.00
Total	$ 23,823.00

Annual expenses begin 2020 and include show/event fees, basic LLC fees, and health insurance for the two full-time employees and two owners.

Revenue Model

We've based our revenue model on four assumptions: Sales growth from Instagram, abandoned cart, eBay, and trade shows and events. From Instagram, we're expecting to see growth through the warmer months, as car enthusiasts will be attending events and posting pictures and more active on social media. We anticipate a sharp decline in late fall as the season dies down. To estimate abandoned cart, we have taken how much abandoned cart will be recoverable and projected four percent conversion to sales. With regard to eBay, we've taken a competitor's product to find a baseline and predict that sales will grow most during tax season, when enthusiasts are searching online for deals. Finally, for trade shows and events, we've incorporated growth, as we plan to take our own vehicles and product showcase to many domestic events, and adjusted for events that take place in certain months. **A full 12-month timeline of all our growth assumptions is available in the appendix (Figure 16.1).** We've based these growth figures on our existing three months' revenue from Q1 2019. The overall growth of sales will be declining. We anticipate year one to carry the highest sales, with brand ambassadors and sponsors most active. Nearing year three, when auto manufacturers are estimated to refresh their designs, we will see sales taper off. Here is a chart showing projected unit sales in our s550 Mustang test market through the end of 2021 (including historical sales from Q1 2019).

Using our growth multiple as described previously, we can project unit sales through the end of 2021 inclusive of new markets we incorporate every quarter. The visual is as follows:

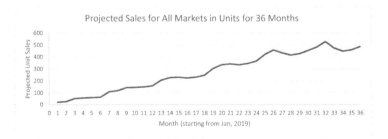

We can derive a five-year revenue projection by using a growth rate compiled from our growth assumptions as shown in the growth and expansion section. Our projected growth rate for year four is 22 percent. To estimate year five, we anticipate the new product line's growth to continue but will exclude the Canada market growth.

Growth Rates	
Industry Growth	4%
New Product Lines Growth	10%
Entry to Canada Growth	8%
Total Projected Growth 2022 (yr 4)	22%
Total Projected Growth 2022 (yr 5)	14%

The projected five-year revenues are displayed in the projected five-year income statement and are represented by this line graph:

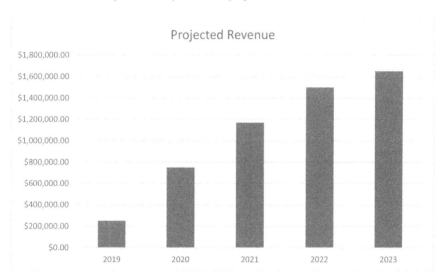

Projected Five-Year Income Statement

	Annual Projected Income Statements				
	2019	2020	2021	2022	2023
	Annual	Annual	Annual	Annual	Annual
Revenue	$ 237,605.67	$ 732,019.78	$ 1,184,650.64	$ 1,445,273.77	$ 1,647,612.10
Cost of Goods Sold					
Material	$ (11,466.51)	$ (36,315.00)	$ (58,769.71)	$ (71,699.05)	$ (81,736.92)
Water Jet Cutting Costs	$ (15,473.01)	$ (46,206.10)	$ (74,776.79)	$ (91,227.69)	$ (103,999.56)
Edge Trim	$ (5,690.46)	$ (19,233.93)	$ (31,126.87)	$ (37,974.78)	$ (43,291.25)
Hardware	$ (17,366.32)	$ (56,426.62)	$ (91,316.98)	$ (111,406.72)	$ (127,003.66)
Labor	$ (15,873.61)	$ (53,653.24)	$ (86,828.73)	$ (105,931.05)	$ (120,761.40)
Cardboard	$ (8,753.02)	$ (29,585.45)	$ (47,879.06)	$ (58,412.45)	$ (66,590.20)
Shipping	$ (27,490.88)	$ (92,919.97)	$ (150,375.31)	$ (183,457.87)	$ (209,141.98)
Total CoGs	$ (102,113.81)	$ (334,340.32)	$ (541,073.45)	$ (660,109.60)	$ (752,524.95)
Gross Profit	**$ 114,458.25**	**$ 397,679.47**	**$ 643,577.19**	**$ 785,164.17**	**$ 895,087.15**
Gross Profit Margin	**48.17%**	**54.33%**	**54.33%**	**54.33%**	**54.33%**
Other Variable Costs					
Sales Commissions	$ (21,657.21)	$ (73,201.98)	$ (118,465.06)	$ (144,527.38)	$ (164,761.21)
Sales Discounts	$ (6,497.16)	$ (21,960.59)	$ (35,539.52)	$ (43,358.21)	$ (49,428.36)
Sales Tax	$ (15,160.04)	$ (51,241.38)	$ (82,925.54)	$ (101,169.16)	$ (115,332.85)
Allowance for defective Products (1%)	$ (2,165.72)	$ (7,320.20)	$ (11,846.51)	$ (14,452.74)	$ (16,476.12)
Total Other Variable Expenses	$ (45,480.13)	$ (153,724.15)	$ (248,776.63)	$ (303,507.49)	$ (345,998.54)
Fixed Expenses (Monthly)					
Insurance		$ (3,708.00)	$ (3,708.00)	$ (3,708.00)	$ (3,708.00)
Internet and Phone Line		$ (1,404.00)	$ (1,404.00)	$ (1,404.00)	$ (1,404.00)
Marketing (Instagram)	$ (4,800.00)	$ (7,200.00)	$ (7,200.00)	$ (7,200.00)	$ (7,200.00)
Office Supplies	$ (250.00)	$ (600.00)	$ (600.00)	$ (600.00)	$ (600.00)
Rent and Utilities	$ (500.00)	$ (20,060.64)	$ (20,060.64)	$ (20,060.64)	$ (20,060.64)
Software and Phone		$ (2,976.00)	$ (2,976.00)	$ (2,976.00)	$ (2,976.00)
Sponsorship/Partnership allowance	$ (1,999.98)	$ (3,999.96)	$ (3,999.96)	$ (3,999.96)	$ (3,999.96)
Truck (Lease, Insurance, Gas)	$ (5,405.00)	$ (12,972.00)	$ (12,972.00)	$ (12,972.00)	$ (12,972.00)
Wages		$ (142,082.04)	$ (142,082.04)	$ (142,082.04)	$ (142,082.04)
Website	$ (200.00)	$ (480.00)	$ (480.00)	$ (480.00)	$ (480.00)
Total Monthly Expenses	$ (13,154.98)	$ (195,482.64)	$ (195,482.64)	$ (195,482.64)	$ (195,482.64)
Fixed Expenses (Annual)					
Trade Shows and Events		$ (5,000.00)	$ (5,000.00)	$ (5,000.00)	$ (5,000.00)
LLC Renewal Fee		$ (15.00)		$ (15.00)	
Health Insurance		$ (18,808.00)	$ (18,808.00)	$ (18,808.00)	$ (18,808.00)
Total Annual Expenses		$ (23,823.00)	$ (23,808.00)	$ (23,823.00)	$ (23,823.00)
Expansion Expenses					
Building upgrade to 220V power supply		$ (4,000.00)			
CAD Training course		$ (6,920.00)			
Safety		$ (2,200.00)			
Security		$ (751.99)			
Total Expansion Expenses		$ (13,871.99)			
Depreciation Expense		$ (44,347.38)	$ (44,347.38)	$ (44,347.38)	$ (44,347.38)
Total Fixed Expenses	$ (13,154.98)	$ (277,525.01)	$ (263,638.02)	$ (263,653.02)	$ (263,653.02)
Total Expenses	$ (58,635.11)	$ (431,249.16)	$ (512,414.65)	$ (567,160.51)	$ (609,651.56)
Operating Income	**$ 55,823.14**	**$ (33,569.70)**	**$ 131,162.54**	**$ 218,003.66**	**$ 285,435.59**
Income Tax	$ (14,932.69)	$ (6,895.13)	$ (35,085.98)	$ (58,315.98)	$ (76,354.02)
Net Income	**$ 40,890.45**	**$ (40,464.83)**	**$ 96,076.56**	**$ 159,687.68**	**$ 209,081.57**

2019 Projected Income Statement

The following income statement details the remaining months in 2019. As previously described, advertising expenses will start now, while some fixed monthly costs will begin when the business relocates to a residential garage in Bloomington for the fall school semester. CoGs are higher in 2019 than they will be in future years, as economies of scale will reduce some costs in 2020.

2019 Projected Income Statement									
	Quarter 1 Accumulated	Apr	May	Jun	Jul	Aug	Sep	Oct	Nov	Dec
Revenue	$ 21,033.61	$ 12,001.69	$ 12,666.57	$ 13,337.16	$ 23,444.91	$ 25,770.08	$ 31,040.84	$ 31,473.47	$ 32,433.69	$ 34,398.63
Cost of Goods Sold										
Material		$ (635.44)	$ (670.64)	$ (706.14)	$ (1,241.30)	$ (1,364.41)	$ (1,643.47)	$ (1,666.38)	$ (1,717.48)	$ (1,821.25)
Water Jet Cutting Costs		$ (857.46)	$ (904.96)	$ (952.87)	$ (1,675.02)	$ (1,841.15)	$ (2,217.72)	$ (2,248.62)	$ (2,317.59)	$ (2,457.61)
Edge Trim		$ (315.35)	$ (332.82)	$ (350.44)	$ (616.02)	$ (677.11)	$ (815.60)	$ (826.97)	$ (852.33)	$ (903.83)
Hardware		$ (962.38)	$ (1,015.70)	$ (1,069.47)	$ (1,879.98)	$ (2,066.43)	$ (2,489.08)	$ (2,523.77)	$ (2,601.17)	$ (2,758.33)
Labor		$ (879.66)	$ (928.39)	$ (977.54)	$ (1,718.39)	$ (1,888.61)	$ (2,275.13)	$ (2,306.84)	$ (2,377.59)	$ (2,521.24)
Packaging (Decals, Packing Tape, Cardboard)		$ (485.06)	$ (511.93)	$ (539.44)	$ (947.55)	$ (1,041.53)	$ (1,254.55)	$ (1,272.04)	$ (1,311.05)	$ (1,390.26)
Shipping		$ (1,523.45)	$ (1,607.85)	$ (1,692.97)	$ (2,976.01)	$ (3,271.16)	$ (3,940.21)	$ (3,995.13)	$ (4,117.65)	$ (4,366.44)
Total CoGs		$ (5,658.80)	$ (5,972.29)	$ (6,288.48)	$ (11,054.29)	$ (12,150.60)	$ (14,635.77)	$ (14,839.75)	$ (15,294.86)	$ (16,218.97)
Gross Profit		$ 6,342.89	$ 6,694.28	$ 7,048.69	$ 12,390.63	$ 13,619.48	$ 16,405.07	$ 16,633.72	$ 17,143.84	$ 18,179.66
Gross Profit Margin		52.85%	52.85%	52.85%	52.85%	52.85%	52.85%	52.85%	52.85%	52.85%
Other Variable Costs										
Sales Commissions		$ (1,200.17)	$ (1,266.66)	$ (1,333.72)	$ (2,344.49)	$ (2,577.01)	$ (3,104.08)	$ (3,147.35)	$ (3,243.87)	$ (3,439.86)
Sales Discounts		$ (360.05)	$ (380.00)	$ (400.11)	$ (703.35)	$ (773.10)	$ (931.23)	$ (944.20)	$ (973.16)	$ (1,031.96)
Sales Tax		$ (840.12)	$ (886.66)	$ (933.60)	$ (1,641.14)	$ (1,803.91)	$ (2,172.86)	$ (2,203.14)	$ (2,270.71)	$ (2,407.90)
Allowance for defective Products (1%)		$ (120.02)	$ (126.67)	$ (133.37)	$ (234.45)	$ (257.70)	$ (310.41)	$ (314.73)	$ (324.39)	$ (343.99)
Total Other Variable Expenses		$ (2,520.35)	$ (2,659.98)	$ (2,800.80)	$ (4,923.43)	$ (5,411.72)	$ (6,518.58)	$ (6,609.43)	$ (6,812.13)	$ (7,223.71)
Fixed Expenses (Monthly)										
Insurance										
Internet and Phone Line										
Marketing (Instagram)			$ (600.00)	$ (600.00)	$ (600.00)	$ (600.00)	$ (600.00)	$ (600.00)	$ (600.00)	$ (600.00)
Office Supplies						$ (50.00)	$ (50.00)	$ (50.00)	$ (50.00)	$ (50.00)
Rent and Utilities						$ (100.00)	$ (100.00)	$ (100.00)	$ (100.00)	$ (100.00)
Software and Phone										
Sponsorship/Partnership allowance					$ (333.33)	$ (333.33)	$ (333.33)	$ (333.33)	$ (333.33)	$ (333.33)
Truck (Lease, Insurance, Gas)						$ (1,081.00)	$ (1,081.00)	$ (1,081.00)	$ (1,081.00)	$ (1,081.00)
Wages										
Website						$ (40.00)	$ (40.00)	$ (40.00)	$ (40.00)	$ (40.00)
Total Monthly Expenses			$ (600.00)	$ (600.00)	$ (933.33)	$ (2,204.33)	$ (2,204.33)	$ (2,204.33)	$ (2,204.33)	$ (2,204.33)
Fixed Expenses (Annual)										
Trade Shows and Events										
LLC Renewal Fee										
Health Insurance										
Total Annual Expenses										
Expansion Expenses										
Building upgrade to 220V power supply										
CAD Training course										
Safety										
Security										
Total Expansion Expenses										
Depreciation Expense										
Total Fixed Expenses			$ (600.00)	$ (600.00)	$ (933.33)	$ (2,204.33)	$ (2,204.33)	$ (2,204.33)	$ (2,204.33)	$ (2,204.33)
Total Expenses		$ (2,520.35)	$ (3,259.98)	$ (3,400.80)	$ (5,856.76)	$ (7,616.05)	$ (8,722.91)	$ (8,813.76)	$ (9,016.46)	$ (9,428.04)
Operating Income		$ 3,822.53	$ 3,434.30	$ 3,647.88	$ 6,533.87	$ 6,003.43	$ 7,682.17	$ 7,819.96	$ 8,127.38	$ 8,751.62
Income Tax		$ (1,022.53)	$ (918.68)	$ (975.81)	$ (1,747.81)	$ (1,605.92)	$ (2,054.98)	$ (2,091.84)	$ (2,174.07)	$ (2,341.06)
Net Income	7980.22	$ 2,800.01	$ 2,515.62	$ 2,672.07	$ 4,786.06	$ 4,397.51	$ 5,627.19	$ 5,728.12	$ 5,953.31	$ 6,410.56

2020 Projected Income Statement

The year 2020 is our expansion year, so we will accrue significant costs in January. Additionally, full monthly expenses as detailed previously, annual expenses, and depreciation from assets purchased in January will begin in this period. CoGs will decrease over one percent as economies of scale take place.

2020 Projected Income Statement

	Jan	Feb	Mar	Apr	May	Jun	Jul	Aug	Sep	Oct	Nov	Dec
Revenue	$ 44,551.06	$ 49,043.69	$ 49,632.26	$ 48,426.26	$ 49,877.82	$ 53,323.21	$ 65,450.31	$ 72,408.35	$ 73,859.55	$ 72,230.80	$ 74,418.23	$ 78,798.25
Cost of Goods Sold												
Material	$ (2,210.15)	$ (2,433.02)	$ (2,462.22)	$ (2,402.39)	$ (2,474.40)	$ (2,645.33)	$ (3,246.95)	$ (3,592.13)	$ (3,664.12)	$ (3,583.32)	$ (3,691.84)	$ (3,909.13)
Water Jet Cutting Costs	$ (2,812.12)	$ (3,095.71)	$ (3,132.86)	$ (3,056.73)	$ (3,148.36)	$ (3,365.84)	$ (4,131.31)	$ (4,570.52)	$ (4,662.12)	$ (4,559.31)	$ (4,697.38)	$ (4,973.85)
Edge Trim	$ (1,170.59)	$ (1,288.63)	$ (1,304.09)	$ (1,272.41)	$ (1,310.55)	$ (1,401.08)	$ (1,719.72)	$ (1,902.54)	$ (1,940.67)	$ (1,897.87)	$ (1,955.35)	$ (2,070.44)
Hardware	$ (3,434.15)	$ (3,780.46)	$ (3,825.83)	$ (3,732.86)	$ (3,844.76)	$ (4,110.34)	$ (5,045.14)	$ (5,581.49)	$ (5,693.35)	$ (5,567.80)	$ (5,736.42)	$ (6,074.04)
labor	$ (3,265.36)	$ (3,594.65)	$ (3,637.79)	$ (3,549.39)	$ (3,655.79)	$ (3,908.31)	$ (4,797.17)	$ (5,307.16)	$ (5,413.52)	$ (5,294.14)	$ (5,454.47)	$ (5,775.50)
Packaging (Decals, Packing Tape, Cardboard)	$ (1,800.58)	$ (1,982.16)	$ (2,005.95)	$ (1,957.20)	$ (2,015.87)	$ (2,155.12)	$ (2,645.25)	$ (2,926.47)	$ (2,985.12)	$ (2,919.29)	$ (3,007.70)	$ (3,184.72)
Shipping	$ (5,655.15)	$ (6,225.43)	$ (6,300.14)	$ (6,147.06)	$ (6,331.31)	$ (6,768.66)	$ (8,308.03)	$ (9,191.26)	$ (9,375.47)	$ (9,168.72)	$ (9,446.38)	$ (10,002.37)
Total CoGs	$ (20,348.10)	$ (22,400.05)	$ (22,668.88)	$ (22,118.05)	$ (22,781.03)	$ (24,354.67)	$ (29,893.56)	$ (33,071.55)	$ (33,734.37)	$ (32,990.46)	$ (33,989.54)	$ (35,990.05)
Gross Profit	$ 24,202.95	$ 26,643.84	$ 26,963.39	$ 26,308.21	$ 27,096.79	$ 28,968.54	$ 35,556.73	$ 39,336.80	$ 40,125.18	$ 39,240.34	$ 40,428.69	$ 42,808.19
Gross Profit Margin	54.33%	54.33%	54.33%	54.33%	54.33%	54.33%	54.33%	54.33%	54.33%	54.33%	54.33%	54.33%
Other Variable Costs												
Sales Commissions	$ (4,455.11)	$ (4,904.37)	$ (4,963.23)	$ (4,842.63)	$ (4,987.78)	$ (5,332.32)	$ (6,545.03)	$ (7,240.83)	$ (7,385.95)	$ (7,223.08)	$ (7,441.82)	$ (7,879.82)
Sales Discounts	$ (1,336.53)	$ (1,471.31)	$ (1,488.97)	$ (1,452.79)	$ (1,496.33)	$ (1,599.70)	$ (1,963.51)	$ (2,172.25)	$ (2,215.79)	$ (2,166.92)	$ (2,232.55)	$ (2,363.95)
Sales Tax	$ (3,118.57)	$ (3,433.06)	$ (3,474.26)	$ (3,389.84)	$ (3,491.45)	$ (3,732.62)	$ (4,581.52)	$ (5,068.58)	$ (5,170.17)	$ (5,056.16)	$ (5,209.20)	$ (5,515.88)
Allowance for defective Produces(1%)	$ (445.51)	$ (490.44)	$ (496.32)	$ (484.26)	$ (498.78)	$ (533.23)	$ (654.50)	$ (724.08)	$ (738.60)	$ (722.31)	$ (744.18)	$ (787.98)
Total Other Venable Expenses	$ (9,355.72)	$ (10,299.17)	$ (10,422.77)	$ (10,169.51)	$ (10,474.34)	$ (11,197.87)	$ (13,744.57)	$ (15,205.75)	$ (15,510.51)	$ (15,168.47)	$ (15,627.83)	$ (16,547.63)
Fixed Eapernos (Monthly)												
Insurance	$ (309.00)	$ (309.00)	$ (309.00)	$ (309.00)	$ (309.00)	$ (309.00)	$ (309.00)	$ (309.00)	$ (309.00)	$ (309.00)	$ (309.00)	$ (309.00)
Internet and Phone Line	$ (117.00)	$ (117.00)	$ (117.00)	$ (117.00)	$ (117.00)	$ (117.00)	$ (117.00)	$ (117.00)	$ (117.00)	$ (117.00)	$ (117.00)	$ (117.00)
Marketing (Instagram)	$ (600.00)	$ (600.00)	$ (600.00)	$ (600.00)	$ (600.00)	$ (600.00)	$ (600.00)	$ (600.40)	$ (600.00)	$ (600.00)	$ (600.00)	$ (600.00)
Office Supplies	$ (50.00)	$ (50.00)	$ (50.00)	$ (50.00)	$ (50.00)	$ (50.00)	$ (50.00)	$ (50.00)	$ (50.00)	$ (50.00)	$ (50.00)	$ (50.00)
Rent and Utilities	$ (1,671.72)	$ (1,671.72)	$ (1,671.72)	$ (1,671.72)	$ (1,671.72)	$ (1,671.72)	$ (1,671.72)	$ (1,671.72)	$ (1,671.72)	$ (1,671.72)	$ (1,671.72)	$ (1,671.72)
Software and Phone	$ (248.00)	$ (248.00)	$ (248.00)	$ (248.00)	$ (248.00)	$ (248.00)	$ (248.00)	$ (248.00)	$ (248.00)	$ (248.00)	$ (248.00)	$ (248.00)
Sponsorship/Partnership allowance	$ (333.33)	$ (333.33)	$ (333.33)	$ (333.33)	$ (333.33)	$ (333.33)	$ (333.33)	$ (333.33)	$ (333.33)	$ (333.33)	$ (333.33)	$ (333.33)
Truck (lease, Insurance, Gas)	$ (1,081.00)	$ (1,081.00)	$ (1,081.00)	$ (1,081.00)	$ (1,081.00)	$ (1,081.00)	$ (1,081.00)	$ (1,081.00)	$ (1,081.00)	$ (1,081.00)	$ (1,081.00)	$ (1,081.00)
Wages	$ (11,840.17)	$ (11,840.17)	$ (11,840.17)	$ (11,840.17)	$ (11,840.17)	$ (11,840.17)	$ (11,840.17)	$ (11,840.17)	$ (11,840.17)	$ (11,840.17)	$ (11,840.17)	$ (11,840.17)
Website	$ (40.00)	$ (40.00)	$ (40.00)	$ (40.40)	$ (40.00)	$ (40.00)	$ (40.00)	$ (40.00)	$ (40.00)	$ (40.00)	$ (40.00)	$ (40.00)
Total Monthly Expenses	$ (16,290.22)	$ (16,290.22)	$ (16,290.22)	$ (16,290.22)	$ (16,290.22)	$ (16,290.22)	$ (16,290.22)	$ (16,290.22)	$ (16,290.22)	$ (16,290.22)	$ (16,290.22)	$ (16,290.22)
Fixed Expenses (Annual)												
Trade Shows and Events	$ (5,000.00)											
LLC Renewal Pee	$ (15.00)											
Health insurance	$ (18,808.00)											
Total Annual Expanses	$ (23,323.00)											
Expansion Expenses												
Building upgrade to 220V power supply	$ (4,000.00)											
CAD Training course	$ (6,920.00)											
Safety	$ (2,200.00)											
Security	$ (751.59)											
Total Expansion Expenses	$ (13,371.99)											
Depreciation Expense	$ (3,695.62)	$ (3,695.62)	$ (3,695.62)	$ (3,695.62)	$ (3,695.62)	$ (3,695.62)	$ (3,695.62)	$ (3,695.62)	$ (3,695.62)	$ (3,695.62)	$ (3,695.62)	$ (3,695.62)
Total Fixed Expenses	$ (57,680.83)	$ (19,985.84)	$ (19,985.84)	$ (19,985.84)	$ (19,985.84)	$ (19,985.84)	$ (19,985.84)	$ (19,985.84)	$ (19,985.84)	$ (19,985.84)	$ (19,985.84)	$ (19,985.84)
Total Expenses	$ (67,036.55)	$ (30,285.01)	$ (30,408.61)	$ (30,155.35)	$ (30,460.18)	$ (31,183.71)	$ (33,730.40)	$ (35,191.59)	$ (35,496.34)	$ (35,154.30)	$ (35,613.66)	$ (36,533.47)
Operating Income	$ (42,833.59)	$ (3,641.37)	$ (3,445.22)	$ (3,847.14)	$ (3,363.39)	$ (2,215.17)	$ 1,826.35	$ 4,145.21	$ 4,628.84	$ 4,086.04	$ 4,815.03	$ 6,274.73
Income Tax	$ -	$ -	$ -	$ -	$ -	$ -	$ -	$ (488.55)	$ (1,108.84)	$ (1,238.21)	$ (1,093.01)	$ (1,288.02)	$ (1,678.49)
Net Income	$ (42,833.39)	$ (3,641.31)	$ (3,445.22)	$ (3,847.14)	$ (3,363.39)	$ (2,215.17)	$ 1,337.80	$ 3,036.36	$ 3,390.63	$ 2,993.02	$ 3,527.01	$ 4,596.24

2021 Projected Income Statement

The year 2021 should reflect our first "normal" operating year after building brand equity in 2019 and the expansion costs of 2020.

	2021 Projected Income Statement											
	Jan	Feb	Mar	Apr	May	Jun	Jul	Aug	Sep	Oct	Nov	Dec
Revenue	$ 90,874.06	$ 98,901.10	$ 93,809.64	$ 89,866.43	$ 92,278.64	$ 97,817.89	$ 104,090.47	$ 113,774.34	$ 102,415.05	$ 96,663.35	$ 99,247.37	$ 104,912.29
Cast of Goods Sold												
Material	$ (4,508.20)	$ (4,906.42)	$ (4,653.63)	$ (4,458.21)	$ (4,577.88)	$ (4,852.68)	$ (5,163.86)	$ (5,644.27)	$ (5,080.74)	$ (4,795.40)	$ (4,923.59)	$ (5,204.63)
Water Jet Cutting Costs	$ (5,736.10)	$ (6,242.77)	$ (5,921.39)	$ (5,672.49)	$ (5,824.76)	$ (6,174.40)	$ (6,570.33)	$ (7,181.59)	$ (6,464.58)	$ (6,101.53)	$ (6,264.63)	$ (6,622.21)
Edge Trim	$ (2,387.73)	$ (2,598.64)	$ (2,464.86)	$ (2,361.25)	$ (2,424.63)	$ (2,570.18)	$ (2,734.89)	$ (2,989.44)	$ (2,690.97)	$ (2,539.44)	$ (2,607.74)	$ (2,756.59)
Hardware	$ (7,004.89)	$ (7,623.64)	$ (7,231.17)	$ (6,927.22)	$ (7,113.16)	$ (7,540.14)	$ (8,023.65)	$ (8,770.12)	$ (7,894.51)	$ (7,451.15)	$ (7,650.33)	$ (8,087.00)
Labor	$ (6,660.60)	$ (7,248.94)	$ (6,875.76)	$ (6,586.74)	$ (6,763.54)	$ (7,169.54)	$ (7,629.29)	$ (8,339.07)	$ (7,506.49)	$ (7,084.92)	$ (7,274.32)	$ (7,689.52)
Packaging (Decals, Packing Tape, Cardboard)	$ (3,672.78)	$ (3,997.21)	$ (3,791.43)	$ (3,632.06)	$ (3,729.55)	$ (3,953.43)	$ (4,206.94)	$ (4,598.32)	$ (4,139.23)	$ (3,906.76)	$ (4,011.20)	$ (4,240.15)
Shipping	$ (11,535.23)	$ (12,554.15)	$ (11,907.86)	$ (11,407.32)	$ (11,713.52)	$ (12,416.65)	$ (13,212.87)	$ (14,442.11)	$ (13,000.20)	$ (12,270.10)	$ (12,598.11)	$ (13,317.19)
Total CoGs	$ (41,505.52)	$ (45,171.77)	$ (42,846.31)	$ (41,045.30)	$ (42,147.04)	$ (44,677.02)	$ (47,541.94)	$ (51,964.92)	$ (46,776.71)	$ (44,149.70)	$ (45,329.92)	$ (47,917.29)
Gross Profit	**$ 49,368.54**	**$ 53,729.34**	**$ 50,963.34**	**$ 48,821.13**	**$ 50,131.60**	**$ 53,140.87**	**$ 56,548.53**	**$ 61.809.42**	**$ 55,638.34**	**$ 52,513.65**	**$ 53,917,45**	**$ 56,994.99**
Gross Plan Margin	**54.33%**	**54.33%**	**54.33%**	**54.33%**	**54.33%**	**54,33%**	**54.33%**	**54.33%**	**5433%**	**54.33%**	**54.33%**	**54.33%**
Other Variable Costs												
Sales Commissions	$ (9,087.41)	$ (9,890.11)	$ (9,380.96)	$ (8,986.64)	$ (9,227.86)	$ (9,781.79)	$ (10,409.05)	$ (11,377.43)	$ (10,241.50)	$ (9,666.34)	$ (9,924.74)	$ (10,491.23)
Sales Discounts	$ (2,726.22)	$ (2,967.03)	$ (2,814.29)	$ (2,695.99)	$ (2,768.96)	$ (2,934.54)	$ (3,122.71)	$ (3,413.23)	$ (3,072.45)	$ (2,899.90)	$ (2,977.42)	$ (3,147.37)
Sales Tax	$ (6,361.18)	$ (6,923.08)	$ (6,566.68)	$ (6,290.65)	$ (6,459.50)	$ (6,847.25)	$ (7,286.33)	$ (7,964.20)	$ (7,169.05)	$ (6,766.43)	$ (6,947.32)	$ (7,343.86)
Allowance for defective Products(1%)	$ (908.74)	$ (989.01)	$ (938.10)	$ (898.66)	$ (922.79)	$ (978.18)	$ (1,040.90)	$ (1,137.74)	$ (1,024.15)	$ (966.63)	$ (992.47)	$ (1,049.12)
Total Other Venable Expenses	$ (19,083.55)	$ (20,769.23)	$ (19,700.03)	$ (18,871.95)	$ (19,378.51)	$ (20,547.76)	$ (21,859.00)	$ (23,892.61)	$ (21,507.16)	$ (20,299.30)	$ (20,841.95)	$ (22,031.58)
Fixed Expenses (Monthly)												
Insurance	$ (309.00)	$ (309.00)	$ (309.00)	$ (309.00)	$ (309.00)	$ (309.00)	$ (309.00)	$ (309.00)	$ (309.00)	$ (309.00)	$ (309.00)	$ (309.00)
Internet and Phone Line	$ (117.00)	$ (117.00)	$ (117.00)	$ (117.00)	$ (117.00)	$ (117.00)	$ (117.00)	$ (117.00)	$ (117.00)	$ (117.00)	$ (117.00)	$ (117.00)
Marketing (Instagram)	$ (600.00)	$ (600.00)	$ (600.00)	$ (600.00)	$ (600.00)	$ (600.00)	$ (600.00)	$ (600.00)	$ (600.00)	$ (600.00)	$ (600.00)	$ (600.00)
Office Supplies	$ (50.00)	$ (50.00)	$ (50.00)	$ (50.00)	$ (50.00)	$ (50.00)	$ (50.00)	$ (50.00)	$ (50.00)	$ (50.00)	$ (50.00)	$ (50.00)
Rent and Utilities	$ (1,671.72)	$ (1,671.72)	$ (1,671.72)	$ (1,671.72)	$ (1,671.72)	$ (1,671.72)	$ (1,671.72)	$ (1,671.72)	$ (1,671.72)	$ (1,671.72)	$ (1,671.72)	$ (1,671.72)
Software and Phone	$ (248.00)	$ (248.00)	$ (248.00)	$ (248.00)	$ (248.00)	$ (248.00)	$ (248.00)	$ (248.00)	$ (248.00)	$ (248.00)	$ (248.00)	$ (248.00)
Sponsorship/partnership allowance	$ (333.33)	$ (333.33)	$ (333.33)	$ (333.33)	$ (333.33)	$ (333.33)	$ (333.33)	$ (333.33)	$ (333.33)	$ (333.33)	$ (333.33)	$ (333.33)
Truck (Lease, Insurance, Gas)	$ (1,081.00)	$ (1,081.00)	$ (1,081.00)	$ (1,081.00)	$ (1,081.00)	$ (1,081.00)	$ (1,081.00)	$ (1,081.00)	$ (1,081.00)	$ (1,081.00)	$ (1,081.00)	$ (1,081.00)
Wages	$ (11,840.17)	$ (11,840.17)	$ (11,840.17)	$ (11,840.17)	$ (11,840.17)	$ (11,840.17)	$ (11,840.17)	$ (11,840.17)	$ (11,840.17)	$ (11,840.17)	$ (11,840.17)	$ (11,840.17)
Welmice	$ (40.00)	$ (40.00)	$ (40.00)	$ (40.00)	$ (40.00)	$ (40.00)	$ (40.00)	$ (40.00)	$ (40.00)	$ (40.00)	$ (40.00)	$ (40.00)
Total Monthly Expenses	$ (16,290.22)	$ (16,290.22)	$ (16,290.22)	$ (16,290.22)	$ (16,290.22)	$ (16,290.22)	$ (16,290.22)	$ (16,290.22)	$ (16,290.22)	$ (16,290.22)	$ (16,290.22)	$ (16,290.22)
Fixed Expenses (Annual)												
Trade Shows and Event,	$ (5.000.00)											
LLC Renewal fee												
Health Insurance	$ (18,808.00)											
Total Annual Expenses	$ (23,808.00)											
Expansion Expenses												
Building upgrade to 220v power supply												
CAD Training course												
Safety												
Security												
Total Expansion Expenses												
Depreciation Expense	$ (3,695.62)	$ (3,695.62)	$ (3,695.62)	$ (3,695.62)	$ (3,695.62)	$ (3,695.62)	$ (3,695.62)	$ (3,695.62)	$ (3,695.62)	$ (3,695.62)	$ (3,695.62)	$ (3,695.62)
Total Fixed Expenses	$ (43,793.84)	$ (19,985.84)	$ (19,985.84)	$ (19,985.84)	$ (19,985.84)	$ (19,985.84)	$ (19,985.84)	$ (19,985.84)	$ (19,985.84)	$ (19,985.84)	$ (19,985.84)	$ (19,985.84)
Total Expenses	$ (62,877.39)	$ (40,755.07)	$ (39,685.86)	$ (38,857.79)	$ (39,364.35)	$ (40,527.89)	$ (41,844.83)	$ (43,878.45)	$ (41,493.00)	$ (40.285.14)	$ (40,827.78)	$ (42,017.42)
Operating Income	**$ (13,505.85)**	**$ 12,974.27**	**$ 11,277.47**	**$ 9,963.35**	**$ 10,767.21**	**$ 12,613.27**	**$ 14,703.70**	**$ 17,930.97**	**$ 14,145.34**	**$ 12.228.51**	**$ 13,089.67**	**$ 14,977.58**
Income Tax	$ 3,613.62	$ (3,470.62)	$ (3,016.72)	$ (2,665.20)	$ (2,880.24)	$ (3,374.05)	$ (31,933.24)	$ (4,796.54)	$ (3,783.88)	$ (3,271.13)	$ (3,501.49)	$ (4,006.50)
Net Income	**$ (9,895.23)**	**$ 9,503.65**	**$ 8,260.73**	**$ 7,298.13**	**$ 7,887.01**	**$ 9,239.22**	**$ 10,770.46**	**$ 13,134.44**	**$ 10,361.46**	**$ 8,957.38**	**$ 9,588.18**	**$ 10,971.08**

Cash Flows

In regard to cash, we have two strategies. We've started off our calculations with our baseline cash at the end of Q1—$8,239.33. Currently, we require customers to use PayPal for all transactions. The result is instantaneous transactions. While we have some credit accounts with suppliers and our shipping solutions, we have chosen to make our payments on the day of transaction. We plan to purchase the sheet materials and hardware one month in advance. The cash injection of $20,000 is necessary for January 2020 expansion costs, but we are looking to secure the cash by November 2019. Following are projected cash flows for five years, then monthly through the end of 2019 and 2020.

Annual Projected Cash Flow

	2019	2020	2021	2022	2023
Starting Cash	$ 8,239.33	$ 80,083.30	$ 40,420.87	$ 176,142.11	$ 343,016.22
New Cash Injection	$ 35,000.00				
Revenue	$ 216,572.06	$ 732,019.78	$ 1,184,650.64	$ 1,445,273.77	$ 1,647,612.10
CoGs (excluding Material and Hardware)	$ (73,280.97)	$ (241,598.69)	$ (390,986.75)	$ (477,003.84)	$ (543,784.37)
Less Other Variable Costs	$ (45,480.13)	$ (153,724.15)	$ (248,776.63)	$ (303,507.49)	$ (345,998.54)
Less Prepay next months Material and Hardware	$ (32,879.31)	$ (98,610.42)	$ (154,789.39)	$ (223,389.03)	$ (254,663.50)
Less Expenses (excluding depreciation)	$ (13,154.98)	$ (233,177.63)	$ (219,290.64)	$ (219,305.64)	$ (219,290.64)
Less Income Tax	$ (14,932.69)	$ (6,895.13)	$ (35,085.98)	$ (55,193.65)	$ (62,920.76)
Less Asset Purchases		$ (37,676.19)			
Cash at End of Period	$ 80,083.30	$ 40,420.87	$ 176,142.11	$ 343,016.22	$ 563,970.51

2019 Projected Cash Flows

	Quarter 1 Accumulated	Apr	May	Jun	Jul	Aug	Sep	Oct	Nov	Dec
Starting Cash		$8,239.33	$10,950.82	$13,377.16	$14,703.57	$19,180.07	$22,875.87	$28,445.46	$34,045.07	$74,737.45
New Cash Injection									$35,000.00	
Revenue		$12,001.69	$12,666.57	$13,337.16	$23,444.91	$25,770.08	$31,040.84	$31,473.47	$32,438.69	$34,398.63
CoGs (excluding Material and Hardware)		($4,060.98)	($4,285.96)	($4,512.86)	($7,933.00)	($8,719.76)	($10,503.22)	($10,649.60)	($10,976.20)	($11,639.38)
Less Other Variable Costs		($2,520.35)	($2,659.98)	($2,800.80)	($4,923.43)	($5,411.72)	($6,518.58)	($6,609.43)	($6,812.13)	($7,223.71)
Less Prepay next months Material and Hardware		($1,686.34)	($1,775.61)	($3,121.29)	($3,430.84)	($4,132.55)	($4,190.15)	($4,318.65)	($4,579.58)	($5,644.30)
Less Expenses (excluding depreciation)			($600.00)	($600.00)	($933.33)	($2,204.33)	($2,204.33)	($2,204.33)	($2,204.33)	($2,204.33)
Less Income Tax		($1,022.53)	($918.68)	($975.81)	($1,747.81)	($1,605.92)	($2,054.98)	($2,091.84)	($2,174.07)	($2,341.06)
Less Asset Purchases										
Cash at End of Period	$8,239.33	$10,950.82	$13,377.16	$14,703.57	$19,180.07	$22,875.87	$28,445.46	$34,045.07	$74,737.45	$80,083.30

2020 Projected Cash Flows

	Jan	Feb	Mar	Apr	May	Jun	Jul	Aug	Sep	Oct	Nov	Dec
Starting Cash	$ 80,083.30	$ 2,699.95	$ 2,679.62	$ 3,082.80	$ 2,747.37	$ 2,643.09	$ 2,587.13	$ 6,739.01	$ 13,287.13	$ 20,579.73	$ 26,991.23	$ 33,658.94
New Cash Injection												
Revenue	$ 44,551.06	$ 49,043.69	$ 49,632.26	$ 48,426.26	$ 49,877.82	$ 53,323.21	$ 65,450.31	$ 72,408.35	$ 73,859.55	$ 72,230.80	$ 74,418.23	$ 78,798.25
CoGs (excluding Material and Hardware)	$ (14,703.81)	$ (16,186.57)	$ (16,380.83)	$ (15,982.79)	$ (16,461.87)	$ (17,599.00)	$ (21,601.48)	$ (23,897.94)	$ (24,376.90)	$ (23,839.34)	$ (24,561.28)	$ (26,006.88)
Less Other Variable Costs	$ (9,355.72)	$ (10,299.17)	$ (10,422.77)	$ (10,169.51)	$ (10,474.34)	$ (11,187.87)	$ (13,744.57)	$ (15,205.75)	$ (15,510.51)	$ (15,168.47)	$ (15,627.83)	$ (16,547.63)
Less Prepay next months Material and Hardware	$ (6,213.48)	$ (6,288.05)	$ (6,135.26)	$ (6,319.16)	$ (6,755.67)	$ (8,292.08)	$ (9,173.62)	$ (9,357.47)	$ (9,151.12)	$ (9,428.25)	$ (9,983.17)	$ (11,513.09)
Less Expenses (excluding depreciation)	$ (53,985.21)	$ (16,290.22)	$ (16,290.22)	$ (16,290.22)	$ (16,290.22)	$ (16,290.22)	$ (16,290.22)	$ (16,290.22)	$ (16,290.22)	$ (16,290.22)	$ (16,290.22)	$ (16,290.22)
Less Income Tax							$ (488.55)	$ (1,108.84)	$ (1,238.21)	$ (1,093.01)	$ (1,288.02)	$ (1,678.49)
Less Asset Purchases	$ (37,676.19)											
Cash at End of Period	$ 2,699.95	$ 2,679.62	$ 3,082.80	$ 2,747.37	$ 2,643.09	$ 2,587.13	$ 6,739.01	$ 13,287.13	$ 20,579.73	$ 26,991.23	$ 33,658.94	$ 40,420.87

Exit and Long-Term Strategy

Assuming we are able to complete the patent process successfully, there are two viable exit strategies to consider: M&A and buyout. The M&A exit strategy would involve selling these rights to a major automotive manufacturer or a competing aerodynamics firm. The alternative is to license to a multitude of firms and expand to manufacture for those firms as well. Unfortunately, highly relevant data on metrics such as EPS and TEV are not available for a comparable firm (aftermarket exterior accessories).

From the "2015 Automotive Aftermarket Merger and Acquisitions Year in Review and Outlook" by BB&T and AASA, we can learn some information on mergers and acquisitions that occurred in relatively recent years. A screenshot is detailed in the appendix (Figure 17.1) in which P/E ratios of automotive aftermarket firms can be observed. These figures seem high, but CSI Market's Auto Industry valuation lists an average P/E of 14.05. The most conservative (low end) estimate in evaluating for exit would be a P/E ratio of 2.35, coming from SORL Auto Parts, Inc.

Beyond M&A, we will consider a buyout exit strategy. The buyout could come from owners, family, or management. We feel strongly that this is a possibility, as many of our current contractors are close friends and have expressed significant interest in taking an ownership stake. Additionally, car enthusiasts love to get wrapped up in all corners of the industry, and there are a plethora of wealthy car enthusiasts with a business mindset. To better make these connections, we will consult with "Fonzie" from our board of advisors due to his automotive business background and business school education.

For the long term, we expect Liquivinyl LLC to branch into new product segments as opportunities arise. As car enthusiasts and entrepreneurs, you could say our gears are always turning as we race to the next opportunity.

Appendix

Tip of Spear Customer Sponsorship Letter (Figure 13.1)

To whom this may concern! I am currently a **20-year-old college student** who works part-time and makes the car culture a part of my lifestyle during my free time! I have **attended/attend numerous local meets** as well as organized meets in my area. I have currently had my car for about five to six months now. Some supporting mods I have done so far are:

MP Concepts GT350 Front Bumper

Airlift Performance 3P Kit

TruFiber Carbon Fiber Hood Vents, Mirror Covers, and Ducktail Wing with Removable Gurney Flap

Farmuh Performance Six-Piece Diffuser

Corsa Xtreme Catback Exhaust

Niche Verona Wheels With Nitto 555 G2 Tires

Finally, some colored badging around the car as well.

I'd love to collaborate with you guys, as I believe I could help reach an audience to help you guys grow as well. If there's anything else you would like to know about my ride, or even myself, do not hesitate, and feel free to let me know!

Sincerely,

Post data and interaction statistics from latest new product posts. Notice profile clicks and comment figures. Small arrow that is third icon (left to right, starting at heart icon) shows how many times post has been sent to another user (word of mouth)

Growth Schedule With Multiples (Figure 8.1)

Q1 2019 is baseline test market (100 percent weight). To derive new weights, divide new total size by Q1 total size. Q1 and Q3 intentionally blank to allow for brand equity development.

Quarterly Growth Plans

2019

Q1		Q2	Q3		Q4
s550 Mustang			**s197 Mustang Early Model**		
2018	75,842		2009	66,623	
2017	81,866		2008	91,251	
2016	105,932		2007	134,626	
2015	122,439		2006	166,530	
			2005	160,975	
Total Size	386,079			620,005	
Weight of Market	100.00%			160.59%	

2020

5th Gen Camaro		Subaru BRZ		7th Gen Charger		BK2 Genesis Coup	
2014	86,297	2018	3,834	2018	80,226	2017	1,055
2013	80,567	2017	4,131	2017	88,351	2016	4,781
2012	84,391	2016	4,141	2016	97,110	2015	6,457
2011	88,249	2015	5,296	2015	94,725	2014	10,859
2010	81,299	2014	7,504	2014	94,099	2013	12,526
2009	61,648	2013	8,587	2013	98,336		
		2012	4,144	2012	82,592		
				2011	70,089		
Total Size	482,451		37,637		705,528		35,678
Weight of Market	124.96%		9.75%		182.74%		9.24%

2021

3rd Gen Challenger		BK1 Genesis Coup		c7 Corvette		Scion FRS	
2018	66,716	2012	11,286	2018	18,791	2018	4,133
2017	64,537	2011	14,148	2017	25,079	2017	6,846
2016	64,478	2010	12,674	2016	29,995	2016	7,457
2015	66,365	2009	8,285	2015	33,329	2015	10,507
2014	51,611			2014	34,839	2014	14,062
2013	51,462					2013	18,327
2012	43,119					2012	11,417
2011	39,534						
2010	36,791						
2009	25,852						
2008	17,423						
Total Size	527,888		46,393		142,033		72,749
Weight of Market	136.73%		12.02%		36.79%		18.84%

SOURCE: carsalesbase.com

Splitter Rod Picture

Common accessory ordered with each splitter. One end screws into the splitter, the other into the bumper. The rods are extendable and come in various colors.

Full Product Line Revenue and Costs (Figure 13.1)

Weights and costs for 2019

Revenue and CoGs 2020

	Splitter	Splitter + Rods	Splitters + Side Fins	Splitter + Rods + Side Fins	Diffuser Kit	Canards	Side Skirts
List Price Revenue	$ 225.00	$ 245.00	$ 255.00	$ 275.00	$ 140.00	$ 150.00	$ 140.00
Material	$ 10.71	$ 13.54	$ 13.54	$ 13.54	$ 6.77	$ 6.77	$ 12.65
Water Jet Cutting Costs	$ 22.00	$ 22.00	$ 22.00	$ 22.00	$ 5.00	$ 5.00	$ -
Edge Trim	$ 5.26	$ 5.26	$ 5.26	$ 5.26	$ -	$ 22.63	$ -
Hardware	$ 5.16	$ 20.03	$ 11.88	$ 26.75	$ 24.48	$ 13.44	$ 6.88
Labor	$ 20.00	$ 20.00	$ 20.00	$ 20.00	$ 20.00	$ 5.00	$ 10.00
Packaging (Decals, Packing Tape, Cardboard)	$ 8.74	$ 8.74	$ 8.74	$ 8.74	$ 8.74	$ 8.74	$ 8.74
Shipping	$ 35.00	$ 35.00	$ 35.00	$ 35.00	$ 10.00	$ 10.00	$ 20.00
Total CoGs	$108.00	$122.87	$116.42	$131.28	$59.99	$76.58	$58.27
Cogs as % of Sales	48%	50%	46%	48%	43%	51%	42%

Revised weights and costs for 2020 given economies of scale

Revenue and CoGs with Economies of Scale (2020)	Splitter	Splitter + Rods	Splitters + Side Fins	Splitter + Rods + Side Fins	Diffuser Kit	Canards	Side Skirts
List Price Revenue	$ 225.00	$ 245.00	$ 255.00	$ 275.00	$ 140.00	$ 150.00	$ 140.00
Material	$ 10.71	$ 11.84	$ 12.24	$ 12.24	$ 6.12	$ 6.12	$ 12.65
Water Jet Cutting Costs	$ 20.00	$ 20.00	$ 20.00	$ 20.00	$ 5.00	$ -	$ -
Edge Trim	$ 5.26	$ 5.26	$ 5.26	$ 5.26	$ -	$ 22.63	$ -
Hardware	$ 4.68	$ 19.55	$ 11.12	$ 25.99	$ 23.60	$ 12.88	$ 6.24
Labor	$ 20.00	$ 20.00	$ 20.00	$ 20.00	$ 5.00	$ 10.00	$ 10.00
Packaging (Decals, Packing Tape, Cardboard)	$ 8.74	$ 8.74	$ 8.74	$ 8.74	$ 8.74	$ 8.74	$ 8.74
Shipping	$ 35.00	$ 35.00	$ 35.00	$ 35.00	$ 10.00	$ 10.00	$ 20.00
Total CoGs	$104.39	$120.39	$112.36	$127.23	$58.46	$70.37	$57.63
Cogs as % of Sales	46%	49%	44%	46%	42%	47%	41%

Expansion Costs (Figure 14.1)

Facilities

As we expand, a larger facility is needed to accommodate equipment, inventory, and more work stations. This will also provide office space. For the purpose of analysis, an example facility has been chosen.

This example is fairly consistent with other market offerings and includes:
Garage square footage 2,500
Office square footage 1,000
Office area with large reception area, bathroom, and two large offices.
HUGE outdoor parking area

We will need to purchase trash services. **Waste Management quoted us $471.72 per month for full service**. This includes a two-yard trash bin alongside a two-yard recycling bin.

Total facility expenses will be $1,671.72 per month.

Upgrades and Furnishings

The space also **includes utilities** and locking gates for the parking/storage area. The only modifications necessary for such a space are converting the power supply to 220 volts. Most garages already have this utility, but we will account for it regardless for the sake of analysis. **The quote we received from our local energy provider was $4,000**.

Finally, we will need to purchase workstations, generic office furniture, and some amenities for our team.

Workstations

Each workstation will include one **Kobalt work bench priced at $199**. Additionally, a Husky rolling tool cart will be provided, with all necessary tools and materials inside. **The cart costs $199. We will allocate an additional $50 per station for items such as trashcans, fans, etc.**

We intend to purchase eight workstations at a total of $3,584 (delivery is included).

Office Furniture

Basic furniture will be purchased from IKEA. We will budget an **additional $100 per desk setup for basic decorations, organizers, power strips, lamps, etc.** **Total furnishing costs: $1,915.96**

Amenities

We will be including common space where our team can take breaks, eat lunch, hang out after hours, and attend company meetings.

After adding a $69.99 shipping fee for some appliances, **total cost of amenities will be $5,800.91.**

Inventory

To store our inventory, we will be purchasing light duty, mini cantilevered racks. Our racks will have eight arms and a 250-pound capacity per arm. As our products are only three millimeters thick, we should be able to store a good amount of each product on every level. We are intending to purchase these racks from materialflow. com.

The racks are priced at $499.42 each. We are looking to purchase **eight racks at a cost of $3,995.36.** We also estimate a cost of $2,000 for shipping, installation, and modification. Modification may mean using wood panels to fill space between the arms or adding rubber traction pads to prevent sliding or even a felt overlay to minimize surface imperfections on the product. **Total cost for storage is $5,995.36**

Security

The system was recommended to us by an automotive business of comparable size. Its features include motion sensing, intercom, real-time alerts, and a slew of others. The basic software package, which has no monthly cost, will suffice. **The system will be a one-time expense of $751.99.**

Safety

As we take care of our customers, we also want to take care of our workers. Compliance is the bare minimum, but the best way to ensure the safety and comfort of our team is bringing on a safety consultant to write a program with procedures and help us purchase the necessary equipment. Kristin Vansoest, owner of Safety Resources, Inc. (specializing in safety consulting and OSHA training), spoke with one of our contractors to give us the upper end of estimated cost. **We can expect to pay $1,200 for written programs and an additional $1,000 for necessary safety tools up front.**

Lifts

As we develop and test products for more vehicles, a lift will be necessary to get the vehicles up and off the ground with ease. Given our intended expansion goals and available space, we will be purchasing two lifts.

While we don't anticipate needing the extra add-ons to the garage door, we will include them as an overestimate for the sake of analysis. **This brings our total cost for two lifts to $9,100.**

Computers

Beyond automotive equipment, we will need four desktop computers for the two owners and two salaried team members. Other small machinery was already purchased by the company (vinyl cutters, printers, etc.) in Q1 2019. We will be purchasing four of these machines.

The total cost is $3,279.96.

Monthly Costs (Figure 15.1)

Software

With any growing company, the necessary steps must be taken to support growth and development. Following are some of the necessary software:

G Suite will provide professional email tools to our team, an organized calendar, online storage, etc. **The appropriate G Suite package will cost $10 per month.**

Grasshopper will provide our team with professional communication tools to better help our customers. The service will give us our own business-specific phone number and allow all texts, calls, and voicemails to be forwarded to any device that is logged into the Grasshopper profile. **The suitable Grasshopper package will cost us $26 per month.**

QuickBooks will be our finance and accounting tool. The **$17 per month package** will suffice, with multiple users, 1099 tracking, invoice ability, expense tracking, etc.

AutoCAD will provide us with the appropriate design software to create new products and relay design specifications to machine shops effectively. **AutoCAD will cost $195 per month.** Additionally, there will be necessary training costs to ensure that we can maximize the potential of the software. As both owners will be involved in handling new product R&D, we will need to purchase training for two people. Certstaff.com estimates the cost for training to be $1,730 per student for essentials and the same for advanced. Assuming two people take both courses, **one-time learning costs will total $6,920.**

Total monthly software costs will be $248.

Internet and Phone Line

After exchanging information with several other local businesses, we can expect to pay **$117 per month** for 150 mbps (plenty quick) and one phone line with Comcast Business Class.

Truck

A truck is necessary to pick up supplies, drop off packages, and run general errands. It may also be utilized to bring materials to shows and events. We met with our local Chevy dealer with our requirements for hauling capacity. The following financials are based on a truck that is the exact model—with the exact options—that we would lease. FitSmallBusiness.com states that we can expect to pay $750–$1,200 annually for insurance. We will estimate $100 in gas every week. Total **monthly cost for the truck is $1,081**.

Full 12-Month Growth Assumptions (Figure 16.1)

Revenue by Sales Platform	Jan	Feb	March	April	May	June	July	August	September	October	November	December
Online Sales Instagram												
% Growth	0%	2%	0%	2%	5%	5%	5%	1%	-20%	-10%	-1%	5%
Online Sales Abandoned Cart												
Converted to Sales	4%	15%	10%	4%	4%	4%	4%	4%	4%	4%	4%	4%
Online Sales eBay												
% Growth	-5%	10%	10%	-15%	1%	1%	1%	1%	-2%	0%	0%	10%
Online Sales from Trade Shows/events												
% Growth	-39%	0%	0%	10%	15%	10%	5%	5%	-50%	0%	0%	50%

P/E Ratios (Figure 17.1)

	Ticker	Stock Price	52 Week High/Low	Market Cap	TEV	Price/ TBV	P/E LTM	P/E CY 2016	P/E CY 2017
Suppliers									
Axalta Coating Systems Ltd.	AXTA	$26.65	$36.50/$23.94	$6,339	$9,835	NM	48.1x	20.0x	16.6x
Cooper Tire & Rubber Co.	CTB	$37.85	$43.94/$31.18	2,121	1,869	2.6x	9.5x	10.5x	10.8x
Dorman Products, Inc.	DORM	$47.47	$53.75/$43.65	1,685	1,777	3.3.x	18.8x	16.4x	14.9x
Federal - Mogul Holdings Corporation	FDML	$6.85	$15.87/$6.01	1,158	4,491	NM	12.3x	8.4x	7.5x
The Goodyear Tire & Rubber Company	GT	$32.67	$35.30/$23.74	8,785	13,110	2.4x	12.4x	8.3x	7.8x
Horizon Global Corporation	HZN	$10.37	$15.88/$8.04	188	378	NM	32.7x	9.6x	7.4x
Motorcar Parts of America, Inc.	MPAA	$33.81	$41.03/$22.12	619	706	3.2x	NM	13.8x	12.4x
Snap-on Incorporated	SNA	$171.43	$174.52/$129.14	9,951	9,879	7.1x	23.6x	18..6x	16.5x
Standard Motor Products Inc.	SMP	$38.05	$45.72/$30.30	862	787	2.8x	17.0x	13.5x	12.3x
Tenneco Inc.	TEN	$45.91	$61.73/$39.13	2,654	3,881	7.2x	12.0x	8.7x	7.7x

Sources of Data in Plan

Auto parts sales trends
https://hedgescompany.com/blog/2012/08/things-to-know-
2012-auto-parts-sales/

SEMA Market report
www.sema.org/products/35384/2018-sema-market-report

Competitor APR product listing page
http://shop.aprperformance.com/index.php?route=product/
category&path=72_128_80

Body kit costs
www.side.cr/how-much-do-body-kits-cost/

Word of mouth
www.mckinsey.com/business-functions/marketing-and-sales/
our-insights/a-new-way-to-measure-word-of-mouth-marketing

Instagram effectiveness
https://go.forrester.com/blogs/15-09-15-how_does_your_brand_stack_up_on_
facebook_twitter_and_instagram/

PRI trade show
https://performanceracing.com/

ACES car show
www.aces-ac.com/

Tuner Evolution car show
http://tuner-evolution.com/

Abandoned cart four percent
www.klaviyo.com/marketing-resources/abandoned-cart-benchmarks

Car sales statistics
http://carsalesbase.com/

Water jet costs and background information
www.techniwaterjet.com/faqs/
how-much-does-a-complete-waterjet-system-cost/?v=7516fd43adaa

Garage insurance
www.insurancejournal.com/magazines/mag-features/2014/02/10/319390.htm
https://fitsmallbusiness.com/garage-liability-insurance/

Secretary pay
www.payscale.com/research/US/Job=Secretary/Hourly_Rate

Health insurance numbers
www.kff.org/other/state-indicator/single-coverage/?currentTimeframe=0&sortMo
del=%7B%22colId%22:%22Location%22,%22sort%22:%22asc%22%7D

2015 Automotive Aftermarket Mergers and Acquisitions report
www.aftermarketsuppliers.org/sites/aftermarketsuppliers.org/files/2015%20
AASA%20%20BB%26T%20Automotive%20Aftermarket%20Mergers%20
and%20Acquisitions.pdf

CSI Market industry report
https://csimarket.com/Industry/Industry_Valuation.php?ind=405

Index

Note: Page numbers in **bold** indicate a table on the corresponding page.

Printed in the United States
By Bookmasters